THE NATIONAL DIRECTORY OF

GRANTS AND AID TO INDIVIDUALS IN THE ARTS,

INTERNATIONAL

*Containing listings of most grants, prizes, and
awards for professional work in
the U.S. and abroad, and information
about universities and schools
which offer special aid to students*

BY DANIEL MILLSAPS
and the Editors
of the
Washington International Arts Letter

*fourth
edition*

4th Edition
The National Directory of
GRANTS AND AID TO INDIVIDUALS IN THE ARTS
International

By DANIEL MILLSAPS
and the editors of the
WASHINGTON INTERNATIONAL ARTS LETTER

Library of Congress Number:
70 – 112695
ISBN:912072-09-1

© Daniel Millsaps, 1980

Address Orders & Inquiries:
WIAL, Box 9005, Washington, DC 20003

PREFACE

The *Washington International Arts Letter* and the various committees which it sponsored, began in 1962 primarily as a lobby effort to influence the necessary elements in American society toward greater recognition of the arts and their subsidy.

One of the most important activities for the first three years of its existence was toward creation of an Act by Congress which would place the arts, their theory, history, creation and performance into the mainstream of activity in this country by official endorsement at the Federal level; to put it more simply, toward establishment of what came into being in 1965 as the National Foundation on the Arts and the Humanities. This would, it was hoped, in turn, spur additional support for cultural activities in this area by other sectors, i.e., active business, tax-exempt foundations, and individuals. To a degree this aim has been accomplished but the efforts of the original citizen-lobby for which the "Letter" was responsible has never been given proper recognition. The purpose of this preface is to help correct that. As for myself, I neither care for the recognition nor seek it. My efforts toward the ends described extended many years prior to the founding of the publication and its committees, and so the success of accomplishment toward the goal is enough reward. It is the others who, like myself, devoted themselves and their fortunes in some cases, to the project unselfishly who deserve the recognition.

Dorothea Crowe Ward, Robert DeShazo and his associates, and Thomas E. Clarke, my associate and companion for eighteen years were the underpins of the undertaking. They worked daily in their various ways to gather influential people to the movement, sustain their interest, and coordinate with the few in Congress who had already become convinced of the Federal level need partly, again, because of my earlier efforts. (Usher L. Burdick, Congressman from the Dakotas in those years, introduced a bill for me as early as 1955 but got trounced. The time was not yet right.)

Mrs. Ward was a Canadian by birth and had lived much of her life there and in Europe. Her wealth, stemming at first from lumber interest in Canada and growing through her intuitive grasp of worldwide money markets, was the most active in her volunteer efforts for the group. She was our hatchet-woman with Members of Congress, heading a large group of young men we enlisted for her as a leg-work committee, convincing the lawmakers that the arts were healthy, worthwhile, useful to society and vigorous as well as sexy and appealing. Our travels to European capitals cornering influential Americans who in turn put pressure on their Congressmen from abroad, as well as the many other, more familiar techniques of entertainment-lobbying in Washington were perhaps the most telling of all the energies spent.

i

Robert DeShazo and especially his lieutenant J.C. (Pat) Patterson who helped with the production and distribution of the early copies of the publication virtually assured that our words and those of the committees of Congress who were on our side were distributed and that communications came back into Washington to appropriate people. Clarke kept the offices of the "Letter" going as a volunteer, devotedly handling the business affairs and recruiting the many unnamed men for the working pool. (Mrs. Ward was responsible for turning, at one crucial point, the vote of John L. Macmillan, Washington's ultra-conservative "mayor" of those years, toward our project, to the astonishment of all others remotely concerned. This act was typical of the many unexpected coups she made in the slow and rather exhausting process we undertook. It influenced the vote of many others who had doubted. Mr. Clarke accompanied her, that day, to make the call on "Johnny Mac," as he was called.)

This preface is too short to mention all the Members of Congress who, once convinced by us and our constituents, worked hard to obtain the legislation, but a few like Frank Thompson of New Jersey, Claiborne Pell of Rhode Island and Jacob Javits of New York did expend extraordinary energies toward the goal. Their efforts were observable and did them no harm in their positions.

The others in the private sector to whom honors are due, though less active on a day to day basis were members of "prestige" name committees, even though some were still working at the time to establish their positions in the worlds of affairs: Warren Robbins, Otho Shaw, J.C. Turner, Leon Kroll, Carolyn J. Proctor (now) Cassilly, Dr. Gilbert Convers, John Wyatt Gregg, Wolf Von Eckardt, Stewart Klonis, Roy Neuberger, Richard C. Muehlberger, Henry Hecht, Jr., Myrtle E. Russell, Rene d'Harnoncourt, and Stanley Marcus.

Upon passage, in 1965, of the first Federal legislation for the arts and humanities, not conceived as welfare such as in the WPA and in elements now of CETA, the "Letter" became not only a catalyst for increased support in other sectors but a critical journal on all kinds of funding in these fields. We are more free than any other journal to draw attention to weaknesses as well as strengths of the Federal subsidies because we did so much to help create them and to those in other sectors because we continue to work on both, and attempt to develop better understanding of these aspects of U.S. cultural life. The pages of the monthly carry information very frequently about new patronage as it develops, to the benefit of all.

Everything we have done has been done without grants or tax-exemption and, we feel, shows what still can be done by concerned citizens, working on their own, purely privately, in American development. The publications which have grown out of the foundation of the Washington International Arts Letter, including this one, show how initiative, single-mindedness and attention to detail can still be rewarded in a free society when they provide an unselfish service to the field.

INTRODUCTION

The Fourth edition of "Grants and Aid to Individuals in the Arts," a national as well as international directory, was, like the Third, a year in the making and expands considerably the earlier work. The first (1970) was spurred by questions of young people and older professionals alike, about where to look for help in their chosen field. It was a skeleton pamphlet but America's first consolidation of the type of information many needed. It and the Second edition both contained errors and no doubt some will be found in this one. We have corrected as many as we could find and trace down but we cannot guarantee that the institutions have not changed their addresses, their ways of giving grants or awards nor the aid itself, even after we received their answers. We hope again that users will call any changes and additions, or, indeed errors, to our attention for later editions. For this one, we sent out questionnaires to all sources previously listed and to newly discovered sources, and followed up in various other ways if they did not return them. For those we could never track down, but whom we believed still to be active, we have inserted the letters "MR" (mail returned) in their listing. Should anyone know more about these entities, including addresses, than appears here, please give us your more complete information for our files.

As we said in the Third edition, we still feel that sources for funding for individuals in America have not expanded as they should have in recent years. The considerably more numerous listings in this edition are accounted for by the fact that we have discovered more that were already in existence but missed and the fact that we have added many prizes and competitions offering monetary awards which were not included, as such, in some earlier efforts.

Private foundations (most of whom are listed in our volume called the *National Directory of Arts Support by Private Foundations,* Volume Three) generally support the organizations listed here, but in days past they also gave out many grants directly to individuals themselves. The Congress, taking with one hand while giving with another, rather well squelched this practice in the Tax Reform Act of 1969. (Some individual aid may still be had from some foundations. Many who do work with individuals in the arts and humanities are listed in the volume mentioned but not all. For the serious student of philanthropy, or those whose need is for considerable aid, or who have projects which could be expanded into "group" efforts, it is suggested that a search in the title mentioned would be helpful. It can be found in almost any library or had from WIAL, Box 9005, DC 20003.)

It was expected that the Federal and State governments would take up the slack in diminishing foundation activity on behalf of individuals but this has not been fully realized. There are some programs in various disciplines from tax monies which may grow with time. Those presently in existence are described more fully in the back section of this book. The National Endowment for the Arts claims much more aid is going to individuals through its broader programs in addition to its outright individual "fellowship" programs. Bureaucratic overheads there—and especially at state level—diminish the trickle-down considerably.

In the Education Act of the 92nd Congress (with amendments), one finds authority for considerable student aid which can be had routinely by people in all fields. These types of grants are not covered in this volume because they are routine and available for the asking. Any school or college student aid office will supply details and forms for them. The assistance for students listed here is, for the most part, in addition to those basic amounts.

Amounts of grants and awards are generally put in when they are $1,000 or more, but many smaller ones have been included this time to emphasize the need for their increase. Deadlines, unless they have become fixed over the years, have been omitted. This work is designed so that the user may (and he should, before applying) contact the organization directly for more information and necessary forms. We have tried to delineate which help is purely "educational" and which is for "professional" work. There is frequently a crossover and interpolations have been liberal on our part. There is no guarantee that we are right. Emphasis has been on finding help for creative professional work but the inclusion of the educational as such provides the best guide available under one cover for teachers and students alike from all levels. In America the distinctions between educational activity and professional work at higher levels, combining as is more and more frequent the community with the institution, are blurred and approach the ambience of the situation of Europe, whether right or wrong.

National restrictions are noted where considered important. Other restrictions such as sex, conventional marital status, age are generally included to save time of applicants, but these too change with time. It is best to check them out. We found no instances where "spouse" provisions included partners of the same sex although it is known that in some institutions such factors are taken into account informally. In reverse, the McDowell Colony, for instance, sometimes allows only the person who is creating to occupy space. Their idea is that the intrusion of family or other encumbrances is against the creative arts process there.

To repeat from an earlier edition: while useful in an uncommon degree, this work is an indictment also, an indictment of America for not having found more ways to support its creative artists and scholars. We hope this work will bring the fact to the attention of all.

A final note for young artists: The private person is still the largest and most generous patron in America and his largesse is not reported anywhere in a formal way. In the days before the welfare agencies, neighbors helped neighbors directly with problems; in a like manner today a person-to-person aid for artists is still possible. As with all such matters, however, when something is given, something in general is expected in return. There are few truly altruistic patrons left, unfortunately. The State generally—more and more recently—asks for "public service" in return for its grants. The private patron expects, whether stated or not, sometimes loyalties, works, amusement or other satisfactions from the artist whom he helps. There is an old saying: "Knock only on doors you wish to enter." It holds true in searches for grants! Good luck!

Daniel Millsaps, Publisher
Washington International Arts Letter
Research Office
Rehoboth Beach, Delaware

ACKNOWLEDGMENTS

The research for this edition was done under the direction of Randy Perkins to whom we are indebted for his attention to detail and thoroughness. Additional editing was done by Dennis Muentnich who also contributed in depth to the second edition. Help in earlier parts of the "Arts Patronage Series" came from Ron Hoskins, Mrs. Frances Neel Cheney (Peabody Library School), Larry Johnson (D.C. Public Library System), Bill Cook (Chelsea Court), and Thomas N. Snyder (Allied Business Consultants, Inc.).

SYMBOLS

The symbols for disciplines are in upper and lower case letters in the margins, with those in upper case being used to indicate aid most predominantly in the "professional" category and those in lower case used for aid most predominantly in "education." See the index by discipline for further notation.

A, or a . . . . .Architecture
ALL, or all . . . . .Generally means all arts are in competition with other disciplines. When "ALL," or "all" of the arts are the sole recipients from a given source it is so noted.
AM . . . . .Arts management.
C, or c . . . . .Crafts
D, or d . . . . .Dance or Ballet.
F, or f . . . . .Film
-H, or -h . . . . .Historian in the field to which attached, i.e., VP-H means art history.
M, or m . . . . .Musicians, music, instrumentalists, composers.
MUS, or mus . . . . .Museum administration.
P . . . . .Prize, award or competition in the field to which attached, i.e., P-F applies to the field of film.
T, or t . . . . .Theater, including actors and playwrights.
VP, or vp . . . . .Visual or plastic arts, painters, sculptors, printmakers, photographers.
WR, or wr . . . . .Writers, all fields.
Anyone . . . . .Generally means persons of any nationality.

ABBREVIATIONS MOST COMMON

Fels . . . . .Fellowships
Grad . . . . .Graduate
Mos . . . . .Months
NYC . . . . .New York, NY
Schols . . . . .Scholarships
Yr-s . . . . .Year, years

OTHER VOLUMES

For the information of librarians, the "Arts Patronage Series" consists of the following publications to date (and in print January 1, 1980):

Arts Patronage Series #2,   "Millions for the Arts: Senate Study of Cultural Programs" with update.

Arts Patronage Series #6,   "National Directory of Arts Support by Private Foundations," Vol. 3.

Arts Patronage Series #7,   "National Directory of Arts Support by Business Corporations," 1st edition.

Inquiries should be directed to: *Washington International Arts Letter* (or *WIAL*), Box 9005, Washington, DC 20003.

T	ABC THEATRE AWARD. See: Eugene O'Neill Theater Center.
P-M,P-m	ABA-OSTWALD BAND COMPOSITION CONTEST, The United States Marine Band, 8th and I Sts., SE, Washington, DC 20390. $500 to $1,500 for original, unpublished composition for band. Deadline Nov. 1.
WR	ABINGDON PRESS, Award Editor, 201 8th Ave. So., Nashville, TN 37202. Prize $5,000 annually for encouragement of writing of books of outstanding quality. To author of an unpublished manuscript. Areas: general books, children, religious.
M	ACADEMIE MUSICALE CHIGIANA, Siena, Italy. Full and half 2 mo. sch. for study at academy to all nationals under 30. Examinations.
WR	ACADEMY OF AMERICAN POETS, Inc., 1078 Madison Ave., NYC 10028. Several prizes for works by American poets. Prizes range from $10,000 to $100. Some with publication of works involved.
P-VP	ACADEMY OF FINE ARTS, 23 Quai de Conti, Paris 75006, France. Drawing Prize: Awarded for the outstanding in drawing. Artist must be under 30 years of age, and must have lived for at least two years in France. All drawing techniques with the exception of Gouache, pastel and watercolor. Ten drawings must be presented by each artist. Monetary prizes of 20,000 france, 15,000 and 10,000 francs are awarded annually.
M (voice)	ACADEMY OF MUSIC, Lothringerstrasse 18, Vienna 3, Austria. International Mozart Singing Competition for all singers under 30 years.
M	ACADEMY OF VOCAL ARTS, Mr. V. Hammond, Dir., 1920 Spruce St., Philadelphia, PA 19103. Full scholarships for exceptional voices with operatic potential. Under 30 years.
M	ACCADEMIA NAZIONALE DE SANTA CECILIA, Via Vittoria 6, Rome, Italy. Cash awards plus concert to conductors under 40 yrs of any nationality.
T	ACTORS FUND OF AMERICA, 1501 Broadway, NYC 10036. Loans for anyone in the theatrical profession.
P-T, P-WR	ACTORS THEATER OF LOUISVILLE, 316-320 West Main St., Louisville, KY 40202. Any U.S. citizen with a play that hadn't been an Equity production.
m,t,vp,c	ADAMS STATE COLLEGE, Alamosa, CO 811202. Contact: Melvin E. Clark, Dir. of Financial Aid. State and Private Grants: For $100 per quarter and $300 per academic year to students recommended by the chairperson of the appropriate division. Undergraduates only.

f   ADELPHI UNIVERSITY, Communications, Blodgett Hall 113, Garden City, NY 11530. Contact: Paul Pitcoff. Two filmmaking grants of $150 per semester from the Film Company of Adelphi University, Inc.

V-P   ADRIAN COLLEGE, Adrian, MI 49221.

M   AEOLIAN ORGAN PLAYING COMPETITION, Secretary for Organ Competitions, Aeolian Hall, Box 2121, London, Ont., Canada. Organ performance. Anyone.

AESOP GOLDEN PRIZE. See: Gabrovo International Biennial of Caricature.

M,T,D   AFFILIATE ARTISTS, Inc., 155 W 68th St., NYC 10023. Arranges assistance for professional singers, actors, dancers and instrumentalists at colleges and universities located away from large urban centers. 3 year contracts. No teaching involved; only performing and talking about work with local groups on and off campus. Artists are free to accept other engagements.

wr   AFGHANISTAN, MINISTRY OF ED., Embassy of Afghanistan, 2341 Wyoming Ave., NW, Washington, DC 20008. Fels. for study of lit. and culture of Afghanistan; 6 months; anyone.

all   AFL-CIO EDUCATION DEPT., 815 16th St., NW, Washington, DC 20006. Attn: Ms. Shields. Some scholarships for the children of Union members. Write for information to the above person.

AFRICAN—AMERICAN SCHOLARS CONFERENCE, 1401 14th St., NW, Washington, DC 20005. Constance Hilliard.

P-WR,M,   AFRICAN ARTS MAGAZINE, African Studies Center, U/Cal at Los Angeles, Los Angeles, CA 90024. African Arts' Annual Competition for African Artists. Awards: Entrants must be citizens and permanent residents of the AFrican continent or the Malagasy Republic. Entries must be original unpublished works. $2,000 to be divided between the works by the judges. Awarded annually: In alternate years the prizes are given: One year literature and plastic and graphic arts are awarded; the next year music and dramatic writings are awarded.

P-WR   AFRICAN STUDIES ASSOCIATION, 218 Shiffman Center, Brandeis University, Waltham, MA 02154. One award: THE HERSKOVITS AWARD. For an outstanding work on Africa published or distributed in the U.S.A. in the previous year; it must be an original scholarly publication. Monetary award, annually.

P-WR   AGA KHAN FICTION PRIZE, The Paris Review, 541 East 72nd St., NYC 10021. $500 and publication given annually.

2

m,t,wr   AGNES SCOTT COLLEGE, East College Ave., Decatur, GA 30030. Scholarships of up to $1,000 or according to need.

m   AGRICULTURAL AND TECHNICAL COLLEGE OF NORTH CAROLINA, Greensboro, NC 27411. To entering fresh. eight $250 voice, eight $250 woodwinds.

all   ALABAMA STATE COUNCIL ON THE ARTS and Humanities, 449 South McDonough St., Montgomery, AL 36130. Artists-in-Schools.

vp,c   ALABAMA STATE UNIVERSITY, Montgomery, AL 36101.

all   ALASKA STATE COUNCIL ON THE ARTS, 619 Warehous Ave., Suite 220, Anchorage, AK 99501. Monies for artists in schools, purchase awards also.

ALL   ALBANY CREATIVE ARTS GUILD, PO Box 841, Albany, OR 97321. Contact: Corrine Woodman. Write for grants information.

m   ALBANY STATE COLLEGE, Holley Dr., Albany, GA 31705. $250-$1,000 to undergrads. Some w/restrictions; some renewable.

WR,VP   THE EDWARD F. ALBEE FOUNDATION, INC., 226 W 47th St., NYC 10036. Limited studio space given with room and sometimes board to writers and visual artists. Center is located on Long Island, NY.

vp,c   ALBERTA COLLEGE OF ART, Southern Alberta Institute of Technology, 1301-16 Ave. NW, Calgary, Alberta, Canada.

vp,m,t   ALBION COLLEGE, Albion, MI 49224. All aid for attendance based on need. $500 to $600. Anyone.

d,m,wr   ALDERSON BROADDUS COLLEGE, Philippi, WV 26416. Contact: Nathaniel G. Jackson, Director of Fin. Aid.
   SUSAN TUTTENBERG SCHOLARSHIP: $750 awarded annually to black student in the field of drama.
   MUSIC AWARD: $2,500 awarded annually to any student displaying skill in music.
   ALDERSON BROADDUS TRUSTEE AWARD: $1,000 awarded annually to any student in the upper 10% of his/her graduating class, only in the field of Humanities.

vp,c   ALLEGHENY COLLEGE, Meadville, PA 16335.

vp,c   ALLEN UNIV., 1530 Harden & Taylor St., Columbia SC 29204.

WR   ALLIANCE FRANCAISE, 101 Boulevard Raspail, Paris 6, France.
   FEDERATION OF ALLIANCES FRANCAISES IN THE UNITED STATES PRIZE: For any literary work written in French, strengthening Franco-

American relations. $2,000 plus translation into English, and publication in the U.S.A. Anyone.

ALLIANCE FRANCAISE OF NEW YORK
SEE: French Institute/Alliance Francaise.

P-VP   **ALLIED ARTISTS OF AMERICA, INC.**, 1083 Fifth Ave., NYC 10028. 15 awards:

ALLIED ARTISTS OF AMERICA GOLD MEDAL OF HONOR: For the the best oil painting, watercolor, and sculpture shown in the Annual Exhibition. One award per media. Gold medal and $200 annually.

ALLIED ARTISTS OF AMERICA MONETARY AWARD: For the outstanding oil painting, watercolor and sculpture shown in the Annual Exhibition. One award per media. Award: $250 given annually.

ASSOCIATE MEMBERS PRIZE: For the best watercolor exhibited in the Annual Exhibition Award of $100 given annually.

ALEX BERT CHASKY AWARD FOR A REPRESENTATIONAL OIL PAINTING: For the best oil painting in the Annual Exhibition. $500 awarded annually.

COUNCIL OF AMERICAN ARTISTS SOCIETIES AWARD: For a traditional oil painting shown in The Annual Exhibition. $100 awarded annually.

GRUMBACHER ARTISTS' MATERIALS COMPANY AWARD: For the outstanding oil painting, watercolor and acrylic painting shown at the Annual Exhibition. Awards: $200 for the oil, $200 for the watercolor, $100 for the acrylic. Awarded annually.

PAULINE LAW PRIZE: For an outstanding sculpture shown in the Annual Exhibition. $50 awarded annually.

EMILY LOWE PRIZE: For an outstanding contemporary oil painting by an American artist. $300 awarded annually.

LINDSEY MORRIS MEMORIAL PRIZES: For the two best bas reliefs shown in the Annual Exhibition. Awards of $150 & $100 annually.

JANE PETERSON PRIZES: For the outstanding oil paintings shown in the Annual Exhibition. Two awards annually of $150: one for still life or landscape, one for figure or portrait.

PAUL PUZINAS MEMORIAL AWARD: For an outstanding oil painting shown in the Annual Exhibition. Award of $100.

THERESE RICHARD MEMORIAL PRIZE: For the best religious sculpture shown in the Annual Exhibition. Annual award of $100.

SALMAGUNDI CLUB AWARD: For an outstanding oil painting shown in the Annual Exhibition. Annual award of $100.

BARBARA VASSILIEFF AWARD: For an outstanding oil painting shown in the Annual Exhibition. Annual award of $100.

TODAY'S ART MEDAL OF MERIT: For an outstanding oil painting. Discussed in an article in Today's Art magazine, awarded annually.

T,WR   **ALL-MEDIA DRAMATIC WORKSHOP**, Chicago Radio Theatre, 812 North Michigan Ave., Room 316, Chicago, IL 60611. Up to $1,500 for radio scripts. MR

4

WR ALL NATIONS POETRY CONTEST, Triton College, 2000 5th Ave., River Grove, IL 60171. Publication for poem of certain length and subject matter.

m,vp,c ALMA COLLEGE, Alma, MI 48801. Academic Schls.

ALL,all ALPHA CHI OMEGA, 8733 Founders Road, Indianapolis, IN 46268. Mrs. Scott Martindill, Exec. Sec. $1,000 fels. to graduating senior & member or alumna for creative, or study or resrches in one of the fine arts: Fels. to Mac-Dowell Colony with expenses paid with varying amounts of time. MR

P-VP ALVA MUSEUM REPLICAS PRIZE
SEE: National Sculpture Society award: $500.

m ALVERNO COLLEGE, 3401 South 39th St., Milwaukee, WI 53215. To entering freshmen. Renewable. $100-$7,000. Women only.

M,D ALVIN AILEY DANCE CO.
SEE: Brooklyn Academy of Music.

vp AMARILLO COLLEGE, PO Box 447, Amarillo, TX 79105.

M AMARILLO NATL. ARTISTS AUDITIONS, c/o Mary Elisabeth Wilson, 903 Sunset Terrace, Amarillo, TX 79106. Award cash & appearance with Amarillo Symphony. MR

ALL AMERICA THE BEAUTIFUL FUND, 219 Shoreham Bldg., Washington, DC 20005. Paul Bruc Dowling, Exec. Dir. This is a non-profit organization, giving seed grants of under $1,000 to artists and architects for public service, environmental, conservation and Americana Projects. Most grants must be matched by community funds. No restrictions, deadlines. Applications sought.

a,vp,wr, AMERICAN ACADEMY IN ROME, 41 East 65th St., NYC 10021. 1 year
m fellowships for U.S. citizens. Also, stipend for travel, supplies, studies, housing.

vp AMERICAN ACADEMY OF ART, 30 E. Adams St., Chicago, IL 60603. MR

P-WR, VP, THE AMERICAN ACADEMY OF ARTS AND LETTERS, 633 West 155th St., NYC 10032.
AWARD OF MERIT: To honor excellent work in one of the following arts, in this order: 1) painting, 2) sculpture, 3) the novel, 4) poetry, 5) drama. To a person in America, cannot be a member of the National Institute of Arts and Letters. Medal and $1,000 awarded annually.
Note: Applications NOT requested. They make their awards on recommendations only.

WR   AMERICAN ACADEMY OF ARTS AND SCIENCE, 165 Allandale Rd., Jamaica Plain Sta., Boston, MA 02130. Grants restricted to Academy sponsored projects or programs.

P-M   AMERICAN ACCORDION MUSICOLOGICAL SOCIETY, Pitman, NJ 08071. $500 and $100 for a composition for accordion. Deadline Dec. 31.

M,m   AMERICAN ACCORDIONISTS' ASSOCIATION, 165 West 10th St., NYC, 10014. Emily Martignoni, Pres. National contest, awards, schols. Anyone.

ALL   AMERICAN ASSOCIATION OF UNIVERSITY WOMEN EDUCATIONAL FOUNDATION, 2401 Virginia Ave., NW, Washington, DC 20037. International fellowship of university women.   Advanced research in any field. Must be used in country other than recipient's own. Any member of IAUW. 6 awards $2,500 each.

M   AMERICAN BANDMASTERS ASSOCIATION, 7414 Admiral Drive, Alexandria, VA 22307. For band composition, awards of $1,000 and expenses to ABA convention. Write: Col. Arnold Gabriel, Director, U.S. Air Force Band, Bolling Air Force Base, Washington, DC 20332.

WR   AMERICAN BOOK AWARDS, Parker Ladd, Exec. Dir., c/o Association of American Publishers, Inc., 1 Park Ave., NYC 10016. Annual. $1,000 each of book published in year. 14 regular categories, plus awards for those fitting none of these: Gen. Fiction; Science Fiction, Mystery, Biography; Autobiography, Childrens, Science, History, General Nonfiction, Religious and Inspiration, Art and Illustrated Books, Current Interest, Reference, etc. Jury. First awards given in Spring of 1980. This is a takeover from what had been the National Book Awards which had suffered much criticism for various reasons. TABA is a non-profit subsidiary of the AAP which committed $200,000 for its operation the first year ('79-80). Publishers submit titles and pay a fee for each entry. Committees of about 30 people for each category nominate, then members of AAP vote on "best." Members are in 4 categories: Publishers, booksellers/distributors, librarians, and authors/critics. Ballots are handled by independent accountants. The new awards announcements met with much criticism and became controversial when made in 1979 with forty former National Book Award winners and a well-known publisher calling for a boycott.

WR   AMERICAN COLLEGE OF HOSPITAL ADMINISTRATORS, 840 N. Lake Shore Dr., Chicago, IL 60611. $500 cash award for book on management and/or administration which, in a special committee's opinion, represents "an original contribution to the literature on the art and science of administration." Award is granted each February; only books published two years prior are eligible. (Ex.: the 1970 award went to a book published in 1968, etc.).

M,m   AMERICAN CONSERVATORY OF MUSIC, 410 So. Michigan Ave., Chicago, IL 60650. No set schols. Awards for study and composition 18-45 yrs by approval and study with individual teachers on application and audition.

WR AMERICAN CONSERVATORY THEATRE, 450 Geary St., San Francisco, CA 94102. Token royalty, travel, per diem. Plays in Progress Program (5 selected each year). Also: Fellowships for Young Playwrights.

WR-H, AMERICAN COUNCIL OF LEARNED SOCIETIES, 800 Third Ave., NYC
wr-h 10022. Post-doctoral research grants in the Humanities and humanistic aspects of the Social Sciences. Maximum of $15,000 awarded.

M,D AMERICAN DANCE THEATER.
SEE: Brooklyn Academy of Music.

P-WR AMERICAN FEDERATION OF FILM SOCIETIES, 3 Wash. Sq. Village, NYC 10012. Wm. A. Starr, Exec. Sec.
FILM CRITIC AWARD: To promote higher standards of socially relevant film criticism among college students in the U.S. Award of $100 and publication of the winning review in the Federation's magazine Film Critic, annually to a presently enrolled undergraduate student.

F,f AMERICAN FILM INSTITUTE, Independent Filmmaker Program, Section N, 501 Doheny Rd., Beverly Hills, CA 90210. Has independent filmmaker program. Awards vary $500-$10,000. Awards are grants in aid, internships, advanced study and film writing, for those who are students; professors usually recommend.

m AMERICAN FOREIGN SERVICE ASSOC., 2101 E St., NW, Washington, DC 20006. Musical students; children of Foreign Service personnel: study in the U.S. Broad.

AMERICAN FRIENDS OF ISRAEL MUSEUM, Suite 1208, 10 E. 40 St., NYC 10016. Leonard Straus.

WR AMERICAN FRIENDS OF THE MIDDLE EAST, 1717 Mass. Ave., NW, Washington, DC 20036. Occasionally travel fels; teacher and professorial placement service for Middle East. Americans.

m AMERICAN GUILD OF MUSICAL ARTISTS, Student Award, 1841 Broadway, NYC 10023. Membership privileges to student of music school selected by faculty or student body. One per school.

M,m AMERICAN GUILD OF ORGANISTS COMPETITION, 630 Fifth Ave., NYC 10020. Organists under 25 years. Winner presented at solo organ recital at AGO Convention.

WR AMERICAN HERITAGE PUBLISHING CO., INC., 551 Fifth Ave., NYC 10021. American Heritage Biography Prize: two books of auto or biography already accepted by publisher. Not limited to American history. TWO prizes of $20,000 each. Annually. Anyone. N.B. Publisher submits nomination to Richard M. Ketchum, Managing Director, at above address. MR

7

WR   AMERICAN HISTORICAL ASSN., 400 A St., SE, Washington, DC 20003. Up to $4,000 for historical books and manuscripts. Write for listing of many awards.

A   THE AMERICAN HOSPITAL ASSOCIATION DIVISION OF HEALTH FACILITIES AND STANDARDS, 840 North Lake Shore Dr., Chicago, IL 60611. Graduate fellowships not to exceed $6,000 for students of architecture and health facilities design. U.S. citizens. Deadline March 15.

P-A   AMERICAN INSTITUTE OF ARCHITECTS, 1735 New York Ave., NW, Washington, DC 20006.
        R.S. REYNOLDS MEMORIAL AWARD FOR COMMUNITY ARCHITEC-TURE: Award of $25,000 and aluminum sculpture to architects and planners of communities without respect to nationality. Every five years.

M   AMERICAN INTERNATIONAL MUSIC FUND, Theodate Johnson, 1 W. 72nd St., NYC 10023. Write for details.

A   AMERICAN INSTITUTE OF ARCHITECTS, NY CHAPTER, 20 W. 40th St., NYC 10018. Lebrun Fellowship. Award in even-numbered yrs for 6 mos in Europe. Competitions for architects 23-30. Min. 1½ yrs experience in architecture office. $3,000. Deadline Feb. 1.
        LOUIS SULLIVAN AWARD FOR ARCHITECTURE: Awarded to an architect whose works in masonry exemplify the ideals and accomplishments of Louis H. Sullivan. $5,000 and plaque awarded to an architect registered and practicing in the U.S. or Canada biennially.

WR   AMERICAN INSTITUTE OF INDIAN STUDIES, Box 100, Logan Hall, University of Pennsylvania, Philadelphia, PA 19104. Faculty research fels. has travel funds and work in India, housing open to Americans also some aliens are eligible.

P-M   AMERICAN INTERNATIONAL MUSIC FUND, INC., 1 W 72nd St., NYC 10023.
        KOUSSEVITZKY INTERNATIONAL RECORDING AWARD: For the recognition of living composer. $2,000 awarded to composer whose commercial recording is selected after invitation to compete by international panel of jurors.

WR   AMERICAN LIBRARY ASSOCIATION, 50 E. Huron St., Chicago, IL 60611. Contact: Ms. Margaret Myers, Exec. Sec. Arts Librarians may possibly find some aid to their professional education through a booklet (50c) "Financial Assistance for Library Education," an annual. It shows sources from state agencies, local libraries, and academic institutions.

P-ALL   AMERICAN MOTHERS COMMITTEE, INC., Waldorf Astoria, 301 Park Ave., NYC 10022. Works compete on a state level before judging for first prize of

8

$1,000 and second prize of $500. Contact: National Art Chairperson, 11939 Waldermar Dr., Houston, TX 77077.

M   AMERICAN MUSIC CENTER, INC., 250 W. 57th St., Suite 626, NYC 10019. $2,000 assistance for reproducing a score which has been contracted for performance. The piece must be for 7 or more performers and at least 10 minutes in length and its composer under the age of 51 unless a New York resident or place of performance is in New York.

M,m   THE AMERICAN MUSIC CONFERENCE, 1000 Skokie Blvd., Wilmette, IL 60091. Currently organizing the Propp Scholarship Fund. Write for developments. They promote "professional performances" in schools with assistance of a trust fund.

P-WR,wr AMERICAN MUSICOLOGICAL SOCIETY, Music Dept., University of Pennsylvania, Philadelphia, PA 19104.
      ALFRED EINSTEIN AWARD: To honor excellence of a published musicological article in an American or Canadian periodical during the preceding year by an author not over 40 years old. Prize of $400 awarded annually.
      OTTO KINKELDEY AWARD: To honor the excellence of a musicological book published within the previous year. By an American or Canadian author. $400 awarded annually.

M,m   AMERICAN MUSICOLOGICAL SOCIETY, New York University, NYC 10003. Travel grants to attend international meetings, sponsored & paid by ACLS for scholars in the field of music only.

WR   THE AMERICAN NATIONAL THEATRE AND ACADEMY, 245 W. 52nd St., NYC 10019. Awards in playwriting; full length play never produced or published; Americans. Apply ANTA Awards in Playwriting, A AP Dept. at above address.

WR   AMERICAN NEWSPAPER GUILD, 1126 16th St., NW, Washington, DC 20036. MR
      HEYWOOD BROUN AWARD: Journalistic work with concern for public interest $1,000.

M   AMERICAN OPERA AUDITIONS, 4511 Carew Tower, Cincinnati, OH 45202. AMERICAN SINGERSONLY. Age limit for sopranos, tenors, baritones, 32 yrs; mezzos, contraltos, bassos, 34 yrs. Award is debut in Milan, Italo, trans. & expenses. For auditions in Italy apply: Assoziazione Lirica e Concertistica Italiana, Via Mazzi 7, Milan, Italy.

vp   AMERICAN ORIENTAL SOCIETY, Freer Gallery of Art, Washington, DC 20560. Louise Wallace Hackney Scholarship administered by the American Oriental Society, for U.S. citizens who are graduate students with three years of Chinese language or its equivalent. For further information apply to John A. Pope, above address.

ALL-H,   AMERICAN PHILOSOPHICAL SOCIETY, 104 S. Fifth St., Philadelphia, PA
all-h   19106. Many small, must have PhD or equivalent.

T,WR   THE AMERICAN PLAYWRIGHTS THEATER, 1102 Drake Union, 1849 Cannon Dr., The Ohio State University, Columbus, OH 43210. Winning play is offered to member groups for production the following year.

WR   AMERICAN POLITICAL SCIENCE ASSOCIATION, 1527 New Hampshire Ave., NW, Washington, DC 20036. The Public Affairs Reporting Award; article or series of articles on any phase of state or local govt. politics. Americans, preferably under 40 years.

M   AMERICAN RECORDER SOCIETY, Seventh Floor, 13 E. 16th St., NYC 10013. Andrew Acs.

ALL-H,   AMERICAN RESEARCH INSTITUTE IN TURKEY, 1155 E. 58th St., Chi-
all-h   cago, IL 60637. Fels. to $10,000 renew., in Turkey. Any nationality, who have PhD's who are members of good standing or educational or research institutions in the U.S. or Canada.

vp,c   AMERICAN RIVER COLLEGE, 4700 College Oak Dr., Sacramento, CA 95814.

all   AMERICAN SAMOA ARTS COUNCIL, Office of the Governor, Pago Pago, American Samoa 96799. Money awarded to artists in schools and occasionally to individual artists.

ALL,all   AMERICAN SCANDINAVIAN FOUNDATION, 127 E. 73rd St., NYC 10021. Must have BA degree. Study or work in any field for Norway, Denmark, Sweden, Finland and Iceland. Annually. Cash grants up to $4,000, rarely renewable. Grants given in recent years have ranged from $150,000 to $250,-000 per year. Contact: Ms. Delores Di Paole, Director of the Exchange Division.

WR-H   AMERICAN SOCIETY OF CHURCH HISTORY, 321 Mill Rd., Oreland, PA 19075. Frank S. and Elizabeth D. Brewer Prize fresearch in the field of American Church History and aid in publication of work $1,000. Once every 2-3 yrs.

WR,M   AMERICAN SOCIETY OF COMPOSERS, AUTHORS AND PUBLISHERS, ASCAP Bldg., One Lincoln Plaza, NYC 10023. Four awards of $500 each for Deems Taylor Awards which are for any work written about music and/or its creators. Can be biographical, critical, reportorial or historical. Deadline June 1.

P-VP   AMERICAN SOCIETY OF CONTEMPORARY ARTISTS, 1916 Avenue K, Brooklyn, NY 11230. Awards temporarily stopped to be an exhibiting organization.

P-VP   AMERICAN SOCIETY OF MAGAZINE PHOTOGRAPHERS, 60 E 42nd St., NYC 10017.

ROBERT LEVITT AWARD: In honorium of continued excellence and contributions in photojournalism. Awarded annually.

PHOTOGRAPHER OF THE YEAR: In honorium of excellent work and outstanding magazine photographic coverage. Awarded annually.

SPECIAL TECHNICAL AWARD: In honor of unusual and unique technical achievements which benefit the art of photography. Awarded irregularly.

TECHNICAL ACHIEVEMENT AWARD: In recognition of achievement in photography, this achievement advancing the technical state of the art. Annually.

WR   AMERICAN SOCIOLOGICAL ASSN., 1722 N St., NW, Washington, DC 20036. Award $500: pulbications contribution to progress of sociology during preceding two yrs. Americans by nomination.

P-T   AMERICAN THEATRE ASSOCIATION, INC., 726 Jackson Place, NW, Washington, DC 20566.

JENNIE HEIDEN AWARD: In honorium of outstanding work in the field of children's theatre, $100 and certificate awarded annually.

m,vp,f   AMERICAN UNIV., Washington, DC 20016, Dr. L. Ultan, Chmn. $1,000 vocal schl. for full time degree as music major in voice. Also Univ. fels. & teaching assists, all $2,000 & tuition. P-t service required. Seven fels. in film to $2,000.

AUDREY WOOD AWARD IN PLAYWRITING: In honorium of the best original script of any length. $500 and production of the play is awarded to the playwright annually.

P-VP   AMERICAN WATERCOLOR SOCIETY, 1083 Fifth Ave., NYC 10028. 33 awards:

THE AMERICAN WATERCOLOR SOCIETY GOLD MEDAL OF HONOR: In honor of achievement in watercolor painting. Medal and $800 awarded to any artist annually.

THE AMERICAN WATERCOLOR SOCIETY SILVER MEDAL OF HONOR: In honor of achievement in watercolor painting. Medal and $700 awarded to any artist annually.

THE AMERICAN WATERCOLOR SOCIETY BRONZE MEDAL OF HONOR: In honor of achievement in watercolor painting. $600 and medal awarded to any artist annually.

THE ARCHES PAPERS AWARD: $222 awarded annually.

THE SAMUEL J. BLOOMINGDALE MEMORIAL AWARD: For recognition of an outstanding watercolor painting. $250 awarded to the artist annually.

THE CFS AWARD: In honor of achievement in watercolor painting. $200 awarded annually.

THE MARIO COOPER AWARD: In honor of outstanding work in watercolor painting. $200 awarded annually.

THE JOHN L. ERNST AWARD: In honor of outstanding work in water-color painting. $250 awarded annually.

THE FAMOUS ARTISTS SCHOOL AWARD: In honor of outstanding work in watercolor painting. $150 awarded annually.

THE FORD TIMES AWARD: In honor of a traditional watercolor painting. $250 awarded annually.

THE ANTOINETTE GRAVES GOETZ AWARD: In honor of an outstanding watercolor painting. $200 awarded annually.

THE HIGH WINDS AWARD: $300 awarded annually.

THE EMILY LOWE MEMORIAL AWARD: To honor outstanding work in watercolor painting. $300 awarded annually.

THE MARTHA T. MC KINNON AWARD: $100 awarded annually.

THE BARSE MILLER MEMORIAL AWARD: To honor achievement in watercolor painting. $300 awarded to the artist annually.

THE GERHARD C. MILLER AWARD: For recognition of a different artist annually with a prize of $250.

THE TED KAUTZKY MEMORIAL AWARD: In honor of outstanding work in watercolor painting. $200 annually awarded to any artist.

CHARLES R. KINGHAN AWARD: For recognition of outstanding work in watercolor painting. $300 awarded to the artist annually.

THE RUDOLPH LESCH AWARD: To honor transparent watercolor painting. Medal and $200 awarded annually.

MARY S. LITT AWARD: To honor achievement in watercolor painting. $250 awarded annually to a non-member.

THE LENA NEWCASTLE MEMORIAL AWARD: In honor of an outstanding work in watercolor painting. $300 awarded to an artist entered in the Society's exhibition, annually.

THE HELEN GAPEN OEHLER AWARD: In honor of an outstanding transparent, traditional watercolor painting. $100 awarded annually.

THE HERB OLSEN AWARD: In honor of outstanding transparent water-color painting. $200 awarded annually.

THE WILLIAM CHURCH OSBORNE MEMORIAL AWARD: To honor achievement in watercolor painting. $200 awarded annually to any artist.

THE LARRY QUACKENBUSH MEMORIAL BIENNIAL AWARD: To honor outstanding work in watercolor painting; $100 awarded every other year, alternating with the Carolyn Stern Award.

THE PAUL B. REMMEY, AWS, MEMORIAL AWARD: To honor outstanding work in watercolor painting. $200 awarded annually.

THE CLARE STOUT AWARD: To honor outstanding work in watercolor painting. $250 awarded annually.

THE WASHINGTON SCHOOL OF ART AWARD: In recognition of outstanding work in watercolor painting. $200 awarded annually.

THE WATERCOLOR USA AWARD: To honor achievement in watercolor painting. $200 awarded annually.

THE EDGAR A. WHITNEY AWARD: For recognition of an outstanding transparent-traditional watercolor painting. Annual award of $200 donated by Mr. & Mrs. Robert A. Blum.

THE WINSOR AND NEWTON AWARD: To honor an outstanding water-

color painting. $150 awarded annually to any artist entered in the Society's exhibition.
THE JOHN YOUNG-HUNTER MEMORIAL AWARD: $100 awarded annually.
THE VERDA KAREN MC CRACKEN YOUNG AWARD: $200 awarded annually.

M   AMICI DELLA MUSICA, Arezzo, Italy. Cash awards for Gregorian, polyphonic & Folk music. All choruses from all countries. Apply: Luigi Colacicchi, Art. Dir.

P-f   AMSTERDAM INTERNATIONAL FESTIVAL OF STUDENT-MADE FILMS (CINESTUD), Office: Roetersstraat 34, Amsterdam, Netherlands.
CINESTUD AWARDS: Two awards—the Prize of the Public of 1,000 Dutch florins for the best film voted by the audience; the Prize of the Press of 1,000 Dutch florins for the best film voted by the Press. The CINESTUD PRIZE of 500 Dutch florins is for work considered worthy of support, and the N.R.C. HANDELSBLAD PRIZE of 500 Dutch florins for the best film made in difficult circumstances. Awarded every two years. Anyone.

ALL   AMVETS MEMORIAL SCHOLARSHOPS, 1710 Rhode Island Ave., NW, Washington, DC 20036. Awards $500-$2,000 scholarships to children of disabled or deceased war veterans.

vp   ANCO WOOD FOUNDATION MERIT SCHOLARSHIP: Awarded through the Art Students League of N.Y. (Talent.).

M   MARIAN ANDERSON SCHOLARSHIP FUND, 762 So. Martin St., Philadelphia, PA 19046. Discontinued.

P-M   ANGELICUM PRIZE, Secretariat, Piazza S. Angelo 2, Milan, Italy.
ANGELICUM PRIZE: For the outstanding chamber orchestra composition, not longer than 20 minutes. First Prize: 800,000 liras, a concert, and publication of the work. Second prize: 300,000 liras.

WR   ANISFELD-WOLF AWARD IN RACE RELATIONS, 321 Cherry Hill Rd., Princeton, NJ 08540. Two prizes, $1,500 each; books on race relations published in preceding yr. Anyone. Submit to: Dr. Ashley Montagu.

F   THE ANN ARBOR 8mm FILM FESTIVAL, The Ann Arbor Film Co-op, PO Box 7592, Ann Arbor, MI 48107. Prize money over $1,000 to nonprofessional regular and super 8mm filmmakers. Deadline Feb. 1.

m   ANTIOCH COLLEGE, Yellow Springs, OH 44074. Some small grants.

M,m   APPALACHIAN STATE UNIV., Boone, NC 28607. 60-$50 marching band; 15-$150 concert band; 15-$15 orch; 6-$150 piano; 6-$150 voice, all renewable. Graduate fels. also.

13

A-H,   ARCHAEOLOGICAL INSTITUTE OF AMERICA, 8th Floor, 53 Park Plaza, NYC 10007, Eugene Sterud, Exec. Dir. U.S. nationals in history, hist. of art, archaeo logy in Mediterranean area, preferably Eastern Mediterranean. Annually to $7,000.

P-VP   THE ARCHES PAPERS AWARD. $200.
SEE: AMERICAN WATERCOLOR SOCIETY.

M   ARCHIVES DU PALAIS PRINCIER, Monaco. Several worthwhile cash awards to composers of all countries. Prizes and requirements vary with categories. Write: Prix de Composition Musicale Prince Rainier III de Monaco.

P-M   GUIDO D'AREZZO INTERNATIONAL POLYPHONIC COMPETITION, Secretariat, Piazza Vasari 6, Arezzo, Italy. PRIZES: A total sum of 3,000,-000 liras are awarded annually to the winning polyphonic choruses, secular folk music and Gregorian chant.

ALL   ARIZONA COMMISSION ON THE ARTS, 6330 No. Seventh St., Phoenix, AZ 85014. Grant Aid to Non-Profit Organizations. Consultant services to Arts Organizations. Travel assistance to artists and small arts organizations. An artists-in-schools program. Awards to visual artists and creative writers.

vp,t,c,a   ARIZONA STATE UNIVERSITY, College of Fine Arts, Tempe, AZ 85281. Contact: William E. Arnold, Acting Dean. Financial Support: For individuals seeking a graduate degree. Currently masters degrees are offered in areas listed, and doctorates in music and art are also available. Stipends range from $2,700 to $3,800 for an academic year. Numerous scholarships & grants to undergraduate students in each of the same areas.

P-VP   ARKANSAS ART CENTER, MacArthur Park, Little Rock, AR 72203.
ANNUAL DELTA ART EXHIBITION PURCHASE AWARDS: For the encouragement and recognition of regional artists born in, or presently living in Texas, Arkansas, Louisiana, Mississippi, Missouri, Oklahoma and Tennessee who entered the Annual Exhibition. Monetary awards totaling $3,500, including a first prize of $1,000. Awarded annually.
ANNUAL PRINTS, DRAWINGS & CRAFTS EXHIBITION PURCHASE AWARDS: For the encouragement and recognition of regional artists who have entered works in the Annual Prints, Drawings & Crafts Exhibition. Artists must be residing in the following states: Arkansas, Louisiana, Mississippi, Missouri, Oklahoma, Tennessee, or Texas. Monetary awards of $500 for the "Best in the Exhibition," $200 for each of the three categories (prints, drawings, crafts). Annual.

vp,c,f   ARKANSAS STATE UNIVERSITY, Jonesboro, AR 72467. Contact: Charles L. Rasberry (for Film). Film Scholarships: Ted Rand Memorial Scholarship—$200 per semester for freshmen; Scripps-Howard Foundation Scholarship—$200 per semester to a student planning a career in Broadcast Journalism.

M   ARLINGTON SYMPHONY ASSOCIATION, Mrs. T. Taylor, 706 N. Fredrick St., Arlington, VA 22203. Small awards ($150).

P-VP JOHN TAYLOR ARMS MEMORIAL PRIZE. Award: $250. SEE: NATIONAL ACADEMY OF DESIGN.

P-WR CHARLOTTE ARMSTRONG NOVEL AWARD. Award: $5,000. SEE: COWARD, MC CANN & GEOGHEGAN, INC.

VP,C ARNOT ART MUSEUM, 235 Lake St., Elmira, NY 14901. $1,000 awards. Must be over 18 years of age and live within 100-mile radius of Elmira, NY. Deadline March 23-April 1.

vp   THE ART ACADEMY OF CINCINNATI, Eden Park, Cincinnati, OH 45202.

P-T,   ART-ACT PLAYWRITING COMPETITION, Box 754, Mt. Sterling, KY 40353. Restricted to current or former Kentucky residents.

ALL   THE ART ANNUAL, PO Box 10300, 410 Sherman Ave., Palo Alto, CA 94303. Exposure and publicity. Selected works will be reproduced in Annual. All. Deadline March 21.

p-vp   ART CAREER SCHOOL, 175 5th Ave., NYC 10010. MR

P-VP,C THE ART CENTER, INC., 120 South St. Joseph St., South Bend, IN 46601. BIENNIAL MICHIANA REGIONAL ART COMPETITION AWARDS: To honor excellent art works by residents or former residents of Indiana or Michigan. Monetary prizes are awarded for first, second & third place winners in the following categories: Drawings, prints, painting, sculpture and crafts. Awarded biennially.

P-VP-H THE ART DEALERS ASSOCIATION OF AMERICA, INC., c/o Ralph F. Colin, Esq., 575 Madison Ave., NYC 10022. At present time no grants are being given.

P-VP, THE ART DIRECTORS CLUB, PO Box 2358, NYC 10001. Makes grants to
P-WR art schools, colleges and organizations in visual arts and communications arts. Send for application.

p-vp   ART INSTITUTE OF BOSTON, 718 Beacon St., Boston, MA 02215.

vp,c   ART INSTITUTE OF CHICAGO, Michigan Ave. at Adams St., Chicago, IL 60603.

p-vp   ART INSTITUTE OF PITTSBURGH, 635 Smithfield St., Pittsburgh, PA 15222. MR

ALL   ARTPARK, PO Box 371, Lewiston, NY 14092. Fee of $300 per week and

$125 per week living expenses given to chosen artist who constructs on the 200-acre site his piece of work. Artist must remove his work at the end of the summer. Deadline Dec. 31.

vp THE ART SCHOOL, 18 N. Park Row, Erie, PA 16501.

vp ART SCHOOL OF W.E. GEBHARDT ASSOCIATES, 124 E. 7th St., Cincinnati, OH 45202.

vp,c ART SCHOOL OF THE SOCIETY OF ARTS AND CRAFTS, 245 E. Kirby, Detroit, MI 48202.

VP,vp ART STUDENTS LEAGUE OF NEW YORK, 215 W. 57th St., NYC 10019. The League does not give Grants or Fellowships to anyone but its own students. The tuition & need scholarships: for study at the Art Students League only.
THE MAC DOWELL SCHOLARSHIP: A traveling grant is awarded competitively to member students of the Art Students League annually. 10 full time scholarships (through the National Scholastic Organization) are awarded for study at the League only. Has several grants-scholarship funds listed in this catalog.

vp ARTESIA COLLEGE, 1400 Richy Ave., Artesia, NM 88210.

M ARTISTS ADVISORY COUNCIL, Mrs. W. Cowen, 55 E. Washington St., Chicago, IL 60602 or Orchestra Hall, 220 S. Michigan, Chicago, IL 60604. Two $1,000, two $500, plus financial and professional help available. Outstanding performers to find engagements. Singers 16-35, anyone. Composers, $1,000 for major orchl. composition 20 minutes' duration, and probable performance. Anyone.

VP ARTISTS EQUITY ASSOCIATION OF NEW YORK (ARTISTS WELFARE FUND), 225 W. 34th St., NYC 10001. Non-interest loans of up to $300 for visual artists with emergency needs.

VP ARTISTS' FELLOWSHIP, INC., 47 Fifth Ave., NYC 10003. Funds for professional artists and their families in financial distress because of age or disability.

M,VP,WR ARTISTS FOR ENVIRONMENT FOUNDATION, Box 44, Wallpack Center, NJ 07881. Residencies at headquarters in Delaware for 14 weeks. Deadline Nov. 15.

ALL,all THE ARTISTS FOUNDATION, INC., 100 Boylston St., Boston, MA 02116. There are 85 grants of $3,500 given annually to residents of Massachusetts who are over 18 years of age and not enrolled in a degree program. In addition to artists-in-residence, artist living-working space and straight-out grant programs, there is a grant program to train artists in management accounting, marketing and handling of legal issues.

16

M   ARTISTS PRESENTATION SOCIETY, 7150 Wise Ave., St. Louis, MO 63117. Auditions young artists within 150-mile radius, and presents winner(s) in personal recital.

VP   ARTISTS SPACE
SEE: COMMITTEE FOR THE VISUAL ARTS.

ALL,all   ARTS COUNCILS OF THE VARIOUS STATES of the U.S. Some States which now have budgets ranging from almost nothing to those which have up to $18 million in appropriated funds in addition to private donations, support various grants to individuals and organizations which, in turn, give such grants both for educational and creative work. Look under other headings for the different councils in the States which are specifically active at the time this edition was edited. If the one in which your interest lies is not listed, check with the office of the governor of the state for the current address of its Council to see if it has funds to the extent that it supports creative work.

ALL,all   ARTS AND EDUCATION COUNCIL AND FUND, 40 No. Kingshighway Blvd., St. Louis, MO 63108.

ALL   ARTS ENDOWMENT (The National Endowment for the Arts, A Federal Agency).
SEE: NATIONAL ENDOWMENT FOR THE ARTS.

ARTS LIBRARIES SOCIETY/NORTH AMERICA, 7735 Old Georgetown Road, Washington, DC 20014. Charles Mundt, Exec. Sec.

P-M   ASBDA-VOLKWEIN BAND COMPOSITION AWARD, 2964 Roberta St., Largo, FL 33541. $1,000 for unrestricted composition. Deadline March 1.

WR,M   ASCAP-DEEMS TAYLOR AWARD. Award: Four awards of $500.
SEE: American Society of Composers, Authors and Publishers.

M,F,vp   ASHLAND COLLEGE, Music Dept., Ashland, OH 44805. Contact: Joseph E. Thomas, Chairman for Music. Small to sizable scholarships for music majors only, renewable pending review, audition required for incoming students. Small to moderate sized grants in aid for participants in music performing groups, no restrictions. Renewable pending review, audition required for incoming students. GRANTS: 15 gifts of $300 to $500 per yr. in the radio-tv division (requires about 10 hrs of work a week), $200 to $1,000 in outright grants for printmaking, painting, sculpture, ceramics, art education.

P-F   ASOLO INTERNATIONAL FESTIVAL OF FILMS ON ART AND BIOGRAPHIES OF ARTISTS, c/o Ms. Flavia Paulon, Director, Calle Avogaria 1633, 30123 Venice, Italy.
THE PRIZE OF THE AIME AND MARGERITE MAEGHT FOUNDATION: For a film which results from the cooperation between the film-

maker and the artist, or the film of an artist as a result of a deep expression. Awarded annually: 6,000 francs. Anyone.

m   ASPEN MUSIC SCHOOL, PO Box AS, Aspen, CO 81611. Partial & full schls. to Summer Institute: instrumentalists pref.

WR   ASSOCIATED WRITING PROGRAMS SERIES FOR CONTEMPORARY POETRY, Washington College, Chestertown, MD 21620. Award is publication and small royalties from books sold.

P-WR   ASSOCIATION DES ECRIVAINS D'EXPRESSION FRANCAISE DE LA MER ET DE L'OUTRE-MER, 41 rue de la Bienfaisance, Paris 8, France.
GRAND FRANCO-BELGIAN LITERARY PRIZE: For the work of a Belgian author written in French, free from any political, religious, or philosophical bias. 2,000 French francs awarded annually.
GRAND FRANCO-CANADIAN LITERARY PRIZE: 2,000 French francs are awarded annually to a Canadian author of a literary work written in French, free from any political or religious bias.
GRAND LITERARY PRIZES OF BLACK AFRICA: 2,000 French francs are awarded annually to an AFrican author writing in French, free from any political, philosophical or religious bias.
GRAND LITERARY PRIZE OF THE REUNION ISLAND, GRAND LITERARY PRIZE OF MADAGASCAR, and GRAND LITERARY PRIZE OF ANTILLES, each of 1,000 French francs are awarded every two years.

AM   ASSOCIATION OF COLLEGE, UNIVERSITY AND UNIVERSITY ARTS ADMINISTRATORS, PO Box 2137, Madison, WI 53701. Full-tuition scholarships for summer workshops made possible through money from the Arts Endowment and otherwise. Basis of financial need and experience in arts administration. ACUCAA has held workshops for over 14 years. Toni Sikes handles applications. Workshops held at different places each year.

ASSOCIATION OF SCIENCE-TECHNOLOGY CENTERS, 1016 16th St., NW, Washington, DC 20037. Michael Templeton, Exec. Dir.

ASSOCIATION OF THEATRE BENEFITS AGENTS, Room 911, 165 W. 46th St., NYC 10036. Ms. Frances Drill.

C,VP ATLANTIC CITY NATIONAL ARTS AND CRAFTS SHOW, 205 N. Montpelier Ave., Atlantic City, NJ 08401. Annual Indian Summer Art Show for all media plus crafts with $3,000 cash awards and $300 purchase award. Due Aug. 15. Annual Boardwalk Art Show with $3,000 in prizes, a trip to Paris for two and purchase awards. No crafts. Deadline June 1.

WR   ATLANTIC MONTHLY, 8 Arlington St., Boston, MA 02116. Atlantic First Awards. Outstanding short stories by new author. $250-$750 annually.

vp,c ATLANTIC UNION COLLEGE, South Lancaster, MA 01516.

WR-VP   ATRAN FOUNDATION, 205 W. 54th St., NYC 10019. Grants, research art & lit; supporting publications furthering these purposes. Anyone.

f,a   AUBURN UNIVERSITY, Speech Communication Haley Center, Auburn, AL 36830. Contact: J.W. Sanders. Graduate assistantships available.

vp   AUGSBURG COLLEGE, 707 21 Ave. S., Minneapolis, MN 55400.

vp   AUGUSTA COLLEGE, 2500 Wolton Way, Augusta, GA 30904.

ALL   AUGUSTANA COLLEGE, Sioux Falls, SD 57102. Faculty members may apply for grants covering cost of research or creative activity in all areas of artistic endeavor.

vp   AUSTIN PEAY STATE COLLEGE, Clarksville, TN 37040. 60-$165-$200 renewable; also Grad. Fels.

P-WR   AUSTRIAN FEDERAL MINISTRY FOR EDUCATION AND THE ARTS, Postfach 65, 1014 Vienna, Austria.
AUSTRIAN NATIONAL BOOK AWARD FOR CHILDREN'S LITERA-TURE: For the best book for children and teenagers. 10,000 Austrian schillings and a certificate are awarded annually to the author.
AUSTRIAN STATE PRIZE FOR EUROPEAN LITERATURE: 100,000 Austrian Schillings and a certificate are awarded to a renowned European author annually. Anyone.

m,wr,vp   AUSTRO-AMERICAN SOCIETY, Stallburggasse 2, Vienna, Austria. Awards covering maintenance and tuition for 6 wk. summer study at Slatzburg Summer school in fields of European Music, German land. Austrian lit & art, int'l relations. 1 yr. of college study, 18-40 yrs. U.S. Nationals. Apply Institute of Int'l Education, 809 United Nations Plaza, NYC 10017.

vp   SHEVA AUSUBEL MEMORIAL SCHOLARSHIP: For females only. SEE: Art Students League of N.Y. (Merit.).

WR   AUTHORS LEAGUE FUND, 234 W. 44th St., NYC 10036. Interest free loans for published artists with sudden financial emergencies. Usually amounts up to $1,000.

vp   AVILA COLLEGE, 11901 Wornall Rd., Kansas City, NO 64145.

P-WR,   AWARD OF MERIT. Award: $1,000 & Medal.
P-VP,P-T   SEE: The American Academy of Arts and Letters.

m   AYUNTAMIENTO DE ALICANTE, Alicante, Spain. Cash awards and study of musical composition in Spain for foreign composer submitting winning composition in orch.

m   AZUSA PACIFIC COLLEGE, Azusa, CA 91702. $100-$250 per semester. Undergrad.

P-M   BACH   INTERNATIONAL   COMPETITION,   c/o Mrs. Raissa Tselentis Chadwell, 1211 Potomac St., NW, Washington, DC 20017. PRIZES: For the outstanding performances of the clavier works of Bach in the age groups 17 to 32. Monetary awards of $1,500, $750 and $500. First place winner has a chance to stay for two months in the Federal Republic of Germany.

P-M   BACH INTERNATIONAL COMPETITION, The Secretariat, Grassistrasse 8, DDR-701 Leipzig, German Democratic Republic. PRIZES: For the outstanding performers in: piano, organ, voice, violin, cello, who are not older than 32. Eight awards from 500 M to 7,500M in each of the 5 divisions except voice competition.

M   BAGBY MUSIC LOVER'S FND., 501 Fifth Ave., NYC 10017. Funds to formerly prominent musicians now aged or physically handicapped.

all   BAKER UNIVERSITY, Miss M. Howen, Dean, Baldwin, KS 66006. Grants given in the arts have to be classified as student scholarships or other forms of financial assistance for undergrads pursuing a baccalaureate degree program at Baker U.

vp,VP   BAKERY SCHOOL OF FINE ARTS OF VERNON COURT JR. COLLEGE, Bellevue Ave., Newport, RI 02840. MR

P-WR   THE EMILY CLARK BALCH PRIZE.
SEE: THE VIRGINIA QUARTERLY REVIEW

vp,c   BALDWIN WALLACE COLLEGE, Berea, OH 44017. Aid based on need utilizing CSS Need Analysis.

f,a   BALL STATE UNIVERSITY, Center for Radio & Television, 2000 University Ave., Muncie, IN 47306. Contact: William H. Tomlinson, Director. Two graduate assistantships at $2,800 each.

M   BALTIMORE OPERA COMPANY, Inc., 40 West Chase Street, Baltimore, MD 21201. Rosa Ponselle is the artistic director. May 21 deadline. Prizes (7) ranging from $500 to $2,500 for contestants between ages 20 and 32 who recite given arias in original language from memory.

WR-H,   BANARAS HINDU UNIV., Varanasi 5, India. SCHLSPS. to graduates of
VP-H,   most countries for study and research. In Indian history, philosophy, culture,
M-H   art, etc. Apply Office of the Registrar above.

P-WR-H   BANCROFT PRIZES, Columbia University, 311 Low Library, NYC 10027. AWARDS: In recognition of best published works in American (i.e.: North, Central & South) History and Diplomacy. Two awards of $4,000 each annually. Entries must be submitted no later than December 10.

vp,c BANFF SCHOOL OF FINE ARTS, Banff, Alberta, Canada.

P-WR BARCELONA INSTITUTE OF HISPANIC CULTURE, Calle de Valencia 231 Barcelona, Spain.
JUAN BOSCAN PRIZE: In honorium of the outstanding Spanish and His-pano-American poets writing in Castilian language. 50,000 awarded annually. Anyone.

m,t,d BARD COLLEGE, Annandale-on-Hudson, NY 12504. Two up-to-full tuition, auditions, to entering freshmen. Renewable. Scholarships are also open, fol-lowing auditions, for Theatre and Dance students.

m BARNARD COLLEGE, Columbia Univ., NYC 10027. Women only, two schls annually.

P-VP HELEN FOSTER BARNETT PRIZE. Award: $350.
SEE: NATIONAL ACADEMY OF DESIGN.

m BARRINGTON COLLEGE, Division of Fine Arts, Middle Highway, Barring-ton, RI. All schls, awards through the Office of the Dean of Students.

P-WR ALICE HUNT BARTLETT PRIZE. See: Poetry Society.

m,vp,c BAYLOR UNIVERSITY, PO Box 6237, Waco, TX 76706. Contact: Arch W. Hunt, Vice Pres. for Student Financial Aid and Placement.
NATIONAL MERIT SCHOLARSHIPS: Ten new scholarships each year and Baylor makes a $200 freshman scholarship award to the high school vale-dictorian. Deadline: March 1 prior to the fall semester, and November 1 prior to the spring semester. Anyone.

M JOSEPH H. BEARNS PRIZES IN MUSIC, 703 Dodge, Columbia, Univ., NYC 10027. Two prizes for outstanding musical composition by U.S. Citizen, 18-25 yrs. old. $900 for composition in smaller form and $1,200 for composi-tion in larger form. Deadline Feb. 1.

vp,t,m BEAVER COLLEGE, Glenside, PA 19038. Contact: Director of Admissions. Scholarships awarded on basis of financial need. Cover tuition and room and board. No set number awarded, amounts up to $3,000.

m BEEBE (FRANK HUNTINGTON) FUND FOR MUSICIANS, c/o Francis C. Welch, 73 Tremont St., Rm 1034, Boston, MA 02108. Two scholarships to American music students for study abroad.

m THE BEETHOVEN CLUB, Mrs. Fred M. Neill, Pres., 263 S. McLean Blvd., Memphis, TN 38104. Non-interest loans to teacher recommended musicians, from $500 to $1,000 for 5-year period.

WR,wr BELGIAN AMERICAN EDUCATIONAL FOUNDATION, 420 Lexington

Ave., NYC 10017. Fellowships for study and work in Belgium to graduates. Knowledge of French or Flemish is essential and a PhD is a prerequisite. Stipend is $350 per month, plus travel for a maximum period of ten months. Applications must be in by January 10.

vp,m   BELOIT COLLEGE, Beloit, WI 53511. Up to full tuition to Beloit, annually and renewable; on academic achievement and need.

m   BEMIDJI STATE COLLEGE, Bemidji, MI 56601. Ten $200; 12 $2,400.

vp,c   BENEDICT COLLEGE, Taylor at Harden Sts., Columbia, SC 29204.

m   BENEDICTINE COLLEGE MUSIC DEPARTMENT, Atchison, KS 66002. Contact: Sister Joachim Holthaus.
      DR. E.F. STEICHEN SCHOLARSHIP: A partial tuition grant is made ao a talented student who intends to study music in college. Based on outstanding performance, ability on audition and ACT scores.
      A no-need grant which varies in amount.

vp   BENNETT COLLEGE, Millbrook, NY 12545.

vp,a,c   BENNINGTON COLLEGE, Bennington, VT 05201. Contact: Dean of Studies and Secretary of Visual Arts Division. Financial aid toward the tuition. Studio facilities. Graduate Fellowships in return for faculty assistance is possible.

vp,c,   BEREA COLLEGE, Berea, KY 40403.
P-WR   THE W.D. WEATHERFORD AWARD: In recognition of excellent published works that best capture the unique atmosphere of the Appalachian South. The work must have been published in the U.S., may be any length, may be fact, fiction, or poetry. $500 is awarded annually to the author, plus a framed certificate.

WR   BERGEN-BELSEN REMEMBRANCE AWARD, World Federation of Bergen-Belsen Associates, Box 333, Lenox Hill Station, NYC 10021. $2,500 for literature on the Nazi holocaust. All.

P-WR   MIKE BERGER AWARDS: To honor New York journalists who are outstanding in their field, as well as New York reporters. $1,000 is to be shared among the winners. Individual framed certificates, however. Annually.
    SEE: COLUMBIA UNIVERSITY.

m   BERKLEE SCHOOL OF MUSIC, 1140 Boylston St., Boston, MA 02215. Two $1,000, 4 $500, 6 $250. Various schls., part-time service required.

VP   BERKS ART ALLIANCE SHOW, 20 West Court Blvd., West Lawn, PA 19609. Purchase and cash awards in regional exhibition.

VP   BERKSHIRE MUSEUM, PO Box 385, Pittsfield, MA 01201. $1,000 prize for annual show of graphics and drawings. New England States and New York. Deadline May 25.

M,m   BERKSHIRE MUSIC CENTER, Symphony Hall, Boston, MA 02115. Daniel R. Gustin, Adm. Many awards for young, active performers, composition, conducting, singers, instrumentalists, various stipends up to $700. Apply Boston. College training prerequisite. Training takes place at Tanglewood in Lenox, MA.

P-F   BERLIN INTERNATIONAL AGRICULTURAL FILM COMPETITION, Bureau des Internationale Agrarfilm-Wettbewerbe Bundesallee 216-218, 1 Berlin 15, West Berlin.
     EDUCATIONAL, DOCUMENTARY, and public relations, advisory and publicity films on agriculture, horticulture, forestry, fishery, rural home economics, production and marketing of food, nutrition, environmental protection are honored with the Golden, Silver and Bronze Ear plus a monetary prize annually. Anyone.

a   BERLIN TECHNICAL UNIV., Akademisches Auslandsamt, Technische Universitat, Hardenbergstrasse 34, 1 Berlin 12, Federal Republic of Germany. Monthly stipend plus tuition of 10 months at Berlin Tech. To Univ. students who are nationals of Unesco Member States. Candidates apply through their Univ. to above address. Knowledge of Germany essential.

vp   THELKA M. BERNAYS MEMORIAL FUND: Founded 1940. See: Art Students League of N.Y. (Merit.).

P-WR   PRINCE BERNHARD FUND, Herengracht 284, Amsterdam, Netherlands.
     MARTINUS NIJHOFF PRIZE: For the best work in translating a literary work into and from Dutch. 3,000 Dutch Florens awarded annually. Anyone.

vp,t,m   BERRY COLLEGE, Art Dept., Drawer V, Mt. Berry, GA 30149. Scholarships and assistantships—several up to $900. Drama and Speech fellowships— Grant given by Berry college $300 to incoming freshmen who show talent and interest in speech/drama activities. Music schols. by audition, renewable, range up to full tuition.

WR   BETA SIGMA PHI SORORITY, c/o Canadian Authors Assn., 22 Yorkville Ave., Toronto 5, Ontario, Canada. For first novel of distinction, $1,000. Annually.

all,all-h   BETHANY COLLEGE, Lindsborg, KS 67456. Joe Newell, Financial Aid Officer. Scholarships awarded in Arts, Humanities, Music and Social sciences. Worth under $1,000—grants are for education only. Apply: Office of Admissions.

vp-c,m   BETHANY COLLEGE, Bethany, WV.

m   BETHANY NAZARENE COLLEGE, 39th Expressway and College Ave., Bethany, OK 73008. R-(20) $100. One assistantship.

m   BETHEL COLLEGE, 1480 No. Snelling, St. Paul, MN 55101. 1-2, $50-$100 to entering freshmen, 3-4 $100.

m   BETHEL COLLEGE, McKenzie, TN 38201. One $960, full tuition and music fees; 10 $135 music fees.

T,WR   BETTER BOYS FDN. FAMILY CENTER, 1512 Pulaski Rd., Chicago, IL 60623. Prize of $400 and production for children's play written by a black playwright.

vp   BIRMINGHAM-SOUTHERN COLLEGE, 800 Eighth Ave., W., Birmingham, AL.

m,t,f,c,   BLACK HAWK COLLEGE, 6600 34th Ave., Moline, IL 61265. Offers stu-
vp   dents complete financial aid programs, including scholarships, National Defense Student Loans, Work-Study, and Educational Opportunity Grants.

P-WR   THE JAMES TAIT BLACK MEMORIAL PRIZES, University of Edinburgh, Dept. of English Literature, David Hume Tower, George Square, Edinburgh EH8 9JX, Scotland. Two prizes of 1,000 pounds annually; one is for a novel and one is for a biography. Submit copies of entries early in the year.

T   BLACK THEATRE ALLIANCE, 410 W. 42nd St., NYC 10036. J. Devore.

P-WR   THE BLACK WARRIOR REVIEW, PO Box 2936, University, AL 35486. Two prizes of $500 and $250. Deadline July 1.

vp   ARNOLD BLANCH MEMORIAL SCHOLARSHIP. SEE: Art Students League of N.Y. (Merit.).

P-VP-H   THE ROBERT WOODS BLISS SCHOLARSHIP. Award: Up to $5,500. SEE: DUMBARTON OAKS CENTER FOR BYZANTINE STUDIES.

M,T   MARC BLITZSTEIN AWARD, c/o National Institute of Art & Letters, 633 W. 155th St., NYC 10032. To encourage creation of works of merit for the musical Theatre, to composers, lyricists or librettist. $2,500 annually.

M   ERNEST BLOCK AWARD, c/o United Choral Society, Box 73, Cedarhurst, NY 11616.

vp   BLOOMFIELD COLLEGE, Bloomfield, NJ 07003.

P-VP   BLOOMINGDALE, SAMUEL J., AWARD. Award: $250. SEE: AMERICAN WATERCOLOR SOCIETY.

vp,c   BLOOMSBURG STATE COLLEGE, Dept. of Art., Bloomsburg, PA 17185.

m   BLUFFTON COLLEGE, Bluffton, OH 45817. One $300 music teacher.

P-WR   BLUMENTHAL-LEVITON-BLONDER PRIZE. Award: $200.
SEE: POETRY MAGAZINE.

WR   B'NAI B'RITH COMMISSION ON ADULT JEWISH EDUCATION, 1640 Rhode Island Ave., NW, Washington, DC 20036. $1,000 for authors' view of Jewish life and values.

vp   BOB JONES UNIVERSITY, Greenville, SC 29614. Dwight Fustafson, Dean.

all   BOISE STATE COLLEGE, 1907 Campus Drive, Boise, ID 83707. Anyone.

m,vp   BOK (MARY LOUISE CURTIS) FND., 1726 Locust St., Philadelphia, PA 19103. Scholarships primary via Curtis Inst. of Music. Other music activities as well as Fine Arts. Write for details.

P-WR   BOLLINGEN PRIZE IN POETRY.
SEE: YALE UNIVERSITY LIBRARY.

P-WR   BOLOGNA UNIVERSITY, Bologna, Italy.
CARDUCCI PRIZE: 1,000,000 liras awarded annually for poetry, monographs and essays on poetry and poets. Anyone.

P-WR   BOOK WORLD, 435 No. Michigan Ave., Chicago, IL 60611.
CHILDREN'S SPRING BOOK FESTIVAL AWARDS: Author of picture book, book for 8-12 year olds and 12-16 year olds. $250 annually.

P-WR   BOOKS ABROAD, University of Oklahoma, Norman, OK 73069.
BOOKS ABROAD/NEUSTADT INTERNATIONAL PRIZE FOR LITERATURE: In honorijm of outstanding work in the fields of poetry, drama or fiction. Must be in either French or English. Silver eagle, certificate, $10,000 and one issue of Books Abroad devoted to the laureate. Awarded every other year.

P-WR   BOOKS FOR ASIA, 149 W. 4th St., NYC 10012. Gilbert Dilucia.

WR   BORESTONE MOUNTAIN POETRY AWARD, Box 653, Solama Beach, CA 92075. $100-$300 for best poem, in magazines. Three times annually.

vp,c   BOSTON CENTER FOR ADULT EDUCATION, 5 Commonwealth Ave., Boston, MA 02116. Contact: Mr. Donnie Curtis, Registrar. SCHOLARSHIPS: Awarded on the basis of need. Not renewable. Apply 3 weeks prior to term start up date.

d,m,t   BOSTON CONSERVATORY OF MUSIC, 8 The Fenway, Boston, MA 02215. Scholarships of $200 to $2,000 based on talent and aptitude.

P-VP,WR BOSTON GLOBE NEWSPAPER CO., Boston, MA 02107.
BOSTON GLOBE—HORN BOOK AWARDS: For the recognition and encouragement of the writing and illustrating of children's books, published during the previous year. Monetary award of $200 in each category of author and illustrator annually.

M,m BOSTON SCHOOL OF MUSIC, 686 Massachusetts Ave., Cambridge, MA 02139. Contact: Mr. Herman Vaun Binns, Supervisor. Grants offered $1,000 or under for professional creative work while a student. Anyone. No facilities for living quarters or board. Anyone.

vp,c,f BOSTON UNIVERSITY, 640 Commonwealth Ave., Boston, MA 02215. Teaching scholarships and assistantships, up to $1,500.

vp BOWDOIN COLLEGE, Brunswick, ME 04011. Students of Bowdoin; write Dir. of Admissions.

m,F BOWLING GREEN STATE UNIV., School of Music, Bowling Green, OH 43403. Various Graduate Assists. Also 9 PhD fellowships with service ($3,000 each); 2 PhD non-serivce fellowships ($3,000 each); 8 MA assistantships ($2,200).

P-VP BRADFORD CITY ART GALLERY AND MUSEUMS, Cartwright Hall, Bradford, Yorkshire, England, UK.
BRITISH INTERNATIONAL PRINT BIENNIAL: Awarded for outstanding work in the printmaking field. Monetary prizes of a total of $3,000 are awarded every two years.

M,m BRADLEY UNIVERSITY SCHOOL OF MUSIC, Peoria, IL 61625. Contact: Dr. Allen Cannon.
SCHOLARSHIPS: (6) $650 annually, renewable for four years. Financial aid based on need.
GRADUATE ASSISTANTSHIPS: ($2,250) for students working towards Master of Music Education.

M BRAEMER COMPETITION, Congregation Adath Jeshurun, York Road at Ashbourne, Elkins Park, PA. $1,000 awards, annual competition for Jewish composers for work based on Hebraic themes. Brochure available.

wr,vp,m, BRANDEIS UNIV., Waltham, MA 02154. Creative Arts. Award, medals,
t,f citations; achievement and promise in Fine Arts, literature, music, and theater arts—8 $1,000. Americans and others. Several scholarships and assistantships. Write.

P-ALL BRANDEIS UNIVERSITY CREATIVE ARTS AWARDS, 12 E. 77th St., NYC 10021. Contact: Marcia Isaacs. AWARDS: Presented annually in the fields of fine arts, music, literature and theatre arts. No applications are accepted, recipients are chosen by professional juries.

vp   MAUD BRANDON MEMORIAL SCHOLARSHIP: created 1959. Awarded as funds accrue.
SEE: Art Students League of N.Y. (Merit.).

wr   BREAD LOAF WRITERS' CONFERENCE, Middlebury College, Middlebury, VT 05753. This conference makes it possible to award fellowships for tuition only.

m,vp   BRENAU COLLEGE, Gainesville, GA 30501. Women undergrads only; renewable schls. & honor schls.

m   BRESCIA COLLEGE, Owensboro, KY 42301. $350 voice; $150 piano; $100 orchestra.

vp   BREVARD COLLEGE, Brevard, NC 28712.

P-VP   THE BREVOORT-EICKEMEYER PRIZE: to honor outstanding additions to the field of design. Award of $1,000 given every five years.
SEE: COLUMBIA UNIVERSITY.

m   BRIAR CLIFF COLLEGE, 3303 Rebecca St., Sioux City, IA 51104. Undergrad. One $250; renewable.

vp   GEORGE B. BRIDGMAN MEMORIAL SCHOLARSHIP.
SEE: Art Students League of N.Y. (Merit.).

m,vp,c,F   BRIGHAM YOUNG UNIV., Provo, UT 84601. Thirty-five scholarships, $200-$400, renewable, with restrictions. Also, Graduate fellowships. Five Film Assistantships ($785 to $1,175).

m   BRISTOL CHAMBER OF COMMERCE, 81 Main St., Bristol, CT 06010. Connecticut Opera Students, ages 14-25. Scholarships up to $300.

P-WR,   BRITISH ACADEMY, Burlington House, Piccadilly, London, W1V 0NS,
WR-H   England. GRANTS: To British or Commonwealth citizens.

vp   BRITISH GOVERNMENT, MARSHALL SCHOLARSHIP. Apply: British Consul-General in NYC, New Orleans, Chicago, Boston, San Francisco by October 22. U.S. nationals, graduates under 26, study for the awarding of a British University Degree.

vp   BRITISH SCHOOL AT ROME, The Hon. General Sec., 1 Lowther Gardens, Exhibition Rd., London, SW 7 England. Nationals of U.S. & U.K., painters under 30 for full-time art courses for study in Italy at British School. Apply to Hon. General Secretary by Jan. 15.

P-WR   BRITISH SOCIETY OF AUTHORS, 84 Drayton Gardens, London SW10, England, UK.

CHOLMONDELEY AWARD FOR POETS: 1,000 pounds are awarded annually for work generally rather than for a specific book of poetry. Anyone.

M-WR   BROADCAST MUSIC INC., 40 W. 57th St., NYC 10019. Several awards $250-$2,000 to student composers in accredited conservatories, university colleges & schools or of private teachers in U.S, Canada & S. America. Apply Allan Beckel. Also Lyricist Award.

WR   BROADMAN PRESS, 127 - 9th Ave. N, Nashville, TN 37203. Frost Fiction Award for original work of fiction representing the Christian missionary and/or evangelist. Writings, contributing to both Christianity & literature. $1,000 and advance against royalties ($1,500).

D,M,d,m   BROOKLYN ACADEMY OF MUSIC, 30 Lafayette Ave., Brooklyn, NY 11217 (part of Brooklyn Institute of Arts and Sciences). Grants for dance through the Academy for work with Merce Cunningham, Alvin Ailey, American Dance Theater and American Ballet Company, as well as dance festivals. For Theater work with Chelsea Theater and the Polish Laboratory Theater.

d,m,t   BROOKLYN COLLEGE SHOOL OF PERFORMING ARTS, City University of N.Y. , Contact Office of the Dean, 11210. Many individual scholarships based on need for undergraduate and graduate students in Dance, Music and Theater.

f   BROOKLYN COLLEGE, CITY UNIVERSITY OF NEW YORK, Film, Television & Radio, Brooklyn, NY 11210. Contact: Mr. Lawrence Kellerman. Thirty television graduate assistantships at $3,200 each.

vp,c   BROOKLYN MUSEUM ART SCHOOL, Eastern Pkwy., Brooklyn, NY 11238.

P-WR   BROOME AGENCY, INC., Box 3649, 3080 No. Washington Blvd., Sarasota, FL 33578. $1,250 for book manuscript and $750 for short story.

wr   BROSS FDN. OF LAKE FOREST COLLEGE, Sheridan and College Roads, Lake Forest, IL 60045. $20,000 awarded every ten years and next award is to be given in 1980. Anyone.

vp,m   BROWN UNIV., Prividence, RI 02912. Scholars and Artist to carry on work; not applicable for graduate study. Annually.
    CHORAL CONTEST FOR AMERICAN COMPOSERS: 3-10 min. suitable for college singers. $200 and royalties from publication.
    HOWARD FND. FELLOWSHIPS, Graduate School: To nationals of all countries 25-45 for productive scholarly work and not for academic degree. Place of study unrestricted. No music schls, as such, general schls which may go to a music major. Graduate assists. may be recommended but as such do not exist.

P-WR   BRUNNER FACT AND FICTION, LTD., c/o Midland Bank, 27 Market Sq.,
            Crewkerne, Somerset, England.
            MARTIN LUTHER KING MEMORIAL PRIZE: 100 pounds sterling
            awarded annually on April 4th for a literary work reflecting the ideals
            to which Dr. King dedicated his life. Prose, verse, fiction, non-fiction, or
            script form. Anyone.

P-AQ   ARNOLD W. BRUNNER MEMORIAL PRIZE IN ARCHITECTURE. Award
            $1,000.
            SEE: NATIONAL INSTITUTE OF ARTS AND LETTERS.

            BUREAU OF CULTURAL AFFAIRS, 317 Marietta St., NW, Atlanta, GA
            30313.

P-WR   BUTLER FAMILY AWARDS IN IRISH LITERATURE. Awards: $1,400 to
            $5,600.
            SEE: THE IRISH AMERICAN CULTURAL INSTITUTE.

vp   BYRON BROWNE MEMORIAL SCHOLARSHIP.
            SEE: Art Students League of N.Y. (Merit.).

all-h   BRYN MAWR COLLEGE, Bryn Mawr, PA 19010.

vp   CHRISTIAN BUCHHEIT SCHOLARSHIP.
            SEE: Arts Students League of N.Y. (Merit.).

m,vp   BUCKNELL UNIVERSITY, Lewisburg, PA 17837. Frances Gilbert Scholar-
            ship Fund, set up by Irving, based on need and scholarship.

P-M   BUDAPEST INTERNATIONAL MUSIC COMPETITION, The Secretariat,
            P.O.B. 80, H-1366 Budapest 5, Hungary. PRIZE: Categories vary annually.
            1976: Best piano performers of Liszt and Bartok music. 330,000 forints
            total.

vp   BUENA VISTA COLLEGE, Storm Lake, IA 50588. Small scholarships avail-
            able annually for arts majors or minors as full-time students. Selection made
            from enrolled students only.   Undergrads. 6-$400, 4-$200, 8-$100. Renew-
            able. Music majors must audition.

M,D,T,A,   BUFFALO FOUNDATION, 812 Genesse Building, Buffalo, NY 14202.
m,d,t,a   Restricted to local area. Numerous awards, scholarships.

P-WR-H   BULGARIAN ACADEMY OF SCIENCES, 7th November 1, Sofia, Bulgaria.
            CYRIL & METHODIUS PRIZE: To scholars for original work in the field
            of old Bulgarian literature, linguistics and art. 2,000 leva and diploma
            awarded annually. Anyone.

P-D,d   BULGARIAN COMMITTEE OF CULTURE AND ART, Office of Bulgarian

Music, Boulevard Stambolijski 17, Sofia, Bulgaria.
VARNA INTERNATIONAL BALLET COMPETITION AWARDS: For the recognition of outstanding work in field of ballet performance. Two age groups: Juniors—up to 19 years of age; Seniors—up to 28 years of age. The Great Prize of the City of Varna of 3,000 leva plus gold statuette is awarded every two years. Anyone.
GOLDEN ORPHEUS INTERNATIONAL FESTIVAL OF THE BULGARIAN MUSIC-HALL SONG: For the best song and performance of a music-hall song. First Prize: Gold statuette of Orpheus and 1,000 leva. Other small awards. Annual. Anyone.

M BULGARIAN CONCERT BUREAU, 1 Benkowsky St., Sofia, Bulgaria. For singers born after Jan. 1, 1934. Write for details attention: INTERNATIONAL COMPETITION FOR YOUNG OPERA SINGERS. Anyone.

P-WR BULGARIAN PEOPLE'S REPUBLIC STATE COUNCIL, Sofia, Bulgaria.
CHRISTO BOTEV INTERNATIONAL PRIZE FOR REVOLUTIONARY POETRY: 2,000 leva, diploma and title of the Poet Laureate of the Botev International. Prize is awarded every five years. For outstanding poetry dealing with the struggle against imperialism and furthering the causes of peace, democracy and social progress. Anyone.

M BUREAU DE CONCERTS MAURICE WERNER, Immeuble Gaveau, 11 Avenue Delcasse, 75 Paris 8, France.
INTERNATIONAL COMPETITION MARGUERITE LONG-JACQUES THIBAUD: Piano and violin. Ages 15-30. Cash awards approx. $4,000. Anyone.
INTERNATIONAL COMPETITION MUSICAL COMPOSITION: $1,000 plus (approx.) to composers under 40; composition for percussion (1 soloist) and 8 accompanying instruments; 15-20 min.

ALL BUSH FOUNDATION FELLOWSHIPS FOR ARTISTS, First National Bank Bldg., St. Paul, MN 55101. Ten grants of up to $14,000 each annually. Applicants must be 25 years of age and lived in Minnesota one year prior to deadline.

P-M BUSONI INTERNATIONAL PIANO COMPETITION, The Secretariat: Conservatorio C. Monteverdi, Piazza Domenicani 19, 1-39100 Bolzano, Italy.
FERRUCCIO BUSONI PRIZE: For the outstanding performances by pianists in the competition. First Prize: 1,000,000 liras and a concert. Other prizes of 500,000; 400,000; 300,000 and 200,000 liras to the other winning contestants. Anyone.

M BUSSETO INTERNATIONAL COMPETITION FOR VERDI VOICES, Via Paola di Cannabio 2, Milan 2, Italy. Sopranos and tenors under 32; messo, baritones, bass under 35; prizes total $2,000. Any nationality.

VP BUTLER INSTITUTE OF AMERICAN ART, 524 Wick Ave., Youngstown,

OH 44502. National Annual Midyear Show for paintings only. $7,500 in purchase prizes. Deadline June 3.

VP   CBBC, Dept. of Art, University of Arizona, Tucson, AZ 85721. Copper II (the CBBC Exhibition) with $5,000 in prizes. Write for further information.

M   CBC OTTAWA ORIGINAL MUSIC COMPETITION, Box 3220, Ottawa, Ont. Canada. SEE: Canadian Music Centre.

WR   MARIA MOORS CABOT AWARDS, Columbia University Graduate School of Journalism, 706 Journalism, Columbia University, NYC 10027. Prize of $1,000 to journalists whose reporting promotes inter-American understanding between North and South America.

vp,c   CABRILLO COLLEGE, 6500 Soquel Dr., Aptos, CA 95003.

VP-H   PAUL CAILLEUX FOUNDATION PRIZE.
          SEE: French Committee for the History of Art.

vp,c,m   CALDWELL COLLEGE, Caldwell, NJ 07006. Contact: Sister Mary Elizabeth Dir. of Admission.
          JOSEPH MURPHY SCHOLARSHIP: A four-year, half tuition scholarship for $3,800. Applicant must be female, and have completed application procedures for admission to Caldwell College.
          MUSIC SCHOLARSHIP: Same requirements as above.
          The following scholarships are for no particular discipline but could be won by a student planning to major in any of the arts: The Mother Mary Joseph Scholarship; The Sister Marguerite Scholarship; The Alumnae Scholarship; The Martin Tiernan Scholarship, The Alumnae Work Scholarship; The Reverend Walter A. Farrell, O.P. Scholarship; N.J. State Scholarship, and the New Jersey Educational Incentive Awards.

WR   THE CALEB AND JULIA W. DULA EDUCATIONAL AND CHARITABLE FDN., c/o Manufacturers Hanover Trust Co., 350 Park Ave., NYC 10022. Grants to many fields including research, education, libraries and literature projects and individuals.

ALL,all   CALIFORNIA ARTS COUNCIL, 1151 I St., Sacramento, CA 95814. Aside from supporting the artist in school and residency, this council also gives several awards. An award of up to $250 for assistance with a public project in a visual art media is given. An award of less than $5,000 for an unfamiliar art project which may answer old art problems (deadline Sept. 1). There is also a program where an artist teacher is chosen and will receive $600 a month and have a chosen apprentice who will receive $400 a month for the length of the apprenticeship.   The California Resale Royalties Act is a law which gives an artist the right to share any profit there may be from the resale of one of his works if sold for over $1,000. Artists who think they may benefit from this must file a visual artists registry form.

31

Each year the State Architect selects from a list of artists compiled by the California Arts Council someone whose work will be placed in one of the public buildings. Interested artists must complete a visual artist registry form.

vp,c,f   CALIFORNIA COLLEGE OF ARTS AND CRAFTS, 5212 Broadway, Oakland, CA 94618. High school seniors and transfer students, annually. Also students who have completed two or more consecutive semesters and currently enrolled. Semi-annually. Film scholarships and assistantships available.

ALL,all-h   CALIFORNIA INSTITUTE OF THE ARTS, 24700 McBean Parkway, Valencia, CA 91355. Anyone. 10 to 20 from $250 to $2,200, also several to MA candidates.

vp   CALIFORNIA INSTITUTE OF THE ARTS, 7500 Glen Oak Blvd., Film & Video School, Burbank, CA 91504. Several small; 10 schols. at $3,000 each.

m,f   CALIFORNIA STATE COLLEGE AT FULLERTON, 800 N. State College Blvd., Fullerton, CA 92631. Graduate assistants, $2,200 and performance grants $50-$400 yearly to talented students in music working on MA degree. 2-3 film assistantships $2,000 per academic year.

vp,vp-h   CALIFORNIA STATE UNIVERSITY SACRAMENTO, Art Department, 6000 J St., Sacramento, CA 95818. AWARDS: For education, history and creation. Kingsley Award $200. R.W. and Joyce B. Witt scholarships are various with annual decisions of the faculty in number and amount.

f   CALIFORNIA STATE UNIVERSITY, San Francisco, Film, Broadcast Communication Arts, San Francisco, CA 94132. Contact: William Kleb, Chairman, Film. SCHOLARSHIPS: 4 assistantships each semester (around $1,150 each).

vp   CALIFORNIA WESTERN UNIV., 3902 Lomaland Dr., San Diego, CA 92106.

ALL   CAMBRIDGE ARTS COUNCIL, 57 Inman St., City Hall Annex, Cambridge, MA 02139. Cambridge residents who have been unemployed for 30 days or more and are registered at the CETA office of Cambridge (51 Inman St.). Judged as to originality, quality and community benefit. Awards range from $600 to $1,000. Apply by August 15 and March 15.

D,M,T,   CAMDEN COUNTY CULTURAL AND HERITAGE COMMISSION, Hopkins
VP   House, South Park Dr. and Shady La., Hadden Twp., NJ 08109. Purchase prizes for annual art competition for Camden Co. residents only. Also, paid services of art groups working for Commission.

m   CAMPBELL COLLEGE, Buies Creek, NC 27506. Twenty $100-$300.

vp,c   CAMPBELLSVILLE COLLEGE, Campbellsville, KY 42718.

32

ALL   CANADA: Among other sources, write to Mr. Rene d'Anjou, Department of Cultural Affairs, 955 St. Louis Road, Quebec, Que., Canada G1S 1C8 and ask for their booklet "Aide Aux Artistes." Theater, music, visual arts, audio visual, literature covered. Maximum: $7,500. Also research grants, aid to exhibitions, art in public buildings, museum acquisitions.

P-ALL   THE CANADA COUNCIL, PO Box 1047, Ottawa, Ontario K1P 5V8.
CANADA COUNCIL MEDALS: In honorium of outstanding work over a span of time in the arts, humanities, and social sciences. Bronze medal and $2,500 are awarded to a Canadian citizen annually.
GOVERNOR GENERAL'S LITERARY AWARDS: In recognition of the best books published during the year by Canadian authors. Six prizes are awarded annually, $2,500 each and a specially bound copy of the book. Three of the prizes go to books in English, three for French.
MOLSON PRIZES: In honorium for outstanding work in the arts, humanities, or social sciences, or to national unity. Awards of $15,000 each, normally three a year.
Basically, in all the disciplines if you are a Canadian or 5-year resident one can receive aid for upgrading their professional skills with institutions or private teachers or for just creative work. Deadlines vary with the many awards.

P-WR   CANADIAN AUTHORS ASSOCIATION, 22 Yorkville Ave., Toronto, Ontario M4W 1L4, Canada.
VICKY METCALF AWARD: In honorium of a piece of writing inspirational to Canadian youths. Award of $1,000 annually.

M   CANADIAN COUNCIL ASSISTANCE TO ARTISTS, Awards Section, The Canada Council, 140 Wellington St., Ottawa 4, Ont., Canada. Awards, Bursaries, Short-Term grants, and travel grants available to Canadian citizens, or permanent residents.

M   THE CANADIAN OPERA CO., 129 Adelaide St., W., Toronta 1 a, Ontario, Canada. Cash prize $500-$1,000 to members of COC only. Age 18-25.

M   CANADIAN WOMEN'S CLUB OF NEW YORK, 140 E. 63rd St., NYC 10021. $300 for Canadian-born singers studying in N.Y. not having made professional debut.

P-M,m   MARIA CANALS INTERNATIONAL MUSIC COMPETITION, The Secretariat, Avenida Jose Antonio 654 Pral, Barcelona 10, Spain. PRIZES: Best piano and violin performers from 15 to 32. Best singers from 18 to 35. Monetary awards amounting up to 300,000 pesetas. Annually, anyone.

P-WR   MELVILLE CANE AWARD.
SEE: THE POETRY SOCIETY OF AMERICA.

m   CANNON MUSIC CAMP, College of Fine and Applied Arts, Appalachian State University, Boone, NC 28607. Scholarships for qualified high school musicians range up to full tuition grants ($250); 4-week term. Must audition.

P-VP   CANNON PRIZE. Award $300.
SEE: NATIONAL ACADEMY OF DESIGN.

P-WR   CAORLE CITY COUNCIL AND THE TOURIST ASSN. OF THE CITY OF CAORLE, Genoa, Italy.
CAORLE CITY PRIZE: To honor the best book for young people which deals with the principles of Modern European education. Must be written by a European. 1,000,000 awarded biennially. Anyone.

D   CAPEZIO, 1841 Broadway, NYC 10023. Capezio Dance Award for contribution to public awareness of the progress of dance in the U.S.A. $1,000.

m,vp   CAPITAL UNIVERSITY, Conservatory of Music, 2199 East Main St., Columbus, OH 43209. Various $200-$900 per year; performance, need and talent. Art Dept.Huber Hall.

ALL   CAPS, SEE: Creative Artists Program Services.

m   THE CARDINAL STRITCH COLLEGE, 6801 No. Yates Rd., Milwaukee, WI 53217. To entering freshmen; restricted and renewable. Two $250 per year. Women only.

ALL   CARNATION CO., Mr. Wallace Jamie, Dir. of Public Relations, 5045 Wilshire Blvd., LA, CA 90036. Elbridge A. Stuart Scholarships. Tuition and stipend. Must be company employee connected. Any field of study. U.S. or abroad.

WR   CARNEGIE FUND FOR AUTHORS, 330 Sunrise Highway, Rockville Center, NY 11570. Maximum of $500. Anyone.

M   CARNEGIE HALL—JEUNESSES MUSICALES, 154 W. 57th St., NYC 10019. Inactive in 1976-77.

m   CARNEGIE INSTITUTE OF TECHNOLOGY, Pittsburgh, PA 15213. Various, to entering freshmen, some require part-time service.

m,vp,c,a   CARNEGIE MELLON UNIV., College of Fine Arts, Schenley Park, Pittsburgh, PA 15213. 8-10 full tuition graduate assistantship; 3 $2,000 & tuition Experienced Teacher Fels.; 1 tuition & $4,800 stipend & dependency allotment for Prospective Teacher Fel.; 4 doctoral Fels. of tuition, stipend & funds for summer study and materials; 2 $2,000 Heinz Fels. to music students.

P-VP   ANDREW CARNEGIE PRIZE. Award: $700.
SEE: NATIONAL ACADEMY OF DESIGN.

P-WR   CAROLINA QUARTERLY CONTEST IN FICTION AND POETRY FOR

34

NEW WRITERS, Fiction Contest or Poetry Contest, Carolina Quarterly, PO Box 1117, Chapel Hill, NC 27514. Up to $125 awarded and publication in the magazine.

c,vp THE EMILY CARR COLLEGE OF ART, 249 Dunsmuir St., Vancouber, B.C., Canada V6B 1X2. Scholarships of $50 to $300 and a loan-grant program which typically yields $2,200.

m CARROLL COLLEGE, Waukesha, WI 53186. Up to one-half tuition, renewable.

vp JOHN CARROLL MEMORIAL SCHOLARSHIP.
SEE: Art Students League of N.Y. (Merit.).

m,vp,c CARSON-NEWMAN COLLEGE, Jefferson City, TN 37660. Five $250, accompanying; 5 $250, band; 7 $250 clerical.

vp ELIZABETH CARSTAIRS SCHOLARSHIP, Est. 1954.
SEE: Art Students League of N.Y. (Merit.).

m,vp,c CARTHAGE COLLEGE, 2001 Alford Dr., Kenosha, WI 53140. Fifteen $100-$700 with restriction, renewable, part-time service.

vp,a CASE WESTERN RESERVE UNIV., Cleveland, OH.

P-M ALFREDO CASELLA INTERNATIONAL COMPETITION, Accademia Musicale Napoletana, Via S. Pasquale a Chiaia 62, 1-80121 Naples, Italy.
PRIZES: The total monetary award in 1976 of 1,500,000 liras goes to the winners of the piano competition, aged from 18 to 32. To the best composer of any age: "Prix Daniele Napolitano," Gold medal and publication for the composition. Anyone.

m,vp,a CATHOLIC UNIVERSITY OF AMERICA, School of Music, 620 Michigan Ave., NE, Washington, DC 20064. Ten performance $800; 36 $400 per semester; 17 partial tuition, varying amounts. Undergraduates, restrictions, renewable, and part-time service required.

VP THE CATSKILL CENTER FOR PHOTOGRAPHY, INC., 59A Tinker St., Woodstock, NY 12498. Purchase considerations and printing of winning works in catalog. Deadline May 1.

WR THE CAXTON PRINTERS, PO Box 700, Caldwell, ID 83605. No grants at present time.

M,m CENTENARY COLLEGE OF LOUISIANA, School of Music, PO Box 4188, Shreveport, LA 71104. Ten $1,000-$1,500 symphony players, renewable; 10 $800 band players.

M CENTRAL CITY OPERA ASSN., 636 University Bldg., 910 16th St., Denver, CO 80202. $500. Colorado residents only.

m CENTRAL COLLEGE, Pella, IA 50219. To entering freshmen, renewable, performance ability, 6-8 $500.

vp,c CENTRAL CONNECTICUT STATE COLLEGE, Stanley St., New Britain, CT 06050.

m CENTRAL METHODIST COLLEGE, Swinney Conservatory of Music, Fayette, MO 65248. Eight $200 to entering freshmen.

d,m,t, vp,wr CENTRAL MICHIGAN UNIVERSITY, School of Fine and Applied Arts, Central Michigan University, Mt. Pleasant, MI 48859. Principally for students, faculty and staff. Award may include up to full tuition, room and board. Other grants for special projects may exceed $1,000.

m,vp CENTRAL MISSOURI STATE COLLEGE, Division of Music, Warrensburg, MO 64903. Graduate assistantships $1,800 up.

vp,c CENTRAL STATE COLLEGE, Edmond, OK 73074.

m CENTRAL STATE UNIV., School of Art and Music, Wilberforce, OH 45384. Various grants-in-aid and N.D.S. loans.

m CENTRAL WASHINGTON STATE COLLEGE, Dept. of Music, Ellensburg, WA 98926. Graduate assistantships $175-$275 per month for academic yr. for MEd. in music education.

vp,c CENTRALIA COLLEGE, PO Box 639, Centralia, WA 98531.

wr CENTRO COLOMBO-AMERICANO, Apartado aereo 38-15, Bogota, Colombia. Teaching Fels. for U.S. graduates for one year in Colombia.

WR CENTRO MEXICANO DE ESCRITORES, Valle-Arizpe 18, Mexico, 12 DF, Mexico.

ALL CERCLE CULTUREL DE ROYAUMONT, 95 Asnieres-sur-Oise, France. Opportunity to scholars and artists to spend a couple of months at the Cercle Culturel de Royaumont to carry out independent work and research. Grants covering room and board.

P-VP THE CFS AWARD. Award: $200.
 SEE: AMERICAN WATERCOLOR SOCIETY.

vp,m,t,c CHADRON STATE COLLEGE, Chadron, NE 68337. Contact: Dr. Harry E. Holmberg.
 TUITION WAIVERS & CASH GRANTS: Applications should be in by

36

April 1 to be considered for following fall term. Cash grants given by Chadron Fine Arts League, renewable. Tuition waiver for first time enrollee. Anyone.

vp,c   CHAFFEY JUNIOR COLLEGE, 5885 Haven Ave., Alta Loma, CA 91701.

VP,vp   CHALONER PRIZE FOUNDATION, William Platt, Pres., 101 Park Ave., NYC 10017. Painting and sculpture creation, approximately $4,000 for one year. Painters and sculptors under 30 for study in Europe, to $3,500.

ALL   CHANGE, INC., PO Box 705, Cooper Station, NYC 10003. Source of emergency funding (i.e. unpaid utility bill or eviction), etc., ranging from $100 to $500. Frequently out of funds.

VP   CHARLOTTE PRINTMAKERS SOCIETY, 110 East 7th St., Charlotte, NC 28202. $2,500 in awards for artists East of Mississippi River with prints only. Deadline Nov. 1.

P-VP   ALEX BERT CHASKY AWARD for a Representational Oil Painting. Award: $500. SEE: ALLIED ARTISTS OF AMERICA.

d,vp,m   CHAUTAUQUA INSTITUTION, Chautauqua, NY 14722. Seven-week summer course or work. Awards $100 to $1,000. Opera production participation, summer season $560 each for 30 apprentices, experienced only. Apply Leonard Trash, 18 Tuxford St., Pittsford, PA 14534.

T   CHELSEA THEATER. SEE: BROOKLYN ADADEMY OF MUSIC.

P-WR   CHIANCIANO CITY COUNCIL, Secretariat of the Chianciano Literary Prize, Chianciano Terme, Siena, Italy.
        CHIANCIANO CITY PRIZE: For the outstanding poetry, fiction or journalism. 1,000,000 liras awarded annually for poetry or novel; 500,000 for journalism. Anyone.

vp   CHICAGO ACADEMY OF FINE ARTS, 84-86 E. Randolph St., Chicago, IL 60601. MR

M,m   CHICAGO CONSERVATORY COLLEGE, 410 So. Michigan Ave., Chicago, IL 60605. Jeanne Howard, Registrar.

m   CHICAGO MUSICAL COLLEGE, Roosevelt University, 430 So. Michigan Ave., Chicago, IL 60605. Contact: Associate Registrar in Music, CMCofRU. All the following awards deal with the field of Music, and are open to ANYONE. Awarded thru competition.
        THE OLIVER DITSON SCHOLARSHIPS: A maximum of six undergraduate schols. of up to $1,000 each toward tuition. Annually for students of unusual ability and in need of financial assistance.

THE H.A. CERTIK VIOLIN SCHOLARSHIP: An annual award to a student.
THE RUTH FRIEDMAN PIANO AWARD: This award provides the sum of up to $1,300 towards tuition for a piano major.
THE MIRIAM MESIROW MARKS MEMORIAL AWARD: This award provides the sum of up to $1,000 toward tuition for a piano major.
THE ROBBONS FOUNDATION MUSIC AWARD: This award provides the sum of $250 towards tuition for a Music History, Theory, or Composition student.
THE MORRIS GOMBERG MEMORIAL STRING AWARD: This award provides a sum of up to $500 towards a full time collegiate violin major's tuition.
THE RABBI NAPHTALI FRISHBERG AWARD: Provides a sum of $150 towards a collegiate violin major's tuition.
THE RUDOLPH GANZ AWARD: Provides the sum of up to $1,300 toward a full year's tuition for a piano student.
THE RAYMOND S. WILSON MEMORIAL SCHOLARSHIP: Provides an annual sum of up to $500 for a full time piano student's tuition.
THE SUE COWAN HINTZ MEMORIAL AWARD: Provides the sum of $120 towards a year's tuition for a full time voice student.
THE MUSARTS CLUB AWARD: Provides the sum of $400 for pre-college, non-credit or college string student in need of financial assistance.
THE CHICAGO MUSICAL COLLEGE STRING AWARD: Provides up to $1,000 to a collegiate, undergraduate string student, chosen annually by competition and deserving of financial assistance. This award may be divided.
THE CHICAGO MUSICAL COLLEGE DEAN'S AWARD: Provides up to $500 annually towards undergraduate tuition for a horn viola, bassoon, harpsichord, classic guitar, trombone or tuba major.
THE DUMAN MUSIC SCHOLARSHOP: Provides $500 towards full time music students in violin, tuition.

P-WR   CHICAGO REVIEW ANNUAL PRIZE AWARDS, Faculty Exchange, Box C, The University of Chicago, Chicago, IL 60637. Award of $100 for works having previously appeared in the magazine.

M   CHICAGO SYMPHONY ORCHESTRA, 220 So. Michigan Ave., Chicago, IL 60604. Contest award to any composer of $1,000 plus probable performance by the Orchestra. Anyone.

m   CHICO STATE COLLEGE, Chico, CA 95926. Four $150 musical talent, 2 $100 string players, undergrad.

wr,hum CHINA, MINISTRY OF EDUCATION, Taipei, Taiwan, Republic of China. Scholarships to students from most countries for study of Chinese culture at National Chengchi U. or National Taiwan U., or Taiwan Norm. U. Knowledge of Chinese.

38

M FREDERIC CHOPIN SOCIETY, Okolnik 1, 00-368 Warszawa, Poland. Annual piano competitions. Anyone between 18-30 yrs. Also grants for research work in music offered. Six prizes awarded to finalists and smaller cash prizes to contestants of certain ranking.

D CHOREOGRAPHERS THEATRE, Suite 906, 225 Lafayette, NYC 10012. John Watts.

F THE CHRIS STATUETTE AWARD, THE CHRIS STUDENT AWARD. SEE: Columbus International Film Festival.

M,m CHRISTIAN EDUCATION FOR THE BLIND, INC., PO Box 6399, Fort Worth, TX 76115. Music Competition for Blind Artists: For the outstanding vocal soloist awards: 1st—$1,000; 2nd—$750; 3rd—$500. Instrumental soloist awards: 1st—$1,000; 2nd—$750; 3rd—$500. Grand Prize—$2,000. Contestants must be under 25.

wr CHUNG-ANG (CENTRAL) UNIVERSITY, Seoul, Korea. Teaching scholarships to those with teaching experience in their own language which they are required to teach while taking courses. For room, board, stipend, tuition. Apply Secretariat above.

wr CHUNG-GU COLLEGE, Taegu, Korea. Scholarships in many fields including Korean language and literature. Apply registrar.

vp,c THE CHURCH COLLEGE OF HAWAII, Laie, HI 96762.

a HENRY S. CHURCHILL FELLOWSHIP. to $1,000.
SEE: American Institute of Architects, NY Chapter, 20 W. 40th St., NYC 10018. Also: A.W. Brunner scholarships, to $6,000.

all WINSTON CHURCHILL TRAVELING FELLOWSHIPS, English Speaking Union of the U.S., 16 E. 69th St., NYC 10021. Fels. to enable travel/consultation in the British Commonwealth countries. U.S. citizens between 25 and 45 eligible for up to 6 mos. travel with between $2,000 and $4,000.

C CINCINNATI CRAFT SHOW, Craft Guild of Greater Cincinnati, 6018 Ridge Ave., Cincinnati, OH 45213. Regional contest with approximately $1,500 in prizes.

ALL CINTAS, c/o Institute of International Education, 809 U.N. Plaza, NYC 10017. Eight annual awards for Cuban citizens or those of Cuban lineage.

vp CITRUS COLLEGE, 18824 Foothill Blvd., Azusa, CA 91702.

wr,m,vp, THE CITY COLLEGE OF NEW YORK, Robert Sherman, Financial Aid
f,a Office, 280 Convent Ave., NYC 10031. Graduate restriction waivers, graduate scholarships up to $1,500, no restrictions. Graduate grants in aid, small,

for those who show unusual promise.
SIDNEY MEYERS MEMORIAL FUND: For the support of deserving film-makers. Others various.

f   CITY COLLEGE OF SAN FRANCISCO, Photography, Broadcasting, 50 Phelan Ave., SF, CA 94112. Contact: B.J. Pasqualetti. SCHOLARSHIPS: Five American Federation for Television & Radio per year ($50); two American Broadcasting Company awards per year ($250 each).

M   CITY OF MONTEVIDEO INTERNATIONAL PIANO COMPETITION, Friburgo 5899, Montevideo, Uruguay. Prizes total $5,000 to pianists 15-32 yrs.

F   CLAREMONT SCHOOL OF THEOLOGY, Clarement, CA 91711. Three to five assistantships, one-half to full tuition.

vp   CLARK COLLEGE, 240 Chestnut St., SW, Atlanta, GA 30314. Contact: Director of Financial Aid. Grants: $550 to full tuition. Scholarships: Averages $1,000 each year; based on need and ability.

m,vp CLARKE COLLEGE, Dubuque, IA 52001. Entering freshmen women, two $800, renewable.

P-VP THOMAS B. CLARKE PRIZE. Award $400.
SEE: NATIONAL ACADEMY OF DESIGN.

wr   CLASS STUDENT SERVICES, INC., PO Box 1006, Rockville, MD 20850. "CLASS—The Student Guide," prizes totaling $400 for best works of fiction, nonfiction, poetry, humor and cartooning by college and university students.

vp,c CLATSOP COMMUNITY COLLEGE, 16th and Jerome Sts., Astoria, OR 97103.

vp,a CLEMSON UNIVERSITY, Dept. of Visual Studies, Clemson, SC 29631.

      CLEVELAND AREA COUNCIL, c/o One Playhouse Sq., Suite 310, 1375 Euclid Ave., Cleveland, OH 44115.

vp,c THE CLEVELAND INSTITUTE OF ART, 11141 E. Blvd., University Circle, Cleveland, OH 44106. Grants for freshmen who major in one of many visual arts fields offered. Many crafts included.

M   CLEVELAND INSTITUTE OF MUSIC, 11021 East Blvd., Cleveland, OH 44106. Contact: Wm. Kurzban, Dean. GRANTS: Up to full tuition ($3,150 for academic year 1976-77) for students offered admission to one of the degree programs, renewable each year, based on need and merit.

C,VP CLEVELAND MUSEUM OF ART, 11150 East Blvd., Cleveland, OH 44106. Annual exhibition with $1,000 reward in 4 categories. A regional competition.

40

WR   CLEVELAND PLAYHOUSE, 2040 E. 86th St., Cleveland, OH 44106. Expenses.

vp   COALINGA COLLEGE, 300 Cherry Lane, Coalinga, CA 93210.

m   COE COLLEGE, 1220 First Ave., NE, Cedar Rapids, IA 52402. Various scholarships to undergrads $120-full tuition. Some renewable, restrictions, need.

vp   COKER COLLEGE, Hartsville, SC 29550. To entering freshmen women only two $2,000 performance.

vp   COLBY JUNIOR COLLEGE, New London, NH 03257.

VP   BLANCHE E. COLEMAN FDN., Boston Safe Deposit and Trust Co., One Boston Pl., Boston, MA 02106. Open to New England Artists. $7,500 was given in 1976. No students. Deadline June 15.

m   COLGATE UNIVERSITY, Hamilton, NY 13346. Men only, various, renewable.

m,d   COLLEGE-CONSERVATORY OF MUSIC, University of Cincinnati, OH 45221. To entering freshmen, continuable, 3-$300, 13-$375; 10-$450; 7-$525; 8-$600; 7-$750; 2-$900; 14-$1,035. Others, restrictions, 31-$300; 5-$375; 11-$450; 9-$525; 15-$600; 5-$900; 3-$1,035. Special ability, 8-$960, dance (ballet emphasis), 25-$1,035, string, woodwind. Graduate fellowships also.

ALL,all   COLLEGE OF CHINESE CULTURE, Hwa Kang, Yang Ming Shan, Taiwan, Republic of China. Facilities and assistance offered by the College of Chinese Culture to foreign artists in art, music, drama, dancing, architectural design, museum management. Special awards to artists having made special attainments in their field.

vp,c   COLLEGE OF EASTERN UTAH, North 4th East, Price, UT 84501.

vp   COLLEGE OF THE DESERT, 43-500 Monterey Ave., Palm Desert, CA 92260.

vp,c   COLLEGE OF THE HOLY NAMES, 3500 Mountain Blvd., Oakland, CA 94619. Women only, 5 renewable $270, 1 $1,000 with part-time services required, 1 $1,000. Undergrad.

vp,m   COLLEGE MISERICORDIA, Lake St., Dallas, PA 18612. Contact: Director of Admissions. Financial aid, work scholarships based on need for those working towards a degree. Scholarships are available to students in top 10% of high school class, regardless of need. Music performance annual schols. awarded.

41

vp,vp-n   COLLEGE OF NEW ROCHELLE, Castle Place, New Rochelle,NY 10801. Contact: Director of Financial Aid.
ART SCHOLARSHIP: Awards are based upon completion of students submitting portfolios which are evaluated by the Art. Dept. Awards range from $250 to full tuition depending upon the recipients' financial need. Deadline: March 1. Applicant must also file a Scholarship application and a Parent's Confidential Statement by February 1st.

vp,m   COLLEGE OF NOTRE DAME, Belmont, CA 94002. $1,000-$4,000, renewable, some performance area. Undergrad.

vp,c,m,   COLLEGE OF NOTRE DAME OF MARYLAND, 4701, N. Charles St., Baltimore, MD 21210. Financial aid for undergraduate student. May be $1,000 or over.
t,w

vp,c   COLLEGE OF THE OZARKS, Clarksville, AR 72830.

vp,c   COLLEGE OF ST. FRANCIS, 500 N. Wilcox St., Joliet, IL 60435.

vp,c   COLLEGE OF ST. MARY, 72 & Mercy Rd., Omaha, NE 68124.

vp   COLLEGE OF THE SEQUOIAS, Mooney Blvd., Visalia, CA 93277.

vp,c   COLLEGE OF SOUTHERN UTAH, 1552 W. 200th North, Cedar City, UT 84720.

all   THE COLLEGE OF WOOSTER, Wooster, OH 44691. Contact: Director of Financial Aid. College of Wooster Grants-in-Aid; College of Wooster Endowed Scholarships and Gifts; Ohio Instructional Grants. Plus grants from other outside agencies.

M   COLLEGES PONTIFICAUX, Saint-Siege, Rome, Italy. Scholarships for postgraduate study of many subjects including Roman sacred music. Anyone. Broad.

P-WR   COLOMBIAN ACADEMY OF LANGUAGE, Bogota, Colombia.
COLOMBIAN ACADEMY OF LANGUAGE: To honor those who make outstanding contributions to the field of Philology. Diploma plus 100,-000 Colombian pesos and cost of publication of the work. Annually. Anyone.

m   THE COLORADO COLLEGE, Colorado Springs, CO 80903. Several full and partial scholarships; based on merit and need by confidential college report. Undergrads.

ALL,all   COLORADO COUNCIL ON THE ARTS, 770 Pennsylvania St., Denver, CO 80203. Monies for artists in schools and some for the placement of artists' works in public places.

42

m,vp,c   COLORADO STATE COLLEGE, Division of Music, Greeley, CO 80631. Various, renewable, restrictions; grad. teaching assistantships in most areas of music. Art Dept.

m,vp,c,f   COLORADO STATE UNIVERSITY, Music Dept., Fort Collins, CO 80521. (Min. of 46) $375, renewable, restrictions, undergrads: Graduate schols. tuition and fees, except $40 per quarter. Two graduate assistantships in Speech Arts.

WR   COLORADO QUARTERLY, Hellems 134, University of Colorado, Boulder, CO 80309. Award of $1,000 and publication in the Spring.

vp,c   COLUMBIA BASIN COLLEGE, 2600 N. Chase, Pasco, WA 99301.

f   COLUMBIA COLLEGE, 925 N. La Brea Ave., LA, CA 90038. Contact: Bruch Shoemaker, Dir. of Admissions.
    SCHOLARSHIPS: Cinema-Three work scholarships for $550 each. Broad-casting-Three work scholarships for $550 each. Seven schols. sponsored by several Los Angeles Television stations.

f   COLUMBIA COLLEGE, Motion Picture Dept., 540 N. Lake Shore Dr., Chi-cago, IL 60611. Six scholarships in Film are available after completion of one semester. MR

vp   COLUMBIA TECHNICAL INSTITUTE, 112 S. Wayne St., Arlington, VA 22204.

m   COLUMBIA UNION COLLEGE, Takoma Park, MD 20012. Five $110 to entering freshmen.

all,wr   COLUMBIA UNIVERSITY, Broadway & W. 116th St., NYC 10027. Travel-ing schls. to men grads at Columbia in Political Science, Philosophy, or Pure Science—at least one academic year. Also Fels. to Col. grads and experienced journalists for Col. course or individual study under faculty supervision. Any-one. Bancroft Prizes for books in field of American History, incl. biography, American diplomacy and U.S. international relations. Americans. Joseph Hearns Prizes in Music, $1,500 & $1,100 to composers 18-25. Anyone. Apply: 703 Dodge St., Columbia U., NYC 10027. For V-P,C: Teachers Col-lege, Dept. of Art & Education, 515 W. 120th St., NYC 10027. For F: Fel-lowships $900, 1st year, $1,500 2nd year. Pulitzer Prizes in Journalism.

WR,wr   COLUMBIA UNIVERSITY TRANSLATION CENTER AWARDS, Transla-tion Center, 307A Mathematics, Columbia Univ., NYC 10027. Fellowships of $10,000 each to proven literary translators to encourage them to learn difficult non-Western languages not generally known in order to tranlate the literature. Also, grants of $500 for booklength translation in progress. U.S. citizens.

vp   THE COLUMBUS COLLEGE OF ART AND DESIGN, 486 Hutton Pl., Columbus, OH 43215.

P-F,f   COLUMBUS INTERNATIONAL FILM FESTIVAL, Film Council of Greater Columbus, 8 East Broad St., Room 706, Columbus, OH
THE CHRIS STATUETTE AWARD: Given for the outstanding 16mm film in Art & Culture; Business & Industry; Education; Education for Social Studies; Health & Medicine; Religion & Ethics; Travel.
THE PRESIDENT'S SILVER CHRIS: For the most unusual and creative film.
THE CHRIS STUDENT AWARD: For the best student film plus $300 and a plaque.
THE MAYOR'S CHRIS: For the most innovative films. Awarded annually in October.

ALL   COMMITTEE OF INTERNATIONAL EXCHANGE OF PERSONS, Senior Fullbright Hays Program, 2102 Constitution Ave., NW, Washington, DC 20418. University lecturing and post-doctoral research abroad under Hays Fullbright Act. Write for details.

VP   COMMITTEE FOR THE VISUAL ARTS, 105 Hudson St., NYC 10013. Helene Winer, Dir., Paul McMahon, Asst., Susan Wyatt, Program Coordinator. Emergency Materials Fund (avg. grant $150) to help meet artists' expenses for shows in non-profit galleries. Also a program providing fees for visiting artists ($75 to $400). Also independent exhibitions program with grants to a group of 3 or more artists who have scheduled a show. All for work inside NY State. Also operates Artists Space Gallery, gives shows to artists and gives aid to non-profit galleries in NY State.

P-WR   COMMONWEALTH INSTITUTE, Kensington High St., London W8 6NQ, England. The Prize of 250 pounds is awarded annually for a first book of poetry in English published by an author from a Commonwealth country other than Britain.

ALL,all   COMMONWEALTH OF PENNSYLVANIA, Council on the Arts, 2001 No. Front St., Harrisburg, PA 17102. Fellowships of $4,000 to enable creative artists to set aside time to continue their work. Deadline Sept. 15.

ALL,all   COMMUNITY ARTS COUNCILS: In some 1,000 different communities in the U.S. there are arts councils supporting organizations in the arts. Some of these organizations and some councils themselves give grants to individuals. Check with your local council to see if they given these. At the time of editing of this edition, there was no central registry of community arts councils with finite information on them. They are growing in number and effectiveness every year and should not be overlooked as a source. Information about new councils and new activities of old councils is published regularly in the Washington International Arts Letter, PO Box 9005, Washington, DC 20003. The community councils known to be active at the time of this edition are listed in it.

44

M,d   COMMUNITY ASSOCIATION OF SCHOOLS FOR THE ARTS—St. Louis, 560 Trinity at Delmar, St. Louis, MO 63130. Contact: Mr. John Bales. Student merit scholarships.

T,WR   THE COMMUNITY CHILDREN'S THEATER OF KANSAS CITY, 1015 West 55th St., Kansas City, MO 64113. Annual award of $500 for unpublished children's play able to be performed by women.

vp,c   COMMUNITY COLLEGE OF BALTIMORE, 2901 Liberty Heights Ave., Baltimore, MD 21215.

M   COMPOSERS THEATRE, Suite 906, 225 Lafayette, NYC 10012. John Watts.

vp,c   COMPTON COLLEGE, 1111 E. Artesia Blvd., Compton, CA 90221.

M   CONCERT ARTISTS GUILD, INC., Carnegie Hall, 154 W. 57th St., Suite 136, NYC 10019. Young professionals building careers, annual auditions, aid through orchestra placement service. Also national competition with awards of recitals, money, etc.

m   CONCORD COLLEGE, Athens, WV 24712. Ten full tuition.

m   CONCORDIA CONSERVATORY OF MUSIC, Concordia College, Moorehead, MN 56560. Many schls. on scholastic aptitude, $100-$800; 2-$150 to entering freshmen; 5-$100; 12-$1,000 renewable, restrictions.

m-P   CONCOURS INTERNATIONAL DE CHANT, Theatre du Capitole, Place du Capitole, 31000 Toulouse, France. Singing competition for all nationalities between ages of 18 and 33. Candidates paid daily allowance of 100 francs and prize winners give performance concerts.

M   CONCOURS INTERNATIONAL D'EXECUTION MUSICAL, Secretariat, Palais Eynard, CH-1204, Geneva, Switzerland. For women 20-30; men 22-32 years, all pianists, viola, clarinetists or percussion players from 15 to 30 years. Sponsored by Radio Geneva and Swiss Romand Orchestra. Substantial prizes and recognition. Annual. Dr. F. Liebstoeckl, General Secretary.

M   CONCURSO VIANNA DA MOTTA, Av. Conselheiro Fernando de Sousa, Srf-rcf, Lisbon, Portugal. International piano competition; 17-30 yrs.; prizes: first $4,000-$100 for 8th.

WR   CONFERENCE BOARD OF ASSOCIATED RESEARCH COUNCILS, SEE: Committee of International Exchange of Persons, 2102 Constitutional AVe., DC 20418.

m   CONGRESS OF STRINGS PROGRAM (AFM), Office of Secy.-Treas., 220 Mt. Pleasant Ave., Newark, NJ 07104. Scholarships to string students 16-23 for 8-week period including room, board, tuition, transportation. Anyone. MR

ALL CONNECTICUT COMMISSION ON THE ARTS, 340 Capitol Ave., Hartford, CT 06106. Assistance for a specific project by a professional artist who is a resident of Connecticut in the amount of $250 to $2,500.

M,m CONNECTICUT OPERA GUILD, Pres., 15 Lewis St., Hartford, CT 06103. Operatic singers, 18-30 yrs. Edrie Van Dore and Frank Pandolfi, Scholarship Awards.

m CONSERVATOIRE DE MUSIQUE BENEDETTO MARCELLO, Direzione Vacanze Musicali, campo S. Stefano 2809, Venice, Italy. Fifty 15-day-1 mo. scholarships open to graduates of all nationalities of a music conservatory or those enrolled in upper level courses. Size of schl. varies.

M CONSERVATORIO C. MONTEVERDI, Bolzano, Italy.
  BUSONI INTL. PIANO COMPETITION: Pianists 15-32. Cash awards. Anyone.

M CONSERVATORIO DE MUSICA DI SANTA CECILIA, Renato Fasano, Via dei Greci 18, Rome, Italy. International "Toscanini" contest for conductors of all countries for opera music under 38. Cash award plus contracts.

M CONSERVATORIA DI MUSICA G. TARTINI, Via Ghega, 12, I-34132 Trieste, Italy. First prize of approximately $3,200 and performance to composers of any age for symphonic composition. 2nd & 3rd prizes.

M CONSERVATORY OF MUSIC, Dreilindenstr. 82, 6000 Lucerne, Switzerland.
  HASKIL (CLARA) COMPETITION: For pianists 18-32. Approximately $2,500. Apply: Hanny Kurzmeyer above. Anyone.

M CONSERVATORY OF ORENSE, Plaza Mayor 2, Orense, Spain. International Competition of Music, Pianists of all ages and nationalities. Cash prizes.

M CONTEMPORARY MUSIC FESTIVAL, Dept. of Music, FA 304, Indiana State Univ., Terre Haute, IN 47809. Award is performance of composition by Indiana Symphony and expenses paid for the performance. Deadline July 15.

m CONVERSE COLLEGE, School of Music, 580 East Main St., Spartanburg, SC 29301. Contact: Financial Aid Office. Undergraduate and graduate financial aid for education at Converse College, in the form of scholarships, general financial aid and graduate assistantships. Admission and audition are required prior to granting of aid.

VP HEREWARD LESTER COOKE FDN., Suite 804, 1200 18th St., NW, Washington, DC 20036. American artists over 40 years of age in need of a subsidized block of time to work in their field. Up to $3,500 given. Deadline Jan. 31.

all COOPERATIVE RESEARCH PROGRAM, Arts and Humanities Program, National Center for Educational Research and Development. U.S. Office of

Education, Washington, DC 20202. Various. Inquire for details. Grants to staff members of institutions of higher education, groups and individuals for conduct of research, surveys and demonstrations.

P-VP   COOPER, MARIO, AWARD. Award: $200.
         SEE: AMERICAN WATERCOLOR SOCIETY.

vp   COOPER SCHOOL OF ART, 2112 Euclid Ave., Cleveland, OH 44115. MR

vp,a   COOPER UNION SCHOOL OF ART & ARCHITECTURE, Cooper Sq., NYC 10003. All students full tuition scholarship.

WR   COORDINATING COUNCIL OF LITERARY MAGAZINES, 80 8th Ave., NYC 10011. Grants to literary magazines and projects to help support non-commercial mags and independent writers. Also to Black literary community.

P-WR   THE COPERNICUS AWARD: $10,000.
         SEE: Academy of American Poets, Inc.

m   THE CORBETT FOUNDATION, 1501 Madison Rd., Cincinnati, OH 45206. In the process of dissolving.

vp   JON CORBINO MEMORIAL SCHOLARSHIP.
         SEE: Art Students League of N.Y. (Merit.).

m,vp   CORNELL COLLEGE, Mt. Vernon, IA 52314. To entering freshmen, four $100-$4,000.

         CORNELL UNIVERSITY, Ithaca, NY 14853. Grants program is no longer in existence.

vp   CORNING MUSEUM OF GLASS, Corning Glass Center, Corning, NY 14830. Qualified graduate students in decorative arts; museum staff to perfect glass knowledge.

m,vp   CORNISH SCHOOL OF ALLIED ARTS, 710 East Roy St., Seattle, WA 98102. Contact: Ms. Karen Killebrew.

vp-p   CORONADO SCHOOL OF FINE ARTS, Monty Lewis, Dir., 176 C Avenue, PO Box 156, Coronado, CA 92118. Scholarship awarded only to students enrolled in the School of Fine Arts.

ALL,all COSMOS CLUB, 2121 Massachusetts Ave., NW, Washington, DC 20008. One annual $1,000 prize awarded to nominees of Cosmos members only.

all   COUNCIL FOR ASSISTANCE TO THE ARTS, 714 S. Hill St., Rm. 405, LA, CA 90014. Wm. R. Meyer, Steering Committee, or Grace T. Bushman, Administrative Assistance. Gives volunteer assistance to individuals in many areas, including finding patrons for small grants of money. Operates with professional volunteer lawyers, businessmen, accountants, and architects to aid in matters such as housing, studio help, legal and other matters. Operates in Los Angeles area with aims toward broader area.

P-ALL   **COUNCIL FOR INTERNATIONAL EXCHANGE OF SCHOLARS**, Eleven Dupont Circle, Washington, DC 20036.
    FELLOWSHIPS: International travel for grantee only (not dependents) plus maintenance allowance covering normal expenses for grantee and accompanying family members; or international travel only; or international travel plus partial maintenance allowance. Contact Director. Open only to American citizens. Fellowship terms range from $1,000 to $1,500 per month. Twelve postdoctoral fellowships with $800 per month. NATO Research Fellowships in the Humanities with grant of 23,000 Belgian francs per month.

WR   **COUNCIL FOR WISCONSIN WRITERS**, PO Box 212, Milwaukee, WI 53216. Awards to Wisconsin residents for literary work in book langth fiction and nonfiction, poetry and plays published in current year.

P-VP   **COUNCIL OF AMERICAN ARTISTS SOCIETIES AWARD.** Award: $100. SEE: ALLIED ARTISTS OF AMERICA, INC.

P-WR   **COUNCIL ON INTERRACIAL BOOKS FOR CHILDREN**, 1841 Broadway, Rm. 300, NYC 10023. Five prizes of $500 for unpublished Third World writers.

D,M   **COUNTRY DANCE AND SONG SOCIETY OF AMERICA**, 505 8th Ave., NYC 10018. Joan Carr.

P-WR   **COWARD, Mc CANN & GEOGHEGAN, Inc.**, 200 Madison Ave., NYC 10016.
    CHARLOTTE ARMSTRONG NOVEL AWARD: In recognition of an outstanding suspense fiction written by a U.S. or British author in the same or similar class of Charlotte Armstrong. $5,000 divided between advances and advertising and promotion. Awarded semi-annually.
    THOMAS R. COWARD MEMORIAL AWARD: For outstanding fictional work, 65,000 words or more, $10,000 awarded to the author annually against the royalties.

m   **TRUSTEES OF LOTTA CRABTREE**, 619 Washington St., Boston, MA 02111. Scholarships, grants, loans to students of the New England Conservatory of Music, and to dependents of deceased or disabled veterans of World War I residing in Mass., Calif. or N.Y. MR

P-F   **CRACOW INTERNATIONAL FESTIVAL OF SHORT FILMS**, c/o Henryk Mocek, Dir., 618 Mazowiecka St., PO Box 61, Warsaw, Poland.
    AWARDS: For the fest films dealing with the advances, the growth of the 20th century, Grand Prix "Golden Dragon" statuette plus 15,000 zlotys

for best short film. Four "Silver Dragon" statuettes plus 10,000 zlotys for best shorts. Anyone.

P-VP   CRACOW OFFICE FOR ARTISTIC EXHIBITIONS, Pl. Szczepanski 3A, Cracow, Poland.
CRACOW INTERNATIONAL GRAPHICS BIENNIAL PRIZES: In honorium of outstanding work in graphic arts. Grand prize: 30,000 zlotys, second prize: 20,000 zlotys, third prize 10,000 zlotys. Awarded annually.

vp   CRAFT GUILD OF THE THOUSAND ISLAND MUSEUM, Old Town Hall, Clayton, NY 13624.

vp,c.a   CRANBROOK ACADEMY OF ART, 500 Lone Pine Road, Bloomfield Hills, MI 48013. Many tuitions and fellowships up to $1,700 each.

ALL   CREATIVE ARTISTS PROGRAM SERVICE (CAPS), 250 W. 57th St., NYC 10019, Rm. 1424. Henry Murphy, Fellowship Application Mgr. Funded by NYSCA. Gives fellowship grants to individual creative artists who are residents of NY state and not enrolled in any school or college. $3,500 to $10,000 non-renewable. Artists must perform some community service for which they are paid in addition to grant. No restrictions otherwise. Fields: choreographers, writers of fiction, filmmakers, graphic artists, mixed media artists, composers, painters, photographers, playwrights, poets, sculptors, video artists.

C,M,T,VP   CREATIVE ARTS LEAGUE, 620 Market St., Kirkland, WA 98033. Services of artists for teaching in exchange for percentage of tuition basis.

VP,WR   CREEKWOOD COLONY FOR THE ARTS, PO Box 88, Hurtsboro, AL 36860. Residencies lasting from one to three weeks in mansion in Alabama. Writers, photographers and artists who have had some recognition may apply. Obtain application from Charles Ghigna, Alabama School of Fine Arts, 820 18th St., N., Birmingham, AL 35203.

m   GEORGE CUKOR SCHOLARSHIP, University of Southern CAlifornis, University Park, LA, CA 90007. $2,000.

P-ALL   CULTURAL LAUREATE FOUNDATION, 2030 No. Lincoln St., Arlington, VA 22207.
CULTURAL LAUREATE AWARDS: To honor outstanding individuals in the areas of cultural endeavor: philosophy, religion, social science, language, pure sciences, technology, fine arts, literature, history, communications, and statesmanship. These international awards are to be initially given on July 4, 1976.

m,vp,c   CULVER-STOCKTON COLLEGE, Canton, MO 63435. Numerous $10-$400, renewable, restrictions.

vp,c   CUMBERLAND COLLEGE, Art. Dept., PO Box 167, Cumberland College Sta., Williamsburg, KY 40764.

ALL   CUMMINGTON COMMUNITY OF THE ARTS, Cummington, MA 01026. Facilities for 15 artists to work together must also help maintain the kitchen and grounds. There are facilities for families. Minimum stay is one month. Some grants in form of tuition abatements. There is a fee involved for use of private room or cabin.

M,D,m,d   MERCE CUNNINGHAM DANCE CO. SEE: Brooklyn Academy of Music.

m   CURTIS INSTITUTE OF MUSIC, 1726 Locust St., Philadelphia, PA 19103. Full scholarship (based on talent) for all students awarded by competitive audition.

m   CUYAHOGA COMMUNITY COLLEGE, 626 Huron Road, Cleveland, OH 44105.

CYRIL AND METHODIUS PRIZE.
SEE: Bulgarian Academy of Sciences.

CZECHOSLOVAK SOCIETY OF ARTS AND SCIENCES IN AMERICA, 12013 Kemp Mill Road, Silver Spring, MD 20902. Vera Z. Boekovec, Sec. Gen.

VP   DALLAS ART INSTITUTE, 8350 N. Central Expy. 1984, c/o Dr. Harvey Davisson, Dallas, TX 75206.

M   DALLAS MORNING NEWS, 3611 Oak Lawn, Dallas, TX 75219. First Prize, $1,000 and contract for featured role with Dallas Civic Opera and possible Dallas Symphony. 17-28 yrs, US or froeign student studying in U.S. MR

P-VP,C   DALLAS MUSEUM OF FINE ARTS, Fair Park, Box 26250, Dallas, TX 75226.
TEXAS CRAFTSMAN EXHIBITION AWARDS: Cash awards awarded triennially to legal residents of the state of Texas for their original craft work.
TEXAS PAINTING & SCULPTURE EXHIBITION AWARDS: To honor artists residing in Texas for their outstanding original works not previously exhibited. Awards from $200 to $1,000 are given biennially.

vp,c   DANA COLLEGE, Blair, NE 68008.

m   DANA SCHOOL OF MUSIC, Youngstown State Univ., 410 Wick Ave., Youngstown, OH 44555. Musical and academic awards.

all   DANFORTH FOUNDATION, 222 So. Central Ave., St. Louis, MO 63105. Various programs of graduate fellowships to men and women in the teaching of all arts and humanities subjects. Usually under 30; numerous full tuition and living expense grants.

ALL   DANISH GOVERNMENT SCHOLARSHIPS, Institute of International Education, 809 United Nations Plaza, NYC 10007. U.S. nationals, under 35 preferable, BA degree, or in creative and performing arts. Four years professional study and/or experience. Apply above by November 1.

T   LOLA D'ANNUNZIO AWARD INC., 10 Manor Drive, West Trenton, NJ 08638. $500 annually in recognition to contribution to Off Broadway Theatre. MR

vp   DARTMOUTH COLLEGE, Hanover, NH 03755.

VP   DAVENPORT MUNICIPAL ART GALLERY, 1737 W. 12th St., Davenport, IA 52804. Regional Mid-Mississippi Annual Art Competition with $2,500 in prizes. Deadline Sept. 26.

P-WR   PRIX DAVID. Award: $5,000.
SEE: MINISTERE DES AFFAIRES CULTURELLES DU QUEBEC.

P-WR   GUSTAV DAVIDSON MEMORIAL AWARD.
SEE: THE POETRY SOCIETY OF AMERICA.

vp   DAVIS & ELKINS COLLEGE, Elkins, WV 26241.

vp   LILLIAN BOSTWICK DAVIS MEMORIAL SCHOLARSHIP.
SEE: Art Students League of N.Y. (Merit.).

vp,c   DAYTON ART INSTITUTE, Forest 7 Riverview Aves., Dayton, OH 45405.

vp   DEAN JR. COLLEGE, Franklin, MA 02038.

vp,m,t   THE DEFIANCE COLLEGE, Gerald E. Mallott, Defiance, OH 43512.

C   DELAWARE ART MUSEUM, 2301 Kentmere Pkwy, Wilmington, DE 19806. Annual contemporary crafts exhibition with cash and purchase prizes.

all,ALL   DELAWARE STATE ARTS COUNCIL, 820 N. French St., Wilmington, DE 19801. Aid for artists in schools and individual artists fellowships for residents of Delaware and not enrolled in school.

M,m   DELIGACION NACIONAL DE LA SECCION FEMMENINA DE FALANGE ESPANOLA Y DE LAS JONS, Almagro 36, Madrid 4, Spain. Fels. (35) for 1-3 yrs travel & maintenance expenses to women with study certificates in music or corresponding university degree. All nationalities, preference to Spanish-Americans.

P-M   DELIUS COMPOSITION AWARDS, Jacksonville University, Jacksonville, FL

51

32211. $200 to $50 for compositions in areas of vocal, instrumental, band and orchestra. Deadline Nov. 1.

WR,D, T,M   DELL PUBLISHING CO. FOUNDATION, 245 E. 47th St., NYC 10011. Grants in civic improvement and performing arts.

P-VP,C   ANNUAL DELTA ART EXHIBITION PURCHASE AWARDS. Monetary awards (also purchase awards in VP and C). SEE: ARKANSAS ART CNTR.

vp   DELTA COMMUNITY COLLEGE, Univ. Center, MI 48710.

WR   DELTA KAPPA GAMMA SOCIETY, International, Box 1589, Austin, TX 78767. Award to one or two women for documented publications in education. U.S. & Canadian women only. $1,500 biennially.

M   DELTA OMICRON INTERNATIONAL MUSIC FRATERNITY, 2410 McCullough, Apt. 209, San Antonio, TX 78212. $500 and performance of composition by women of college age or older. Award is given triennially.

vp   DELTA PHI DELTA ALUMNI SCHOLARSHIP FOUNDATION, Mrs. R.B. Stewart, Sec.-Treas., RR#10, W. Lafayette, IN 47906. Seniors and graduate students. MR

WR   DELTA PRIZE NOVEL AWARD, Dell Publishing Co., 750 Third Ave., NYC 10017. $5,000 plus advance on royalties biennially for best unpublished work in fiction.

vp,c   DELTA STATE COLLEGE, Art Dept., Cleveland, MS 38732.

ALL   EBEN DEMAREST TRUST, Secretary, 4601 Bayard St., Apt. 807, Pittsburgh, PA 15213. Annual grant of $4,500 can be given for one or more yrs. Designed as a living stipend for the devoted artist or archeologist who has no other income from any source that equals the income from the trust. Deadline June 1.

WR   DENMARK: Ministry of Education, Frederiksholms Kanal 21, Copenhagen K, Denmark. Short-term Schls. for study in Denmark. Graduates with specific research program. Apply: Institute of International Education, 809 U.N. Plaza, NYC 10017. Post doctoral or advanced, research candidates apply: Conference Board of Associated Research Councils Committee on International Exchange of Persons, 2101 Constitution Ave., NW, Washington, DC 20418.

ALL,all   DEPARTMENT OF AGRICULTURE, Farmers Home Administration (FMHA), Washington, DC 20250. Nonfarm Enterprise Loans: Loans approximately $28,000 for up to 40 years available to owner/operators of family farms for operation of artist or craftperson's studio. Upon request will provide permits to allow visual artists to gather materials from forests.

c,d,f,t, vp	DEPARTMENT OF JUSTICE, Administrator, Education Branch, Federal Bureau of Prisons, Washington, DC 20537. Prison Art Programs: teaching positions for those interested in working in federal prisons.
m	DEPAUL UNIVERSITY, School of Music, Greencastle, IN 46135. Twenty-five $1,500 to undergraduates, on financial need. Renewable.
m	DE PAUL UNIVERSITY, School of Music, 804 W. Belden Ave., Chicago, IL 60614. Several scholarships from $500 to $1,200 for entering freshmen.
T	DES MOINES COMMUNITY PLAYHOUSE, 831 42nd St., Des Moines, IA 50312. Winner of award gets $375 plus travel expenses to see the premier performance.
M	DETROIT GRAND OPERA ASSOCIATION, Ford Auditorium, 20 E. Jefferson, Detroit, MI 48226. Cash $2,500 and participation in Metropolitan Opera National Council Regional Auditions and one year study with Detroit Grand Opera. To American citizens 18-33 residing in Michigan or Lucas, Fulton, or Ottawa counties in Ohio. Apply: Grinnell Fnd. of Music Scholarship. Additional $1,000 Elizabeth Hodges Donovan Scholarship.
all	DEUTSCHER AKADEMISCHER AUSTAUSCH DIENST, Kennedy Allee 50, 532 Bad Godesberg, Germany. Foreign students and graduates, no restrictions. Various with travel and depenents allowance. Apply: Stipendenabteilung DAAD, above.
WR	THE DEVINS AWARD, Breakthrough Editor, University of Missouri Press, 107 Swallow Hall, Columbia, MO 65201. Award of $500 for book of poetry.
P-WR	ALICE FAY DI CASTAGNOLA AWARD. SEE: THE POETRY SOCIETY OF AMERICA.
VP	DICKINSON ART AWARD, Dickinson College, Carlisle, PA 17013. To honor achievements in the arts, letters or humanities. $1,000 biennially.
P-WR	EMILY DICKINSON AWARD. SEE: THE POETRY SOCIETY OF AMERICA.
vp,c	DICKINSON STATE COLLEGE, Dickinson, ND 58601.
P-VP	C. PERCIBAL DIETSCH SCULPTURE PRIZE. Award: $200. SEE: NATIONAL SCULPTURE SOCIETY.
P-WR	GEORGE DILLON MEMORIAL PRIZE; Award: $100. SEE: POETRY MAGAZINE.
P-F	DINARD INTERNATIONAL FESTIVAL FILMS FROM FRENCH SPEAKING REGIONS, 105 ter. Avenue de Lille, 75 Paris, France.

AWARDS: For best work from a country using French as its first and second language. Monetary prize of $20,000 for the best script, and $2,000 each for the best feature and short. Anyone.

vp   NATHANIEL DIRK MEMORIAL SCHOLARSHIP.
SEE: Art Students League of N.Y. (Merit.).

all   DISNEY FOUNDATION, 500 So. Buena Vista St., Burbank, CA 91505. A small scholarship program limited to the children of employees of Walt Disney Productions. Support includes assistance to hospitals, higher educational institutions, youth organizations and federated and organized charities of the United Fund type.

M   ALICE M. DITSON FUND OF COLUMBIA UNIV., Jack Beeson, Sec. of the Advisory Committee, Music Dept., NYC 10027. Some individual aid, though mostly through institutions, publishers and recording companies.

P-VP   DIXIE ANNUAL, Montgomery Museum of Fine Arts, 440 S. McDonough St., Montgomery, AL 36104. Only two-dimensional works from artists residing in one of 13 states. Selected works are shown in annual exhibit in March or April.

vp,c   DIXIE COLLEGE, St. George, UT 84770.

ALL,all   DOBIE-PAISANO FELLOWSHIPS, Office of Vice Pres. and Dean of Graduate Studies, Main Bldg. 101, University of Texas, Austin, TX 78712. Residency at a ranch and a stipend of $500 for a month. Applicants must be residents of Texas or associated with the state. Writers and artists are welcome to apply by March 15.

vp   DOMINICAN COLLEGE, 2401 E. Holcombe Blvd., Houston, TX 77021.

all   DOMINICAN COLLEGE OF SAN RAFAEL, Sister M. Richard Rhodes, Office of Financial Aid, San Rafael, CA 94901. Independent liberal arts college grants to individuals for study within institution. Room, board, facilities, tuition only, no personal restrictions. Deadline Feb. 15.

P-WR   DOUBLEDAY & CO. INC., 245 Park Ave., NYC 10017.
O. HENRY AWARDS: Discontinued. Inquire as to any new ones now instituted.

VP   DOUGLAS ART CENTER, Box 256, Douglas, AZ 85607. Two Flags International Juried Exhibit with $1,000 in awards. Deadline April 20.

vp   DOUGLASS COLLEGE OF RUTGERS UNIV., New Brunswick, NJ 08903. NJ prospective sophomore, junior or senior in art. NJ Residents only, also same scholarship of lesser amount apparently open to residents out of NJ.

vp,m,c DRAKE UNIV., Des Moines, IA 50311. Art Majors, renewable: College of Fine Arts. For music: Honor awards for band, choral and orchestra. Other grants via Drake in music.

WR DRAMATISTS GUILD, 234 W. 44th St., NYC 10036. $7,000 Warriner Award to playwright dealing with controversial matter. Interest-free loans for produced playwrights with sudden emergencies. Occasionally loans made for script duplication and transportation.

vp DREW UNIV., Madison, NJ 07940.

m, vp DRURY COLLEGE, Springfield, MO 65802. Twenty-four renewable, half tuition, based on musicianship and need.

VP "DUCK STAMP" DESIGN CONTEST, Public Affairs-Audio/Visual, U.S. Fish and Wildlife Service, Dept. of the Interior, Washington, DC 20240. An annual competition for the best design for Migratory Bird Hunting Stamp. Artist issued $150 sheet of stamps with his/her design if selected. Deadline Oct. 15.

VP THE DULIN GALLERY OF ART, 3100 Kingston Pike, Knoxville, TN 37919. National Print and Drawing Competition with $2,000 in purchase awards. Deadline is March 26.

P-VP-H, DUMBARTON OAKS CENTER FOR BYZANTINE STUDIES, The Ass't.
vp-h Dir., 1703 32nd St., NW, Washington, DC 20007. Offers Junior Fellowships of $5,000 and Fellowships with a minimum of $7,000 for postdoctorate studies in late Roman, early Christian, Middle Ages and Byzantine cultures. Recipient is expected to reside at Dumbarton Oaks. Allowances made for dependents. All.

vp FRANK VINCENT DUMOND MEMORIAL SCHOLARSHIP.
SEE: Art Students League of N.Y. (Merit.).

vp DUNBARTON COLLEGE OF HOWARD UNIVERSITY, 2935 Upton St., NW, Washington, DC 20008.

m DUQUESNE UNIV., Pittsburg, PA 15219. One Graduate Assist. of $1,000 to student in music, plus tuition.

P-M DUSEK COMPETITION OF MUSICAL YOUTH, c/o Prof. Anna Ditetova, Pohranicni straze 1, Prague 6, Czechoslovakia. PRIZES: For recognition of the outstanding classical music interpretation in the following categories: 1) piano, ages 13-21; 2) string instruments, ages 13-21; 3) chamber music, ages 13-21; 4) singing, ages 17-25.

P-F DUTCH FILM FESTIVAL, Cinemanifestatie, c/o Hubert Bals, Dir., Oudegracht 156, Utrecht, Netherlands.

CINEMANIFESTATIE AWARDS: 24 feature films are presented from all over the world; there are no official awards, but there is voting for a Public and a Critic's Award. A festival of Dutch short films is held, the outstanding film is given the Pepsi Award of $1,000. Awarded every other year. Anyone.

vp,c   DUTCHESS COMMUNITY COLLEGE, Poughkeepsie, NY 12601.

WR   E.P. DUTTON AND COMPANY, 201 Park Ave. South, NYC 10003. The Man and His Environmental Book Award with an annual award of $10,000 as an advance toward the book's earnings. The Dutton Animal Book Award with an annual award of $15,000 toward the book's earnings. The Dutton Junior Animal Book Award with an annual award of $3,500.

vp   WINTHROP EARLE MEMORIAL FUND FOR ENCOURAGEMENT OF SCULPTURE, Est. 1936. SEE: Art Students League of N.Y. (Merit.).

m   EARLHAM COLLEGE, Richmond, IN. 47375. $250 to freshmen string quartet, renewable.

T,WR   EARPLAY, WHA Radio, Vilas Communication Hall, 821 University Ave., Madison, WI 53706. Award (purchase) up to $3,000 for original play to be aired on the radio.

P-M   EAST AND WEST ARTISTS ANNUAL COMPETITION FOR COMPOSERS, 310 Riverside Dr., #313, NYC 10025. Cash and performance at Carnegie Recital Hall for composition for one to four instruments. Deadline May 20. Anyone. Also, Annual Young Performers Auditions Award for chamber ensembles up to 32 yrs. old and singers up to 35 yrs. old. Award is debut at Carnegie Recital Hall and some New York City radio engagements.

m   EAST CAROLINA UNIV., School of Music, PO Box 2517, Greenville, NC 17834. Various, $100-$500 to string majors, renewable and with restrictions.

t,vp,wr,m,   EAST MISSISSIPPI JUNIOR COLLEGE, Box 176, Scooba, MS 39358, Con-
c,-h   tact: Terry Cherry, Art Director. SCHOLARSHIPS: Renewable each year, all are departmental scholarships and they cover room and matriculation fees. Anyone.

m   EAST TENNESSEE STATE UNIV., Johnson City, TN 37601. To entering freshmen, 250 tuition, state residents only, with restriction; 3 tuition for student members of the Kingsport Symphony Orch.; EOP and work schols. for stipend.

m   EAST TEXAS BAPTIST COLLEGE, Marshall, TX 75670. Twenty $30-$90 per semester (applied music fees); 10 $50 per semester, band, renewable, restrictions.

m   EAST TEXAS STATE UNIV., Commerce, TX 75428. One $550 per yr. bassoon performance; 15 $550 per yr. dance band ability with p-ts service; 14 $360 with p-t service; Graduate Assists. 13 $2,250.

vp,c   EASTERN ILLINOIS UNIV., School of Music, Charleston, IL 61920. Undergrads, 6-$310, renewable. Graduate assistantships.
       GRANTS, TALENTED STUDENT AWARDS: From $100 to $1,769, and are renewable. May include room and board, tuition and fees. Must be enrolled as an Art Major. Deadline March.

m   EASTERN KENTUCKY UNIV., Richmond, KY 40475. Fifteen $200-$300 with special service required; 10 $200-$400 renewable, restrictions, special part-time service; Graduate fels. (assistantships).

m   EASTERN MICHIGAN UNIV., Ypsilanti, MI 48197. $300 per yr. to Michigan residents, $750 to out of state students; federal matching funds for acute financial need $600-$1,500.

m,vp,c EASTERN MONTANA COLLEGE, Division of Humanities, 1500 No. 30th St., Billings, MT 59101. Twenty instr. and/or vocal, to entering freshmen.

m,vp,c,d,t EASTERN NEW MEXICO UNIV., School of Fien Arts, Portales, NM 88130. Contact: Dr. David Willoughby, Dean. Grad. Assistants: $3,600 max. per yr; Cash awards: $500 max. per yr; Tuition waivers, acacemic and individual scholarships.

m,vp,c EASTERN WASHINGTON STATE COLLEGE, Cheney, WA 99004. Various, part-time service; Graduate fels.

VP   EASTMAN KODAK COMPANY, Rochester, NY. Over $50,000 annually for awards in photography. Competitive. $100 to $5,000.

M,m   EASTMAN SCHOOL OF MUSIC, Univ. of Rochester, 26 Gibbs St., Rochester, NY 14604. Contact: James Harden.
       TUITION REMISSION: For undergraduate degree candidates, up to $3,525.
       FELLOWSHIPS AND ASSISTANTSHIPS: For graduate degree candidates – up to $3,525 plus stipend for duties performed.

vp   ECOLE SUPERIEURE DES BEAUX ARTS D'ATHENES, School of Fine Arts, Patission 42, Athens, Greece.

vp   EDGECLIFF COLLEGE, 2220 Victory Pkwy, Cincinnati, OH 45206. Four-year scholarships leading to the BA degree with major in Fine Arts. Schols. for one year value $1,000, renewable for three yrs. No restrictions.

vp   EDGEWOOD COLLEGE OF THE SACRED HEART, 855 Woodrow St., Madison, WI 53711.

vp,c   EDINBORO STATE COLLEGE, Edinboro, PA 16412.

P-F   EDUCATIONAL FILM LIBRARY ASSOCIATION, 17 W. 60th St., NYC 10023.
JOHN GRIERSON AWARD: To reward a filmmaker who has not more than three films to his/her credit. A wooden plaque with gold seal and engraved plate and $500 is awarded annually at the American Film Festival.

P-WR,   ALFRED EINSTEIN AWARD. Award: $400.
wr   SEE: American Musicological Society.

WR   EISENHOWER EXCHANGE FELLOWSHIPS, Inc., 256 S. 16th St., Philadelphia, PA 19102. Fellowships to those who have already achieved considerable success in their fields, to enable potential leaders to take period of training abroad; age 30-45.

m, cp,c   ELIZABETH CITY STATE COLLEGE, Elizabeth City, NC 27909. Eleven $100; 8 $150; 3 $175; 4 $200; 5 $270; 2 $300; 3 $320; 4 $350 all renewable, part-time service required.

m   ELKS FND. SCHOLARSHIP AWARDS, 2750 Lakeview Ave., Chicago, IL 60614. 150 scholarships, $800-$1,500, to any high school or college student in the U.S. under jurisdiction of the Order of the Elks.

WR,wr   THE ELLISTON BOOK AWARD, University of Cincinnati, Dept. of English, 248 McMicken Hall, Cincinnati, OH 45221. Annual of $1,000 to be divided between the author and publisher.

vp,c   ELMIRA COLLEGE, Elmira, NY 14901.

m   ELON COLLEGE, Elon College, NC 27244. Various renewable.

all   EMERSON COLLEGE, 130 Beacon Street, Boston, MA 02116.

P-WR   EMERSON-THOREAU MEDAL. Award: Bronze medal and moneatry sum. SEE: American Academy of Arts and Sciences.

WR   EMORY UNIVERSITY, Atlanta, GA 30322. Teaching position as visiting lecturer in creative writing to authors of standing, poets, novelists, dramatists, (T.F. or T.V.). $5,000 per quarter, i.e. 10-12 weeks for one or more quarters. Anyone. Apply: Prof. Frank Manley, Dept. of English, above.

vp,c   ENDICOTT JR. COLLEGE, Hale St., Beverly, MA 01915.

P-WR   ENGLISH ACADEMY OF SOUTHERN AFRICA, Ballater House, 35 Melle St., Braamfontein, Johannesburg 2001, South Africa. Contact: The Administrative Officer.

THE OLIVE SCHREINER PRIZE: Three categories: prose, poetry, and drama. Awarded every three years for work published—or in the case of plays produced—in the last three years in South Africa.

THE PRINGLE AWARD: Three categories are awarded every year. 1) Book & Play reviews in newspapers and magazines; 2) Literary articles & articles dealing with language and the teaching of languages in academic and other journals; 3) Creative work in journals & magazines. Restricted to work only appearing in South African publications.

M   ENTE AUTONOMO TEATRO ALLA SCALA, Via Filodrammatici, 2, Milan, Italy. Open to all composers. Cash prize for symphonic composition.

VP   ENVIRONMENTAL PROTECTION AGENCY (EPA), Project Documeria, Office of Public Affairs, EPA, Washington, DC 20460. Awarded thirty-day assignments for photographing environmental conditions in the U.S. Per diem rate and expenses covered.

P-VP   ERNST, JOHN L., AWARD. Award: $250.
SEE: American Watercolor Society.

VP   EVANSVILLE MUSEUM OF ARTS AND SCIENCE, 411 S.E. Riverside Dr., Evansville, IN 47713. Mid-States Art Exhibit for most media except photography. $5,900 in awards. Deadline Sept. 23.

M   EVANSVILLE PHILHARMONIC, PO Box 84, Evansville, IN 47701. Rosanna M. Enlow Young Artists Award of $500 and Solo Appearance with Evansville Philharmonic to residents or natives of Indiana, Illinois or Kentucky, under 28 yrs.

vp   WALKER G. EVERETT MEMORIAL SCHOLARSHIP. Awarded as funds accrue from monies he left the Art Students League of N.Y. (Talent.).

D   EXOTIC DANCERS LEAGUE OF AMERICA, 2321-17 So. Pacific Ave., San Pedro, CA 90731. Two annual prizes with bookings and artist-in-residence award.

P-WR FABER AND FABER LTD., 3 Queen Square, London WC1 N3AU, England, UK.
GEOFFREY FABER MEMORIAL PRIZE: For the best volume of verse or prose fiction first published in the united Kingdom during the two previous years. Under 40. Citizens of Britain; any other Commonwealth state; Republic Of Ireland, or Republic of South Africa. 250 pounds annually.

V-P,C FAIRMONT STATE COLLEGE, Fairmont, WV 26554.

P-VP THE FAMOUS ARTISTS SCHOOL AWARD. Monetary award.
SEE: AMERICAN WATERCOLOR SOCIETY.

| M | FARGO-MOORHEAD SYMPHONY, Box 1753, Fargo, ND 58102. The Sigvald Thompson Composition Award Competition. $500 plus allowance up to $300 for cost of copying parts and possible premier with symphony. |

M   FARGO-MOORHEAD SYMPHONY, Box 1753, Fargo, ND 58102. The Sigvald Thompson Composition Award Competition. $500 plus allowance up to $300 for cost of copying parts and possible premier with symphony.

VP,C   FASHION INSTITUTE OF TECHNOLOGY, Mrs. Marion Brandriss, Dean, 227 W. 27th St., NYC 10001.

ALL,all   FEDERAL ARTS ENDOWMENT. SEE: National Endowment for the Arts.

ALL-H,   FEDERAL HUMANITIES ENDOWMENT. SEE: National Endowment for
all-h   the Humanities.

WR   FEDERATION OF FRENCH ALLIANCES, 22 E. 60th St., NYC 10022. Literature prize for non-political book on France-America relations to U.S. or French writer. One $2,000 biennially; anyone.

M   FEDERATION OF JEWISH PHILANTHROPIES, 130 E. 59th St., NYC 10022. Mitropoulis (Dimitri) International Music Competition to conductors 20-33 of all countries. Four $5,000 first prizes each and appointments as Assistant Conductors of the NY Philharmonic (3) or National Symphony of DC. (1). Also $2,500, $1,000 and $750 prizes.

M   EMMA FELDMAN MEMORIAL COMPETITION, c/o Philadelphia All-Star Forum Series, 1530 Locust St., Philadelphia, PA 19102. Singers from 16-35 yrs. $1,000 first prize and appearance with Philadelphia Orchestra at Robin Hood Dell, in summer.

P-WR   FELLOWSHIP OF THE ACADEMY OF AMERICAN POETS, $10,000. SEE: ACADEMY OF AMERICAN POETS.

P-VP   FELTRINELLI FOUNDATION, c/o National Academy of Sciences, Via della Ungara 10, Rome 00165, Italy. ANTONIO FELTRINELLI PRIZES: In honorium of excellence in 1. Moral and historical science; 2. Physical, mathematical and natural sciences; 3. Literature; 4. Arts; and 5. Medicine. A monetary award of 5,000,000 liras and other cash prizes plus gold medals are awarded annually in the five areas in alternating order.

P-WR   FICTION INTERNATIONAL MAGAZINE, St. Lawrence University, Department of English, Canton, NY 13617. ST. LAWRENCE AWARD FOR FICTION: To the author of an outstanding first collection of short fiction published by an American publisher. $1,000 awarded to the author. Submit entries by Jan. 31st for the preceding year. Announcement of the award is made in issues of Fiction International magazine. Contact: Joe David Bellamy.

vp   ERNEST FIENE MEMORIAL SCHOLARSHIP. SEE: Art Students League of N.Y. (Merit.).

P-WR   FILM CRITIC AWARD. AWARD: $100 and publication of winning review in Film Critic magazine. SEE: American Federation of Film Societies.

M   FINDLAY COLLEGE, Music Dept., Div. Chairman, 1000 N. Main St., Findlay, OH 45840.

all   FINE ARTS COUNCIL OF FLORIDA, The Capitol Bldg., Tallahassee, FL 32304. Fellowships of up to $2,000 for Florida artists.

VP,WR   FINE ARTS WORK CENTER IN PROVINCETOWN, INC., 24 Pearl St., Provincetown, MA 02657. Twenty Fellows accepted for 7-month sessions. Stipends are from $50 to $150 a month. No facilities for filmmakers, photographers or video artists. Deadline Feb. 1.

M   FIRESTONE CONSERVATORY OF MUSIC, The Univ. of Akron, Akron, OH 44304. Renewable, 3 $100 performance & need; 1 $150 performance; 2 $150 scholarship and perform.; 3 $125 scholarship; 2 $150 scholarship; renew. with restrictions; 1 $500 male student in the NY area, schol., perform., and need; renew., 5 $200, 3 for upper strings, 1 for lower strings, 1 for theory. Also approx. 100 $40-$50 membership in Univ. Marching Band (Fall Semester).

M   FISK UNIV., Seventeenth Ave., North, Nashville, TN 37203. Various $200-$800. No music schls, as such but music majors eligible for financial aid.

P-M   CARL FLESCH INTERNATIONAL VIOLIN COMPETITION, Barbican Arts Centre, Cromwell Tower, Barbican, London EC2Y 8DD, England, UK.
         PRIZES: For the best violin performances by an artist no older than 30 years of age. First—1,000 pounds, Second—750 pounds, Third—300 pounds, Fourth—200 pounds, and Fifth—100 pounds sterling. Carl Flesch Medal and engagements. Biennially.

VP,C   FLINT COMMUNITY JR. COLLEGE, Fine Arts Div., 1401 E. Court St., Flint, MI 48503.

P-WR   FLORENCE CITY PRIZE, c/o Nuovo Cenacolo Fiorentino, Piazza Pietro Leopoldo II, Florence, Italy.
         FLORENCE CITY INTERNATIONAL POETRY PRIZE: For the best book of poetry. 1,000,000 liras and Dante Alighieri Medal annually. The Medal of the Community of Florence (Comune di Firenze) awarded to the publisher of the winning poetry. Anyone.

M   FLORENCE STATE COLLEGE, Florence, AL 35630. Several undergrad. schols. from $20-$540 in areas of instr., accompanists, librarians and general service. Some renewable, some part time service required.

M   FLORIDA AGRICULTURAL AND MECHANICAL UNIV., Tallahassee, FL 32307. (90) up to $600, band, inst., voice, piano, organ, renewable, part-time

time service required, undergrads.

ALL   THE FLORIDA ARTS COUNCIL OF FLORIDA, Dept. of State, Div. of Cultural Affairs, The Capitol, Tallahassee, FL 32314. Fellowships of up to $2,000 for adult residents of Florida who are creative artists as opposed to interpretive artists.

m,M,D FLORIDA ATLANTIC MUSIC GUILD, INC., PO Box 512, Boca Raton, FL 33432. Monies for music scholarships. Also, awards of up to $1,000 for competitions for voice, piano, violin, depending on the officials choice.

VP   FLORIDA GULF COAST ART CENTER, INC., 111 Manatee Rd., Belleair, Clearwater, FL 33516.

WR,wr FLORIDA INTERNATIONAL UNIVERSITY, English Dept., Florida International University, Miami, FL 33199. The Anne Sexton Poetry Prize of $250 for best unpublished poem by a woman.

VP,C   FLORIDA JR. COLLEGE AT JACKSONVILLE, Jacksonville, FL 32205.

VP,C   FLORIDA MEMORIAL COLLEGE, 15800 NW 42nd Ave., Miami, FL.

vp,m,d, FLORIDA SCHOOL OF THE ARTS, 5001 St. Johns Ave., Palatka, FL
t,f   32077. Prize and scholarships from $100 to $3,500.

vp,c   FLORIDA SOUTHERN COLLEGE, Lakeland, FL 33802.

vp,vp-h,f FLORIDA STATE UNIVERSITY, Art Dept., Dr. Jerry L. Draper, Chm. FSU, Fine Arts Bldg., Rm 236, Tallahassee, FL 32306. Assistantships, $1,800/yr; Fellowships $3,900/yr in Graduate level; lesser for undergraduates.

f   FLORIDA TECHNOLOGICAL UNIV., Communication, PO Box 25000, Orlando, FL 32816. Contact: Raymond W. Buchanan. Graduate Assistantships of varying amounts.

T,WR, FLORIDA THEATER CONFERENCE, FTC Playwriting Contest, 2232 NW
t,wr   19th La., Gainesville, FL 32605. Award of $250 and reading for Florida residents or playwrights enrolled in a Florida University.

V-P   FLORISSANT VALLEY COMMUNITY COLLEGE, 3400 Pershall Rd., Ferguson, MO 63135.

T-H   FOLGER SHAKESPEARE LIBRARY, 201 E. Capitol St., Washington, DC 20003. Contact: Director. Three categories, applications must be received by October 15, or February 1. Research concerning English drama and theatre, non-dramatic literature and history.
       DISSERTATION FELLOWSHIPS: For those working for their PhD. Sti-Stipends vary according to the period of grant and individual circumstances.

FOLGER FELLOWSHIPS: PhD required; up to 4 months study. Up to $600 a month.

SENIOR FELLOWSHIPS: 5 years study beyond PhD. $15,000 for one academic year; $7,500 for one semester. Submit application a year or more in advance.

M,T,D,   FOLKWANG-HOCHSCHULE ESSEN, Administration Office, 43 Essen-
m,t,d   Werden, Abtei, Federal Republic of Germany. 1-15, 1 term awards for study at Folkwang-Hochschule, Essen. Knowledge of German for M&D required. For T, a mastery of spoken and written German essential. 16-30 yrs. Preference for foreign students from developing countries.

WR   FOLLETT PUBLISHING CO., 201 No. Wells St., Chicago, IL 60606. Award for fiction or nonfiction; readers 9-12 yrs 25,000-35,000 words; 12 yrs up 40,000-60,000 words; $3,000 annually plus royalties.

vp,m   FONDATION DES ETATS-UNIS, 15 Boulevard Jourdan 75690, Paris-Cedex 14, France.

HARRIET HALE WOOLLEY SCHOLRASHIPS: Five or six scholarships of $3,000 each, payable in francs; an extra $600 for pianists and $200 for artists. 21 to 34 years of age. American citizenship; graduate level study.

M   FONDATION PRINCE PIERRE DE MONACO, Prix de Composition Musicale, Rene Novella, Secretary-General, Ministere d'Etat, Monaco. 20,000 French francs for composition whose category changes annually (i.e. 1978—chamber music, 1979—sacred). Anyone. Deadline April 1.

wr   FONDATION ROYAUMONT, 95, Asnieres-sur-Oise, France. Grants cover room and board so writers may work on or finish their creative work, at Val d'Oise.

VP,WR,   FONTBONNE COLLEGE, Leo Range, Dir. of Financial Aid, 6800 Wydown
M,T   Blvd., St. Louis, MO 63105. Federal grants and loans (EOG, NDSL, work study, institutional) up to entire tuition. Anyone having need is eligible.

f   FOOTHILL COLLEGE, Mass Communications, 12345 El Monte Road, Los Altos Hills, CA 94087. Contact: Stuart Roe, Chairman, SCHOLARSHIPS: Three part-time work/study schols. at $550 each.

P-WR   CONSUELO FORD AWARD.
SEE: THE POETRY SOCIETY OF AMERICA.

T,D,AM   FORD FOUNDATION, 320 E. 43rd St., NYC 10017. Administrative internships for those who have completed basic education to work in theater, opera, symphony or dance organization administration. Certain other small programs for individuals from time to time. Foreign people given considerable attention. Ford is diminishing support of arts-humanities during the 70's decade.

P-VP   THE FORD TIMES AWARD. Monetary Award.
SEE: AMERICAN WATERCOLOR SOCIETY.

f   FORDHAM UNIVERSITY, Communication Arts Dept., Bronx, NY 10458.
General scholarships available.

P-WR   E.M. FORSTER AWARD. Award: $5,000.
SEE: National Institute of Arts and Letters.

M   FORT COLLINS SYMPHONY SOCIETY, 801 E. Elizabeth St., Fort Collins,
CO 80521.
FORT COLLINS SYMPHONY YOUNG ARTIST COMPETITION in piano,
violin, viola, cello, flute, oboe, clarinet, bassoon, French horns, trumpet,
voice. Prize of $100 plus appearance as soloists and consideration of 4-yr
scholarship at Colorado State Univ. Apply: Mrs. Walter E. Snyder, Secretary, above.

m,vp,c   FORT HAYS KANSAS STATE COLLEGE, Hays, KS 67601. To entering
freshman, by audition full tuition 1-2 semesters, also partial-full tuition schl.
1 semester. Grad. assistantships.

vp   FORT WAYNE SCHOOL OF FINE ARTS, 1026 W. Berry St., Ft. Wayne, IN
46804.

VP,C   FT. WORTH ART CENTER MUSEUM & SCHOOL, 1309 Montgomery, Ft.
Worth, TX 76107.

vp   FT. WRIGHT COLLEGE, RT 4, Spokane, WA 99202. MR

P-AM   FOUNDATION FREIHERR-VON-STEIN OF HAMBURG, Bellindamm 6, 2
Hamburg 1, Federal Republic of Germany.
FRITZ SCHUMACHER PRIZE: For recognition of excellence in the preservation of architecture, monuments, and urban areas. Monetary prize of
20,000 German marks. Awarded annually.

D,F,M,T   FOUNDATION OF CONTEMPORARY PERFORMANCE ARTS, 225 East
Houston, NYC 10002. Grants for artists involved in performance of $1,000
to $2,000 given yearly. Anyone.

M   FOUNDATION ROYAUMONT, 23 bis, rue de L'Assumption, Paris 16,
France. All nationalities, 35 or under; publication award for instrumental or
vocal composition for an orchestra or ensemble, no more than 25 min.

VP   FOUNDERS SOCIETY, Detroit Institute of Art, 5200 Woodward Ave.,
Detroit, MI 48202. Michigan artists, Craftsmen; exhibition. Founders Prize,
monetary prizes; biennially.

vp   ROBERT LAWRENCE FOWLER ART SCHOLARSHIPS, c/o Univ/So. California, University Park, LA, CA 90007. $1,000.

All FRENCH MINISTRY OF FOREIGN AFFAIRS, Direction generale des affaires culturelles, 23 rue La Perouse, 75 Paris 16, France. Grants for foreign national grads for advanced study in all fields in France; 9 months to 1 yr. Apply: Institute of International Education, 809 UN Plaza, NYC 10017.

T,WR THE MILES FRANKLIN AWARD, Permanent Trustee Co., Ltd., CPO Box 4270, 23-25 O'Connell St., Sydney, Australia 2000. Award annual of $2,250 Australian dollars for best novel concerning Australian life.

P-VP THE FRANKLIN MINT GALLERY OF AMERICAN ART, Franklin Center, PA 19063.
 THE FRANKLIN MINT GOLD MEDAL FOR DISTINGUISHED WATERCOLORS: To artists who have won a major award in competitions of the American Watercolor Society in the previous five years. Gold medal and $5,000 to painters of each of the 12 winning watercolors. Anyone.
 THE FRANKLIN MINT GOLD MEDAL FOR DISTINGUISHED WESTERN ART: To artists who specialize in Western Art. Gold medal and $5,000 for the painters of each of the 10 winning pieces. Annual.

T FREE SOUTHERN THEATRE, 601 So. Scott St., New Orleans, LA 70119. John O. Neal.

P-VP-H FRENCH COMMITTEE FOR THE HISTORY OF ART, 3 rue Michelet, Paris 6, France.
 PAUL CAILLEUX FOUNDATION PRIZE: In recognition for outstanding work on French art of 18th century. A monetary prize of 10,000 francs is awarded annually.

ALL,all FRENCH INSTITUTE/ALLIANCE FRANCAISE, 22 East 60th St., NYC 10022. $1,400 to $3,000 for work in all disciplines to American or French citizens under 35 years of age. Americans apply: The Institute of International Education, 809 UN Plaza, NYC 10017. French applicants write: La Commission Franco-Americaine d'echanges Universitaires et Culturels, 9 rue Chardin 75016 Paris.

WR FRENCH P.E.N. CLUB, 66 rue Pierre Charron, Paris 8, France.
 KATHERINE MANSFIELD MENTON SHORT STORY PRIZE: For the best short story in English or French. Two monetary prizes: One English (100 pounds) and one French (1,500 francs) every other year in Menton, France. Anyone.

m FRIDAY MORNING MUSIC CLUB FOUNDATION, 8121 Rayburn Road, Washington, DC 20034. Mrs. Thea D. Woolsey, Competition Chairman.
 WASHINGTON INTERNATIONAL COMPETITION AWARDS: Monetary awards totaling $2,500 presented to the best performances in various categories by artists 18 to 29, not yet launched on their professional careers.

vp,c FRIEND UNIV., Hiram & Univ. St., Wichita, KS 67201.

P-WR FRIENDS OF AMERICAN WRITERS, Mrs. Norman A. Parker, 540 William St., River Forest, IL 60505.
FRIENDS OF AMERICAN WRITERS $1,000 AWARD: To an author who has had less than six books published, and was born in the Mid-West or has been a resident of the area for more than five years. The award of $1,000 is awarded annually in April.
FRIENDS OF AMERICAN WRITERS DISTINGUISHED RECOGNITION AWARD: Requirements similar to those of the $1,000 award. Monetary prize is $100 or more. Annually.
JUVENILE AWARD: Requirements similar to those of the $1,000 award, only that this award of $100 or more is to honor juvenile literature.

M FRIENDS OF HARVEY GAUL COMPOSITION CONTEST, c/o Mrs. D.V. Murdoch, Pres., 105 Bevington Rd., Pittsburgh, PA 15221. American composers; categories change every year. Annual composition contest with monetary award.

WR FRIENDS OF LITERATURE, PO Box 8198, Chicago, IL 60680. Cash awards up to $500 for works published the previous year and written by Chicago authors.

VP FRIENDS OF PHOTOGRAPHY, Box 239, Carmel, CA 93921. Award of $1,500. Anyone working with photographic materials or imagery who has achieved some recognition.

M FROMM MUSIC FND., at Harvard University, Music Bldg., Cambridge, MA 02138. Encourates contemporary musical composition; commissions new works, awards prizes for existing works, sponsors the study, performance, publication and recording of contemporary music. Anyone.

All FULBRIGHT ACT AND BUENOS AIRES CONVENTION, Counseling Div., Inst. of International Education, 809 United Nations Plaza, NYC 10017. U.S. Grads, with BA or in creative & performing arts 4 yrs of professional study and/or experience having knowledge of language of country for which application is made.

WR FUND FOR INVESTIGATIVE JOURNALISM, 1346 Connecticut Ave., NW, Rm. 1021, Washington, DC 20036. Contact: Howard Bray, Exec. Dir. GRANTS: To investigative writers.

m FURMAN UNIV., Greenville, SC 29613. 10-20 $250 and over, renewable.

P-VP GABROVO INTERNATIONAL BIENNIAL OF CARICATURE, Home of Humor and Satire, Gabrovo, Bulgaria.
AESOP GOLDEN PRIZE: For recognition of excellence in the field of caricature. A monetary prize of 1,000 leva is awarded every two years.

P-ALL GALLERY NUKI (see Nuki Award).

vp   GANNON COLLEGE, 109, W. Sixth St., Erie, PA 16501.

P-M   GASPAR CASSADO INTERNATIONAL CELLO COMPETITION, Maggio Musicale Fiorentino, Teatro Comunale, Via Solferino 15, Florence, Italy. PRIZE: 1,500,000 liras to the best cellist in the competition plus a performance with the orchestra of Maggio Musicale in Florence. Biennially. Anyone.

C,VP   GASPARILLA SIDEWALK ART FESTIVAL, PO Box 10591, Tampa, FL 33679. Arts/Crafts festival with $10,000 in prizes and awards. Deadline is Nov. 30.

VP,C   GASTON COLLEGE, PO Box 1397, Gastonia, NC 28052.

M   GAUDEAMUS INTERNATIONAL COMPETITION FOR COMPOSERS, Gaudeamus Fdn., Postbox 30, Bilthoven, Netherlands. Awards of Dfl 4,000 to Dfl 1,000 to composers born after January 1, 1943.

P-C   GDANSK CITY COUNCIL, Department of Culture, Ul. Torunska 1, Gdansk, Poland.
           GDANSK INTERNATIONAL CERAMICS TRIENNIAL PRIZES: For the outstanding work in ceramics. Five prizes of 15,000 zlotys each; awarded every three years.

all   GENERAL MOTORS SCHOLARSHIP PROGRAM, 8-163 GM Bldg., Detroit, MI 48202. 300 4-year scholarships from $200-$2,000. No restrictions on course of study or career.

C,VP   GENERAL SERVICES ADMINISTRATION (GSA), Assistant Commissioner for Construction Management, Public Buildings Service, Washington, DC 20405. Commissions for works of art for new federal buildings. U.S. citizens.

all   GENESEE COMMUNITY COLLEGE, 1401 E. Court St., Flint, MI 48503. R. Johnson. $500-$1,000 per year available to needy students.

P-M   GENEVA INTERNATIONAL COMPETITION FOR MUSICAL PERFORMERA, The Secretariat, Palais Eynard, Geneva, Switzerland. Five regular prizes amount to over 5,000 francs. In 1975 there were 23 other special prizes, smaller in amounts than the above.

P-M,T   GENEVA INTERNATIONAL COMPETITION FOR OPERA AND BALLET COMPOSITION, The Secretariat, Maison de la Radio, CH-1211 Geneva 8, Switzerland. PRIZES: Categories vary annually. In 1975 the first prize was 15,000 Swiss francs, for the best musical theatre composition.

vp,m,t   GEORGETOWN COLLEGE, Georgetown, KY 40324. Contact: Mr. Don DeBorde. GRANTS: For those pursuing a degree. Min. $250, max. depending on need. Avg. $1,000. Judged on ability, portfolio or tryout. Anyone.

all   GEORGETOWN UNIVERSITY, Dept. of Fine Arts, 37th and O Sts., NW, Washington, DC 20007.

vp,c   GEORGIA COLLEGE AT MILLEDGEVILLE, Dept. of Art, Milledgeville, GA 31061.

all   GEORGIA COUNCIL FOR THE ARTS AND HUMANITIES, 225 Peachtree St., NE, Suite 1610, Atlanta, GA 30303. Aid for artists in schools.

A   GEORGIA INSTITUTE OF TECHNOLOGY, Atlanta, GA 30332.

VP,C   GEORGIAN COURT COLLEGE, Lakewood, NJ 08701.

m   GEORGIA SOUTHERN COLLEGE, Landrum, Box 8052, Statesboro, GA 30458. Undergrads. Four $100 renewable; 3 $150 renewable accompanying ability.

P-ALL   GERMAN BOOKSELLERS ASSOCIATION, Grosser Hirschgraben 17-21, 6 Frankfurt/Main, Federal Republic of Germany.
GERMAN BOOK TRADE PEACE PRIZE: For outstanding contributions to literature, science, and art in the name of peace. 10,000 German marks awarded annually.

P-WR   GERMAN COMMITTEE FOR JUVENILE LITERATURE, Kaulbachstr. 40, D 8 Munich 22, Federal Republic of Germany.
GERMAN YOUTH BOOK AWARD: For noteworthy contributions to books for the young. Three awards for 7,500 German marks annually. Anyone.

all   GERMAN ACADEMIC EXCHANGE SERVICE, Kennedyallee 50, 532 Bad Godesberg, Germany. Scholarships to graduates of all countries for study and research in Germany, 10-12 months. Apply Institute of International Education, 809 UN Plaza, NYC 10017.

WR,HUM   INSTITUTE FUR EUROPAISCHE GESCHICTE, Alte Universitatsstrasse 19, 65 Mainz, Germany. GRANTS to nationals and graduates of all countries for study and research in German in European history or religious European history. Apply: Eur. Hist. Professor M. Gohring, Abteilung fur Universalgeschichte; Religion, Professor J. Lorz, Abteilung fur Abendlandische Religionsgeschichte.

F,M,T,   GERMANY ARTISTS-IN-BERLIN PROGRAM (BERLINER KUNSTLER-
VP,WR   PROGRAMM), German Academic Exchange Service (Deutscher Akademischer Austauschdienst), Bureau Berlin, PO Box 126240, Steinplatz 2, 1,000 Berlin 12, West Germany. Residency of 6 to 12 months in Berlin. Anyone.

P-WR   CHRISTIAN GAUSS AWARD. Award: $2,500.
SEE: PHI BETA KAPPA.

WR   JAMES HERRICK GIBSON BOOK AWARD, c/o Caxton Printers Ltd., PO Box 700, Caldwell, ID 83605. $2,000 for unpublished non-fiction work in field of Western Americana.

ALL,all   GIRTON COLLEGE CAMBRIDGE, Cambridge CB3 OJG, England, UK. Contact: Secretary to the Council.
RESEARCH FELLOWSHIPS AND STUDENTSHIPS: Awarded through competition. Annually. Fellowships provide residence and facilities, deadline: January 8. Studentships: University fees paid. Deadline: mid-May.

m   GLASSBORO STATE COLLEGE, Glassboro, NJ 08028. Five $100-$200 Graduate fels.

P-WR   JACOB GLATSTEIN MEMORIAL PRIZE. Award: $100.
SEE: POETRY MAGAZINE'

vp,c   GLENVILLE STATE COLLEGE, Glenville, WV 26351.

f   GODDARD COLLEGE, Film Dept., Plainfield, VT 05667. General scholarships.

P-VP   GOETZ, ANTOINETTE GRAVES, AWARD. Monetary Award.
SEE: AMERICAN WATERCOLOR SOCIETY.

WR,T   JOHN GOLDEN FUND, 274 Madison Ave., NYC 10016. Grants for the advancement of American legitimate theater or of individual associated in any way with it. Financial assistance to playwrights, relief grants, awards to actors, etc.

M   GOLDOVSKY OPERA INSTITUTE, Boris Goldovsky, Carnegie Hall, NYC 10019. Tuition and subsistence for singers in training in language and acting. Seminars for directors, conductors, lighting and set designers who work in opera.

P-VP   GOLDSMITH, EMILY, AWARD. Monetary award.
SEE: AMERICAN WATERCOLOR SOCIETY.

m   GONZAGA UNIVERSITY, E 502 Boone Ave., Spokane, WA 99202. Financial Aid Office.

vp   GOUCHER COLLEGE, Towson, MD 21204.

P-WR   GOVERNOR GENERAL'S LITERARY AWARDS. Award: Six $2,500.
SEE: THE CANADA COUNCIL.

VP,A   GRAHAM FOUNDATION FOR ADVANCED STUDIES IN THE FINE ARTS, 4 W. Burton Place, Chicago, IL 60610. Advanced study in architecture, and those of the Fine Arts that contribute to it. Primarily to Americans working in U.S. having outstanding talent and specific work objectives. No loans.

f   GRAHM JUNIOR COLLEGE, Communications, 632 Beacon St., Boston, MA 02215. Contact: George Schwartz. SCHOLARSHIPS: WCVB-TV scholarship for a minority student; three other scholarships available for communications students.

m   GRAMBLING COLLEGE, Grambling, LA 71245. Various band, orchestra, piano and voice.

P-WR   GRAND PRIX DE LA VILLE DE MONTREAL. Award: $3,000.
SEE: The Greater Montreal Council of Arts.

C,VP   GRAND PRIX INTERNATIONAL D'ART CONTEMPORAIN DE MONTE-CARLO, Comite d'Organisation du Grand Prix International d'Art Contemporain de Monte-Carlo, Musee National, 17, Avenue Princess Grace, Monte-Carlo. Awards range from 1,000 to 5,000 francs. Contact local consul of Monaco for more information. Anyone. Deadline August 31.

vp   GRAND RAPIDS JR. COLLEGE, 143 Bostwick Ave. NE, Grand Rapids, MI 49502.

M   GRAN TEATRO DEL LICEO, Calle de San Pablo 1 bis, Barcelona, Spain.
(voice)   OPERA PRIZE OF THE CITY OF BARCELONA. Opera competition open to anyone.

WR,wr   GREAT LAKES COLLEGES ASSN., GLCA New Writers Award, English Dept., Wabash College, Crawfordsville, IN 47933. Author of chosen book will visit different colleges and receive $100 from each. Deadline Feb. 28.

P-WR   THE GREATER MONTREAL COUNCIL OF ARTS, 700 Craig St. East, Suite 112, Montreal, Quebec H2Y 1A6, Canada.
GRAND PRIX DE LA VILLE DE MONTREAL: In honorium of an outstanding literary work published for the first time in the previous year, $3,000 is awarded to the author annually. Must have been published in Montreal.

WR,-H   GREEK INTERNATIONAL FEDERATION OF UNIVERSITY WOMEN, 17 A King's Road, Sloane Sq., London, SW 3, UK. Hellenic Assoc. Grant; postgraduate research or advanced study in Greece in Greek lit., history, archaeology, or appropriate field; 2-3 months; members of American Association of University Women only. Apply: Amer. Assoc. of Univ. Women, 2401 Virginia Ave., NW, Washington, DC 20037.

V-P   GREENFIELD COMMUNITY COLLEGE, 125 Federal St., Greenfield, MA 01301.

vp   MACCABI GREENFIELD MEMORIAL SCHOLARSHIP.
SEE: Art Students League of N.Y. (Merit.).

70

VP GREEN RIVER COMMUNITY COLLEGE, 12401 SE 320, Auburn, WA 98002.

M GREENSBORO COLLEGE, Greensboro, NC 27402. Various renewable.

VP GREENSHIELDS FOUNDATION, 1814 Sherbrooke St. W., Montreal H3H 1E4, Canada. Six various, to nations of any country for study in any country in painting and sculpture.

M GREENVILLE COLLEGE, Greenville, IL 62246. To entering freshmen 5, one-half applied music, tuition.

VP,C GREENWICH HOUSE POTTERY, 16 Jones St., NYC 10014. Scholarships available for children and adults to study pottery. Deadlines Sept. 1 and Dec. 1.

M GREENWOOD PRESS CHORAL COMPETITION, 2145 Central Parkway, Cincinnati, OH 45214. This has been cancelled.

WR GREGG DIVISION, McGraw-Hill Book Co., 330 W. 42nd St., NYC 10036. Award for contribution to business education sustained during two previous calendar years. By nomination.

T,WR, THE HORACE GREGORY AWARD, H. Gregory Foundation, c/o The New School, 66 W. 12th St., NYC 10011. Annual award of $2,000 for U.S. citizen who is both teacher and writer.

P-VP JOHN GREGORY AWARD. Award: $500.
  SEE: NATIONAL SCULPTURE SOCIETY.

P-F JOHN GRIERSON AWARD. $500.
  SEE: Educational Film Library Association.

vp SIDNEY GROSS MEMORIAL SCHOLARSHIP.
  SEE: Art Students League of N.Y. (Merit.).

vp GEORGE GROSZ MEMORIAL SCHOLARSHIP.
  SEE: Art Students League of N.Y. (Merit.).

WR GROVE PRESS, B. Rosset, 80 Univ. Pl., NYC 10003. International Literary Prize $10,000 biannually for published work by living author. Anyone.

P-VP GRUMBACHER ARTISTS' MATERIALS CO. Award: $200 & $100.
  SEE: Allied Artists of America, Inc.

P-WR GUARDIAN NEWSPAPER, 164 Deansgate, Manchester M60 2RR, England, UK.
  GUARDIAN AWARD FOR CHILDREN'S FICTION: 100 pounds sterling

awarded annually for the outstanding novel for children published in Britain. Anyone.

all   JOHN SIMON GUGGENHEIM MEMORIAL FOUNDATION, 90 Park Ave., NYC 10016. Adjusted to needs of Fellows re their resources and scope of studies. Citizens or permanent residents of U.S., Canada, and other American states, Caribbean, Philippines, French, Dutch and British Possessions in Western Hemisphere, normally 30-45 yrs. For 12 months. some are 6. Deadline: October 1. In 1975 the Foundation awarded a total of $4,025,467. Send for application.

P-M   GUIDO CANTELLI INTERNATIONAL COMPETITION FOR YOUNG CONDUCTORS, The Secretariat, Ente Provinciale per il Turismo, Corso Cavour 2, 28100 Nivara, Italy. PRIZE: To best young conductor, under 32. 1,000,000 liras plus two appearances with the orchestra of the Teatro alla Scala in Milan, biennially.

M   GUILDHALL SCHOOL OF MUSIC AND DRAMA, John Carpenter Street, London, EC 4, England. London International Violin Competition, biennial, Carl Flesch Medal, cash prizes and possible orchestra contracts. Next, summer of 1980.

VP   GUILDORD TECHNICAL INSTITUTE, PO Box 309, Jamestown, NC 27282.

M   GUSTAVUS ADOLPHUS COLLEGE, St. Peter, MI 57082. Special awards in music based on ability.

M   HAGUE CHOIR FESTIVAL, PO Box 496, The Hague, Netherlands. International Choir festival in Holland for mixed, male, female and youth choirs. Directors should apply by April.

P-VP-H,   HAILE SELASSIE 1 PRIZE TRUST, PO Box 2320, Addis Ababa, Ethiopia.
WR,VP   ETHIOPIAN STUDIES AWARD: For the outstanding in recent contribution to research on Ethiopia in history, languages, literature, arts, customs, natural history. Gold medal, diploma and monetary prize of 20,000 Ethiopian dollars is awarded annually. Anyone.

M   REID HALL INC. AWARDS, Mrs. J. Elliot Jr., Chairman Music Schl. Comm., 767 Lexington Ave., NYC 10021. For women music majors with knowledge of French: $1,500 for study in France. MR

P-VP   JULIUS HALLGARTEN PRIZES. Awards: $350, $250 and $150. SEE: NATIONAL ACADEMY OF DESIGN.

all   HALTON FOUNDATION, 3114 NW Verde Vista, Portland, OR 97210. Mrs. W.S. Findlay. Many small, to children of current, disabled, or deceased employees of Halton Tractor Company.

C,M,VP, WR THE HAMBRIDGE ART CENTER, PO Box 33, Rabun Gap, Georgia 30568. Craftsmen, visual artists, musicians and writers are invited to stay in self-sufficient apartment/studios at a cost of $50 a week. Deadlines are Oct. 15 and April 15.

M,V-P HAMLINE UNIV., St. Paul, MN 55101. Two $200 renewable; various based on need.

P-WR HAMMOND INCORPORATED LIBRARY AWARD. Award: $500 and citation. SEE: AMERICAN LIBRARY ASSOCIATION.

V-P,C,A HAMPTON INSTITUTE, Hampton, VA 23364.

vp HANOVER COLLEGE, Hanover, IN 47243. Grants from $100 to $2,400. Awards through National Merit Scholarship Corp., Presbyterian Schol. Program, Schols. Service, and Fund for Negro Students.

WR THE HARIAN PRESS, 47 Hyde Blvd., Ballston Spa, NY 12020. Annual award of $500 worth of copies of work if published.

VP HARNESS TRACKS OF AMERICA, 333 No. Michigan Ave., Chicago, IL 60601. Art competition with $7,000 in awards. Deadline Aug. 15.

WR HARPER-SAXTON FELLOWSHIPS, Harper and Row Publishers, Inc., 10 E. 53rd St., NYC 10022. Prize is contract for book which is unfinished but is at least 10,000 words long. $7,500 is given, $5,000 of which is an advance against earnings.

WR HARTFORD JEWISH COMMUNITY CENTER, 3 Brighton Rd., West Hartford, CT 06117. Edward Lewis Wallant Memorial Award has a small cash prize for an American Jewish writer.

V-P,C HARTNELL COLLEGE, 156 Homestead Ave., Salinas, CA 93901.

M HARTT COLLEGE OF MUSIC, Univ.. of Hartford, 200 Bloomfield Ave., West Hartford, CT 06117. Various, renewable, partial-full. Talent, career potential and auditions required. Undergrad.

M HARTWICK COLLEGE, Oneonta, NY 13820. Five $400, restrictions, renewable.

WR HARVARD UNIVERSITY PRESS, 79 Garden St., Cambridge, MA 02138. Prize of $1,000 for work between 25,000 and 60,000 words in prose form to promote writing of the short novel.

c,vp,m HASTINGS COLLEGE, Hastings, NE 68901. Ten $100-$300 per year to entering freshmen, renewable, restrict., part-time service; 10 $100-$300 per year, renew., restrict., part-time service.

73

ALL,all   HAWAII STATE FOUNDATION ON CULTURE AND THE ARTS, 250 So. King St., Room 310, Honolulu, HI 96813. Aid for artists in schools, artists' works in state buildings and a $500 award for the Annual Hawaiian Writers Contest.

vp,c   HAYSTACK MOUNTAIN SCHOOL OF CRAFTS, Deer Isle, ME 04627. Contact: Ms. Ethel Clifford, Admin. Asst. Scholarship Grants cover tuition, board and room for six weeks summer study in areas listed in exchange for technical assistance. Anyone.

VP   HAZELTON ART LEAGUE, 225 East Broad St., Hazelton, PA 18201. Regional exhibition with U.S. Savings Bonds, purchase awards. Deadlines: March 31 and April 1.

wr   EDWARD W. HAZEN FND., 400 Prospect St., New Haven, CT 06511. Fellowships and grants for research or consultation especially for those preparing for university teaching and international and intercultural cooperation. Apply Administrative Assistant above.

M   JOSEPH HEARNS PRIZE IN MUSIC, Columbia University, 703 Dodge St., NYC 10027. $1,000-$1,500 — composers 18-25 yrs of age. Anyone.

m,vp   HEIDELBERG COLLEGE, Tiffin, OH 44883. George W. Deinzer, Dir. of Financial Aid.

P-T   JENNIE HEIDEN AWARD. Award: $100 and certificate. SEE: AMERICAN THEATRE ASSOCIATION, INC.

P-WR   CECIL HEMLEY AWARD. SEE: THE POETRY SOCIETY OF AMERICA.

m   HENDERSON STATE COLLEGE, Arkadelphia, AR 71923. $100-$340, some under restrictions, some renewable. Undergrad.

m   HENDRIX COLLEGE, Conway, AR 72032. Some continuing scholarships. $200-$400, undergrad.

all   HENRY FELLOWSHIPS, c/o Chas. & Julia Henry Fund, 17 Quincy St., Cambridge, MA 02138. Fellowships up to $2,600 only to graduates of Yale and Harvard. Must be single. Deadline December 12.

P-VP   HERRON SCHOOL OF ART, INDIANA-PURDUE UNIV. AT INDIANAPOLIS, 1701 No. Pennsylvania St., Indianapolis, IN 46202. Contact: Asst. to the Dean, Business Affairs. Scholarships based on portfolio competition— limited number. Value: full or half tuition. Tenable at the School for one yr. Open to U.S. and foreign art students. Undergraduates. Other financial assistance available through Indiana-Purdue Univ. at Indianapolis. Anyone.

P-WR   HERSKOVITS AWARD. Monetary prize.
SEE: AFRICAN STUDIES ASSOC.

vp   HELEN HERZBERGER SCHOLARSHIP.
SEE: Art Students League of N.Y. (Talent.).

P-VP   DR. MAURICE HEXTER PRIZE. Award: $500.
SEE: NATIONAL SCULPTURE SOCIETY.

P-VP   THE HIGH WINDS AWARD. Monetary award.
SEE: AMERICAN WATERCOLOR SOCIETY.

vp   HIGHLAND PARK COLLEGE, Glendale at Third, Highland Park, MI 48203.

vp   HIGHLINE COMMUNITY COLLEGE, Midway, WA 98031.

T,WR   SIDNEY HILLMAN FDN., INC., 15 Union Square, NYC 10003. $750 annually for published manuscripts only.

m   HILLSDALE COLLEGE, Hillsdale, MI 49242. Ten $1,000 per yr., 4 yrs to entering freshmen, variable according to need; assistantships, $100 per semester (accompanying; band, orchestra, choir perf., contribution of merit).

P-M   WALTER HINRICHSEN AWARD: To recognize and encourage composers in midcareer. Award of $3,000 to be used towards a new work, record or publish an existing work, annually awarded.
SEE: COLUMBIA UNIVERSITY.

M   HOCHSCHULE FUR MUSIK, Grassistrasse 8, DD-701 Leipzig, DDR, Germany.
BACH (J.S.) INTERNATIONAL COMPETITIONS: Piano, organ, voice and violin. Must be born after Dec. 31, 1935. Apply: Secretariat du Concours International J.S. Bach above. Anyone.

M,VP,C   HOFSTRA COLLEGE, 1000 Fulton Ave., Hempstead, NY 11550. Student assistance grants.

P-WR   BESS HOKIN PRIZE. Award: $100.
SEE: POETRY MAGAZINE.

vp   HOLDEN SCHOOL OF ART AND DESIGN, 1924 Arlington Blvd., S 200, Charlottesville, VA 22903. Maximum of $500 per recipient from Holden Fdn., part-time employment. MR

VP   HOLDEN SCHOOL OF FINE AND APPLIED ARTS, 215 East High St., Charlottesville, VA 22902. MR

m,vp   HOLLINS COLLEGE, Hollins College, VA 24020. $400, music ability; renewable. Women only.

75

WR   HOLT, RINEHART AND WINSTON, INC., 383 Madison Ave., NYC 10017. Henry Holt Public Affairs Award for outstanding nonfiction in current history or biography. $5,000 plus royalties. Annually.

vp   HOLYOKE COMMUNITY COLLEGE, 170 Sargent St., Holyoke, MA

VP   HONOLULU ACADEMY OF ARTS, 900 So. Bretania St., Honolulu, HI 96814. National Print Exhibition with $3,000 purchase awards. Prints only.

M,VP   HOPE COLLEGE, Holland, MI 49423. Twelve $100, performance audition, to entering freshmen; 4 $100 junior or senior majors.

P-WR   HORN BOOK AWARDS, The Boston Globe, Boston, MA 02107. Three different categories with a $200 award for each.

     BARON HORTA PRIZE.
     SEE: ROYAL ACADEMY OF BELGIUM.

m   HOUGHTON COLLEGE, Houghton, NY 14744. Two $100-$200 organ majors; Presser Fnd. $400 prospective music teacher, renewable.

WR   HOUGHTON MIFFLIN COMPANY, 2 Park St., Boston, MA 02107. Award of $2,500 cash and $7,500 advance against royalties. This award is for the Literary Fellowship and The New Poetry Series.

t,m,vp,c HOUSTON BAPTIST COLLEGE, 7502 Fondren Road, Houston, TX 77036. Contact: Ken Rogers, Director of Financial Aid. Grants in Aid are awarded annually, and range from $150 to $750 per year.

ALL   HOWARD (GEORGE A. AND ELIZA GARDNER) FDN., Box 1867, Brown Univ., Providence, RI 02912. Contact: Michael J. Brennan, Secy. FELLOW-SHIPS: In the arts and humanities to individuals, as well as other areas. Applicants must apply through a professional in the field he or she wants to work in (i.e.: museum director, critic, editor, head of a university, etc.). This is not for degree work. Stipends range from $3,000 to $7,000. Deadline Dec. 10.

all   HOWARD UNIVERSITY, Cambridge, MA 02138. Various small.

m,a,vp,c HOWARD UNIVERSITY, Washington, DC Various, renewable, restrictions, undergrads.

VP,WR   HUDSON ARTS FESTIVAL INC., 909 Bergenline Ave., Union City, NJ 07087. Mawy Vargas, Exec. Dir. MR

WR   THE HUDSON REVIEW, 65 E. 55th St., NYC 10022. The Bennett Award: Biennially gives $12,500 for author who feels he or she is at a critical state in their career and have not yet received recognition.

P-WR THE HUMAN FAMILY EDUCATIONAL AND CULTURAL INSTITUTE, PO Box 861, Pacific Palisades, CA 90272. THE HUMANITAS AWARD: To writers of teleplays that have ALREADY been broadcast by National Commercial Networks. Annual. $25,000 for teleplay 90 min. or longer; $15,000 for teleplay of 60 min.; $10,000 for teleplay of 30 min.

H,WR HUMANITIES ENDOWMENT (National Endowment for the Humanities, A Federal Agency).
SEE: National Endowment for the Humanities.

f HUMBOLDT STATE UNIVERSITY, Theater Arts, Arcata, CA 95521. Contact: Mr. Richard R. Rothrock, Chairman. SCHOLARSHIPS: One technical assistant at $387 a month; two graduate assistants at $311 a month each.

m,vp HUNTER COLLEGE OF CITY UNIV. OF NEW YORK, Dept. of Music, 695 Park Ave., NYC 10021. N.Y. State regents teaching fels. $500-$2,500. NDEA fels. Teaching fels. $2,900. Univ. fels. up to $2,500 for PhD's.

vp HUNTINGDON COLLEGE, 1500 E. Fairview Ave., Montgomery, AL 36106.

WR,WR-H HUNTINGTON LIBRARY AND ART GALLERY, San Marino, CA 91108. Contact: James Thorpe, Dir. Grants of $600 per month, for one to twelve months, for projects using the Huntington collections extensively. NOT for dissertations, or persons already having reasonable access to the Library. Applications invited from scholars having publications of merit.

m HURON COLLEGE, Seventh & Illinois Ave., SW, Huron, SD 57350. Ten to fifteen $100-$200 per year performing, in orchestra, band or choir required.

WR
all
ICELAND, Ministry of Education, Reykjavik, Iceland. Award for advanced study and research of language, literature and history of Iceland; 7 months; one to U.S. or Canadian student of Icelandic origin. Apply: Institute for International Education, 809, UN Plaza, NYC 10017.

ALL,all IDAHO STATE COMMISSION ON THE ARTS AND HUMANITIES, State House, Boise, ID 83720. Monies for artists in schools. Fellowships for Idaho residents. Touring programs for professional artists.

a,vp,c IDAHO STATE UNIV., Fine Arts Bldg., Pocatello, ID 83201.

ALL,all ILLINOIS ARTS COUNCIL, 111 No. Wabash Ave., Chicago, IL 60602. Grants of up to $500 to complete a work in progress by an Illinois artist. Applications accepted in August. There are also monthly exhibitions of Illinois visual artists in the council's offices.

A ILLINOIS INSTITUTE OF TECHNOLOGY, Chicago, IL 60616.

M	WGN ILLINOIS OPERA GUILD, WGN, 2501 Bradley Pl., Chicago, IL 60657. Dick Jones. To $3,000 – 20 to 34 yrs. Tape with application; live auditions in NY, LA, Chicago.
vp,m,c, f,vp-h, m-h	ILLINOIS STATE UNIV., College of Fine Arts, Normal, IL 61761. Contact: Dean Charles W. Bolen. Graduate assistantships, tuition waivers and grants given by theatre, music and art departments. Contact individual schools within University.
vp	ILLINOIS TEACHERS COLLEGE CHICAGO, 5500 N. St. Louis Ave., Chicago, IL 60625.
m,vp	ILLINOIS WESLEYAN UNIV., School of Music, Bloomington, IL 61701. Financial aid available to all qualified undergrads; auditions required. Grad, assistantships.
P-WR	IN A NUTSHELL, Hibiscus Press, PO Box 22248, Sacramento, CA 95822. $100 and $25 for original short story or poem.
vp	INCARNATE WORD COLLEGE, 4301 Broadway, San Antonio, TX 78209.
VP	INCORPORATED E.A. ABBEY SCHOLARSHIPS FOR MURAL PAINTING IN THE U.S.A., 1083 Fifth Ave., NYC 10028. $3,750 to American Academy in Rome for study in mural painting. U.S. citizens not more than 35 yrs of age. Biennially.
ALL,all	INDIANA ARTS COMMISSION, 155 East Market St., Suite 614, Indianapolis, IN 46204. Monies given for arts education and as a matching cash basis for residencies of performing artists. Competitive system of grants. Deadlines March 1 and October 1.
m,vp,c	INDIANA STATE UNIV., Terre Haute, IN 47809. Undergrads, 20 $250 per yr.; 10 $100, special services required; 5 $100-$300. Twelve grad assistantships, $1,500 plus remission of tuition.
vp	INDIANA UNIV., NORTHWEST, 3400 Broadway, Gary, IN 46408.
f,t	INDIANA UNIVERSITY AUDIO VISUAL CENTER, Bloomington, IN 47401. Associate instructorships at $2,700 each; several fels.
VP,VP-H	INDIANA UNIV., Dept. of Fine Arts, Bloomington, IN 47401. Contact Mrs. Ann O'Neill, Graduate Secretary.

FORD FOUNDATION FELLOWSHIPS: For 1976-77 (about $2,000 each plus in-state fee reduction) for graduates in Creative Arts.

UNIVERSITY GRADUATE SCHOOL FELLOWSHIPS: About $2,000 plus privilege of in-state fee rates.

ASSOCIATE INSTRUCTORSHIPS: For art history and visual arts (about 60 in 1976-77) in an amount about $2,200 plus full fee remission. Not usually awarded to first-year student.

UNIVERSITY FELLOWSHIP: For graduate student $2,000 plus fee reduction.

m INDIANA UNIV., School of Music, Bloomington, IN 47401. Undergraduate scholarships from $100-$1,000; over 200 teaching assistantships valued at $2,000; fellowships to $1,500.

vp INDIANA UNIVERSITY MUSEUM, Wesley R. Hurt, Dir., 107 Student Bldg., Indiana Univ., Bloomington, IN 47401. Disciplines: Fine Arts/Audio-Visual; Exhibition Design (design, photography). Factors: Graduate Assistantship $1,800 for period Aug.-May (reg. academic yr.). May be renewed. Issued in bi-weekly payments of $112.50. Appointee also receives Indiana University Museum Fee Remission Award for Fall and Spring semesters. Requirements: Must be enrolled as a graduate student in Fine Arts or Audio/Visual Depts., must maintain a B average; 12 hrs of work per week during regular classes. Apply Director, Indiana Univ. Museum, no recommendation needed.

vp INDIANA UNIV. OF PENNSYLVANIA, Indiana, PA 19103. Various amounts. String Scholshp. Fund; NDEA Loans; Work-Study Programs. Graduate work-study. Dept. of Art & Art Education.

WR INDONESIA, Ministry of Foreign Affairs, Djakarta, Indonesia. Scholarships for postgraduate study in Indonesia to graduates. Apply to Embassy of Indonesia, 2020 Mass. Ave., NW, Washington, DC 20036.

VP,C INSTITUTE FOR THE ARTS, 6702 Marlboro Pike, Washington, DC 20028. Award of exhibition in a Washington gallery, commissions for the artist who uses his talents to express "spiritual truths." A religious oriented requirement. Anyone.

H INSTITUTE FOR THE STUDY OF HISTORY THROUGH ARTS AND ARTIFACTS, 2512 33rd Ave., South, Seattle, WA 98144. Alan Gowans.

WR INSTITUTE FOR WORLD ORDER, 777 United Nations Plaza, NYC 10017. GRANTS to writers who help bring the topic of war prevention to the surface of the contemporary mind. Anyone. Apply: Mrs. Close Zerwick, above.

WR INSTITUTE OF EARLY AMERICAN HISTORY AND CULTURE, Box 220, Williamsburg, VA 23185. AWARD $1,000 plus book publication biennially, for nonfiction ms in Early American History and Culture from 1760 to 1815. Apply Director above.

all INSTITUTE OF EUROPEAN STUDIES, 710 North Rush St., Chicago, IL 60611. Contact: Joan Racki, Admissions & Financial Aid Officer. GRANTS: Available to those students studying on one of the Institute's programs. $500 to $1,200 for the academic year are available to College level sophomores, juniors and seniors, studying abroad for academic credit for either a semester or academic year. Based on need, and submit a Parents' Confidential Stmt.

ALL   INSTITUTE OF INTERNATIONAL EDUCATION, Information Services
809 UN Plaza, NYC 10017.
GRANTS FOR GRADUATE STUDY ABROAD: Opportunities for candidates in the Creative and Performing Arts: Fulbright-Hays (U.S. Government) Grants, Germanistic Society of America, Alliance Francaise de New York, French Government, Austrian Government, and Italian Government grants are offered under IIE's auspices. Plus many more.

all   INSTITUTE OF PUERTO RICAN CULTURE, Apartado Postal, 4184, San Juan, Puerto Rico 00905. Aid for artists-in-schools.

M   INSTITUTIO DE ESTUDIOS GIENNESES, Delegado del Concorso de Piano, Palacio Provincial, Jean, Spain. International competition for piano. Apply: Sr. Consejero.

VP,WR,   INSTITUTO ALLENDE, San Miguel Allende, Guanajuato, Mexico. Grants
T,C   for full or partial tuition after one trimester of attendance. Anyone.

M   INSTITUTO MUSICALE PAGANINI, Palazzo della Meridiana, 4 Salita di San Francesco, Genoa, Italy. Paganini International Violin Contest: Violinists under 35 yrs. First prize over $3,000. Anyone.

ALL   EMBASSY OF IRAN, Educational Affairs Section, 2135 Wisconsin Ave., NW, Washington, DC 20007. Many scholarships and grants for foreign students, at six of Iran's universities. Inquire for more information at above address.

all   INSULAR ARTS COUNCIL OF GUAM, PO Box Ek (Univ. of Guam), Agana, Guam 96910. Aid for artists-in-schools.

WR   INTER-AMERICAN PRESS ASSOC. SCHOLARSHIP FUND, 2911 NW 39th St., Miami, FL 33142. Scholarships and stipends to journalists for advanced study for one year in Latin America. U.S. and Canadian citizens. Apply: The Scholarship Awards Committee. James B. Canel, Gen. Mgr. MR

F,f   INTERFILM FESTIVAL, Zrinjekega 9 61000, Ljubljana, Yugoslavia. Contact: Dragan Jankovic, Festival Director.
INTERFILM FESTIVAL SPORT AND TOURISM KRANJ

P-VP   INTERNATIONAL ART DEALERS ASSOCIATION, 575 Madison Ave., NYC 10022. AWARD: In recognition of outstanding work in modern art. The prize of $3,854 is awarded annually.

M-P   INTERNATIONAL BEETHOVEN PIANO COMPETITION, c/o L. Bosendorfer Klavierfabrik AG, Bosendorferstrasse 12, A-1010, Wien, Austria. Three prizes of 75,000, 50,000 and 35,000 Austrian Sch. and grand piano. Deadline March 1.

P-M   INTERNATIONAL BEL CANTO COMPETITION, c/o Secretariat of the

Competition, Quai de Cendroz 5, Liege, Belgium. PRIZE: For the outstanding performances by singers ages 20 to 35 years. Prizes totaling over 30,000 Belgium francs.

P-WR   INTERNATIONAL BOOK FESTIVAL, c/o Bruno La Grange, 38 Avenue de l'Opera, Paris 2, France.
GOLDEN EAGLE AWARD: To an excellent writer for the sum of his outstanding work. 30,000 francs awarded annually. Anyone.

M   INTERNATIONAL COMPETITION "GEORGE ENESCO," Secretariate, 1 Stirbei Voda St., Bucharest, Rumania. Voice, piano, violin, age 33 and under. Up to $4,250. Anyone.

M   INTERNATIONAL COMPETITION FOR EXCELLENCE IN THE PERFORMANCE OF AMERICAN MUSIC. $83,500 annually in prizes, including cash, contracts, tours. (Rockefeller Foundation or Stevens' Office, Kennedy Center, Washington, DC.)

M   INTERNATIONAL COMPETITION FOR MUSICAL COMPOSITION— OPERA AND BALLET, Maison De La Radio, 66, BD Carl-Vogt, CH-1211, Geneva 8, Switzerland. Up to 12,000 Swiss francs for biennial competition for music with or without a story. Anyone.

M   INTERNATIONAL CONTEST FOR STRINGS, Administration du concours, 66, rue de Joie, Liege, Belgium. Guitar, strings, etc. Changes yearly. Write for details of next competition. Anyone.

M   INTERNATIONAL CONTEST FOR YOUNG CONDUCTORS, Secretariat du concours, Promenade Chamars, Besancon (Doubs), France. Cash awards to professional and non-professional conductors 30 or under.

M
(voice)   INTERNATIONAL COMPETITION OF INDIVIDUAL SINGING, 6 rue du Gynmase, Verviers, Belgium. Anyone under 35 yrs. Contest held in April at Verviers Grand Theater. Apply to Miss Yvonne Kaivers, above.

M   INTERNATIONAL COMPETITION OF MUSICAL PERFORMERS, Palais, Eynard, CH-1204 Geneva. First Prize $1,400, 2nd $800, 3rd $400, medals and other awards. Men, 22-32, women 20-30. MR

WR   INTERNATIONAL CREATIVE WRITERS LEAGUE, Atlanta Metro, 3682 Carriage Way, East Point, GA 30344. Dr. C.E. Stovall, Pres.

INTERNATIONAL FOUNDATION FOR ART RESEARCH, 46 E. 70th St., NYC 10021. Elizabeth B. Burns, Exec. Secy.

WR,M,T,   INTERNATIONAL HUMANITIES, 1000 Connecticut Ave., Suite 1208,
D   Washington, DC 20036. Previously listed for international cooperation and performing arts grants but now inactive.

M INTERNATIONAL INSTITUTE OF MUSIC OF CANADA, 106 Dulwich Ave., St. Lambert, Montreal, Quebec, Canada.
MONTREAL INTERNATIONAL COMPETITION. Category changes annually. First prize $10,000. Anyone.

VP INTERNATIONAL JEWISH ART COMPETITION, Haifa, Israel. Summer. $1,000 first prize, two- and three-dimensional fine art. Sponsored by WUJS and the City of Haifa. Forms and competition rules from WUJS, 247 Grays Inn Rd., London WC1, England.

AM INTERNATIONAL MUSEUM OF PHOTOGRAPHY, 900 East Ave., Rochester, NY 14607. Three one-year internships available at International Museum of Photography for training of museum and academic professionals. Must have completed a Master's degree in either science, fine arts, history, art history, literature, film or design. Stipends are $7,200 ($3,600 is tax free). Deadline March 1.

M INTERNATIONAL MUSIC COMPETITION, Lothringerstrasse 18, A-1030 Vienna 3, Austria. Categories vary. Anyone. Apply: Secretariat du concours.

M INTERNATIONAL MUSIC COMPETITION (Geneva), Palais Eynard, 4 rue de la Croix-Rouge, CH-1204 Geneva, Switzerland. Categories vary. Anyone. Apply: Secretariat du concours, above. MR

M INTERNATIONALER MUSIKWETTBEWERB, Bayerischer rundfunk, D-8 Munich 2, Germany.
MUNICH INTERNATIONAL MUSIC CONTEST. Prizes up to and over $1,000. Categories vary. Anyone.

P-M INTERNATIONAL MUSIC INSTITUTE OF THE CITY OF DARMSTADT, Roquetteweg 31, 61 Darmstadt, FDR.
KRANICHSTEINER MUSIC PRIZE: Monetary prize of 1,000 German marks annually for these different categories: percussion, flute, piano, and a prize for interpretation of contemporary music.

M INTERNATIONAL ORGAN COMPETITION (Bruges), Sekretariaat International Musikdagen, Gistelstennweg 285, Bruges 3, Belgium. Anyone. Write for details.

M INTERNATIONAL PIANO CONTEST "ETTORE POZZOLI," Segreatia del concorso presso, Palazzo Muncipale, Seregno, Seregno, Italy. Pianists age 35 or younger. Anyone.

WR,wr INTERNATIONAL POETRY FORUM, University of Pittsburgh Press, 127 North Bellefield Ave., Pittsburgh, PA 15260.
THE INTERNATIONAL POETRY FORUM'S UNITED STATES AWARD: For recognition for a U.S. citizen who has not published a volume of poetry, other than a limited private printing. Award of $2,000 plus the

publication of the manuscript. The Press will pay a standard royalty to the author.

P-WR INTERNATIONAL READING ASSOCIATION, c/o Dr. Ruth K. Carlson, 800 Barksdale Rd., Newark, DE 19711.
CHILDREN'S BOOK AWARD: For the outstanding contribution to children's books by an author who shows unusual promise. $1,000. Anyone.

ALL INTERNATIONAL RESEARCH AND EXCHANGE BOARD, 655 Third Ave., NYC 10017.

M INTERNATIONAL SINGING COMPETITION OF BELGIUM, 15 Blvd. de
(voice) L'Empereur, Brussels 1, Belgium. Open to all singers 20-35. Awards totaling $8,000. Apply to: Secretariat du Concors de Chant de Belgique above.

M INTERNATIONAL TCHAIKOVSKY COMPETITION, Organizing Committee, 15 Neglinnaya St., Moscow, USSR. Piano, violin and voice. Pianists and violinists 16-30 yrs., singers 20-33. Quadrennial, next in '70.

WR,T INTERNATIONAL THEATRE INSTITUTE, 6 Rue Franklin, 75 Paris 16e, France. Fellowships for young theater professionals to study theater. including playwriting in other International Theater Inst. member countries; min. 3 months. Nationals of ITI Membership Countries. Apply: ITI, 245 W. 52nd St., NYC 10019. MR

M INTERNATIONAL TRUMPET GUILD, Crane School of Music, State University College at Potsdam, Potsdam, NY 13676. Dr. Gordon Mathie, Pres.

M INTERNATIONAL VOICE COMPETITION, Secretariat du Concours, Don-
(voice) jon du Capitole, Toulouse, France. Open to all singers 18-33. Prizes total $2,500 including concert presentation.

P-WR INTERNATIONAL WHO'S WHO IN POETRY, INTERNATIONAL BIO-GRAPHICAL CENTRE, Cambridge CB2 3QP, England, UK.
CHARLES BAUDELAIRE POETRY PRIZE: $500 awarded every two years to encourage a young poet (under 21 years). Anyone.
INTERNATIONAL WHO'S WHO IN POETRY AWARDS: Awards amounting to $2,500 every two years to encourage existing poets, and bring out new ones. Anyone.

P-F INTERNATIONALE FILMWOCHE MANNHEIM, Rathaus, E 5, 68 Mannheim 1, Germany. Eight prizes with awards from 2,000 Deutsch Marks to 10,000 Deutsch Marks for original fiction films for cinema and TV.

WR IONA COLLEGE WRITERS' CONFERENCE, Advisory Council, New Rochelle, NY 10801. Prizes in fiction and nonfiction.

V-P IOWA LAKES COMMUNITY COLLEGE, Rotunda Bldg., Estherville, IA 51334.

P-WR   IOWA SCHOOL OF LETTERS, English-Philosophy Bldg., The University of
        Iowa, Iowa City, IA 55242.
        IOWA SCHOOL OF LETTERS AWARD FOR SHORT FICTION: For the
        recognition of unpublished authors of booklength short fiction. Publi-
        cation of the book by the Univ/Iowa Press and $1,000 to the author
        annually.

ALL,all IOWA STATE ARTS COUNCIL, State Capitol Bldg., Des Moines, IA 50319.
        Grants for workshops, individual artists, classes, artist-in-residence. Art works
        are purchased for state buildings.

WR,F,a IOWA STATE UNIV. PRESS, Press Bldg., Ames, Iowa 50010. I.S.U.P. Award
        for unpublished work in English to residents of iowa. Four graduate film
        assistantships ($3,000 each plus 50% tuition remitted) in Journalism.

VP,M   IOWA WESLEYAN COLLEGE, Mt. Pleasant, IA 52641. Many small. Four-
        year liberal arts college with majors in art and music.

P-WR,M,T, IRISH AMERICAN CULTURAL INSTITUTE, 683 Osceola Ave., St. Paul,
        MN 55105. Grants of $10,000 in fiction, poetry or drame. Only for Irish
        artists. Prize of $7,500 for American's book on Irish theme.

P-WR   IRISH ARTS COUNCIL, 70 Merrion Square, Dublin 2, Ireland.
        POETRY IN IRISH AWARD: To award the best book of poetry in the
        Irish language, being published in the previous 3 years. 300 Irish pounds
        awarded triennially. Anyone.

wr   ISRAEL MINISTRY OF EDUCATION AND CULTURE, Jerusalem, Israel.
        Scholarships to grads for postgrad studies in Israel; any grad,. Apply: Insti-
        tute of International Education, 809 UN Plaza, NYC 10017.

        ITALIAN CULTURE COUNCIL, c/o Patricia A. Berreman, Dir., 549 Edgar
        Road, Westfield, NJ 07090.

M-P   ITALIAN NATIONAL ACADEMY OF SANTA CECILIA, 11087 Rome,
        Italy.
        SANTA CECILIA ACADEMY COMPETITION FOR ORCHESTRAL CON-
        DUCTORS PRIZE: A monetary prize of 2,000,000 liras and the oppor-
        tunity to conduct a subscription concert at the Academy is awarded
        every three years to the best conductor.

wr   ITALY, MINISTRY OF FOREIGN AFFAIRS, Palazzo della Farnesina, Rome
        Italy. Scholarships for the study of Italian language and literature, research,
        9 months; teaching fels. in English at Italian Univ. to those with MA and
        teaching experience and working knowledge of Italian. American lit. back-
        ground preferred. Apply: Inst. of Intnl. Ed., 809 UN Plaza, NYC 10017.
        Schols. to Italians abroad, grads to study in Italy, 1-8 months. Apply: Em-
        bassy of Italy, 1601 Fuller St., NW, Washington, DC 20009.

84

m,f ITHACA COLLEGE, School of Music, Ithaca, NY 14850. Various, renewable schls., Grad. fels. T.V., Radio Dept. Gen. U. Schls. Nat'l. Academy of Television Arts & Sciences schol. $500.

all IVY FUND, INC., 65 Broadway, Rm. 2100, NYC 10006. GRANTS for international activities, emphasis on education in foreign countries, higher education, intercultural relations, etc. MR

vp,c JACKSON STATE COLLEGE, Lynch at Dalton St., Jackson, MS 39207.

P-T,p-t JACKSONVILLE UNIVERSITY PLAYWRITING COMPETITION, College of Fine Arts, Jacksonville University, Jacksonville, FL 32211. $2,000 for full-length manuscript and production of winning play. Anyone. Deadline Jan. 1.

P-M JAEN INTERNATIONAL PIANO COMPETITION, c/o Sr. Consejero Delgado del Concurso de Piano "Premio Jaen," Secretaria del Instituto de Estudios Giennenses, Palacio Provincial, Jaen, Spain.
JAEN PRIZE: Totaling 75,000 pesetas and diplomas annually awarded for the outstanding performances on the piano. Anyone.

P-M JAMES MADISON UNIVERSITY FLUTE CLUB, James Madison University, Music Dept., Harrisonburg, VA 22807. $300 prize for best competition for flute choir. Winning entry considered for publication. Deadline Oct. 1.

m,t JAMESTOWN COLLEGE, Box 62, Jamestown, ND 58401. $100-$400 Tuition grants; $400-$800 tuition grants for technical assts. Anyone.

P-ALL, JAPAN FOUNDATION, Daito Bldg., 3-7-1 Kasumigaseki, Chiyoda-ku, Tokyo
all 100, Japan.
JAPAN FOUNDATION AWARD AND JAPAN FOUNDATION SPECIAL PRIZE: Recipient judged for contribution to international cultural exchange.

WR JAPAN MINISTRY OF EDUCATION, 2, Kasumigaseki, 3-chome, Chiyoda-ku. Foreign Schlrshps. tenable in Japan to grads. in Jap. culture and science or to those whose study in Japan will enhance value of their specific program; nationals of most countries, grads.

P-VP JAPAN SOCIETY OF INTERNATIONAL CULTURAL RELATIONS, 55, 1-chome Shiba Shirokane-daimachi, Minato-ku, Tokyo, Japan.
JAPAN INTERNATIONAL BIENNIAL EXHIBITION OF PRINTS PRIZE: Awarded to the artist of the best prints. Monetary prize of 400,000, awarded biennially. MR

M JAZZ COMPOSERS ORCHESTRA ASSOCIATION, 500 Broadway, NYC 10012. Michael Mantler.

P-WR PRIX JEAN-BERAUD. Award: $1,000.
SEE: LE CERCLE DU LIVRE DE FRANCE.

vp   JEFFERSON COLLEGE, Hillsboro, MO 63050.

P-A   THOMAS JEFFERSON MEMORIAL FOUNDATION, Montecello, Box 316, Charlottesville, VA 22901.
              THOMAS JEFFERSON MEMORIAL FOUNDATION MEDAL: To honor outstanding architecture. Medal and $5,000 to the architect regardless of nationality. Awarded annually at Founder's Day Ceremony at the Univ/Virginia. Anyone.

WR   JEFFERSON POETRY AWARD, JNR Publishing, 691 Broadway, NYC 10022. $1,000 annually for unpublished poetry.

all   JELKE FND. INC., 40 Wall St., NYC 10005. Fels. to support higher education, international studies. MR

VP   GEORG JENSEN INC., Madison Ave. at 57th St., NYC 10022.
              LUNNING PRIZE: Awarded to Scandinavian craftsmen and designers, preferably 30 to 35 years of age. $10,000 awarded annually. MR

M   JERUSALEM INTERNATIONAL HARP COMPETITION, Midgal Shalom, 5th Floor, 9 Ahad Haam St., Tel-Aviv, Israel. Harpists under 35, First Prize: concert grand harp from Lyon & Healy. Other prizes, $200-$2,000.

P-WR   JERUSALEM MUNICIPALITY, International Book Fair, PO Box 91000, Israel.
              JERUSALEM BOOK PRIZE: $2,000 awarded to author of outstanding literature expressing man's struggle for freedom. Every 2 yrs. Anyone.

P-T,   THE JERUSALEM PRIZE, Jerusalem International Book Fair, 22, Jaffa Rd., Jerusalem 91000, Israel. Cash prize of $2,000 annually.

          JEWISH ACADEMY OF ARTS AND SCIENCES, Inc., 123 Gregory Ave., West Orange, NJ 07052. Contact: Dr. Hirsch Lazaar Silverman, Secretary for information.

P-WR   JEWISH CHRONICLE, 25 Furnival St., London EC4A IJT, England, UK.
              ANNUAL BOOK AWARD: For the outstanding best fiction or nonfiction dealing with a Jewish interest, in English, by a living Jewish author in the UK or the Commonwealth. 250 pounds sterling, annually.

WR   JEWISH PUBLICATION SOCIETY OF AMERICA, 117 S. 17th St., Philadelphia, PA 19103. Bernard I. Levinson, Exec. V. Pres.
              FRANK AND ETHEL COHEN AWARD: Writing dealing with aspects of Jewish thought; citizen of USA & Canada. $500 annually; many other small.

WR   JEWISH PUBLICATION SOCIETY OF AMERICA, 222 No. 15th St., Philadelphia, PA 19102. Outstanding booklength manuscript dealing with Jewish life: $4,000.

m   JOHN BROWN UNIV., Siloam Springs, AR 72761. Five $700 for instr.; some $200 for voice, renewable, undergrad.

T   MARGO JONES AWARD, INC., 250 W. 57th St., NYC 10019. For new dramatic works of professional or nonprofessional groups To producing managers of American and Canadian theatres; several small annually. MR

m,d   JORDAN COLLEGE OF MUSIC OF BUTLER UNIV., 4600 Sunset Ave., Indianapolis, IN 46208. Contact: Dr. Louis F. Chenette, Dean.
AUDITION AWARDS: Ranging from ¼ to full tuition.

m   JOY IN SINGING INC., Secretary, One W. 72nd St., NYC 10023. Series of lecture-recitals, treating the art song conducted by Winifred Cecil before a discriminating audience in the auditorium of the Library and Museum of the Performing Arts, Lincoln Center Singers are chosen by audition, the one judged most outstanding by distinguished panel is presented in a debut recital in Alice Tully Hall, all expenses paid. If accepted, registration is $30.

P-WR   JAMES JOYCE AWARD.
SEE: THE POETRY SOCIETY OF AMERICA.

vp,c   JUDSON COLLEGE, Marion, AL 36756.

m,t,d   THE JUILLIARD SCHOOL, Lincoln Center, NYC 10023. Grants are for education. Grants are from School itself, private individuals, foundations, business organizations. Made on yearly basis and are most often under $1,000. No restrictions. New program now exists to enable young writers to obtain practical experience at the theater center.

WR,V-P,M,   ALFRED JURZYKOWSKI FND. INC., 200 Park Ave., NYC 10017. Awards
T,D $5,000 to scholars, writers, composers and artists for distinguished service to the arts and science and emphasis on Polish contributions of mankind. Translation grants (Polish) also. Anyone by nomination, annual.

P-WR   JANET KAFKA MEMORIAL PRIZE, University College of Liberal and Applied Sciences, Univ/Rochester, Rochester, NY 14627. Prize is given periodically for outstanding woman writer. Exact amount not yet determined.

vp   KALAMAZOO COLLEGE, Kalamazoo, MI 49001. Schols. based on need, renewable, restrictions, part-time service.

all   KANSAS ARTS COMMISSION, 509A Kansas Ave., Topeka, KS 66603. Artists-in-Schools.

V-P   KANSAS CITY ART INSTITUTE, Kansas City, MO 64111. High school and college transfers.

vp,a   KANSAS STATE UNIV., Dept. of Art, Manhattan, KS 66502. Teaching assistantships for students working for Master's degree.

M   KAUFMAN (MINNA)-RUDD FND, Chatham College, Pittsburgh, PA 15232. Unmarried women 18-29 yrs. only. Financial assistance based on needs and requirement for studies in a concert and operatic career. Apply to: Edward Eddy, Pres., above. Also $1,000 Distinguished Performance Award-5 annually.

P-VP   KAUTZKY, TED, MEMORIAL AWARD. Monetary Award.
         SEE: AMERICAN WATERCOLOR SOCIETY.

m   KEARNEY STATE COLLEGE, Kearney, NE 68847. Four $50 various applied music schls, audition to entering freshmen; $250 Cosmopolitan Club Schl. $50 Phi Mu Alpha Schl., $50 Menc student schl. Grad. assists.

VP   KELLOGG COMMUNITY COLLEGE, Battle Creek, MI 49106.

P-M   JOHN F. KENNEDY CENTER FOR THE PERFORMING ARTS, Kennedy Center, Washington, DC 20566. The Friedheim Award is given to three American composers with works at least 20 minutes long. Prizes are $5,000, $2,000 and $500.

WR   ROBERT F. KENNEDY JOURNALISM AWARDS, 1035 30th St., NW, Washington, DC 20007. Cash prizes of up to $3,000 for media of print and broadcasting. Deadline last week of January.

WR   JOHN F. KENNEDY MEMORIAL AWARD, 10 E. 53rd St., NYC. Literary work in field of biography or history illuminating the influence of individuals to foster understanding of this country and its role in the world. $2,000 and guarantee, awarded irregularly.

vp,c,a   KENT STATE UNIV., Kent, OH 44240.

all   KENTUCKY ARTS COMMISSION, 100 W. Main St., Frankfort, KY 40601. Artists-in-schools.

m,vp,c   KENTUCKY WESLEYAN COLLEGE, Owensboro, KY 42301. Six $400, renewable.

wr,vp   KENYON COLLEGE, Gambier, OH 43022. Kenyon Review Fels. $2,700 (single), $4,000 (married) on basis of published works. By nomination for study in any country.

WR   KEVORKIAN FND., 1411 Third Ave., NYC 10028. Grants to promote interest in Near and Mid-East art through exhibitions and schlsps for study in this field.

vp   KILGORE COLLEGE, 1100 Broadway, Kilgore, TX 75662.

all   KIMBER FARMS, Div. of Dekalbag Research, Inc., Sycamore Rd., Dekach, IL 60115. To employees' children only. Leland C. Cerruti, Pres.

vp   REV. MARTIN LUTHER KING, JR. MEMORIAL SCHOLARSHIP.
SEE: Art Students League of N.Y. (Merit). A scholarship in perpetuity.

P-VP   KINGHAN, CHARLES R., AWARD. Monetary award.
SEE AMERICAN WATERCOLOR SOCIETY.

m   KING'S COLLEGE, Briarcliff Manor, NY 10510. Four $500 renewable,
restrictions.

P-WR,wr   OTTO KINKELDEY AWARD. Award: $400.
SEE: AMERICAN MUSICOLOGICAL SOCIETY.

a,a-h,d,f,   THE KATE NEAL KINLEY MEMORIAL FELLOWSHIP, College of Fine
m,t,vp,wr   and Applied Arts, Univ/Illinois at Urbana-Champaign, 110 Architecture Bldg.,
Urbana, IL 61801. Fellowship of $3,500 given once yearly to graduates of
higher education institutions. Preference to persons under 25 yrs of age.
Deadline April 15.

VP   KITCHENER WATERLOO ART GALLERY, 43 Bento St., Kitchener, Ontario N2G 3H1, Canada. Grants of up to $4,000 are given annually to On-
tario artists. Emergency aid is also given.

P-WR   ROGER KLEIN FOUNDATION, INC., c/o Berlack, Israels & Liberman, 26
Broadway, NYC 10004.
         ROGER KLEIN AWARD FOR CREATIVE EDITING: To honor the excel-
lence of a trade book editor for his work over at least the previous five
years. You must be under 40 yrs of age; textbook, magazine and children's book editors need not apply. Scroll and $1,000 awarded bi-
ennially.

vp   BERNARD KLONIS MEMORIAL SCHOLARSHIP.
SEE: Art Students Leage of N.Y. (Merit).

VP-P   KNICKERBOCKER ARTISTS OF AMERICA, Virginia Goldberg, Pres., 126
Princeton Rd., NYC 11570. Annual exhibition with purchase awards, medals,
cash awards. Deadline Sept. 28.

WR   ALFRED A. KNOPF, INC., 210 E. 50th St., NYC 10022. Knopf Western
History Prize: $5,000 biennially for best ms. in Western American History.

m   KNOXVILLE COLLEGE, Division of Music, Knoxville, TN 37921. To
entering freshmen. Five-ten $200-$500; others: 3-5 $200-$500 renewable.

M,m   KONSERVATORIUM DER STADT WIEN, SR Prof. Erwin Weiss, Director,
Johannesgasse 4a, 1010 Vienna, Austria. Competitions in various subjects
and fields of music since 1966 (jazz), Schubert and the 20th Century.

WR   KOREAN LANGUAGE RESEARCH SOCIETY, 58-14 Shimmoon-ro 1 ka,

Chongno-ku, Seoul, Korea. Fels. for study of Korean language, literature or culture. Males, 31-35 yrs, academic or professional qualifications, pref. in exchange for similar opportunity to a Korean teacher or research worker.

WR   KOREA UNIV., 1 Anam-dong, Seoul, Korea. Scholarships to grads for study in Korean history, language, literature and Far Eastern affairs. Two years.

wr,m   KOSCIUSZKO FND., 15 E. 65th St., NYC 10021. Scholarships to be used in U.S. or Poland for study of Polish language, literature, history; research and publication of books pertaining to Polish history and culture, etc., to promote Polish cultural heritage. Apply: Scholarship Committee, above. Chopin Schlrshp. 15-21, $1,000 for study in conservatory, music schook, or competent private teacher.

wr   KOSSUTH FND., c/o Butler Univ., Indianapolis, IN 46208. Grants to Hungarian refugee scholars, acts as cultural and study center in Hungarian academic and literay subjects. Exchange program. Dr. Janos Horvath, Pres. MR

M   KOUSSEVITZKY MUSIC FOUNDATION, c/o Freeman & Kohns, 415 Madison Ave., NYC 10017. General purpose to foster the development of music and music education. Commissions compositions and provides schls. for study at the Berkshire Music Center.

vp   YVONNE KRAMER SCHOLARSHIPS, c/o Univ/Southern California, University Park, Los Angeles, CA 90007. $2,000.

P-F   KRANJ INTERNATIONAL FESTIVAL OF SPORT AND TOURIST FILMS, c/o Me. Dragan Yankovic, Dir., Interfilm Festival, Zrinjskega 9, Ljubljana, Yugoslavia.
AWARDS: UNESCO Prize for the film which best shows the connection between sport and tourism. Prize for direction: 8,000 dinars. Prize for screenplay: 6,000 dinars. Prize for music: 3,000 dinars. Biennially. Anyone.

wr,v-p,   SAMUEL H. KRESS FND., 221 W. 57th St., NYC 10019. Grants for general
vvp-h   philanthropic programs; studies in art history; support for conservative works of art. Anyone.

P-WR   ALFRED KREYMBORG MEMORIAL AWARD.
SEE: THE POETRY SOCIETY OF AMERICA.

vp   YASUO KUNIYOSHI MEMORIAL SCHOLARSHIP.
SEE: Art Students League of N.Y. (Merit).

vp,c   KUTZTOWN STATE COLLEGE, Kutztown, PA 19530. Various small.

VP   LAFAYETTE ART CENTER, 101 South 9th St., Lafayette, IN 47901. Tippecanoe Biennial for painting, print, sculpture and photography with over $1,000 in prizes.

vp   LAGUNA BEACH SCHOOL OF ART AND DESIGN, 630 Laguna Canyon Rd., Laguna Beach, CA 92651. MR

P-WR   GORDON LAING PRIZE. Award: $1,000.
SEE: UNIVERSITY OF CHICAGO PRESS.

all   LAKE ERIE COLLEGE, Painesville, OH 44077. Many small, anyone.

all   LAKE FOREST COLLEGE, Lake Forest, IL 60045. Various, small.

vp   LAKE PLACID ART SCHOOL, Victor Herbert Road, Lake Placid, NY 12946.

vp   LAMBUTH COLLEGE, Lambuth Blvd., Jackson, TN 38301. Scholarships up to $700 for music education.

P-WR   THE LAMONT POETRY SELECTION AWARD: Publication of the manuscript with guaranteed distribution of 1,000 copies of the book. SEE: Academy of American Poets, Inc.

M   THE LAMONT SCHOOL OF MUSIC OF THE UNIVERSITY OF DENVER, 2370 East Evans Ave., Denver, CO 80210. Many academic schols. partial-full tuition. One Presser Fnd. $400; many activity grants $300-$1,500. Many $180-$420 applied music. Opera Workshop $328, audition and some operatic experience; Grad. fels.

WR,AM   LANNAN FND., 175 West Jackson Blvd., Rm. 1541, Chicago, IL 60604. Grants for the preservation and exhibition of art of all kinds; gifts and loans to promote creative imagination through poetry.

vp   LANGSTON UNIV., Langston, OK 73750.

P-VP   LARAMIE ART GUILD, 603½ Ivinson Ave., Laramie, WY 82070. Two-dimensional media may apply. Four prizes given of $200 and $100. Deadline Sept. 15.

vp,c   LASELL JR. COLLEGE, 1844 Commonwealth Ave., Auburndale, MA 02166.

vp   ANNA LAUER SCHOLARSHIP: Small. SEE: Art Students League of N.Y. (Talent).

ALL,all   D.H. LAWRENCE SUMMER FELLOWSHIP, Dept. of English, Humanities Bldg., 217, Univ/New Mexico, Albuquerque, NM 87131. Any U.S. citizen may apply for summer residency at a ranch and a stipend of $700. Deadline Jan. 15.

m,vp,c   LAWRENCE UNIV, Conservatory of Music, Appleton, WI 54911. To entering freshmen, various; need and talent.

V-P   LAYTON SCHOOL OF ART, 1362 N. Prospect Ave., Milwaukee, WI 53202. MR

m LEBANON VALLEY COLLEGE, Annville, PA 17003. To entering freshmen, schols. on competitive basis (second week in December).

P-WR LE CERCLE DU LIVRE DE FRANCE, 8955 Boulevard St. Laurent, Montreal, Quebec, Canada.
PRIX DU CERCLE DU LIVRE DE FRANCE: To honor a French-Canadian novel of outstanding quality. $1,000 awarded plus publication of the book by the Cercle du Livre annually.
PRIX JEAN-BERAUD: To honor a work of fiction in the French language by a Canadian citizen. $1,000 awarded plus publication by the Cercle du Livre.

P-M LEEDS PIANO INTERNATIONAL COMPETITION, c/o Leeds University, Leeds LS2 9JT, England, UK. PRIZES: To the outstanding professional pianists, not older than 30. Twenty awards of 2,850 pounds sterling awarded triennially.

VP,vp LEE-STACEY (JOHN F. AND ANNA) SCHOLARSHIP FUND, V.E. Box 2, Quemado, NM 87829. Approximately $4,000 given annually to further the artists education.

P-F LEIPZIG INTERNATIONAL FILM FESTIVAL, Organizing Committee, Otto-Nuschke-Strasse 27, 108 Berlin, GDR.
AWARDS: For the outstanding documentary and short film made for cinema or television. For cinema: First: Two Golden Doves each with 5,000 marks; Second: Three Silver Doves each with 3,000 marks; Three Special prizes for the best animated film of 1,000 marks. Anyone. For television: First: Two Golden Doves each with 5,000 marks; Second: Three Silver Doves each with 3,000 marks; Third: Special award of the Association of Film and Television Film Makers of 2,000 marks.

m LENOIR RHYNE COLLEGE, Hickory, NC 28601. $500 usually divided, and work scholarships.

M LES AMIS DE L'ART LYRIQUE, Siege Social, 10 rue des Dominicans, Liege, Belgium. Cash awards for all singers. No restrictions.

M LES AMIS DE MOZART, 15 Boulevard de L'Empereur, Brussels, Belgium.
(voice) BRUSSELS INTERNATIONAL SINGING CONTEST, singers 20-35. Any nationality, prizes totaling $8,000. MR

P-VP LESCH, RUDOLPH, AWARD. Monetary award.
SEE: AMERICAN WATERCOLOR SOCIETY.

M EDGAR LEVENTRITT FND., 1175 Park Ave., NYC 10028. International Competition categories vary. Up to $1,000 with appearances with major orchestras. Anyone. MR

92

P-WR   LEVINSON PRIZE. Award: $500.
SEE: POETRY MAGAZINE.

P-VP   ROBERT LEVITT AWARD. Photo-journalism.
SEE: AMERICAN SOCIETY OF MAGAZINE PHOTOGRAPHERS.

m   LEWIS AND CLARK COLLEGE, SW Palatine Hill Rd., Portland, OR 97219.
All scholarships based on need. No limit to amount.

vp   JEAN LIBERTE MEMORIAL SCHOLARSHIP.
SEE: Art Students League of N.Y. (Merit).

M,WR   LIBRARY OF CONGRESS, Transcript Division, Washington, DC 20540.
Award is one year employment at the Library of Congress as a consultant.
No application is possible. The Librarian of Congress selects the poet. The
music department commissions works from different composers with amounts
varying from $1,000 to $3,000. Anyone.

p-wr   ELIAS LIEBERMAN STUDENT POETRY AWARD.
SEE: THE POETRY SOCIETY OF AMERICA.

M   LIEDERKRANZ FND., 4 E. 87th St., NYC 10022. Singers 18-35 of all
(voice)   nationalities. Prizes up to $1,000 plus presentation in recital at Carnegie Hall.

P-M   LIEGE COMPETITION FOR STRING QUARTETS, 57 rue de Joie, Liege,
Belgium. AWARDS: Totaling over 235,000 Belgian francs, awarded every
other year for the best achievements in 1) composing; 2) performing, 3) bowed
string instrument making.

VP   LIGHT WORK, 316 Waverly Ave., Syracuse, NY 13210. Residencies in photography with stipends of $1,000 in addition for one month.

vp,c   LINFIELD COLLEGE, McMinnville, OR 07128.

vp   MRS. JANET O. LIPPER SCHOLARSHIP FOR WOMEN. Founded 1928.
SEE: Art Students Leage of N.Y. (Talent).

WR   LITERARY PRIZE OF THE FEDERATION OF FRENCH ALLIANCES
IN THE USA, 22 E. 60th St., NYC 10022. Writers whose non-political book
deals with Franco-American relations in all cultural or fictional aspects.
American or French author, $2,000, every two years.

P-PV   LITT, MARY S., AWARD. Monetary award.
SEE: AMERICAN WATERCOLOR SOCIETY.

WR   LITTLE BROWN & CO. (CANADA) LTD., 25 Hollinger, Toronto 16, Ontario, Canada. Canadian Childrens Book Award: Fiction or nonfiction, unpublished juvenile manuscript to Canadian citizen only. $1,000, plus royal-
ties biennially.

vp,c   LITTLE ROCK UNIV., Little Rock, AR 72294.

P-WR   RUSSELL LOINES AWARD FOR POETRY. Award: $2,500.
SEE: NATIONAL INSTITUTE OF ARTS AND LETTERS.

M   LONG (KATHRYN) TRUST, c/o Metropolitan Opera Assn., Lincoln Center
Plaza, NYC 10023. No restrictions; auditions for schls to Kathryn Long
classes at the Metropolitan Opera Fnd. Apply to: John Gutman, Dir.

P-M,m   MARGUERITE LONG AND JACQUES THIBAUD INTERNATIONAL
PIANO AND VIOLIN COMPETITION, The Secretariat, 11 Avenue Delcasse,
F-75008 Paris 8, France. PRIZES: For the outstanding work with a violin
and with a piano by a performer aged 15 to 30. Two monetary awards of
30,000 French francs each. Annually; anyone.

VP-H   ROBERT LONGHI FOUNDATION FOR THE STUDY OF THE HISTORY
OF ART, Via Benedetto Fortini 30, Instituto Longhi, 50125 Florence, Italy.
Fellowships for postdoctoral work for a period of 8 months with lire 250,000
per month. Must have doctoral degree in art history, non-Italian citizen and
under 30 years of age.

m   LONGWOOD COLLEGE, Farmville, VA 23901. $300 yearly teaching schol,
cancelled for year's teaching in Virginia after graduation.

M   LONGY SCHOOL OF MUSIC, 1 Follen St., Cambridge, MA 02138. Contact:
Ms. Christina Baena. Scholarships based on talent and need. Occasional
prizes for musical composition.

vp   LORAIN COUNTY COMMUNITY COLLEGE, 1005 N. Abbe Rd., Elyria,
OH 44035.

f   LOS ANGELES VALLEY COLLEGE, Theater Arts Dept., Van Nuys, CA
91401. One Assistantship; amount varies.

vp,c   LOUISIANA COLLEGE, Box 327, Pineville, LA 71360.

vp,c,a   LOUISIANA POLITECHNIC INSTITUTE, Ruston, LA 71270. Assistantships to $2,400.

ALL,all   LOUISIANA STATE ARTS COUNCIL, Division of Arts, Old State Capitol,
Baton Rouge, LA 70801. Limited number of highly selective grants to individual artists.

vp,m,a,c   LOUISIANA STATE UNIV., Baton Rouge, LA 70803. Qualified students;
renewable; for music, honor award, tuition waiver, Presser Fnd. schols, Rotary (women only) Fels. Restriction: perf. cash grants, orch., band and choir;
Grad assistantships.

P-WR   LOUISIANA STATE UNIV PRESS, Baton Rouge, Louisiana 70803. Grant
            $1,000 to author of book adding to the distinction of the Press' list. Anyone.

vp,f,c,   LOUISVILLE SCHOOL OF ART, 100 Park Road, Anchorage, KY 40223.
vp-h   Seventeen schols. for full tuition $1,000 per yr, renewable. Restrictions: high
            school grad. No others. Also Black schols. Anyone.

VP   JOE AND EMILY LOWE FOUNDATION, 720 Fifth Ave., NYC 10022. Poli-
            cies changing. Inquiry suggested.

vp   LOWE, EMILY, MEMORIAL SCHOLARSHIP.
            SEE: Art Students League of N.Y. (Merit).

vp   JOE LOWE MEMORIAL SCHOLARSHIP.
            SEE: Art Students League of N.Y. (Merit).

P-VP   EMILY LOWE PRIZE. Award: $300.
            SEE: ALLIED ARTISTS OF AMERICA, INC.

vp-c   LOWELL STATE COLLEGE, Lowell, MS 01854.

vp,c   LOWER COLUMBIA COLLEGE, Longview, WA 98632.

m,vp   LOYOLA UNIVERSITY, New Orleans, LA 70118. Two small undergrad to
            $650 each.

vp   LUBNER-DIMONDSTEIN STUDIO, School of Fine Art, 530 N. La Cienega
            Blvd., Los Angeles, CA 90048.MR
WR,wr   LUCIUS N. LITTAUER FOUNDATION, 622 Third Ave., NYC. Grants for
            higher education, studies on Near and Mid-East, Hebrew literature and phil-
            osophy, research and publication in Hum. and social science.

vp   GLEN LUKENS AWARD, c/o University of Southern Calif., University Park,
            Los Angeles, CA 90007.

VP   LUNNING PRIZE. SEE: GEORG JENSEN, INC.

vp   LYCOMING COLLEGE, Art Dept., Williamsport, PA 17701.

vp,c   LYNCHBURG COLLEGE, Lynchburg, VA 24504.

WR   THE LYRIC, Bremo Bluff, VA 23022. Nathan Haskell Dole Prize Poetry:
            $100; several other small.

F,M,VP,   THE MAC DOWELL COLONY, INC., 680 Park Ave., NYC 10021. Thirty-
WR   four cabins available on a 400-acre estate in Peterborough, NH. Accepted
            applicants receive room, board, studio space for a fee of $10 per day.

m   MAC MURRAY COLLEGE, Jacksonville, IL 62650. Numerous schls. up to full tuition, room & Board, renewable, on performance, talent and academic standing.

VP   CHARLES H. MAC NIDER MUSEUM, 303 2nd St., SE, Mason City, IA 50401. Annual show with $200 first prize and 3 $100 awards. Deadline April 29.

all   FAYE MC BEATH FOUNDATION, 161 W. Wisconsin Ave., Suite 5146, Milwaukee, WI 53203. Scholarships for art exposure for children and students.

vp   EDWARD G. MC DOWELL TRAVELING SCHOLARSHIPS: 2 awards yrly. About $3,500 for travel and study abroad. To unmarried people of any sex. Administered by Art Students League of N.Y.

WR   MC GRAW-HILL BOOK CO., 330 W. 42nd St., NYC 10036. Fiction award for unpublished work, $2,500 plus advance and royalties, awarded irregularly.

wr   THE MC GREGOR FUND, 2486 First National Bldg., Detroit, MI 48226. Several grants for general philanthropic purposes also for translation of American children's books. MR

P-VP   MC KINNON, MARTHA T., AWARD. Monetary award.
SEE: AMERICAN WATERCOLOR SOCIETY.

wr,am   MC KINSEY FND. BOOK AWARD, McKinsey Fnd. for Management Research, 245 Park Ave., NYC 10017. Support for literature on management; research, on management and business.

m   MC MASTER UNIVERSITY, Hamilton, Ont., Canada. Write: W.N. Paterson, Assistant to the President.

m   MC MURRAY COLLEGE, Abilene, TX 79605. Various, performance.

m   MC NEESE STATE COLLEGE, Lake Charles, LA 70601. Various schls. in band, orchestra, piano, opera, composition. Grad. fellowships.

vp   WILLIAM G. MC NULTY MEMORIAL SCHOLARSHIP.
SEE: Art Students League of N.Y. (Merit).

all   MACALESTER COLLEGE, 77 Macalester, St. Paul, MN 55105. Contact:Ms. Mary Lunblad, Dir. of Admissions; Ms. Ruthena Fink, Dir. of Financial Aid.
EDWARD DUFFIELD NEILL SCHOLARSHIP PROGRAM: Recipients receive a $500 renewable award to be used toward tuition costs, on the basis of academic performance and potential, talent in the arts and social commitment. No special application, just general application to the College. Must be incoming freshman. Anyone.

vp,c   MACOMB COUNTY COMMUNITY COLLEGE, 14500 E. 12 Mile Rd, Warren, MI 48093.

vp,f   MADISON COLLEGE, Art Dept., Asst. Provost for Graduate Studies, Harrisonburg, VA 22801. For current grad. study . Limited number of Grad. Asstship $3,000, annually, not renewable. Few outright grants to students no more than $1,000. Applicants must have "B" average or better. Some schls. are available to Virginia teachers only. Virginia Assn. of Broadcasters Scholarship $500.

VP-C   MADOC-TWEED ART CENTER, Madoc, Ontario, Canada.

P-WR   MADRID INSTITUTE OF HISPANIC CULTURE, Avenida Reyes Catolicos, Ciudad Universitaria, Spain.
             LEOPOLDO PANERO PRIZE: 100,000 awarded annually for the best poetry. Anyone.

P-T,VP   JOSEPH MAHARAM FOUNDATION, INC., 4500 Fefion Court, Lake Worth, FL 33460.
             JOSEPH MAHARAM DESIGN AWARD FOR BEST COSTUME DESIGN: To reward the best costume design done by an individual on the graduate school level in an American college or university. The $200 award is given annually.
             MAHARAM THEATRICAL DESIGN AWARDS: In honorium of excellence in scenic and costume design in plays and musicals, on/off Broadway. $1,000 for the Best Scenic Design. $500 for Broadway; $500 for Off Broadway. $500 for Best costume design. Awards annually at Drama Desk-Sardi Luncheon.

all   MAINE STATE COMMISSION ON THE ARTS AND HUMANITIES, State House, Augusta, ME 04330. Artists-in-schools.

M   MAISON DES ARTISTES, Praha 1, Czechoslovakia. Prague Spring International Music Contest, for vocalists of all nations under 30 years. Cash awards. Apply: Printemps de Prague, above.

P-WR   MAISON DE POESIE, 11 bis Rue Ballu, Paris 9, France.
             EDGAR POE PRIZE: 100 francs awarded annually to the best foreign poet writing in the French language. Anyone.

M   MAISON DE LA RADIO, 66, Blvd. Carl Vogt, CH-1211 Geneva, Switzerland. $2,500 approx. ot all composers of all ages for a ballet composition 15-40 min. Anyone.

vp,vp-h   MANHATTAN COLLEGE, Manhattan College Parkway, Bronx, NY 10471. Contact: Admissions Office, Financial Aid. SCHOLARSHIPS/FINANCIAL AID: Up to full tuition awarded on need and ability and academic record to students working towards a BA degree.

M   MANHATTAN SCHOOL OF MUSIC, 120 Claremont Ave., NYC 160 renewable totaling $120,000.

VP   MANHATTANVILLE COLLEGE, Purchase, NY 10577.

M   MANKATO STATE COLLEGE' Mankato, MN 56001. Several symphony orchestra schols (full tuition). Private lessons fees to qualified music majors; Grad. assistantships 2 $1,200.

m   MANNES COLLEGE OF MUSIC, 157 E. 74th St., NYC 10021. Contact: Director of Student Financial Aid.
             MANNES COLLEGE OF MUSIC GRANTS: Range from $200 to $2,500. All grants are for full time study at the institution. Recipients must be accepted into the full-course program at Mannes, must demonstrate financial need, and must maintain satisfactory scholastic and performance standards.

P-F   MANNHEIM INTERNATIONAL FILM FESTIVAL.
             SEE: Internationale Filmwoche Mannheim.

m   MANSFIELD STATE COLLEGE, Mansfield, PA 16933. Grad. assists.

m,wr   MARIAN COLLEGE, 3200 Cold Spring Road, Indianapolis, IN 46222. Contact: Mark J. Tobin, Dir. of Fin. Aid, Richard Scott, Dir. Admissions.
             LORETTA MARTIN MUSIC SCHOLARSHIP: Winning selection based on academic criteria, renewable w/a 3.00 grade point average, $200 a year.
             ARTHUR JORDAN MUSIC SCHOLARSHIP: Winning selection based on academic criteria, renewable, $500 per year.
             DRUM & BUGLE CORPS GRANTS: Winning selection based on participation in Drum & Bugle Corps. $200 a year.
             OUR SUNDAY VISITOR SCHOLARSHIP (Journalism): Winning selection based on academic criteria demonstrated leadership, past journalistic experience, and extracurricular involvement in college publications.

vp   MARIAN COLLEGE OF FOND DU LAC, 45 National Ave., Fond du Lac, WI 54935.

vp   MARIETTA COLLEGE, Marietta, OH 45750.

all   MARSDEN FND., Box 5170, F.D.R. Station, NYC 10022. Grants to anyone or projects for self-understanding and fostering interpersonal relationships of a high quality in science, arts, philosophy, anthropology, etc. Anyone. MR

m,f   MARSHALL UNIV., Huntington, WV 25701. Grad. Assists. of $2,000 plus remission of fees in applied music or conducting. Three undergraduate scholarships $150-$300. Number of grad. Assists. $1,200-$1,800, plus waiver of fees.

vp   REGINALD MARSH MEMORIAL SCHOLARSHIP.
SEE: Art Students League of N.Y. (Merit).

M,T,WR   THE DAVID B. MARSHALL AWARD, Professional Theater Program, 227 S. Ingalls, Univ/Michigan, Ann Arbor, MI 48109. Award of $2,000 to stimulate collaboration between composer, lyricists and playwright to create a complete full-length musical. No previously produced material or previous Marshall Award winners are considered. Deadline Jan. 31.

wr   THE MARSHALL BOARD, George C. Marshall Fels., Copenhagen, Denmark. G.C. MARSHALL FELS. up to $3,000 for study in Denmark; usually resrch at grad level; short-term professional observation, or academic yrs resrch. Apply: Exchange Div., American-Scandinavian Fnd., 127 E. 73rd St., NYC 10021.

P-WR   THE LENORE MARSHALL PRIZE. Award: $3,500.
SEE: THE NEW HOPE FOUNDATION.

all   MARSHALL SCHOLARSHIPS, c/o British Embassy, Washington, DC. Marshall Schols. offered by British gov't. to U.S. grads; tenable at any Univ. in U.K. Recipients required to take a degree at their British Univ. Age: 25-26 (25 at time of application). Cash plus trans. tuition, books, & travel. Fields of study unrestricted. Substantial amounts.

M   MARS HILL COLLEGE, Mars Hill, NC 28754. Fifteen $200 renewable, with part-time service.

vp   ISABEL B. MARVIN SCHOLARSHIP.
SEE: Art Students League of N.Y. (Talent).

all   MARY BALDWIN COLLEGE, Staunton, VA 24401. Contact: Ellen Holtz, Dir. of Financial Aid.
    PRESSER SCHOLARSHIP: For music. Approx. $400 per year, based on need. Deadline March 1.
    BENN SCHOLARSHIP: For creative wriring. Approx. $200 per year. Same requirements as above.
    LAMBERT SCHOLARSHIP: For the visual arts. Approx. $250 per year. Same requirements as above.
    OVERBEY SCHOLARSHIP: For the visual arts. Approx. $1,300 per year. Same requirements as above.
    FINANCIAL AID: Grants, jobs, loans awarded based on need.

ALL   MARYLAND ARTS COUNCIL, 15 West Mulberry St., Baltimore, MD 21201. Fellowships of $5,000 to residents of Maryland over the age of 18 and not enrolled in any degree course.

vp,c   MARYLAND INSTITUTE, College of Art, 1300 Mt. Royal Ave., Baltimore, MD 21217. $200 to $1,000 a year (renewable) for study at the Institute. Deadline March 1.

D,M,T, THE MARYLAND-NATIONAL CAPITAL PARK AND PLANNING
VP COMMISSION, 6600 Kenilworth Ave., Riverdale, MD 20840. Grants on
annual basis ranging from $300 to $5,000 for support of arts related activities. Deadline Nov. 1.

vp,c MARYLAND STATE COLLEGE, Princess Anne, MD. MR

m MARYMOUNT COLLEGE, Tarrytown, NY 10591. Women only, 3 $300,
renewable, audition.

vp,c MARYMOUNT COLLEGE, 7750 Fordham Rd., Los Angeles, CA 90045.

m,vp MARYVILLE COLLEGE, Maryville, TN 37801. Entering freshmen 5 $300
one in each: piano, organ, strings, wind instrument, based on audition. Each
spring to high school seniors entering as music majors. Press Fnd. Schls. for
teaching majors.

m MARYWOOD COLLEGE, Scranton, PA 18509. Women only, entering freshmen, restrictions, part-time service, various partial or full.

P-WR JOHN MASEFIELD MEMORIAL AWARD.
SEE: THE POETRY SOCIETY OF AMERICA.

M MASON (FANNY PEABODY) MUSIC FND., INC., 59 Fayerweather St.,
Cambridge, MA 02138. Promotion of musical composition, education, and
enjoyment and culture. MR

WR,VP,F MASSACHUSETTS ARTS AND HUMANITIES FOUNDATION, INC., 14
Beacon St., Room 606, Boston, MA 02108. FELLOWSHIPS: $3,000 for
each fel. awarded to Massachusetts artist in the following disciplines: sculpture, painting/printmaking, photography, poetry, fiction and playwriting.
Also inquire about artists-in-residence programs at schools, etc., and artists-in-
schools. Amounts and numbers vary each year, depending on appropriations.
Mass. residents . MR

vp,f,c, MASSACHUSETTS COLLEGE OF ART, 364 Brookline Ave., Boston, MA
a,vp-h 02215. Contact: Fin. Aid Dir. Work Study programs and tuition waivers;
small prizes of $50 to $200. Graduate Fellowship program under change,
write to determine current status. Anyone.

ALL,all MASSACHUSETTS COUNCIL ON THE ARTS AND HUMANITIES, 1 Ash-
burton Pl., Boston, MA 02108. Aid for arts organizations but some monies
for the individual artist.

ALL MASSACHUSETTS FOUNDATION FOR HUMANITIES AND PUBLIC POL-
ICY, 237E Whitmore Adm. Bldg., Univ/Mass., Amherst, MA 01002. Distrib-
utes federal funds for projects relating the humanities to public policy. Range
is from $6,000 to $30,000. Deadlines are March 1, May 1 and September 1.

a   MASSACHUSETTS INSTITUTE OF TECHNOLOGY, Cambridge, MA 02139.

WR   FRANKLIN K. MATHIEWS AWARD.
SEE: G.P. PUTNAM'S SONS.

all   WILLIAM AND FLORENCE MATTHEW FUND, Univ/California, Santa Barbara, Santa Barbara, CA 93106. Competitive, need to file financial aid application & Parents Confidential Statement. Deadline Dec. 15 each year.

vp   MAWY ART SCHOOL/GALLERY, 909 Bergenline Ave., Union City, NJ 07087. MR

VP,C   MECHANICS INSTITUTE, 20 W. 44th St., NYC 10036.

P-WR   LUCILLE MEDWICK MEMORIAL AWARD.
SEE: THE POETRY SOCIETY OF AMERICA.

M,m   MEET THE COMPOSER, 250 W. 57th St., NYC 10019. Contact: John Duffy, Dir. Financial assistance for composer appearance programs in communities and neighborhoods throughout New England states. Funds provide from 20-50% of the total cost of each program. Range: $50 to $750. Deadlines Sept. 15 and Jan. 3.

P-F   MELBOURNE FILM FESTIVAL, PO Box 165, Carlton South, Melbourne, Victoria 3053, Australia.
AWARDS: For the outstanding in short films: Grand Prix: Gold Boomerang & $2,500; Second Prize: Silver Boomerang & $1,500; Third Prize: Silver Boomerang & $1,000. Annually. Anyone.

WR   THE FREDERICK G. MELCHER BOOK AWARD, 25 Beacon St., Boston, MA 02108. Award is $1,000 for works submitted by publisher.

all   MEMPHIS ACADEMY OF THE ARTS, Jameson M. Jones, Asst. Dir., Overton Park, Memphis, TN 38112. Offering four-year program leading to BFA; endeavors to furnish financial asst. to qualified applicants who can demonstrate need. VP ONLY: Several prize awards to graduates to assist in continuing studies. MAA participates in federal College Work Study Program, educational opportunity grants, etc.

m,f   MEMPHIS STATE UNIV., College of Communication & Fine Arts, Memphis, TN 38152. Various; Grad. assists: 7 $2,000. $500 film schol, 3 assist. of $2,200. Undergrad. schols which can go up to $3,000.

M   MENDELSSOHN-BARTHOLDY STIPENDIUM, Dr. Werner Rachwits, Chmn, Curatorium of Mendelssohn-Stipendium, Molkenmarkt 1-3, Berlin 102, Germany. Monthly stipend for young composers, conductors and soloists. Anyone.

WR,wr   KATHERINE MANSFIELD MENTON SHORT STORY PRIZE.
SEE: FRENCH P.E.N. CLUB.

m   MERCY COLLEGE OF DETROIT, 8200 West Outer Dr., Detroit, MI 48105.
       Ten $50-$300 restrictions, renewable.

vp,c   MERCYHURST COLLEGE, Glenwood Hills, Erie, PA 16501.

m   MEREDITH COLLEGE, Raleigh, NC 27611. Three music talent schols. each
       year. Stipends from $100-$800, renewable.

WR   MEREDITH IOWA WRITERS AWARD, Meredith Press, 750 3rd Ave., NYC
       for outstanding novel and short story collection, $1,250 advance on royalties,
       annually.

vp   MERMEC COMMUNITY COLLEGE, 959 S. Geyer Rd., Kirkwood, MO
       63122.

M   MEROLA MEMORIAL FUND, San Francisco Opera Assn., SF Opera House,
       San Francisco, CA 94102.   Training Program at SF Opera. Audition winners
       and other by audition are eligible; 7-week operatic training course by SF
       Opera members during summer.

ALL,all INGRAM MERRILL FND., 29 W. 57th St., NYC 10019. Grants for the ad-
       vancement of the cultural and fine arts; to individuals, educational institu-
       tions and performing groups. Projects and Indivs. MR

P-WR   VICKY METCALF AWARD. Award: $1,000.
       SEE: CANADIAN AUTHORS ASSOCIATION.

ALL   METROPOLITAN ARTS COMMISSION, Corbett Bldg., Room 314, 430 SW
       Morrison, Portland, OR 97204.   Annual grants of possibly over $1,000 for
       local individuals, and two CETA-funded programs for residents of Portland.

M   METROPOLITAN OPERA ASSN.
       SEE: KATHRYN LONG TRUST.

M   METROPOLITAN OPERA NATIONAL COUNCIL, Regional Auditions Pro-
(voice) gram, Lincoln Center Plaza, NYC 10023. No prizes and/or grants awarded
       without participation in competition. Age requirements varying according
       to voice category. Cash awards and/or study grants awarded at various levels
       of competition. Write Nat'l. Chmn above.

all   MEXICAN EMBASSY, 2829 16th St., NW, Washington, DC 20009.   c/o
       Counselor for Cultural Affairs. Abraham Lincoln Fund Schols. Grad study,
       to 35 yrs, know Spanish. Small awards, 1-4 yrs.

F   SIDNEY MEYERS MEMORIAL FUND, c/o Museum of Modern Art, 11 W.
       53rd St., NYC. Annual awards to purchase and/or subsidize movies made by
       "deserving filmmakers."

                                    102

VP   MIAMI BEACH FINE ARTS BOARD, PO Bin O, Miami, FL 33139. $4,350 in awards for outdoor annual arts festival. Deadline Dec. 1.

vp,c   MIAMI DADE JR. COLLEGE (North Campus), 11380 NW 27th Ave., Miami, FL 33167.

VP   MIAMI INTERNATIONAL PRINTS BIENNIAL, PO Box 440826, Miami, FL 33144. Over $6,000 in prizes for original graphics completed within last two years. Deadline Nov. 1.

vp,c,a   MIAMI UNIV., Dept. of Art, Oxford, OH 45956.

M   MICHAELS AWARD, c/o Ravinia Festival Assoc., 22 W. Monroe St., Chicago, IL 60603. $1,500 plus solo appearance with the Chicago Symphony Orch. at Ravinia Festival during summer. For voice, piano, and strings, ages 18-29.

ALL,all MICHIGAN COUNCIL ON THE ARTS, 1200 Sixth Ave., Detroit, MI 48226. Funding of Michigan artists up to $1,000.

f   MICHIGAN STATE UNIV., TV & Radio Dept., East Lansing, MI 48823. Three Grad. Assists. for $3,200, half-time; 6 PhD assistantships for $3,500 half-time.

vp,t,m MIDWESTERN STATE UNIV., 3400 Taft Blvd., Wichita Falls, TX 76308. Contact: Financial Aid Dir. SCHOLARSHIPS: In Art, Drama, and Music, for education. Auditions required for Drama and Music.

WR   HOUGHTON MIFFLIN CO., 2 Park St., Boston, MA 02107. FELLOWSHIPS, $7,500 for promising writers of fiction or nonfiction to complete their works as prepayment. Unpublished in English. Anyone.

vp,wr,m,t MILES COMMUNITY COLLEGE, 2715 Dickinson St., Miles City, MT 59301. Contact: Steve Maier, Registrar. Tuition waivers: On basis of talent.

VP   MILFORD FINE ARTS COUNCIL, 5 Broad St., Milford, CT 06460. Over $1,200 in purchase awards for all media except photography. Deadline April 20.

ALL   MILLAY COLONY FOR THE ARTS, Steepletop, Austerlitz, NY 12017. Studio and living space available for 5 artists at a time from June to September.

P-VP   MILLER, BARSE, MEMORIAL AWARD. Award: $300. SEE: AMERICAN WATERCOLOR SOCIETY.

P-VP   MILLER, GERHARD C.F., AWARD. Monetary award. SEE: AMERICAN WATERCOLOR SOCIETY.

vp   KENNETH HAYES MILLER MEMORIAL SCHOLARSHIP.
SEE: Art Students League of N.Y. (Talent).

vp,c   MILLERSVILLE STATE COLLEGE, Millersville, PA 17551.

vp   MILLIKIN UNIV. DEPT. OF ART, Decatur, IL 62522.

m,vp   MILLS COLLEGE, Oakland, CA 94613, Imogen Walker, Dir. of Grad. Study.
Several, and grad. assistantship.

P-VP   MILLSAPS AWARD, PO Box 9005, Washington, DC 20003. Administrator:
Ladine Webster. Monetary award for painting, graphics or sculpture given
irregularly. Submit slides and resume, artist's picture and return postpaid
envelope. Age restriction: under 25.

vp   MILTON COLLEGE, Milton, WI 53563. Twelve $540, renewable.

VP   MINIATURE ARTS SOCIETY OF FLORIDA, Lillian Stroud, 14158 88th
Ave., North, Seminole, FL 33542. Over $1,500 in prizes for works in all
media not over 10 inches by 10 inches. Deadline Nov. 8.

P-WR   MINISTERE DES AFFAIRES CULTURELLES DU QUEBEC, c/o Lorenzo
Pare, Hotel du Government, Quebec 4, Canada.
PRIZ DAVID: To the author of outstanding talent for the totality of his
literary production. A monetary prize of $5,000 is awarded annually.
PRIZ FRANCE-CANADA: In honorium of excellent writing in the French
language. For a piece published during the previous year, in either
France or Quebec. A monetary prize is awarded annually.
PRIX FRANCE-QUEBEC: To recognize talent of Quebec French-language
writers. For an outstanding book published either in Quebec or in
France in the previous year. A monetary prize awarded annually.

vp   THE MINNEAPOLIS SCHOOL OF ART, 200 E. 25th St., Minneapolis, MN
55404.

ALL,all   MINNESOTA STATE ARTS BOARD, 314 Clifton Ave., Minneapolis, MN
55403. Three fellowships of $10,000 to Minnesota residents. Deadline Feb.
15. Also, grants of $2,500 or less for aid in the production of an art work in
progress. Deadline Oct. 15.

P-M   MIN-ON CONCERT ASSOCIATION, No. 18, Shinanomachi, Shinjuku-ku,
Tokyo 160, Japan.
MIN-ON COMPETITION AWARDS: Four awards totaling $4,155 for out-
standing work in different areas of music. Annually. MR

vp,c   MINOT STATE COLLEGE, Minot, ND 68701.

vp   MISSISSIPPI ART ASSOCIATION, PO Box 824, Jackson, MI 39205. College students in Mississippi.

all   MISSISSIPPI ARTS COMMISSION, 301 No. Lamar St., PO Box 1341, Jackson, MS 63105. Aid for artists in schools.

m   MISSISSIPPI COLLEGE, Clinton, MS 39056. Two $1,000 to entering freshmen; 1 $4,000 part-time service.

m   MISSISSIPPI STATE UNIV., State College, MS 39762. 150 $35 band schls. per semester, $60 per sem. first chair; 2 $70 voice schls; 10 $75 per month work schls; Grad. fels.

vp,c   MISSISSIPPI UNIVERSITY FOR WOMEN, Art Department, Box 70-W MUW, 39701. Contact: Charles E. Ambrose, Chmn.
PAUL ROBERTSON SCHOLARSHIPS: For entering freshmen or transfer students, $250 not renewable. Applicant must submit portfolio and transcript of credits. Women only. Anyone.

ALL,all   MISSOURI STATE COUNCIL ON THE ARTS, Raeder Pl., 727 N. First St., St. Louis, MO 63102. Some aid to individual artists but most is given for artists-in-schools.

vp,m,wr, MISSOURI WESTERN COLLEGE, George Ashworth, Dir. of Development,
h,t   4525 Downs Dr., St. Joseph, MO 64507. Fee waivers, covering tuition and fees up to $365, per semester, depending on residence.

M   MOBILE OPERA GUILD WORKSHOP, 6 N. Springbank Road, Mobile, AL 36608. $25-$200 to workshop members of outstanding talent in community.

P-WR   MODERN HISTORY SELECTION AWARD. Award: Publication of the book and an advance of $10,000 on the royalties.
SEE: HARPER & ROW, publishers, 10 E. 53rd St., NYC 10022.

vp,c   MODESTO JR. COLLEGE, College Ave., Modesto, CA 95350.

vp,c   MOLLOY COLLEGE, Hempstead Ave., Rockville Center, NY 11570.

P-ALL   MOLSON PRIZES. Awards: Three $15,000.
SEE: THE CANADA COUNCIL.

P-VP   MONEGASQUE NATIONAL COMMITTEE OF THE INTERNATIONAL ASSOCIATION OF ART-PAINTING, SCULPTURE, GRAPHIC ART (IAA), Monaco.
PRINCE RAINIER III PRIZE: Awarded to the artist of an outstanding work in contemporary painting or sculpture. Monetary prize of 5,000 francs. Awarded annually.
SPECIAL PRIZE: For a work with the Principality of Monaco as the main theme. 2,000 francs conferred annually.

vp   MONMOUTH COLLEGE, Art Dept., Monmouth, IL 61462.

WR   HARRIET MONROE POETRY AWARD, Univ/Chicago, 5801 Ellis Ave., Chicago, IL 60637. Notable achievement or distinguished promise to advancement of poetry $500. Applications not accepted; the committee makes its own nomination and decision.

all   MONTANA ARTS COUNCIL, 235 East Pine, Missoula, MT 59801. Artists-in-schools.

a,f   MONTANA STATE UNIV., Bozeman, MT 59715.
CONNIE R. CRANEY SCHOLARSHIP: $600 plus summer apprenticeship in TV station.
MONTANA CABLE TV ASSOCIATION: Annual award of $250.

f,m,t,vp   MONTCLAIR STATE COLLEGE, School of Fine and Performing Arts, Upper Montclair, NJ 07043. Tuition remission and $3,000 per year for graduate assistants.

P-M,m   MONTEVIDEO INTERNATIONAL PIANO COMPETITION, The Secretariat, Rio Branco 1342 Apto. 101, Montevideo, Uruguay. PRIZES: Totaling $5,000, medals and concerts bestowed on the outstanding pianists, aged from 15 to 32.

P-M   MONTREAL INTERNATIONAL MUSIC COMPETITION, Institut International de Musique du Canada, 106 Avenue Dulwich, St. Lambert, Quebec J4P 4Y7, Canada. PRIZES: A total of $22,000 is awarded annually for one of three categories, either piano, violin, or voice. For 1976: To the best piano performers.

vp   MOORE COLLEGE OF ART, Philadelphia, PA 19103. Partial and full tuition to undergrads, and entering freshmen.

T,WR,   JENNY MC KEAN MOORE FUND FOR WRITERS, Dept. of English, George Washington Univ., Washington, DC 20052. Award is one year visiting salary from the University which is approximately $16,500. Deadline Jan. 15.

vp   NANCY MOORE MEMORIAL FUND, c/o Univ/Southern Calif., Univ. Park, Los Angeles, CA 90007. Award for an outstanding student in printmaking.

m   MOORHEAD STATE COLLEGE,Moorhead, MN 56560. Two grad. assists., $1,350 performance & ed.

m   MORAVIAN MUSIC FND. INC., Ewald V. Nolte, Dir., Salem Station, Winston-Salem, NC 27108. Established to make materials related to the early history of music in the Eastern U.S. available for research and publication.

ALL   MOREHEAD STATE UNIV., Research and Development, Morehead, KY 40351. Contact: Dr. Morris L. Norfleet. GRADUATE ASSISTANTSHIPS: For an academic year (nine months) for $2,200. Possibly renewable. Awarded on the basis of grade point.

P-WR   CHRISTOPHER MORLEY AWARD.
SEE: THE POETRY SOCIETY OF AMERICA.

m,vp   MORNINGSIDE COLLEGE, Sioux City, IA 51106. Undergrads, 10 up to $500 need and ability. Some to successful applicants for membership in Sioux City Symphony.

ALL   E.M. MORRIS FOUNDATION, Inc., 205 W. Jefferson Blvd., Office 505, South Ben, IN 46601. MR

P-VP   LINDSEY MORRIS MEMORIAL PRIZES. Awards $150 and $100.
SEE: ALLIED ARTISTS OF AMERICA, Inc.

WR   THE MORROW HONOR AWARD, William Morrow & Co., Inc., 105 Madison Ave., NYC 10016. $500 and publicity for new fiction and nonfiction.

VP   MOSTRA INTERNAZIONALE DEL FILM D'AUTORE, 24100, Bergamo, Italy — Rotonda dei Mille 1. Prize of 5 million lire for film which is written by the director of the film. Money split between director and producer.

m,vp   MOUNT ALLISON UNIV., Sackville, N.B., Canada. To entering freshmen, renewable various schls. $300-$1,500.

m,vp   MOUNT ALOYSIUS JUNIOR COLLEGE, Cresson, PA 16630. George Letcher. Anyone.

m,vp   MOUNT HOLYOKE COLLEGE, South Hadley, MA 01075. Women only. Music majors eligible for general schols. to be applied to fees for instrumental and voice lessons awarded by Dept. of Music.

vp,c   MT. MARY COLLEGE, 2900 N. Menomonee River Pkwy., Milwaukee, WI 53222.

m,vp,c   MOUNT MARTY COLLEGE, Yankton, SD 57078. Women only, 2 $150 applied music, renewable.

m   MOUNT ST. MARY'S COLLEGE, Sister Rose Gertrude, Dir. of Financial Aid, 12001 Chalon Rd., Los Angeles, CA 90049. Financial Aid application, parents' statement, auditions.

m   MOUNT ST. SCHOLASTICA COLLEGE, Atchison, KS 66002. Undergrads, $100-$350, renewable.

m   MOUNT UNION COLLEGE, 1972 Clark Ave., Alliance, OH 44601. Contact: Bridget F. Edwards. Various schols. based on academic performance as well as excellence in a particular field of study.

M   MOZART MEMORIAL PRIZE, 4 Pont St., London SW1, England. Award of $300 plus performances with London Mozart Players to all singers under 30.

vp   MUNCIE ARTS ASSOCIATION, Ball State Univ., Muncie, IN 47306. Grad students for Grad. Assistantships, one and two years.

all   MUNDELEIN COLLEGE, 6363 Sheridan Road, Chicago, IL 60626. Up to $1,000, renewable.

P-M   MUNICH INTERNATIONAL MUSIC COMPETITION, Broadcasting Corporation of the FDR, Internationaler Musikwettbewerb, Bayerischer Rundfunk, D-8000 Munich, FDR. PRIZES: Categories change annually. In 1976: voice, alto, harpsichord, oboe, guitar. 78,000 German marks awarded in 1975.

vp   MUNICIPAL ART SOCIETY OF BALTIMORE, Baltimore, MD 21218. Students of the Rinehart School of Sculpture, Maryland Institute, Baltimore. MR

vp   ALICE HAROLD MURPHY MEMORIAL SCHOLARSHIP.
SEE: Art Students League of N.Y. (Talent).

m,f   MURRAY STATE UNIV., Univ. Station, Murray, KY 42071. 50 $100-$500 renewable; 10 $100-$250 restrictions to entering freshmen; grad fels. Two grad. assistantships ($900 to $1,800 per academic year plus remission of out-of-state fees). Schols. at $150 per year.

vp,c   MUSEUM ART SCHOOL, 1219 SW Park, Portland, OR 97205.

vp,vp-h MUSEUM OF FINE ARTS, Houston School of Art, 1001 Bissonet, PO Box
c   6826, Houston, TX 77005. Ruth Pershing Uhler Scholarship Fund: Full tuition schol. Bob McIntyre Memorial Art Scholarship Fund: Full or partial tuition schol. for students 16 to 21 yrs. of age.

P-C   MUSEUM OF INTERNATIONAL FOLK ART CRAFTSMEN AWARDS. Award: Monetary.
SEE: MUSEUM OF NEW MEXICO.

VP,F   MUSEUM OF MODERN ART, 11 W. 53rd St., NYC 10019. Sidney Meyers Memorial Fund for support of deserving filmmakers. SEE: City College. Others at MOMA various.

P-VP,C MUSEUM OF NEW MEXICO, PO Box 2087, Santa Fe, NM 87501. Currently no financial aid programs.

m,vp   MUSIC AND ART FND. AWARDS, 117 Second Ave., Bldg., Rm. 205, Seattle, WA 98101. Schls. programs in various areas in music. New career awards under consideration. Write. MR

m,t   MUSIC AND ARTS INSTITUTE OF SAN FRANCISCO, 2622 Jackson St., San Francisco, CA 94115. Contact: Ross McKee, Dir. For students in College of Music, Drame and Opera full time. $500 towards full time tuition, for outstanding students, by audition. $100 per semester grants toward full tuition (renewable) to enable students of limited means to attend full time college programs. Additional schols. available.

m   MUSIC CRITICS ASSN., 2211 Midridge Rd., Timonium, MD 21093. Annual institute for young professionals, 2-4 weeks at various locations. Ten fellowships at $1,000 each.

M   MUSIC LIBRARY ASSOCIATION, 2017 Walnut St., Philadelphia, PA 19103. D.J. Hull.

M   MUSIC PERFORMANCE TRUST FUNDS (of the Recording Industries), Jerome H. Adler, Trustee, 1501 Broadway, NYC 10036. Expends over $6 million annually in payment to instrumental musicians for performance at free admission performances as part of community public cultural, educational, entertainment and therapy service and for student awards. Ninety percent of expenditures made according to area allocations throughout U.S. and Canada. Trustee seeks recommendations from local organizations for projects and performances. Funds financed by producers of phonograph records, tapes, electrical transcriptions and distributors of some films exhibited on television.

M   MUSIC TEACHERS NATIONAL ASSOCIATION, 408 Carew Tower, Cincinnati, OH 45202. Mariann H. Clinton, Exec. Dir. Several contests involving composition, keyboard achievement and achievement on other instruments (i.e, guitar, brass, strings, voice) with prizes up to $1,000. There is a state, regional and national judging.

M   MUSICAL MERIT FOUNDATION OF GREATER SAN DIEGO, 1401 Mariposa St., San Diego, CA 92114. William Vere Wolf. $2,500-$3,000 in tuition schols. Residents of San Diego, instrumentalists to 22, vocalists to 25.

M   MUSICIANS CLUB OF NEW YORK ANNUAL YOUNG ARTISTS AWARD, 200 Cabrini Blvd., NYC 10033. Miss Jean Patterson. Categories rotate annually: voice, piano, strings, woodwinds & harp. Ages 18-28. Anyone.

M   MUSICIANS EMERGENCY FUND, Rm 778, 35 W. 4th St., NYC 10003. Brent Williams, Secy-Treas. Offers employment or limited financial aid for musician in immediate financial crisis.

M   MUSICIANS FOUNDATION, Inc., 200 W. 55th St., NYC 10019. Stipends ranging from $25 to $300 a month. $60,000 distributed in 1978 to 45 musicians, mostly retired.

vp   MUSKEGON COUNTY COMMUNITY COLLEGE, 221 S. Quarterline Rd., Muskegon, MI 49442.

vp,m MUSKINGUM COLLEGE, New Concord, OH 43762. Contact: Admissions Office.

109

HONOR AWARDS: A $300 grant extended to a limited number of outstanding incoming freshmen at the time of their admission. This award is for the freshman year only and cannot be renewed.

MUSKINGUM COLLEGE SCHOLARSHIPS: Will be awarded to the valedictorian of each high school so that his complete need will be met by a financial aid package, or if he has no need, a $2,000 scholarship ($500 for each year in school). Persons in the top ten percent of their class will be "considered."

VP NATIONAL ACADEMY OF DESIGN, 1083 Fifth Ave., NYC 10028.

BENJAMIN ALTMAN PRIZE FOR FIGURE PAINTING: $1,250-$2,500 annually. Landscapes, $1,250-$2,500 annually.

JOHN TAYLOR ARMS MEMORIAL PRIZE: For outstanding work in the graphic arts. $250 awarded annually at the Academy's Exhibition.

ARTISTS FUND PRIZE: For outstanding work in sculpture. $400 awarded annually at the Academy's Exhibition.

HELEN FOSTER BARNETT PRIZE: For outstanding work of sculpture by an artist under 35 years of age. The sculptor cannot have previously received the award. $350 awarded annually at the Academy's Exhibition.

WALTER BIGGS MEMORIAL AWARD: For the outstanding work in watercolor, $200 is awarded annually at the Exhibition.

CANNON PRIZE: For outstanding work in the graphic arts. $300 awarded annually at the Academy's Exhibition.

ANDREW CARNEGIE PRIZE: For recognition of excellence in oil painting by an American artist. $700 awarded annually at the Exhibition.

THOMAS B. CLARKE PRIZE: For recognition of the most outstanding figure composition painted in oil in the U.S. by an American citizen without limitation of age. Members of the National Academy of Design are not eligible. $400 awarded annually.

DESSIE GREER PRIZE: For outstanding portrait bust in sculpture. $150 awarded annually at the Exhibition.

JULIUS HALLGARTEN PRIZES: For outstanding oil paintings done in the U.S. by citizens under 35 years of age. $350, $250 and $150 awarded annually at the Exhibition.

FRANK C. KIRK MEMORIAL AWARD: For outstanding oil painting of a figure, still life or landscape. $100 awarded each year at the Exhibition.

ISAAC N. MAYNARD PRIZE: For outstanding work in oil portrait painting. $100 awarded each year at the Exhibition.

NATIONAL ACADEMY OF DESIGN PRIZE: For outstanding work in watercolor. $200 awarded annually at the Exhibition.

ADOLPH AND CLARA OBRIG PRIZE FOR PAINTING IN OIL: For recognition of excellence in oil painting by an American citizen. $500 awarded annually at the Exhibition.

ADOLPH AND CLARA OBRIG PRIZES FOR PAINTING IN WATERCOLOR: For recognition of two outstanding paintings in watercolor by an American artist. $350 and $200 awarded annually at the Exhibition.

THE EDWIN PALMER MEMORIAL PRIZE: For outstanding painting of marine life. $1,500 awarded annually at the Exhibition.

THE WILLIAM A. PATON PRIZE: For outstanding watercolor by an American born citizen who must have lived in the U.S. for three years previous to the award. $750 awarded annually at the Exhibition.
THOMAS R. PROCTOR PRIZE: For outstanding portrait in oil or sculpture. $350 awarded annually at the Exhibition.
SALMAGUNDI CLUB PRIZE: For outstanding oil painting by an American citizen. $100 awarded annually at the Exhibition.
ELLIN P. SPEYER PRIZE: For recognition of an outstanding painting or piece of sculpture depicting an act of humaneness towards animals, or a painting or sculpture of animals. $300 awarded annually at the Exhibition.
S.J. WALLACE TRUMAN PRIZE: For recognition of excellence in landscape painting in oil by an artist under 35 years of age. $700 awarded annually at the Exhibition.
ELIZABETH N. WATROUS GOLD MEDAL: For outstanding work in sculpture. Medal and $300 awarded annually at the Exhibition.

vp   NATIONAL ACADEMY SCHOOL OF FINE ARTS, 5 E. 89th St., NYC 10028.

M   NATIONAL ARTIST AUDITIONS, 903 Sunset Terr., Amarillo, TX. No restrictions. Cash prize and appearance with the Amarillo Symphony. Apply: Mary Elisabeth Wilson, Auditions Committee, above. MR

P-M   NATIONAL ARTS CLUB, Music Chrmn., 15 Gramercy Park, NYC 10003. U.S. citizens 18-30 for fels.; 18-35 for music prize, $500 plus presentation at recital at no cost.
NATIONAL ARTS CLUB YOUNG ARTISTS MUSIC AWARDS: To encourage young musicians who show great promise, emphasis is on singers. To American citizens living within a radius of 100 miles of NY. $500 and $300 awarded annually in November.

A   NATIONAL ASSOCIATION OF SCHOOLS OF ART, 11250 Roger Bacon Drive, #5, Reston, VA 22090. Paul Arnold, Pres.

M   NATIONAL ASSOCIATION OF TEACHERS OF SINGING, 250 W. 57th St., NYC 10019. Annual Artist Awards Auditions to singers 21-30. $1,000, $600, $400 awarded. Apply by Oct. 15.

P-WR   NATIONAL BANK, c/o Antonio Olinto, a/c "O Globo," Rua Irineu Marinho, s/n, 20000 Rio de Janeiro, Brazil.
WALMAP PRIZE: For outstanding literary works in the Portuguese language. $13,000 in awards is given biennially. Anyone.

WR   NATIONAL BOOK AWARDS, c/o National Institute of Arts & Letters, 633 W. 155th St., NYC 10032.

WR   NATIONAL BOOK AWARDS AND COMMITTEE.
SEE: THE AMERICAN BOOK AWARDS – TABA.

111

VP   NATIONAL CAPE CORAL ANNUAL ART EXHIBITION, PO Box 931, Cape Coral, FL 33904. Painting and sculpture entries accepted for possible $1,000 prize. Deadline Oct. 10.

P-C,P-VP   NATIONAL COMPETITION FOR AMERICAN INDIAN ARTISTS, Philbrook Art Center, PO Box 52510, Tulsa, OK 74152. North American Indian descendants working in paint, sculpture and the graphic arts may be awarded up to $1,000.

NATIONAL COUNCIL FOR CRITICAL ANALYSIS, Department of Philosophy, Jersey City State College, 2039 Kennedy Blvd., Jersey City, NJ 07305. Pasqual S. Schievella, Pres.

T   NATIONAL CRITICS INSTITUTE, 1860 Broadway, NYC 10023. Lillian Marus, Exec. Sec.

D   NATIONAL DANCE ASSOCIATION, 1201 16th St., NW, Washington, DC 20036. Gives no grants but does consider 6-month or more volunteer internships.

ALL   NATIONAL ENDOWMENT FOR THE ARTS. A Federal Agency, simply addressed at Washington, DC 20506. See special section for program information. All disciplines. Various categories and ways of giving grants in all disciplines. Amounts vary with Congressional appropriations each year with roughly one-fourth of money going to individuals. There are no set forms for the given grants. Grants reported in the Washington International Arts Letter and continuing info about the National Foundation on the Arts and the Humanities is published in the ten yearly issues. Write W.I.A.L., Box 9005, Washington, DC 20003.

H,WR   NATIONAL ENDOWMENT FOR THE HUMANITIES. A Federal Agency, addressed simply at Washington, DC 20506. Various categories and ways of giving and most grants to individuals must go through educational institutions. Amounts vary with Congressional appropriations each year with roughly one-fourth of the money going to individuals. New developments are reported about "Humanities" in the Washington International Arts Letter, published ten times a year. Write: W.I.A.L, Box 9005, Washington, DC 20003. See also notes after main listings in this book.

M,m,   NATIONAL FEDERATION OF MUSIC CLUBS, National Headquarters, 310
D,d   So. Michigan Ave., Suite 1936, Chicago, IL 60605. Mrs. John McDonald, Office Mgr.
     AWARD PROGRAM FOR SUMMER FESTIVALS (5/15 to 9/1): Contact: Dr. Katherine Mahan, Chairman, 2339 Burton St., Columbus, GA 31904.
     SCHOLARSHIP DEPARTMENT AND SCHOLARSHIP BOARD: Contact: Mrs. William B. Millard, 144 No. Dithridge St., Pittsburgh, PA 15213.
     YOUNG ARTIST AUDITIONS: A competition concerning piano, strings,

man's or woman's voice, opera. Age groups: Instrumentalists 18-30; vocalists 23-35. $2,000 in each category, including $2,500 International and optional contract with NYC Opera. Held in odd-numbered years. Deadline January 22.

IRENE S. MUIR SCHOLARSHIP IN VOICE: Concerning man's and woman's voice. Age group 18-25. $1,000 each category and performance at Biennial Convention to voice major towards a music degree. Held in odd-numbered years. Deadline January 22.

THE OPERA WORKSHOP, INC. SCHOLARSHIP: $475 for Opera, man's or woman's voice. Special consideration for man's voice. Age group 21-25. Deadline February 1.

VERA WARDNER DOUGAN AWARD: For recognition of young artist who has attained professional excellence. $500 presented to an NFMC artist who will perform during the Peninsula Music Festival, Fish Creek, WI. No age limit. By invitation of Committee.

ANNE M. GANNETT AWARD: For a veteran whose musical career has been interrupted by service in the Armed Forces. $500 award. No age limit. Deadline March 15.

MUSIC FOR THE BLIND HINDA HONIGMAN SCHOLARSHIP FOR THE BLIND: For instrumentalists and vocalists, aged 16 to 25. $500 for continued study. Deadline March 25.

VICTOR HERBERT—ASCAP, YOUNG COMPOSERS AWARD: For best composition: Class 1 sonata for solo Wind or String Instrument with piano or 3 to 5 Orchestral Instruments; Class 2 Choral; Class 3 Piano Solo. Age groups 18 to 26. First Prize $1,000; Second $500; Third $250. Deadline April 1.

MANY OTHER SUBSTANTIAL SCHOLARSHIPS AND AWARDS BOTH IN MUSIC AND DANCE. Send for listing at Nat'l Hqs.

P-WR NATIONAL FEDERATION OF STATE POETRY SOCIETIES, INC., c/o Lee Mays, Contest Chairman, 2221 Woodview Dr., Birmingham, AL 35216. Many small awards.

ALABAMA STATE POETRY SOCIETY AWARD, ARIZONA STATE POETRY SOCIETY AWARD, BEAUDOIN GEMSTONE AWARD I., BEAUDOIN GEMSTONE AWARD II., C. FAYE BENNETT MEMORIAL AWARD: THE BIBLE AWARD, AGNES C. BROTHERS SIGNIFICANT POETRY AWARD, SUSAN A. CALLAHAN AWARD, ALMA PARTELL CARLSON MEMORIAL AWARD, COLORADO AWARD, ELEANOR AMAN CRUMP MEMORIAL AWARD, SARAH CURTIS MEMORIAL AWARD, ETERNITY AWARD, GRAFIKON AWARD, KATE HEANUE MEMORIAL AWARD, CLEMENT HOYT MEMORIAL HAIKU AWARD, HUMOROUS POETRY AWARD, ILLINOIS STATE POETRY SOCIETY AWARD, INDIANA CONTEST AWARD, KALEIDOGRAPH AWARD, EUNICE POND LASELLE MEMORIAL AWARD, THE LISA LYRIC PRIZE, LITTLE TWIGS AWARD, LOUISIANA STATE POETRY SOCIETY AWARD, WALTER R. LOVEL MEMORIAL AWARD, LUBBE CINQUAIN AWARD, LYRIC POEM AWARD, THE MANNINGHAM AWARD, ROSA ZAGNONI MARINONI MEMORIAL AWARD, THE MARYLAND AWARD.

ALL   NATIONAL FOUNDATION ON THE ARTS AND THE HUMANITIES. A Federal Agency. SEE: National Endowment for the Arts and National Endowment for the Humanities entries.

VP-H   THE NATIONAL GALLERY OF ART, Washington, DC 20565. Contact: Dr. Douglas Lewis, Curator of Sculpture. Advanced doctoral-level research and publication only, in art history of Western World; support restricted to PhD dissertation completion grants or post-doctoral grants. Eight nonrenewable Fellowships of $8,000 per academic year are awarded annually for museum training and completion of PhD dissertations in art history of Western world, or of books arising from such completed dissertations. Nominations are accepted only from heads of university graduate departments of art history, before Jan. 31 of each year, and Fellowships are restricted to U.S. citizens who have already accomplished at least one full year's research on their dissertation projects. Six of the grants are tenable at any place of research, while two are similarly open to half an academic year, with the other half spent as a resident Fellow in museum training at the Gallery. An office, but no other services, is provided for Fellows in residence.

M   NATIONAL GUILD/COMMUNITY MUSIC SCHOOLS, c/o Harlem School of the Arts, 141st St. and Nicholas Ave., NYC 10031.

M   NATIONAL GUILD OF PIANO TEACHERS, PO Box 1807, Austin, TX 78767.
             BREWSTER-ALLISON BIENNIAL PIANO COMPETITION: Award $1,000. International Quadrennial Piano Recording Competition: To best guild students for recording. Prizes up to $1,000. Scholarships for piano to high school graduates who studied with Guild member teachers.

P-A   NATIONAL HOUSING INSTITUTE, Boulevard St. Lazare 10, 1030 Brussels, Belgium. Contact: Secretariat of the Architecture Prize of the National Housing Institute.
             INTERNATIONAL ARCHITECTURE PRIZE: In recognition of outstanding work that best incorporates progressive ideas of esthetic beauty, population distribution, building materials, cost, etc. There are 2 categories: single-family houses and apartments. Monetary prizes totaling 200,000 Belgian francs awarded every other year. To a practicing architect of a European Community member country.

VP,A   NATIONAL INSTITUTE FOR ARCHITECTURAL EDUCATION, 139 E. 52nd St., NYC 10022. Lillian Marus, Exec. Sec. U.S. citizens under 30 with architectural degree or equivalent, annually by national competition.

WR,VP,M THE NATIONAL INSTITUTE OF ARTS AND LETTERS, 633 W. 155th St., NYC 10021. Many awards and grants over $2,500 for work of distinction with the purpose of furthering literature and fine arts and to stimulate and encourage the arts in the U.S. Only by nomination. Russell Loines Award for Poetry open to British citizens as well as U.S. citizens.

ARTS AND LETTERS AWARDS: To help encourage the creative achievement of art, music, and literature. To all except members of the Institute. Citation and $3,000. Twenty-one awarded annually in cooperation with the American Academy of Arts and Letters.

MARC BLITZSTEIN AWARD FOR THE MUSICAL THEATRE: For the encouragement of works for the musical theatre. To a composer, lyricist, or librettist. Award of $2,500.

ARNOLD W. BRUNNER MEMORIAL PRIZE IN ARCHITECTURE: For recognition of an individual who contributes to architecture as an art. $1,000 awarded annually.

E.M. FORSTER AWARD: For the outstanding work by a Young English writer, the award of $5,000 helping to finance his stay in the United States. Awarded periodically.

RUSSELL LOINES AWARD FOR POETRY: To help promote poetry of value that has not yet been widely recognized. To an American or British poet. $2,500 awarded periodically.

RICHARD AND HINDA ROSENTHAL FOUNDATION AWARDS: Two awards, one for a literary piece, one for a painting, neither of which have been accredited with their due honors. $2,000 each, annually.

MARJORIE PEABODY WAITE AWARD: In recognition of continuing achievement in the arts. To an older artist, writer, or composer in rotation. $1,500 awarded annually.

MORTON DAUWEN ZABEL AWARD: For the original and experimental tendencies rather than of academic and conservative in writing. To an American poet, writer of fiction, or critic, in rotation. $2,500 awarded annually. Note: Applications NOT requested. They make their awards on recommendations only.

WR NATIONAL JEWISH BOOK COUNCIL, 15 E. 26th St., NYC 10010. Each of the following eight awards consists of $500: Frank and Ethel S. Cohen Award for Jewish Thought, William and Janice Epstein Award for Jewish Fiction, Leon Jolson Award for a book on the Nazi Holocaust, Harry and Florence Kovner Memorial Awards for books of Poetry, Morris J. Kaplun Memorial Award for a book on Israel, Bernard H. Marks Award for a book on Jewish History, Charles and Bertie G. Schwartz Juvenile Award, Rabbi Jacob Freedman Award for an English Translation of a Jewish Classic.

all NATIONAL MERIT SCHOLARSHIP Corp., 990 Grove St., Evanston, IL 60201. National Achievement Scholarship Program for Negro Students: $1,000-$6,000 for study at any accredited U.S. college or university. Also 4 year schols. $100-$1,500 to anyone of any nationality or financial need for study in U.S. colleges or university. RCA schols. in music for undergrads; RCA merit schols. to children of RCA employees.

AM,M,T, NATIONAL OPERA INSTITUTE, 726 Jackson Place, NW, Washington, DC
VP,WR 20566. Grants range from $150 to $7,800 for U.S. citizens who are professionals working in opera and/or musical theatre.

115

P-VP,p-vp NATIONAL PAINTING SHOW, Washington and Jefferson College, Washington, PA 15301. Over $1,500 available in prizes. Deadline Jan. 31.

all NATIONAL SCHOLARSHIP SERVICE AND FUND FOR NEGRO STUDENTS, 1776 Broadway, NYC 10019. Supplementary schols. to $600 per student per year as result of NSSFNS college advisory service are awarded college schls. insufficient for their needs.

M NATIONAL SCHOOL ORCHESTRA ASSN., 2209 Abbot Martin Road, Nashville, TN 37215, John R. Bright, Pres. Roth Orchestra Composition Award, $1,000 to any composer for full or string orchestra, not to exceed 7 minutes and playable by any average high school orchestra.

VP NATIONAL SCULPTURE, Department of Art, Uniiversity of South Carolina, Columbia, SC 29208. Competition for annual tour in southeastern museums. Awards are $750, $500 and $250. Deadline Nov. 10.

P-VP NATIONAL SCULPTURE SOCIETY, 777 3rd Ave., NYC 10017. Many small prizes annually in various sculpture media.
ALVA MUSEUM REPLICAS PRIZE: To honor an outstanding small sculpture that is suitable for reproduction. $500 plus reproduction contract if sculptor is agreeable is awarded annually to an entry in the Society's Annual Exhibition.
MRS. LOUIS BENNETT PRIZE: For bas-relief, a prize of $50 is annually awarded to a young sculptor.
C. PERCIVAL DIETSCH SCULPTURE PRIZE: In honorium of outstanding sculpture in the round, $200 is awarded annually.
JOHN GREGORY AWARD: For outstanding sculpture by U.S. citizens under 45 years of age, for work completed in the last 10 years. $500 is awarded annually.
DR. MAURICE HEXTER PRIZE: In honorium of creative sculpture in the round, $500 is awarded annually to an entry in the Annual Exhibition.

P-VP NATIONAL SOCIETY OF PAINTERS IN CASEIN AND ACRYLIC, 1083 Fifth Avenue, NYC 10028. Mark Freisman, Pres. AWARDS: For outstanding art shown in the Society's Annual Exhibition. Cash prizes are awarded annually.

M NATIONAL SYMPHONY ORCHESTRA, The Kennedy Center, Washington, DC 20566. Merriweather Post Contest of $1,500 for violin and cello. Also guest appearances with National Symphony. Second and third prizes are $750 and $350.

F NATIONAL TRUST FOR HISTORIC PRESERVATION, 740-748 Jackson Pl., NW, Washington, DC 20006. National Film and Video Competition "Preserving the Historic Environment" with 6 $1,000 prizes. Deadline Aug. 1.

WR NATIONAL WRITERS CLUB, Suite 620, 1450 So. Havana, Aurora, CO 80012.

116

M   WALTER W. NAUMBURG FOUNDATION, 144 W. 66th St., NYC 10023. Award goes to American composer. No cash involved.

vp,c   NAZARETH COLLEGE, Gull Road, Kalamazoo, MI 49074.

vp,c   NAZARETH COLLEGE OF KENTUCKY, Dept. of Art, 851 So. 4th St., Nazareth, KY 40203.

WR   NEAR EAST COLLEGE ASSOCIATION, 380 Madison Ave., NYC. Recruits teachers for private nonsectarian institutions in Greece, Lebanon, Turkey.

all   NEBRASKA ARTS COUNCIL, 8448 West Center Rd., Omaha, NE 68124. Artists-in-schools.

m,vp,c NEBRASKA WESLEYAN UNIV, Lincoln, NE 68504. Various.

all   NETHERLAND AMERICA FOUNDATION, Inc., One Rockefeller Plaza, NYC 10020. Limited number of outright grants to citizens of the USA for graduate or postgrad. study in the Netherlands. Awards are given to supplement schols. from other sources or a student's own funds—usually $300 to $500. Applications should be submitted prior to March 1.

P-WR   NETHERLANDS GOVERNMENT, c/o Ministry of Culture, Recreation & Social Welfare, Steenvoordelaan 370, Rijswijk Z-H, Netherlands, and BELGIAN GOVERNMENT, Ministry of Culture, Brussels, Belgium.
         DUTCH (FLEMISH) LITERATURE GRAND PRIZES: For outstanding work by a prose writer/poet living in Belgium or Netherlands. Work must be in Dutch or Flemish. $12,000 Dutch florens awarded annually.

P-WR   NEUSTADT INTERNATIONAL PRIZE FOR LITERATURE. Award: Silver eagle, certificate, one issue of Books Abroad devoted to the laureate, and $10,000. SEE: BOOKS ABROAD.

vp,c   NEVADA SOUTHERN UNIV., 4505 Maryland Pkwy, Las Vegas, NV 89108.

All   NEVADA STATE COUNCIL ON THE ARTS, 560 Mill St., Reno, NV 89502. Program under change. MR

vp,c   NEWARK STATE COLLEGE, Union, NJ 07083.

P-VP   NEWCASTLE, LENA, MEMORIAL AWARD. Award: $300. SEE: AMERICAN WATERCOLOR SOCIETY.

m   NEWCOMB COLLEGE, Tulane Univ., New Orleans, LA 70118. Women only, Presser Fnd. Schol. entering freshmen; $800 voice.

vp   NEW COLLEGE, DIVISION OF HUMANITIES, SARASOTA, FL 33578.

| m | THE NEW ENGLAND CONSERVATORY OF MUSIC, Barbara Chapin Fin. Aid. Officer, 290 Huntington Ave., Boston, MA 02115. Music, anyone. |

m THE NEW ENGLAND CONSERVATORY OF MUSIC, Barbara Chapin Fin. Aid. Officer, 290 Huntington Ave., Boston, MA 02115. Music, anyone.

vp NEW ENGLAND SCHOOL OF ART, 26 Newbury St., Boston, MA 02116. Two schols to freshmen; partial schols to upper classmen.

WR NEW ENGLAND QUARTERLY, Houghton Mifflin Co., 2 Park St., Boston, MA 02107. Literary Fels. to complete work in progress for use in any country. Anyone.

T NEW ENGLAND THEATRE CONFERENCE, 50 Exchange St., Waltham, MA 02154. $200 award for unpublished play with running time of no longer than one hour. Deadline April 15.

C,VP NEW HAMPSHIRE COMMISSION ON THE ARTS, 40 No. Main St., Concord, NH 03301. Artists-in-schools and works purchased for New Hampshire public buildings.

all THE NEW HAVEN FOUNDATION, One State St., New Haven, CT 06511. Community foundation restricted by its charter to making grants only within Greater New Haven Area. No individual grants. Nonprofit orgs only, tax exempt in Greater New Haven Area.

P-VP NEW HAVEN PAINT AND CLAY CLUB, 26 Fern Dr., Northford, CT 06472. Cash prizes and purchases annually for artists from New England and New York. MR

P-WR THE NEW HOPE FOUNDATION, 430 Park Ave., NYC 10022.
THE LENORE MARSHALL PRIZE: In honorium of excellence in a book of poems published by a living american poet during the previous year. $3,500 awarded annually.

ALL,all NEW JERSEY STATE COUNCIL ON THE ARTS, 109 West State St., Trenton, NJ 08608. Up to $3,000 for a New Jersey artist. Deadline Feb. 1.

ALL NEW JERSEY STATE MUSEUM, 205 West State St., Trenton, NJ 08625. Purchase awards for all media except crafts. Artists must be over 18 years or working in New Jersey. Deadline Sept. 10-15.

vp MARVIN NEWMAN MEMORIAL SCHOLARSHIP.
SEE: Art Students League of N.Y (Talent).

all NEW MEXICO ARTS COMMISSION, Lew Wallace Bldg., State Capitol, Santa Fe, NM 87503. Monies for artists-in-schools.

m NEW MEXICO HIGHLANDS UNIV., Las Vegas, NM 87701. Various.

m,vp,c,f NEW MEXICO STATE UNIV., Fine Arts Dept., Las Cruces, NM 88001. Various.

P-M,p-m NEW MUSIC FOR YOUNG ENSEMBLES, INC., 490 West End Ave., NYC 10024. Prizes of $300 and $100 for composition for 3 to 5 instruments. Deadline May 15.

m NEW ORLEANS BAPTIST THEOLOGICAL SEMINARY, 3939 Gentilly Blvd., New Orleans, LA 70126. Grad. music schols. $1,200 restrictions, academic achievement; 10 $200 women's academic achievement; grad fels.

M NEW ORLEANS EXPERIMENTAL OPERA, 420 St. Charles Ave., New Or-
(voice) leans, LA 70130. Award is appearance with New Orleans Opera Assn. Age limitations only for vocal register. Anyone.

T NEW PLAYWRIGHTS' THEATER OF WASHINGTON, Script Dept., 1742 Church St., NW, Washington, DC 20036. Looking for scripts for their use in labs, workshops, and readings. Award is from $4,000 to $10,000 for full-time residency. Playwrights whose works are chosen receive royalties based on box office percentages.

P-WR NEW STATESMAN PUBLISHING COMPANY, Great Turnstile, London WCIV 7HJ, England, UK.
  JOCK CAMPBELL NEW STATESMAN AWARD: In honorium of outstanding work by writers born in Africa or the Caribbean, work that is published in English. 1,000 pounds sterling every three years.

vp NYC COMMUNITY COLLEGE OF THE CITY UNIV. OF NY, Commercial Art Dept., 300 Jay St., Brooklyn, NY.

T,M NEW YORK DRAMA CRITICS' CIRCLE, 29 W. 46th St., NYC 10036. $1,000 for best NYC production nominated. Also awards given for best musical and best foreign NYC play production.

vp,f,a NY INSTITUTE OF TECHNOLOGY, Fine Arts Dept., Wheatley Rd., Old Westbury, NY 11568. Full and part tuition schols renewable annually for studies leading to BFA in painting, sculpture, printmaking, advertising design or interior design. Contact: Dr. F.T. Lassiter, Chmn of Fine Arts Dept.

M NEW YORK JAZZ MUSEUM, Box 4228, Grand Central Stn., NYC 10017.

vp NEW YORK-PHOENIX SCHOOL OF DESIGN, 160 Lexington Ave., NYC 10016.

  NEW YORK SHAVIANS, Box 3314, Grand Central Stn., NYC 10017. Douglas Laurie, Sec.

vp NEW YORK STATE COLLEGE OF CERAMICS AT ALFRED UNIV., Alfred, NY 14802. Contact: Div. Head, Art & Design.
  ASSISTANTSHIPS: 8 $1,200 Grad. Assist. per year, plus ½ tuition remission. Ten Teaching Internships—grad—$1,000 per semester, teaching one

119

course per semester.
LOW INCOME AWARDS: $200 per year.

all   NEW YORK STATE COUNCIL ON THE ARTS, 80 Centre St., NYC 10013.
Mostly aid to nonprofit arts organizations in the state but there is aid for
artists-in-schools.

f   NY UNIVERSITY, Cinema Studies, 51 W. 4th St., NYC 10003. Several to
$2,000.

t,f,d   NEW YORK UNIV., Dir. Financial Aid, 10 Wash. Place, Rm 350, NYC
10003. Limited to students admitted to the NYU School of the Arts, amts
based on individual need analysis.

f   NYU SCHOOL OF ARTS, Graduate Institute of Film and TV, 40 E. 7th St.,
NYC 10003. Approximately $19,450 is distributed in schols among nine
students plus the Martin Luther King grants annually. Five student assistantships are also available, tuition remission and stipends of $1,800 each.

all   NEW ZEALAND GOVERNMENT SCHOLARSHIPS, Univ. Grants Committee, PO Box 8035, Wellington, New Zealand. $1,300 for 2½ yrs to candidates
eligible for PhD in New Zealsnd; $2,000 for 2 yrs, number of awards limited
to PhD's.

WR   THE NEWSPAPER GUILD, 1125 15th St., NW, Washington, DC 20005,
Charles A. Perlick, Jr., Pres.

P-M   NIHON GAKKI CO., 10-1 Nakazawa-cho, Hamamatsu-shi, Shizuoka-ken,
Japan.
    WORLD GRAND PRIZE OF POPULAR MUSIC: Gold medal and $1,000
    awarded annually for the best performance and composition of popular
    music.

P-WR   NOBEL FOUNDATION, Hobel House, Sturegatan 14, 11436 Stockholm,
Sweden.
    NOBEL PRIZE FOR LITERATURE: For the most outstanding, distin-
    guished work having to do with an idealistic nature. Nobel Gold Medal,
    Nobel Diploma and cash honorarium of varying amount. 1974 amount:
    $126,000. Anyone. Applications not accepted.

all   NORFOLK FOUNDATION, R.L. Sheets, Ex. Dir., 406 Royster Bldg., Norfolk, VA 23510. A limited number of designated schols available to students
primarily residents in 50 mile radius of Norfolk. Less than $1,000.

WR   NORTH AMERICAN MENTOR MAGAZINE, John Westburg Associates,
Contest Editor, 1745 Madison St., Fennimore, WI 53809. $125 award divided
among 10 winners for poetry entries.

ALL,all NORTH CAROLINA ARTS COUNCIL, Dept. of Cultural Resources, Raleigh,

NC 27611. Programs for the hiring of professional artists by community groups for teaching their art form and a nine-month residency program for visiting artists.

vp,c   NORTH CAROLINA COLLEGE AT DURHAM, Fayetteville St. & Lawson Ave., Durham, NC 27707.

a   NORTH CAROLINA STATE UNIV., Raleigh, NC 27607.

M   NORTH CAROLINA SYMPHONY SOCIETY, Chapel Hill, NC 27514.
EDWARD B. BENJAMIN AWARD: $500 for "restful" composition, to students of Eastman School of Music. Additionally "restful" works are commissioned for the Philadelphia Orchestra, North Carolina Symphony, and New Orleans Symphony. Apply during summer to: Edw. B. Benjamin, Greensboro, NC.

all   NORTH DAKOTA COUNCIL ON THE ARTS AND HUMANITIES, 320 Minard Hall, North Dakota State Univ., Fargo, ND 58102. Artists-in-schools.

m   NORTH TEXAS STATE UNIV., Denton, TX 76203. Grad. Assists. and part-time teaching positions for grad. students to 60 students. $2,800-$4,800.

m,vp,c   NORTHEAST LOUISIANA UNIVERSITY, School of Music, Monroe, LA 71201.

m,vp   NORTHEAST MISSOURI STATE COLLEGE, Division of Fine Arts, Dr. Dale A. Jorgenson, Head, Div. Fine Arts, Kirksville, MO 63501.Music schols. and grad assistantships in various areas. Vp schols. for freshmen based on portfolio, $260 per academic year.

vp   NORTHEASTERN ILLINOIS STATE COLLEGE, Bryn Mawr at St. Louis Ave., Chicago, IL 60625.

vp   NORTHEASTERN JUNIOR COLLEGE, Sterling, CO 80755.

f,m,vp,t   NORTHERN ARIZONA UNIVERSITY, Telecommunications, Box 6006, Flagstaff, AZ 86001. Contact: Dr. Ron. L. McIntyre. One scholarship in Telecommunications for full year's tuition.

all   NORTHERN ILLINOIS UNIVERSITY, DeKalb, IL 60115. Dr. Wm. A. Herrmann, Dir. Grants in Aid to talented students in all disciplines consisting of tuition waivers, numerous governmental and private sources of funds.

vp,c   NORTHERN MICHIGAN UNIV., Marquette, MI 49855.

M   NORTHERN PLAINS TRI-STATE FESTIVAL OF MUSIC, Div. of Music, Dickinson State College, Dickinson, ND 58601. Approx. $1,000 for commissioned work of instrumental or choral nature.

vp,c   NORTHERN STATE COLLEGE, S. Jay St., Aberdeen, SD 57401.

vp,c   NORTHWEST MISSOURI STATE COLLEGE, Marysville, MO 64468.

m,vp   NORTHWEST NAZARENE COLLEGE, Nampa, ID 83651. Activity schols, varying amounts (50), some renewable, undergrads.

vp   NORTHWESTERN COLLEGE, 101 7th St., Orange City, IA 51041.

m   NORTHWESTERN STATE COLLEGE OF LOUISIANA, Natchitoches, LA 71457. Many for undergraduates.

m   NORTHWESTERN UNIVERSITY, School of Music, Evanston, IL 60201. Many for undergrads; grads to $2,300.

vp   NORTHWOOD INSTITUTE, Cook Rd., Midland, MI 48640.

A,VP-H   NORWEGIAN RESEARCH COUNCIL FOR SCIENCE AND THE HUMANI-
         TIES, The Royal Ministry of Church and Education, Oslo, Norway. Re-
         search schols for U.S. nationals to study in Norway and vice-versa. Projects
         should be sponsored by institution in Norway or U.S.

vp,c   NOTRE DAME COLLEGE, 2321 Elm St., Manchester, NH 03104.

vp,c   NOTRE DAME COLLEGE OF OHIO, 4545 College Rd., Cleveland, OH 44121.

wr   NOVALICHES ACADEMY SCIENTIFIC AND EDUCATIONAL FND., PO
         Box 1644, Manila, Philippines. Research fels in field of folklore to grads
         with good knowledge of English. Anyone.

P-ALL   NUKI Award for erotic drawings and paintings done by males under 25. Cita-
         tion, showing, possible gallery contract. Send slides or photographs. If origi-
         nals are sent they must be no larger than 18"x24" and sent in mailing tube.
         No responsibility taken for materials submitted. Ladine Webster, Adm., Box
         9005, Washington, DC 20003.

m   NYACK MISSIONARY COLLEGE, Div. of Music, Nyack, NY 10906. Vari-
         ous schols. from $50-$1,000.

P-VP   OAKLEY FELLOWSHIPS, c/o Univ/Southern Calif., University Park, Los
         Angeles, CA 90007. $2,400.

P-F   OBERHAUSEN INTERNATIONAL FESTIVAL OF SHORT FILMS, Schwartz
         strasse 71, 42 Oberhausen/Rhld, FDR. For the encouragement of young film-
         makers and their first films of documentaries, animated and experimental
         films. Five grand premiums of 5,000 German marks; five principal premiums
         of 2,500 German marks and Max Ernst Award. Anyone.

P-F   OBERHAUSEN SPORTS FILM FESTIVAL, Schwartzstrasse 71, 42 Ober-hausen, FDR.
AWARDS: For the outstanding feature films and shorts having to do with sports:
OBERHAUSEN CATHOLIC PRIZE; OBERHAUSEN PROTESTANT PRIZE;
GRAND PRIZES with a monetary value of $1,250, and MAIN PRIZES with a monetary value of $250. Every other year. Anyone.

vp,m   OBERLIN COLLEGE, Oberlin, OH 44074. Assistantships to grads with BA who qualify, renewable. Conservatory of Music - write for details.

P-VP   ADOLPH AND CLARA OBRIG PRIZE FOR PAINTING IN OIL. Award $500. SEE: NATIONAL ACADEMY OF DESIGN.

P-VP   ADOLPH AND CLARA OBRIG PRIZES FOR PAINTING IN WATER-COLOR. Awards: $350 and $200.
SEE: NATIONAL ACADEMY OF DESIGN.

m   OCCIDENTAL COLLEGE, Los Angeles, CA 90041. Grad. fel. $2,500.

vp,c   ODESSA COLLEGE, Box 3752, Odessa, TX 79760.

P-VP   OEHLER, HELEN GAPEN, AWARD.
SEE: AMERICAN WATERCOLOR SOCIETY.

ALL,all   THE OFFICE OF ARKANSAS STATE ARTS AND HUMANITIES, Conti-nental Bldg., Suite 500, Markham and Main, Little Rock, AR 72201. Grants for both artists in schools and in residence.

m   OGLEBAY INSTITUTE, Opera Workshop, Oglebay Pk., Wheeling, WV 26003. Mrs. Chase Greer, Dir. of Performing Arts. Tuition and partial tuition schols available to male singers. Application deadline May 1.

WR   THE FRANK O'HARA FOUNDATION, 145 W. 45th St., NYC 10036. Award of $1,000 plus publication of book of poems at Columbia Univ. Press for securing recognition and publication for poets who are creating experi-mental poetry that may be difficult to publish.

P-WR   FRANK O'HARA PRIZE. Award: $500. SEE: POETRY MAGAZINE.

F   OHIO ARTS COUNCIL, 50 West Broad St., Columbus, OH 43215. Contact: 1) Ira Weiss, Performing Arts coord., 2) Alice Wright, Visual Arts coord., 3) Susan Neumann, Grants coord. Individual artists must apply through a nonprofit organization which is willing to sponsor their project. Write for guideline booklet "Aid to Individual Artist."

m,f   OHIO STATE UNIVERSITY, Columbus, OH 43210. Film Contact: Robert

Wagner. Two teaching assists in Music; many teaching and research assists in Film.

vp,f OHIO UNIVERSITY, College of Fine Arts, Seigfred Hall, Athens, OH 45701. Two grad assists to $2,400 in visual arts. 4 grad assistants in film (starting at $2,610 plus full tuition waivers). Production grants to advanced students (up to $400).

vp OHIO UNIVERSITY, 940 Second St., Portsmouth, OH 45662.

WR OHIO UNIVERSITY PRESS, 208 Cutler Hall, Ohio Univ., Athens, OH 45701. Discontinued.

vp,c OHIO WESLEYAN UNIV., Delaware, OH 43015. Students (BFA) recommended by undergrad instructors for exceptional application - 4 yrs.

all OKLAHOMA ARTS AND HUMANITIES COUNCIL, 2101 No. Lincoln Blvd, Oklahoma City, OK 73105. Artists-in-schools.

m OKLAHOMA BAPTIST UNIV., College of Fine Arts, Shawnee, OK 74801. Thirty $200, renewable, restirctions.

vp OKLAHOMA CHRISTIAN COLLEGE, N. Eastern and Memorial Rd., Oklahoma City, OK 73111.

m OKLAHOMA CITY UNIV., School of Music, Oklahoma City, OK 73106. To entering freshmen, orchestra, band, piano, voice; talent, need, renewable.

m OKLAHOMA COLLEGE OF LIBERAL ARTS, Chickasha, OK 73018. To women only, entering freshmen, $1,000; others women only, 10 $250 renew, restrict.; 14 $250 members of stage band.

M OKLAHOMA MUSICIAN OF THE YEAR AWARD, c/o Mrs. Denzil C. Pope, Loyal, OK 73756. Performer, composer, or educator.

m,a,f OKLAHOMA STATE UNIV., Stillwater, OK 74074. Various, plus film Assistantships from $1,170 to $3,000 per year.

m OLD DOMINION SYMPHONY COUNCIL, 4802 Kensington Ave., Richmond, VA 23226.
YOUNG VIRGINIA ARTISTS COMPETITION: Cash prizes to Virginia residents under 26 yrs, pianists and orchestral instrumentalists.

wr,m F.E. OLDS & SON, INC., 350 So. Raymond Ave., Fulerton, CA 92631. Olds Schol. in music. Awards to anyone writing on subjects related to musical instruments.

P-WR JOHN M. OLIN AWARD. SEE: WINCHESTER PRESS.

124

vp   IVAN OLINSKY MEMORIAL SCHOLARSHIP.
SEE: Art Students League of N.Y. (Talent).

M   OLIVER MESSIAEN COMPETITION, Secretariat du concours, Bureau de Concerts, Maurice Werner, 1 Ave Delcasse, Pairs 8, France. Performance of contemporary music on piano. To any pianists of any nationality under 33 yrs. First prize approx. $2,000, concert with orch. appearance on French TV.

vp   OLIVET COLLEGE, Olivet, MI 49076.

P-VP   OLSEN, HERB, AWARD. Monetary Award.
SEE: AMERICAN WATERCOLOR SOCIETY.

vp   OLYMPIC COLLEGE, 16th & Chester, Bremerton, WA 98310.

T   OMAHA COMMUNITY PLAYHOUSE, 6915 Cass St., Omaha, NE 68132. Award of $2,000 which includes production of chosen play. Deadline Nov. 21.

wr   THE EUGENE O'NEILL FOUNDATION—WESLEYAN UNIV., Fellowship Program, Middletown, CT 06457. Grants (4) $3,500 to enable playwrights to live and work at the Fnd's estate in Conn. and to take courses at the Univ.

T   THE O'NEILL THEATER CENTER, 1860 Broadway, Suite 1012, NYC 10023. National Playwrights Conference is for unproduced plays and if chosen gives the playwright a chance to work with actors, technicians and professional director and/or will be eligible for TV production by ABC-TV and the ABC Theater Award of $10,000. Deadline between Sept. 15 and Dec. 31.

T,WR   OPEN CIRCLE THEATRE, Goucher College, Towson, MD 21204. Annual award of $200, production and residency expenses, to encourage writing of roles for women. Apply between Sept. 1 and Dec. 31.

ALL,all   OREGON ARTS COMMISSION, 316 Oregon Bldg., 494 State St., Salem, OR 97301. Ten grants of up to $1,000 to Oregon artists who are not students. Deadline Oct. 15.

vp,c   OREGON COLLEGE OF EDUCATION, Monmouth, OR 97361.

vp,c   OREGON STATE UNIV., Dept. of Art, Corvallis, OR 97331.

M   ORGANIZATION COMMITTEE OF WORLD WIDE MME. BUTTERFLY COMPETITION, Inoue Bldg., 4-4 1-chome, Akasaka, Minatoku, Tokyo, Japan. Women of all nations. Award $2,780. Date of next contest not known.

all   ORGANIZATION OF AMERICAN STATES, Pan American Union, Washington, DC 20006. Several grants and fels., 3 mos. to two yrs, for adv. study in another member state. To U.S. nationals for adv. study in Latin America, permanent residents of OAS member states. Apply: Dept. of Technical Secretariat, above.

T   ORIENTAL ACTORS OF AMERICA, c/o Alvin Lum, Pres., 392 Union St., Brooklyn, NY 11231.

P-VP   OSBORNE, WILLIAM CHURCH, MEMORIAL AWARD. Monetary award. SEE: AMERICAN WATERCOLOR SOCIETY.

P-M   THE OSCAR ESPLA PRIZE, Director, Oscar Espla Prize, Excmo, Ayuntamiento de Alicante, Spain. 250,000 pesetas for original composition lasting at least 20 minutes in the symphonic genre. Anyone. Deadline March 15.

ALL,all   OSSABOW ISLAND PROJECT, c/o Ford West, Ossabow Island, PO Box 13397, Savannah, GA 31406. Accommodation for 10 artists on an island off the coast of Georgia. Open from October 1 to June 1. Private room, meals and studio space for $50 per week which can be waived for qualified applicants.

vp   OTERO JUNIOR COLLEGE, La Junta, CO 81050.

vp,c   OTIS ART INSTITUTE, 2401 Wilshire Blvd., Los Angeles, CA 90057. Contact: Office of Financial Aid. Full and partial tuition grants, Grad. Assistantships and Scholarships available.

vp,c   OTTAWA UNIV., 10 & Cedar Sts., Ottawa, KS 66067.

all   OTTUMWA HEIGHTS COLLEGE, Max J. Miller, Dir. of Adm., Grandview at North Elm, Ottumwa, IA 52501. $500 toward tuition, renewable, application and ref required, no restricts, mut be full-time student. Eight Leader Scholar Awards for education given to persons showing potential.

m   OUACHITA BAPTIST UNIV., School of Music, Arkadelphia, AR 71923. Schols in music education from $200 to $1,710.

vp,c   OUR LADY OF CINCINNATI COLLEGE, Edgecliff, Walnut Hills, Cincinnati, OH 45206.

m,vp   OUR LADY OF THE LAKE COLLEGE, 411 SW 24th St., San Antonio, TX 78207. Various.

vp   PACE COLLEGE, NY & Westchester, 41 Park Row, NYC 10038, & Pleasantville, NY.

wr   PADEREWSKI FND., 3 W. 51st St., NYC 10019, Alvin Lum, Pres. Grants $900-$1,200, 9-12 mos. for advanced study to U.S. grads preferably of Polish descent.

P-M   NICOLO PAGANINI INTERNATIONAL VIOLIN COMPETITION, Palazzo

Tursi, Via Garibaldi 9, Genoa, Italy.
NICOLO PAGANINI PRIZE: Monetary award of 6,050,000 liras divided among the best violinists no older than 35 years. Annually. Anyone.

WR   ROBERT TROUP PAINE PUBLICATION FUND, Harvard Univ. Press, 79 Garden St., Cambridge, MA 02138. Robert Troup Paine Prize $3,000 every 4 yrs for author(s) manuscript on specified subject accepted by Harvard Univ Press during preceding 4 yrs. Present category: history and/or philosophy of medicine.

P-VP   THE EDWIN PALMER MEMORIAL PRIZE. Award: $1,500.
SEE: NATIONAL ACADEMY OF DESIGN.

WR   PANACHE, Box 77, Sunderland, MA 01375. The Frances Steloff Prize for fiction or poetry entries amounts to at least $100 and publication in Panache.

m   PAN AMERICAN COLLEGE, Edinburg, TX 78539. Various.

P-M   PARIS INTERNATIONAL HARPSICHORD COMPETITION, Festival de Paris, 5 Place des Ternes, F-75017 Paris, France. PRIZES: For the outstanding performers from ages 20 to 32 yrs. The total monetary awards in 1975 were 14,000 French francs, concerts, records, and radio performances. Biennially.

P-M   PARIS INTERNATIONAL VOICE COMPETITION, 14 bis, Avenue de President-Wilson, F-75016 Paris, France. PRIZES: To the best vocalists. Women: 32 or younger; men: 35 or younger. Monetary prizes (50,000 French francs in 1975) and engagements for many music festivals.

WR   PARIS REVIEW, Inc. 45-39 171 Place, Flushing, NY 11358. $500 for unpublished contemporary work of literature. Unpublished humorous fiction 2 monetary awards annually.

V-P   PARSONS SCHOOL OF DESIGN, 66 Fifth Ave., NYC.

vp,c   PASADENA COLLEGE, 1530 E. Elizabeth St., Pasadena, CA 91104.

P-VP   THE WILLIAM A. PATON PRIZE. Award: $750.
SEE: NATIONAL ACADEMY OF DESIGN.

WR   ALICIA PATTERSON FUND, 535 Fifth Ave., NYC 10017. Fellowships totaling $15,000 for journalists and editors for 1 year abroad to examine and write on areas of their interest. Five yrs editorial or journalistic experience and approval of editor or publisher.

m   HOWARD PAYNE COLLEGE, Brownwood, TX 76801. Various.

m,vp,c   GEORGE PEABODY COLLEGE FOR TEACHERS, Nashville, TN 37203.

Blair fels. of $1,000 to music grads; NDEA fels of $2,400 plus tuition & fees; Epda fels $4,800. Tuition waivers $600-$1,200.

m PEABODY CONSERVATORY OF MUSIC, 1 East Mt. Vernon Pl., Baltimore, MD 21202. Many, up to $1,500; Grad fels.

P-WR THE DREW PEARSON FOUNDATION, Suite 200, 1300 19th St., NW, Washington, DC 20036.
THE DREW PEARSON PRIZE: For outstanding work in investigative reporting. Not only newspaper reporters, but authors of books and magazine articles, and writers involved with radio and television are also eligible. $5,000 awarded annually.

WR P.E.N. AMERICAN CENTER (P.E.N. Writers' Fund), 47 Fifth Ave., NYC 10003.
P.E.N. TRANSLATION PRIZE: $1,000 for best translation into English from any language and published in U.S. in preceding calendar year. Technical, scientific or reference work not eligible. Anyone. Apply: Chmn, Trans. Committee above. Grants and loans given every 6 weeks for emergency needs of professional writers.

P-VP THE PENNSYLVANIA ACADEMY OF FINE ARTS, Broad & Cherry Sts., Philadelphia, PA 19002.
FELLOWSHIP PRIZE: For the outstanding in painting or sculpture entered in the Annual Exhibition, done by either a member of the Fellowship or a former student of the Academy. $100 is awarded annually.
TEMPLE PURCHASE PRIZE FUND: For the outstanding in oil painting. This is awarded annually to an American artist.

vp PENNSYLVANIA FEDERATION OF WOMENS CLUBS SCHOLARSHIPS, (Penny Art Fund), Kutztown State College, Dir. of Financial Aid, Kutztown, PA 19530.

m,vp,a,f PENNSYLVANIA STATE UNIVERSITY, Arts Bldg II, University Park, PA 16802.

vp,c PEPPERDINE COLLEGE, 1121 W. 79 St., Los Angeles, CA 90044.

C,VP PETER'S VALLEY CRAFTSMEN, Star Route, Layton, NJ 07851. Artists community in the Delaware Water Gap National Recreational Area which offers free use of studio space and equipment. Housing is available at $50 per month. Professional artists who can support themselves during the residency are considered.

m PFEIFFER COLLEGE, Misenheimer, NC 28109. $1,000 to entering freshmen per year; $3,000 for 4-yr period renewable. Accompanying assistantships $300.

WR THE CARL & LILY PFORZHEIMER FND., INC., 70 Pine St., NYC 10005.

128

Several grants in connection with American and English literature.

P-VP   JANE PETERSON PRIZES. Awards: $150 & $150.
        SEE: Allied Artists of America, Inc.

WR   JAMES D. PHELAN AWARDS IN LITERATURE, 401 DuBore St., San
        Francisco, CA 94117. To $1,000 in literature or art for native-born Califor-
        nians only, 20-40 yrs of age.

P-WR   PHI ALPHA THETA, 2812 Livingston St., Allentown, PA 18104.
        BOOK AWARD: For outstanding work in the field of history, must be the
        author's second, third or subsequent book. $500 awarded annually to
        members only.
        FIRST BOOK AWARD: For outstanding work in the field of history which
        is the author's first book. $500 awarded annually to members only.
        MANUSCRIPT AWARD: For innovative and challenging new concepts in
        the field of history, or for presenting new materil on subjects already re-
        searched. Author must be a member; manuscript must be book length.
        The prize of underwriting the cost for publishing the book is awarded
        annually.

P-WR   PHI BETA KAPPA, 1811 Q St., NW, Washington, DC 20009.
        CHRISTIAN GAUSS AWARD: In honorium of a book of literary scholar-
        ship or criticism. $2,500 awarded annually to author.

M   PHI MU ALPHA—SINFONIA (Sinfonia Fund), Lyrecrest, 10600 Old State
        Rd., Evansville, IN 47711. Alan Adams, Exec. Dir.

vp,c,f PHILADELPHIA COLLEGE OF ART, Broad & Pine Sts., Philadelphia, PA
        19101. Photography and film; general schls. available.

vp,c   PHILADELPHIA COLLEGE OF TEXTILES AND SCIENCE, School House
        Lane and Henry Ave., Philadelphia, PA 19144.

M,m   PHILADELPHIA MUSICAL ACADEMY, Dr. Maria Ezerman Drake, Chmn,
        Composition Competition, 1617 Spruce St., Philadelphia, PA 19103. To
        women of any nationality, college age or over, $200 and premiere at Delta
        Omicron Int'l. Conf. for string quartet composition of moderate difficulty,
        10-20 minutes. Also various to entering freshmen. MR

vp   PHILANDER SMITH COLLEGE, 812 W. 13th, Little Rock, AR 72203.

WR   MINDANAO STATE UNIV., Marawi City, Philippines. Visiting Professor-
        ship Program for summer; room, board & transp. Anyone.

m   PHILLIPS UNIV., Music Division, Enid, OK 73701. Various scholarships for
        scholastic and musical ability.

vp,c   PHOENIX COLLEGE, 1202 W. Thomas Rd., Phoenix, AZ 85013.

VP   PHOTO CLUB OF ROYAN, SIRP-Animation, B.P. 102, 17201 Royan Cedex, France. 5,000 French francs for international photography contest. Deadline March 30-April 20.

P-VP   PHOTOGRAPHER OF THE YEAR: Photojournalism. SEE: American Society of magazine photographers.

m   PITTSBURGH FLUTE CLUB, 6310 Darlington Rd., Pittsburgh, PA 15217. c/o Bernard Z. Goldberg, or c/o Mrs. R.K. Sayre, 244 Hazel Drive, Pittsburgh, PA 15219. Several, for flute study; one woodwind.

vp,m   PIUS XII INSTITUTE COMMITTEE, Rosary College, Rivers Forest, IL 60305. U.S. nationals for study in Italy at Pius XII Inst., Villa Schifanoia, Florence, for study in music, painting & sculpture. To women 21-45, BA equiv., knowledge of Italian. Apply at College. Taylor Schol. in music for women for MA degree, $1,000.

P-WR   PLANETA PUBLISHING HOUSE, Calvet 51-53, Barcelona, Spain.
PLANETA PRIZE: For the outstanding unpublished novel by an author from a Spanish-speaking country. 2,000,000 pesetas and publication awarded annually.

P-WR   PLAYBOY MAGAZINE, 919 No. Michigan Ave., Chicago, IL 60611.
EDITORIAL AWARD WINNER: In honorium of the outstanding writing contributions published in Playboy. For the following: Best Major Work, Best Short Story (fiction), Best New Contributor (fiction), Best Essay, Best Article, Best Humor, Best Satire, Best New Contributor (nonfiction). Engraved silver medallion and $1,000 awarded annually.
EDITORIAL AWARD RUNNER-UP: Same requirements as above, only that this award is for second best in each category. Silver medallion and $500 awarded annually.

T   THE PLAYWRIGHTS' LAB, 2301 Franklin Ave., E., Minneapolis, MN 55406. Six playwrights-in-residence positions are awarded with a public reading of their works and $2,000 to each.

vp,c   PLYMOUTH STATE COLLEGE OF THE UNIV/NEW HAMPSHIRE, Plymouth, NH 03264.

P-WR   THE EDGAR ALLEN POE AWARD. Award: $5,000. SEE: ACADEMY OF AMERICAN POETS, INC.

WR   POET LORE, John William Andres, Poetry Editor, 52 Cranbury Rd., Westport, CT 06880. $1,000 for Narrative Poetry.

WR   POETRY, 1018 No. State St., Chicago, IL 60610. Many small, annually.

WR   POETRY MAGAZINE, 601 So. Morgan St., PO Box 4348, Chicago, IL 60680.

Prizes of $100 to $300 annually for works previously published in "Poetry" during preceding year.

P-WR POETRY SOCIETY, 21 Earls Court Sq., London SW5, England, UK.
ALICE HUNT BARTLETT PRIZE: 200 pounds sterling to a young poet for a collection of his work, not less than 20 poems. Annually.

P-WR POETRY SOCIETY OF AMERICA, 15 Gramercy Park, NYC 10013. Nine prizes ranging from $100 to $2,000 for poetry.

P-WR POETRY SOCIETY OF TEXAS, c/o Jack E. Murphy, Pres., 10436 Creekmere Dr., Dallas, TX 75218. Annual contest of about 70 categories for poets. Write for information.

m POINT LOMA COLLEGE, Dept. of Music, 3900 Lomaland Dr., San Diego, CA 92106. Scholarships of $225 to $600 annually for music students in addition to any academic schols. Awarded on basis of performance ability.

vp POINT PARK COLLEGE, Wood St. & Blvd of the Allies, Pittsburgh, PA 15222.

P-WR POLISH-AMERICAN POSTER CONTEST, 3712 Fulton St., NW, Washington, DC 20007. Awards of $500, $300 and $200.

P-M POLISH ARTISTIC AGENCY (PAGART), The Secretariat, Pl. Zwyciestwa 9, Warsaw, Poland.
SOPOT INTERNATIONAL SONG FESTIVAL PRIZES: To performers of the best songs: 1st, $15,000 zlotys; 2nd, 10,000 zlotys. To performers of Polish songs: 1st, 20,000 zlotys; 2nd, 15,000 zlotys. Annually.

P-WR POLISH AUTHORS ASSOCIATION (ZAIKS), Ul. Hipoteczna 2, Warsaw, Poland. PRIZES: Two awards of 15,000 zlotys bestowed annually for the best translations of Polish literature into another language.

P-VP POLISH CENTRAL OFFICE OF ARTISTIC EXHIBITIONS, Pl. Malachowskiego 3, Warsaw, Poland.
POLISH INTERNATIONAL POSTERS BIENNIAL: For best posters: 1st prize: Gold medal & 30,000 zlotys; 2nd Prize: Silver medal and 20,000 zlotys; 3rd Prize: Bronze medal and 10,000 zlotys. Awarded biennially.

T POLISH LABORATORY THEATER. SEE: Brooklyn Academy of Music.

P-M POLISH MINISTRY OF CULTURE AND ART Frederic Chopin Association, Okolnik 1, Warsaw, Poland.
FREDERIC CHOPIN INTERNATIONAL PIANO COMPETITION PRIZE: For the outstanding interpretations of Chopin compositions: Six prizes of from 20,000 to 60,000 zlotys.

P-M POLISH MINISTRY OF CULTURE AND ART, Henryk Wieniawski Asso-

ciation, Ul. Wodna 27, Poznan, Poland.
HENRYK WIENIAWSKI INTERNATIONAL COMPETITION FOR LUTE
MAKERS PRIZE: For the best instruments presented: Six prizes from
10,000 to 30,000 zlotys. Every 5 years.
HENRYK WIENIAWSKI INTERNATIONAL COMPETITION FOR VIOLIN
COMPOSITION PRIZE: To the best composers, 12,000 and 8,000
zlotys. Every 5 years.
HENRYK WIENIAWSKI INTERNATIONAL VIOLIN COMPETITION
PRIZE: For the best interpretation of violin compositions: Three prizes
of from 30,000-50,000 zlotys and bronze, silver and gold medals, plus
four honorary awards of 5,000 zlotys each every five years.

P-WR   P.E.N. CENTRE (Polski Klub Literacki PEN), 1 Nauki, Palac Kultury, Warszawa. Six annual awards in writing and translation from Polish into other
languages and vice versa.

vp   POLK JR. COLLEGE, 999 Ave. H NE, Winter Haven, FL 33880.

wr   PONTIFICIA UNIVERSIDAD JAVERIANA, Carrera 7a, No. 40-62, Bogota,
Colombia. Two grants, 2 yrs for exchange of students and professors from
U.S. Apply: Secretary General, above.

m,a,t,h   POMONA COLLEGE, Claremont, CA 91711. All schols based on need.

WR   ARTHUR KINGSLEY PORTER PRIZE, University of Chicago, 5801 Ellis
Ave., Chicago, IL 60637. $400 annually for best article published in the Art
Bulletin. Author must be under 40 yrs of age. MR

M   COLE PORTER SCHOLARSHIP, University/Southern Calif., University
Park, Los Angeles, CA 90007. $5,000.

vp,c   PORTLAND SCHOOL OF ART, 97 Spring St., Portland, ME 04101. Contact: Joan P. Uraneck, Dir. Financial Aid. For Maine high school graduates
only: the Maine State Tuition Equalization Plan. Seog. PSA Scholarship
Trust Fund: Max. amount is $200.

C,VP   PORTSMOUTH PARKS AND RECREATION DEPT., 430 High St., Portsmouth, VA 23704. Annual Seawall Art Show for all art forms. Over $5,000
in awards, purchase and special awards. Deadline May 1.

P-WR   PORTUGAL STATE SECRETARIAT FOR INFORMATION AND TOUR-
ISM, Palacio Foz, Lisbon 2, Portugal.
CAMOES PRIZE: Award of 30,000 escudos and a two-week stay in Portu-
gal for the best work written on Portuguese life and culture by a non-
Portuguese writer, published outside Portugal in its first edition, in a lan-
guage other than Portuguese. Biennial.

V-P   POSITANO ART WORKSHOP, PO Box 3129, Grand Central Post Office,

NYC 10017. Three 1-mo. attendance at workshop in Positano, Italy with funds to cover residence in pensione. Application made through institution where applicant is working must be accompanied with curriculum vitae and recommendation. MR

WR POYNTER FUND, Times Bldg., 440 First Ave. So., St. Petersburg, FL 33701. Several grants and fels. to projects and individuals to train and assist, inspire journalists of all media for improving the reporting and objective interpretation of news of domestic governments to link academic study of political science with practice of journalism and government. Also for editorial and cultural projects primarily in Florida.

P-M PRAGUE SPRING INTERNATIONAL MUSIC COMPETITION, Dum Umelcu, 11000 Praha 1, Czechoslovakia. PRIZES: Categories change annually. Monetary awards.

vp,c PRATT-N.Y. PHOENIX SCHOOL OF DESIGN, 160 Lexington Ave., NYC 10016. Contact: Roz Goldfarb, Dir. PRATT GRANTS: Grants in aid from the Institute to help meet student tuition costs. Write for brochure.

M PREIS DES SCHUBERT WETTBEWERBES, Vienna Conservatory, Johannesgasse, 4A, Vienna, Austria. Three prizes in voice; men aged 20-32; women 20-30.

vp PRESBYTERIAN COLLEGE, Broad St., Clinton, SC 29325.

all PRESSER FOUNDATION, Presser Place, Bryn Mawr, PA 19010. Contact: Dr. John R. Ott, Pres.

m PRESSO ACCADEMIA MUSICALE NAPOLETAN, Via San Pasquale a Chiaia 62, Naples, Italy. Piano and composition. Ages 15-32. Biennial. Anyone. Apply Secretary Concours Casella, re International Contest above.

vp PRINCE GEORGES COMMUNITY COLLEGE, 301 Largo Rd., Largo, MD 20870.

P-M PRINCE PIERRE DE MONACO FOUNDATION, Ministere d'Etat, Monaco. PRINCE PIERRE DE MONACO PRIZE FOR MUSICAL COMPOSITION: Basically the award is for the best musical composition, although the subject of the composition changes every year. 20,000 French francs awarded annually. Anyone.

P-VP PRINCE RAINIER III PRIZE. SEE: Monegasque National Committee of the International Association of Art, Painting, Sculpture, Graphic Art.

WR PRINCETON SERIES OF CONTEMPORARY POETS, Poetry Editor, Princeton Univ. Press, Princeton, NJ 08540. Publication of poetry chosen in the annual The Press. Submit manuscripts between June and October. An aid for publication; no grants are given.

m,a PRINCETON UNIV., Princeton, NJ 08540. Each accepted grad. student having no outside support is offered fellowship sufficient to enable him realistically to accept admission.

P-VP THE PRINT CLUB, 1614 Latimer St., Philadelphia, PA 19103.
BERTHE VON MOSCHZISKER AWARD: In honorium of excellence in the print medium. $500 awarded annually.
WILLIAM H. WALKER PRIZE FOR LITHOGRAPHY: In honorium of excellence in the lithography medium. $100 plus inclusion of the work in the Philadelphia Museum of Art awarded every two years.

P-VP THE PRINT MAGAZINE, 19 W. 44th St.,NYC 10036.
PRINT MAGAZINE INTERNATIONAL COVER DESIGN PRIZE: For the best cover design made by a student designer. A monetary prize of $100 is awarded annually.

VP PROVINCETOWN WORKSHOP, Provincetown, MA.

P-M PUCCINI FOUNDATION, Lucca, Italy.
GIACOMO PUCCINI PRIZE: For the outstanding vocal interpretation of Puccini's music. First Prize: 500,000 liras and statue; Second Prize: 300,000 liras. Annually; anyone.

M,T,WR THE PULITZER PRIZES, Columbia University, NYC 10027. Prizes given for chosen book, play, or musical composition. Twelve prizes in journalism with $1,000 award each, with one exception. Six prizes of $1,000 each for works in letters. One $1,000 award annually for music. Three fellowships of $3,000 made to graduates of journalism for travel abroad.

all PURDUE UNIVERSITY, Dept. of Creative Arts, Lafayette, IN 47907. Grad. Teaching Assists., half and full-time, $1,500-$3,000, one year, renewable. Portfolio and interviews required; request application. Deadline April 1.

P-WR PUTNAM AWARDS, c/o G.P. Putnam's Sons, 200 Madison Ave., NYC 10016.
PUTNAM AWARDS: For outstanding manuscripts fiction or nonfiction already under contract to the House. Advance of $7,500 against royalties plus $7,500 for advertising and promotion. Annually.

P-VP PAUL PUZINAS MEMORIAL AWARD. Award: $100.
SEE: Allied Artists of America, Inc.

m QUACHITA BAPTIST UNIVERSITY, School of Music, Dr. Wm. Trantham Dean, Arkadelphia, AR 71923. Schols ranging from $150-$300 annually.

P-VP QUACKENBUSH, LARRY, MEMORIAL BIENNIAL. Monetary award.
SEE: AMERICAN WATERCOLOR SOCIETY.

P-M QUEEN ELIZABETH OF BELGIUM INTERNATIONAL MUSIC COMPETI-

TION, The Secretariat, 11 rue Baron Horta, B-1000 Brussels, Belgium.
PRIZES: Awards for the best performances; categories change annually.
1,045,000 Belgian francs awarded in 1975 (totao).

P-M   QUEEN MARIE-JOSE PRIZE FOR MUSICAL COMPOSITION, The Secretariat, Ch-1249 Merlinge-Gy, Geneva, Switzerland.
QUEEN MARIE-JOSE PRIZE: A monetary prize for 10,000 Swiss francs is awarded biennially to the outstanding musical composition by composers of any age. Anyone.

vp,c   QUEENS COLLEGE, Selwyn Ave., Charlotte, NC 28207. Various for applied music lessons and fees.

WR   QUEEN'S UNIVERSITY AT KINGSTON, Kingston, Ontario, Canada. Schol. grant of $1,800 for 12 months, candidate must be grad. and assist the department in teaching composition. Apply: School of Grad. Studies.

all   THE QUEEN'S UNIV. OF BELFAST, The Secretary, Academic Council, Belfast 7, Northern Ireland. Visiting studentships for 2 yrs, renewable for 3rd yr. $1,275-$1,900. For grads of any other Univ. than Queen's, must have ability to pursue postgrad. work in English language.

m   QUINCY COLLEGE, Quincy, IL 62301. Several, partial-full varying with need and ability. Undergrads.

P-WR   QUINTO SOL PUBLICATIONS, INC., PO Box 9275, Berkeley, CA 94709.
QUINTO SOL AWARD: In honorium of outstanding literary work, either novel, collection of short stories, book-length essay or experimental writing by a person of Mexican descent living in the U.S. $1,000 awarded annually to the author.

all   RADCLIFFE COLLEGE INSTITUTE FOR INDEPENDENT STUDY, 3 James St., Cambridge, MA 02138. Two Fellowships: Radcliffe Fellows and Non-Tenured Faculty Fellows. Stipends have totaled up to $12,000 per year. Must be professional women from post-doctoral level to senior professional level. Deadlines are Oct. 15 for Radcliffe Fellows and December 1 for Non-Tenured Faculty Fellows.

P-WR,VP   RAMON MAGSAYSAY AWARD FOUNDATION, Ramon Magsaysay Center, 1680 Roxas Blvd., Manila, Philippines.
RAMON MAGSAYSAY AWARD: For recognition of service to the people in the following fields: 1) government service; 2) public service; 3) community leadership; 4) journalism, literature and creative communication arts; 5) international understanding. Five annual awards of $10,000 each. Anyone.

vp   RANDOLPH MACON WOMEN'S COLLEGE, 2500 Rivermount Ave., Lynchburg, VA 24505.

all   READER'S DIGEST FND., Pleasantville, NY 10570. Several grants to projects and individuals, for higher education, scholarships in various areas.

WR-L   REAL ACADEMIA ESPANOLA, Felipe IV No. 6, Madrid, Spain. Prize for unpublished work in linguistics or Spanish literature in Spanish by a Spanish or foreign national. Anyone, biennially.

P-WR   REDBOOK YOUNG WRITERS' CONTEST, Box 2-F, 230 Park Ave., NYC 10017. Prizes from $100-$1,000 for short story on first years of adulthood.

VP   RED CLOUD INDIAN SCHOOL, Holy Rosary Mission, Pine Ridge, SD 57770. Indian Art Show for all media. $1,500 purchase award and $1,150 in prizes. Deadline May 1.

vp   GEORGE A. REDLING MEMORIAL SCHOLARSHIP.
              SEE: Art Students League of N.Y. (Talent).

P-WR   WILLIAM MARION REEDY AWARD.
              SEE: THE POETRY SOCIETY OF AMERICA.

WR   HELEN DWIGHT REID AWARD, Reid Educational Fund, c/o American Political Science Association, 1527 New Hampshire Ave., NW, Washington, DC 20036. Grants for int'l understanding via various educational projects including fels. to outstanding scholars in relevant fields. MR

VP,C   REHOBOTH ART LEAGUE, Henlopen Acres, Rehoboth Beach, DE 19971.

vp   FRANK J. REILLY MEMORIAL SCHOLARSHIP.
              SEE: Art Students League of N.Y. (Talent).

P-WR   REINA PRINSEN GEERLIGS PRIZE FOR SOUTH AFRICA, c/o Het Algemeen Nederlands Verond, Afd. Kaapstad, PO Box 4543, Cape Town 8000, South Africa.
              REINA PRINSEN GEERLIGS PRIZE FOR SOUTH AFRICA: 350 Dutch florins annually to Dutch and Flemish writers between 20-30; to writers of Afrikaans every third year.

T,WR   RELIGIOUS ART GUILD, 25 Beacon St., Boston, MA 02108. Prize of $200 for short play involving few people to be presented Sunday morning during service. Award for poetry dealing with the "spirit of humanity."

wr   RELM FOUNDATION, 9021 First National Bldg., Ann Arbor, MI 48108. Grants for higher education, 8 fels.

P-VP   REMMEY, PAUL B., AWS, MEMORIAL AWARD. Award: $200.
              SEE: AMERICAN WATERCOLOR SOCIETY.

VP,WR   RENAISSANCE ARTISTS AND WRITERS ASSOCIATION, 1240 So. Emerson St., Denver, CO 80206. Mark Friedmen.

P-A   R.S. REYNOLDS MEMORIAL AWARD FOR COMMUNITY ARCHITEC-
        TURE. Award: $5,000 and plaque. SEE: American Institute of Architecture.

vp,c   RHODE ISLAND COLLEGE, 600 Mt. Pleasant Ave., Providence, RI 02908.

vp,c,a,f RHODE ISLAND SCHOOL OF DESIGN, Film Studies, 2 College St., Provi-
        dence, RI 02903. $1,500 Grad Assist.

ALL,all RHODE ISLAND STATE COUNCIL ON THE ARTS, 334 Westminster Mall,
        Providence, RI 02903. In 1977-78 5 grants of $2,500 were given to RI artists.
        Six artists-in-residence are employed working in different media for the Coun-
        cil's Artists-in-Education program.

all   THE RHODES TRUST, c/o Wm. Barber, Wesleyan Univ., Middletown, CT
        06457.

C,VP   RHODODENDRON STATE OUTDOOR ART AND CRAFT FESTIVAL,
        3804 Noyes Ave., SE, Charleston, WV 25304. State Outdoor Art and Craft
        Festival with $3,000 in awards. Deadline May 12.

vp,a   RICE UNIV., Dept. of Fine Arts, 6100 Main St., Houston, TX 77001.

P-VP   THERESE AND EDWIN H. RICHARD MEMORIAL PRIZE. Award: $300.
        SEE: NATIONAL SCULPTURE SOCIETY.

P-VP   THERESE RICHARD MEMORIAL PRIZE. Award: $100.
        SEE: Allied Artists of America, Inc.

f   RICHMOND COLLEGE, City Univ/New York, Div. of Humanities, Staten Is-
        land, NY 10301. General schols.

c,f,vp RIDGEWOOD SCHOOL OF ART AND DESIGN, 83 Chestnut St., Ridge-
        wood, NJ 07450. Contact: Robt. Crawford, Dir. Two $700 schols each yr.

vp,a,t RIJKSAKADEMIE VAN BEELDENDE KUNSTEN, Stadhouderskade 86,
        Amsterdam Z, The Netherlands. One-year schols to advanced students from
        all countries for study in the fine arts; 20-30 yrs.

vp-h   RIJKSUNIVERSITEIT, St. Pietersnieuwstraat 25, Ghent, Belgium. Archae-
        ology and art history post grad. work only.

P-M   RIO DE JANEIRO INTERNATIONAL VOICE COMPETITION, Sociedade
        Brasileira de Realizacoes Artistico-Culturais, Avenida Franklin Roosevelt 23,
        Sala 310, Rio De Janeiro, Brazil. PRIZES: For the best singer not over 32
        years. 41,500 awarded biennially.

m,t,c, RIO HONDO COLLEGE, Fine Arts Dept., 3600 Workman Mill Rd., Whittier,
f,vp   CA 90608. Yoshio C. Nakamura. Outright grants.

137

m   RIVIER COLLEGE, Nashua, NH 03060. Various, women only.

P-WR   RIVISTA ULISSE, Sezione Premio Europeo Cortina Ulisse, Via Po, 11, Rome, Italy. Contact: The Editor.
CORTINA ULISSE PRIZE: For the best work dealing with the history and criticism of European literature. 1,000,000 liras awarded to an individual when merited, but not more than once a year.

vp   RIVERSIDE CITY COLLEGE, 3650 Fairfax Ave., Riverside, CA 92506.

vp,c   ROANOKE COMMONWEALTH UNIV., School of Art, Richmond, VA 23220.

WR   MARY ROBERTS RINEHART FOUNDATION, 516 Fifth Ave., Rm 504, NYC 10036. Contact: Exec. Dir. Grants up to $1,000 will be made to creative writers in the fields of fiction, dramw, poetry, biography, autobiography, autobiography—occasionally history. Amount of grant determined by applicant's need, merit of the project and the funda available. No set deadline. Completed works are ineligible, grants are made on behalf of works-in-progress.

m   ROBERTS WESLEYAN COLLEGE, North Chili, NY 14514. Various up to $450 per yr.

M   ROCHESTER CIVIC MUSIC, City Hall, Rochester, NY 55901. Awards discontinued.

vp,c   ROCHESTER INSTITUTE OF TECHNOLOGY, College of Fine and Applied Art, School of Art and Design, School for American Craftsmen, 1 Lomb Memorial Dr., Rochester, NY 14623.

WR,VP,T,   J.D. ROCKEFELLER III FUND, 30 Rockefeller Plaza, NYC 10020. Grants
D,M,F,C   in all the arts for encouraging understanding and cooperation between Asia and U.S.

ALL   ROCKEFELLER FOUNDATION HUMANITIES FELLOWSHIPS, The Rockefeller Foundation, 1133 Avenue of the Americas, NYC 10036. FELLOWSHIPS: Available to support the production of works of humanistic scholarship intended to illuminate and assess the values of contemporary civilization. Support will be given to applicants in the traditional areas of the humanities but proposals in fields not generally considered as humanities will also be encouraged as long as their humanistic implications and methodology are made clear. In all instances applicants must demonstrate the broad implications of their project for a deeper understanding of contemporary values. Awards cannot be made for the completion of graduate or professional studies; nor can proposals for the writing of poetry or fiction be entertained. Foreign citizens and subjects from abroad may apply, but applications must be in the English language. The ordinary grant will be of the magnitude of $10,000 to $15,000; generally no award will exceed $20,000. Stipends may cover cost of salary, travel, secretarial or research support, or research materials. Address inquiries/requests to above. Deadline for first-stage applications: October 1. Also, see Int'l. Competition for Excellence in Performance of American Music financed by this foundation.

m   ROCKEFELLER (MARTHA BAIRD) FUND FOR MUSIC, INC., One Rockefeller Plaza, Rm 3315, NYC 10020. Assists young solo performers, composers and doctoral candidates in music via individual grants towards advancement in a career.

vp   ROCKLAND COMMUNITY COLLEGE, 145 College Rd, Suffern, NY 10901.

ALL   ARTS COUNCIL OF ROCKVILLE, PO Box 1264, Rockville, MD 20850. Local awards in visual arts, music, drama, dance, film. Up to 21 yrs. Must still be students. This typifies grants made by community arts councils throughout the U.S. although many are for older professionals. Check with the arts groups of the local areas.

m   ROCKY MOUNTAIN COLLEGE, Billings, MT 59102. Various, based on need and ability.

VP   ROCKY MOUNTAIN NATIONAL WATERMEDIA EXHIBITION, Foothills Art Center, 809 15th St., Golden, CO 80401. $9,000 in awards for artists working in watermedia on paper.

vp   ROCKY MOUNTAIN SCHOOL OF ART, 1441 Ogden St., Denver, CO 80218. Several tuition award possibilities from partial to full payment in Commercial Art and Fine Art.

WR,D,   RODGERS AND HAMMERSTEIN FND., 598 Madison Ave., NYC 10022.
T,M   Several grants to projects and individuals for the advancement of the composition of music, lyrics, and writing of dramatic and musical plays, improvements of choreography and public presentation of such.

f   ROGER INSTITUTE OF TECHNOLOGY, College of Graphic Arts and Photography, Motion Picture School, One Lomb Memorial Dr., Rochester, NY 14623. Award $2,500.

m   ROLLINS COLLEGE, PO Box 160, Rollins College, Winter Park, FL 32789. Schol based on need and ability, undergrad.

vp   ROSARY HILL COLLEGE, 4380 Main St., Buffalo, NY 14226.

m   ROSARY COLLEGE GRADUATE SCHOOL OF FINE ARTS, 7900 W. Division St., River Forest, IL 60305. Contact: S. Sigrid Simlik. Approximately 10 $1,000 schols. toward tuition for graduate school of painting, sculpture, printmaking, art history and conservation in Florence, Italy. Deadline Feb. 1.

WR-H, BILLY ROSE FOUNDATION, 120 Broadway, Suite 3220, NYC 10020.
VP-H,WR Institute of Fine Arts Revolving Publication Fund. For writings in art history and other fields.

W.K. ROSE FELLOWSHIP COMMITTEE, c/o Vassar College, Poughkeepsie, NY 12601.

vp ROSEMONT COLLEGE, Rosemont, PA 19010.

P-WR, RICHARD AND HINDA ROSENTHAL FOUNDATION. Awards: Two for
VP $2,000. SEE: NATIONAL INSTITUTE OF ARTS AND LETTERS.

C,VP ROSWELL MUSEUM AND ARTS CENTER, Artist-in-Resident Program, 100 W. 11th St., Roswell, NM 88201. Grants are given for periods of 6 to 12 mos with house, studio, materials, and monthly stipend provided. Stipends can vary from $275 for the single artist to $325 plus $50 per every dependent in the family. Non-obligatory situation. Deadline March 15.

a ROTCH TRAVELLING SCHOLARSHIP, c/o Walter E. Campbell, Secy., 100 Boyleston St., Boston, MA 02116. $7,000 to U.S. citizens under 31 years, having either professional experience or education in Massachusetts. For young men and women with completed primary architectural education and one year's professional office experience to travel and study abroad. MR

ALL ROTARY FOUNDATION FELLOWSHIPS, Rotary International, 1600 Ridge Ave., Evanston, IL 60201. World-wide program of travel study, average $3,100. Single or married. Apply Rotary Club nearest you.

ALL THE MARK ROTHKO FDN., INC., Cleary, Gottlieb et al., 1 State St., Plaza, NYC 10004. $500 to $5,000 for the mature artist in an emergency situation.

WR,VP,T, HERBERT AND NANNETTE ROTHSCHILD FND., INC., 205 E. 58th St., NYC 10022. Grants with emphasis on the arts, art museums, education, projects and indiv.

P-WR ROY PUBLISHERS, INC., 30 E. 74th St.,NYC 10021.
MARIAN KISTER MEMORIAL AWARD: For the outstanding literature translation (Polish-into-English or English-into-Polish). Monetary awards of $250 and $200 annually. Anyone.

t ROYAL ACADEMY OF DRAMATIC ART, 62-64 Gower St., London WC1E 6ED England. Several scholarships possibly for up to full fee remission. There is a scholarship strictly for Americans who audition in New York for consideration.

P-M,A ROYAL ACADEMY OF BELGIUM, Division of Fine Arts, Palais des Academies, Brussels, Belgium.
IRENE FUERISON PRIZE: Monetary prize of 80,000 francs awarded to

140

the best unpublished composition in chamber music, orchestral music and vocal music. To a Belgian or foreign that has lived in Belgium for three years, not more than 35 yrs.

BARON HORTA PRIZE: In recognition of outstanding architectural work that has already been built or studied as a project. The finished work must be in one of the Common Market countries; or it must be planned to be built in one of the Common Market countries. A monetary prize of 250,000 francs is awarded every five years.

m,t   ROYAL IRISH ACADEMY OF MUSIC, 36 Westland Row, Dublin, Ireland. International Summer School of Music and Drama. Two schols. for 2 weeks in July. Anyone.

m   ROYAL OPERA HOUSE, Covent Garden, London WC2, England. Scholarship for singers any nationality. Cash plus 4 mos. training at La Scala Milan. Apply: Count Cinzano Scholarship, above.

P-WR   ROYAL SOCIETY OF LITERATURE, 1 Hyde Park Gardens, London W2, England, UK.

HEINEMAN AWARD FOR LITERATURE: To encourage and promote high quality contributions to literature. Books must have been published in the preceding year, in English. Publishers, not authors, submit books to the committee. Up to three awards, 300 pounds sterling annually.

P-WR   ROYAL SPANISH ACADEMY, Felipe IV No. 6, Madrid, Spain.

RAMON MENENDEZ PIDAL PRIZE: For outstanding work dealing with Spanish linguistics or Spanish literature. 30,000 pesetas awarded biennially.

vp,c,m   RUTGERS UNIV., Dept. of Music, New Brunswick, NJ 08903. Fund $2,500 for grad in music history or theory and composition. NDEA fel. Also MA grants restricted to faculty members.

m   MINNA KAUFMANN RUUD FOUNDATION, Chatham College, Pittsburgh, PA 15232. Contact: Peggy O'Hara, Secy to the Board. Up to $1,000. Schols awarded to students with exceptional ability in vocal music with priority to those that plan to follow careers in concert, operatic or teaching fields. Foundation sponsors Distinguished Performance Awards auditions each spring in NYC. Three $1,000 and 2 $500 awards given to women between 18-29 for exceptional ability in vocal music.

m,vp,c   SACRAMENTO STATE COLLEGE, 6000 J St., Sacramento, CA 95819. Undergrad scholarships by audition; grad. fels.

D   SACRED DANCE GUILD, Box 129, West Barnstable, MA 02668. Martha Yates.

m   SACRED HEART DOMINICAN COLLEGE, 2401 E. Holcombe Blvd., Houston, TX 77021. To entering freshmen, $2,000 scholastic ability; 4 $400 with restrictions.

WR   SACRED HEART UNIV., Bridgeport, CT 06604.
AWARD FOR EXCELLENCE IN ECUMENICAL LITERATURE: Every three years to author(s) for book best furthering knowledge of ecumenism. Book must be published by American firm three years prior to award.

m   ST. AMBROSE COLLEGE, Davenport, IA 52803. Various, for men, up to $1,050. Also Presidential schol. of $1,050 (full tuition).

m,vp   ST. ANDREWS PRESBYTERIAN COLLEGE, School of Music, Laurinburg, NC 28352. Several $200-$1,500, restrictions, renewable.

m   ST. CLOUD STATE COLLEGE, St. Cloud, MN 56301. Several $150; Grad. Assistantships.

m,vp,c   ST. JOHN'S UNIV., Collegeville, MN 56321. Mr. Bela Pethed, Off. of Financial Aid. Work and tuitional schols.

P-WR   ST. LAWRENCE AWARD FOR FICTION. Award: $1,000.
SEE: FICTION INTERNATIONAL MAGAZINE.

vp   ST. LEO COLLEGE, St. Leo, FL 33574.

m.   ST. LOUIS INSTITUTE OF MUSIC, 13550 Connway Rd, St. Louis, MO 63141. Several up to $1,000, renewable, restrict.

m   SAINT MARY COLLEGE, Xavier, KS 66098. Various small, renewable.

m   ST. MARY OF THE PLAINS COLLEGE, Dodge City, KS 67801. Various small, yearly.

m   ST. MARY'S UNIV., 2700 Cincinnati, San Antonio, TX 78228. To entering freshmen, various small, some full tuition.

m,t,vp,   SAINT MARY-OF-THE-WOODS COLLEGE, Saint Mary-of-the-Woods, IN 47876. Contact: Sister Delia Leonard, Dir. of Fin. Aid. Awards up to $500. Renewable, for demonstrated ability in the performing or creative arts and for demonstrated ability in a specific field.

vp,c   ST. NORBERT COLLEGE, West De Pere, WI 54178.

m   ST. OLAF COLLEGE, Northfield, MN 55057. Various, small.

vp,c   ST. PAUL ART CENTER SCHOOL, 30 E. 10th St., St. Paul, MN 55101.

m   SALEM COLLEGE, School of Music, Winston-Salem, NC 27108. Various, renewable. Some based on need, part-time service required.

P-VP   SALMAGUNDI CLUB AWARD. Award: $100.
SEE: ALLIED ARTISTS OF AMERICA, INC.

vp   J. SANFORD SALTUS SCHOLARSHIP.
SEE: Art Students League of N.Y. (Talent).

M,m   SAM HOUSTON STATE UNIVERSITY, Huntsville, TX 77340. Dr. Fisher A. Tull Dir. Dept. of Music. Music schols up to $150 per semester. Renewable. Audition (live or tape) required. Application and recommendation forms available from address above. Teaching assistantships for graduate students up to $3,000 per academic year.

m   SAMFORD UNIV., 800 Lakeshore Dr., Birmingham, AL 35209. Several small.

M   SAN ANGELO SYMPHONY AWARD, 607 San Angelo Nat'l. Bank Bldg., San Angelo, TX 76903. Award of $250 plus appearance with orchestra to Texans by birth or residence, under 30 yrs.

vp,c,f   SAN ANTONIO COLLEGE, 1300 San Pedro, San Antonio, TX Several small.

vp   DOROTHY SANDERS MEMORIAL SCHOLARSHIP. Recipient selected by Mrs. Ethel Katz (or her successor) as funds accrue. SEE: Art Students League of N.Y. (Talent).

m   SAN DIEGO CHORAL CLUB, 3777 44th St., San Diego, CA 92116. Ines Davenport Memorial Scholarship. Cash prize varies; age 18-25, must be studying. Two songs or arias, one in English.

f   SAN DIEGO CITY COLLEGE, Telecommunications, 1425 Russ Boulevard, San Diego, CA 92101. Contact: James Dark, Chmn. Two TV Schols. at $300 a year.

f   SAN DIEGO STATE COLLEGE, Telecommunications and Film, San Diego, CA 92115. Schols., Kogo & Linkletter $500 yearly; Merino Internship $2,500 per year.

VP   SAN DIEGO WATERCOLOR SOCIETY NATIONAL EXHIBITION, 463 Chestnut Lane, Escondido, CA 92025. National exhibit with awards and purchases. Deadline May 8 for slides of works submitted.

m,vp,c   SAN FERNANDO VALLEY STATE COLLEGE, 18111 Nordhoff St., Northridge, CA. Music achievement awards (tuition); Grad assists $1,000 per sem.

vp   SAN FRANCISCO ACADEMY OF ART, 627 Sutter St., San Francisco, CA 94101.

vp   SAN FRANCISCO ART INSTITUTE, 800 Chestnut St., SF, CA 94133. Contact: Financial Aid Ofc. SCHOLARSHIP: SFAI scholarships based on ability and need up to full tuition. Renewable, available to all.

m   SAN FRANCISCO CONSERVATORY OF MUSIC, 1201 Ortega St., San Francisco, CA 94122. Several, to $1,150.

all   THE SAN FRANCISCO FOUNDATION, 425 California St., Suite 1602, SF, CA 94104.
JAMES D. PHELAN AWARDS IN ART: Totaling $2,000 annually. Inquiries are invited each year in January, applicants must be natives of California, and between 20 & 40. Also, the Joseph H. Jackson Award of $2,000 to an author of an unpublished partly completed fiction work. Deadline Jan. 15.

M,m   SAN FRANCISCO OPERA, San Francisco/Affiliate Artists-Opera Program, c/o San Francisco Opera, War Memorial Opera House, SF, CA 94102. There are two contests in which either regional audition winners or professional operatic singers will by audition be employed year-round by San Francisco Opera or receive living stipend and housing assistance to attend a 10-week tuition-free summer training and performing program.

f   SAN FRANCISCO STATE COLLEGE, Film Dept., 1600 Halloway Ave., SF, CA 94132. Schols. to $1,130 per semester.

m,vp,c   SAN JOSE STATE COLLEGE, San Jose, CA 95114. Several, undergrads.

P-F   SAN REMO FILM FESTIVAL, c/o Nino Zucchelli, Rotonda Dei Mille, 24100 Bergamo, Italy. Prizes for the outstanding films, written and produced by the same person. Films may not have been entered in any other international festival. Grand Prize of 5,000,000 liras to be split equally between the director and producer. Grand Prize of 1,000,000 for the best artistic short. Annually. Anyone.

vp,wr,c   SANTA FE WORKSHOPS OF CONTEMPORARY ART, Box 1344, Santa Fe, NM 87501. Scholarships: For partial tuition for education in the fine arts.

P-WR   SCARECROW PRESS AWARD FOR LIBRARY LITERATURE. Award: $500 and citation. SEE: AMERICAN LIBRARY ASSOC.

P-M   SCANDINAVIAN COUNCIL, Gamla Riksdagshuset, Helgeandsholmen, Fack Stockholm 2, Sweden.
SCANDINAVIAN COUNCIL MUSIC PRIZE: Monetary award of 50,000 Swedish crowns annually to the best composition written by a living artist and performed for the first time in the last few years.

P-WR   SCANDINAVIAN COUNCIL, Helgeandsholmen, Fack, Stockholm 2, Swedenn
SCANDINAVIAN COUNCIL LITERARY PRIZE: For an outstanding

work of literature, that is current, in one of the Scandinavian languages. 50,000 Danish crowns annually.

vp   RUDOLPH SCHAEFFER SCHOOL OF DESIGN, 2255 Mariposa St., SF, CA 94110. E. Peter Docili, Secy. Tuition-free schol to high school senior sponsored through Scholastic Magazine.

all   LEOPOLD SCHEPP FND., 551 Fifth Ave., NYC 10017. Limited number of grants for independent study to highly qualified candidates under 40 yrs.

M   SCHNABEL SCHOLARSHIP FUND. Donated by Sir Robert and Lady Mayer of London. SEE: CLEVELAND, OH, INSTITUTE OF MUSIC.

vp   DANIEL SCHNAKENBERG SCHOLARSHIP: Created by 1925 gift and continued as a fund after Schnakenberg's death for gifted and worthy students. SEE: Art Students League of N.Y. (Talent).

M   SCHNITGERPRIJS ZWOLLE INT'L COMPOSITION CONTEST FOR ORGAN, Secretariat: Stichting "Schnitgerprijs Zwolle," Emmawijk 2, Zwolle, Netherlands. Cash award for organ solo composition approx. 10 minutes. Also performance at St. Albans International Organ Festival, England.

vp,wr   SCHOLASTIC MAGAZINES, INC., 50 W. 44th St., NYC 10036. More than 90 scholarship grants of up to $2,000 in writing, visual arts and photography for high school seniors only.

VP   SCHOOL OF THE ASSOCIATED ARTS, 344 Summit Ave., St. Paul, MN 55102. Contact: Virginia Rahja, Dir. Assistantships: Both masters and fellowships in commercial art, fine art and interior design.

vp   THE SCHOOL OF FASHION DESIGN, 136 Newbury St., Boston, MA 02116.

VP   SCHOOL OF FINE ARTS, Fort Wayne Art Institute, 1026 West Barry St., Fort Wayne, IN 46804.

f,vp,c   SCHOOL OF THE MUSEUM OF FINE ARTS, 230 The Fenway, Boston, MA 02115. Grant for 2 yrs study, full tuition, small stipend, restricted to natives of one of 13 southern states that comprised the Confederacy. Sixteen traveling fellowships annually; awards from $2,000-$6,000.

vp   SCHOOL OF THE PENNSYLVANIA ACADEMY OF THE FINE ARTS, Philadelphia, PA 19102. Awards for students of the school, renewable.

vp,f   SCHOOL OF VISUAL ARTS, 209 E. 23rd St., NYC 10010. Contact: Office of Vice Pres. for Academic Affairs. All of the following scholarships cover the cost of tuition for the full four years; renewable each year: SCHOOL OF VISUAL ARTS COMPETITION SCHOLARSHIPS; NEW YORK CITY

SCHOOL ART LEAGUE COMPETITION SCHOLARSHIP; NATIONAL SCHOLASTIC ART AWARD SCHOLARSHIP; THIRD WORLD SCHOLARSHIP.

vp SCHOOL OF THE WORCESTER ART MUSEUM, 55 Salisbury Street, Worcester, MA 01608. Contact: Adm. Ofc. SCHOLARSHIPS: For tuition at the School of Worcester Art Museum only. Amounts vary depending on financial need as calculated by the College Schol. Service, PCS or SFS. Required by April 1st. Maximum $1,500.

c,f,a,vp SCHOOLS OF THE ART INSTITUTE OF CHICAGO, Michigan Ave. at Adams St., Chicago, IL 60603. Schols. and loans for full-time professional degree students accepted for admission and documenting financial need. From $200-$2,000. No restrictions. Travel fels. from $1,000-$4,000 annually to 8 or 10 Grad. students.

P-M SCHUBERT INTERNATIONAL COMPETITION, Konservatorium of City of Vienna, Johannesgasse 4A, 1010 Vienna, Austria. Prizes: Monetary prizes and concerts awarded every four years to: Best pianists aged 17 to 30; Best male singer aged 22 to 32; Best female singer aged 22 to 32.

FRITZ SCHUMACHER PRIZE
SEE: FOUNDATION FREIHERR-VON-STEIN OF HAMBURG.

M ROBERT-SCHUMANN KONSERVATORIUM, Crimmitschauer Strasse 1b, Zwickau, DDR. International Robert Schumann Contest. Awards from $200 to $2,000 to all singers under 30 yrs. Apply: Sekretariat Internationaler Robert-Schumann-Wettbewerb.

P-WR DELMORE SCHWARTZ MEMORIAL POETRY AWARD.
SEE: Washington Square University College of Arts and Science of NYU.

vp,wr,m, SCRIPPS COLLEGE, 9th & Columbia Ave., Claremont, CA 91711. Contact:
d,t,f, Mrs. Elizabeth Johnson, Mrs. Patricia Martin.
c,-h SCRIPPS COLLEGE GRANTS: And scholarships to students studying the listed arts. All grants are based on financial need as determined by the information submitted on the Parents' Confidential Statement and the Student Financial Statement. Grants range from $500 to $4,500; all are renewable if need continues. File the PCS and SFS by February 1 for Fall enrollment.

P-ALL SEATTLE ART MUSEUM, Volunteer Park, Seattle, WA 98112.
  PACIFIC NORTHWEST ARTS AND CRAFTS FOUNDATION AWARD: For an accepted work in any medium in the Northwest Annual Exhibit $300 awarded.
  SEATTLE PRINT INTERNATIONAL BIENNIAL AWARD: A purchaser fund of $1,000 is awarded at the Seattle Art Museum Pavillion, Seattle Center.

CHARLES AND ESTER WEBSTER PRIZES: In honorium of excellence in art works by individuals of the Northwest region. $500 for first place, $300 for second, $200 for third. Annually.

WEST SEATTLE ART CLUB, KATHERINE B. BAKER MEMORIAL AWARD: For excellent work shown at the Annual Exhibition of Northwest Artists. Award of $100.

IRENE D. WRIGHT MEMORIAL AWARD: For the best painting and sculpture alternately, that have been entered in the Annual Exhibition by an artist living in the Northwest region. $200 awarded annually.

M   SEATTLE OPERA ASSN., INC., 158 Thomas St., Seattle, WA 98109. Singer in residence program, age 21 to 45; travel, time for other engagements.

m,vp,c   SEATTLE PACIFIC COLLEGE, School of Music, Third Ave. West at Nickerson, Seattle, WA 98119. Various.

P-WR,   THE CHARLES H. SERGEL DRAMA PRIZE. Awards totaling $3,000.
P-T   SEE: UNIVERSITY OF CHICAGO THEATER.

ALL   SEVEN LIVELY ARTS FESTIVAL, PO Box 737, Hollywood, FL 33020. Cash awards for Lively Arts Circle Art Show.

P-VP,   SEVENTEEN MAGAZINE, 320 Park Ave., NYC 10022.
WR   ART CONTEST AWARDS: For the best unpublished work that shows outstanding skill, originality, and suitability for publication. Boy or girl ages 13 through 19. Nine awards of $500, $300 and $200; six awards of $50 and publication of the winning works in the January issue of Seventeen Magazine. Annually awarded.

PHOTOGRAPHY CONTEST AWARDS: For the best unpublished work that shows outstanding skill, originality and suitability for publication. Boy or girl ages 13 through 19. Six awards of $100 each, and publication in the January issue of Seventeen Magazine. Annually awarded.

SHORT STORY CONTEST AWARDS: For the best original short story of 2,000 to 5,000 words. Boy or girl ages 13-19. Nine monetary awards: $500 for first, $300 for second, $200 for third, and six honorable mentions at $50 each. Awarded annually. Top three stories published in January issue of Seventeen Magazine.

P-WR   THE ANNE SEXTON POETRY PRIZE.
SEE: Florida International University.

vp   SHELDON JACKSON COLLEGE, Box 479, Sitka, AK 99835.

all   SHELL SCHOLARSHIPS, University of Hong Kong,. Undergrad. schols in arts, science or engineering for 4 yrs. $5,500 per annum; Grad schols for study at UK or Australian univ. Max. of 2 years, $1,500 plus transportation. Open to all nationals, preference to those in Hong Kong and Far East.

m   SHENANDOAH CONSERVATORY OF MUSIC, Winchester, VA 22601. Various up to $300.

vp,c   SHEPARD COLLEGE, Shepardstown, WV 25443.

P-M   S'HERTOGENBOSCH INTERNATIONAL COMPETITION FOR SINGERS, Hotel de Ville, s'Hertogenbosch, Netherlands. PRIZES: For the outstanding singer in each area of voice, under 32 yrs. 2,500 Dutch florins First prize; 1,000 Dutch florins, Second prize.

m   SHERWOOD MUSIC SCHOOL, 1014 So. Michigan Ave., Chicago, IL 60605. Various, up to $480.

VP   ALEXANDER SHILLING FUND AWARD. Administered by the ART Students League of N.Y. (Talent).

VP   THE SHIP SCHOLARSHIP, Scholarship Award Committee, 1464 Merchandise Mart, Chicago, IL 60654. Awards $1,000 a year to a member in good standing in the National Art Education Association. Financial need, must have had 2 yrs teaching in the profession and not be receiving other schols or grants. Applications due by Jan. 31.

m,vp   SHORTER COLLEGE, Rome GA 30161. Various mostly undergrad.

M   SHREVEPORT SYMPHONY SOCIETY, PO Box 4057, Shreveport, LA 71104. $100 and performance with Symphony, 18-32 yrs; two arias, one English, one foreign language.

WR   SHUBERT FELLOWSHIP IN PLAYWRITING, c/o Indiana Univ., Dept. of Theater and Drama, Bloomington, IN 47401. $2,500 per year, not renewable.

WR,T   SAM S. SHUBERT FND., 234 W. 44th St., NYC 10036. The Foundation no longer makes grants to individuals due to restrictions imposed by the Internal Revenue Act of 1969.

M   SIGMA ALPHA IOTA, 165 W. 82nd St., NYC 10024. Composition award to encourage Americans to write meritable works.

vp   THE SILVERMINE GUILD OF ARTISTS, INC., 1037 Silvermine Road, New Canaan, CT 06840. New England Exhibition of Painting and Sculpture for outstanding works in painting, sculpture, watercolors, etc., totaling over $5,000 annually.

d   SIMONE SUTER SCHOOL OF DANCE, Caroline 7, CH-1003 Lausanne, Switzerland.

M,m   SINFONIA FOUNDATION, 10600 Old State Rd., Evansville,IN 47711. Small grants for music research and commissioning scholarships.

M   SINGERS CLUB, Mrs. James C. Noel, Pres., 81 Bourndale Rd., Manhasset, NY 11030. $500 educational voice schols every other odd yr; 19-25, to residents of Nassau or Suffolk County or NY State.

m,vp,c,wr,   SKIDMORE COLLEGE, Saratoga Springs, NY 12866, Contact: Frampton
h,d,t,f   Davis, Dir. Finan. Aid. Various schols, loan and work awards. Anyone.

vp   SKOWHEGAN SCHOOL OF PAINTING & SCULPTURE, 329 E. 68th St.,
             NYC 10021 or Box 449, Skowhegan, ME 04976. Nine-week summer work
             program for 65 advanced students. Financial aid up to $1,950. Deadline
             Feb. 28.

VP   SLATER MEMORIAL MUSEUM, 108 Crescent St., Norwich, CT 06360.
             Awards of $50 to $250 for Connecticut residents.

vp   JOHN SLOAN MEMORIAL SCHOLARSHIP.
             SEE: Art Students League of N.Y. (Talent).

vp   SMITH COLLEGE, Northhampton, MA 01060.

P-WR   W.H. SMITH AND SON, LTD., Strand House, London WC2, England, UK.
             LITERARY AWARD: For the recognition of outstanding work in litera-
             ture by residents of the British Commonwealth; published in the previous
             two yrs, in English. 1,000 pounds annually.

P-ALL   SMITHSONIAN INSTITUTION, 1000 Jefferson Drive, SW, Washington, DC
             20560 (Office of Academic Studies). Pre- and postdoctoral fellowships pro-
             grams; summer under- and graduate programs. About $385,000 was appro-
             priated for these programs in FY '76. The SI also has foreign currency pro-
             grams for work abroad such as in archaeology and museum programs. Dead-
             lines vary each year but are generally around the first of October and March.
             For summer work the deadlines are around January 1st each year. Inquire
             of Office of Academic Services above. S. Dillon Ripley is Secretary of the
             Smithsonian and his office will supply information on new programs for
             individuals on request.
             SMITHSONIAN FELLOWSHIPS: Granted only to investigators pursuing
                research training in Smithsonian facilities and are not granted to support
                research outside the Smithsonian and its facilities. Candidates must have
                approval of their university to conduct their research at the Smithsonian.
                Postdoctoral fellowships $10,000; predoctoral $5,000. Each fellowship
                is augmented by an allowance of $1,000 to help defray the research-
                related costs incurred by the Institution. Deadline: January 15. Date
                that candidates are notified: March 15.
             SMITHSONIAN FELLOWSHIPS FOR GRADUATES AND UNDERGRAD-
                UATES: A few fellowships are available for students enrolled in formal
                university training at the graduate level, ranging from $800 to $1,000 for
                ten to twelve week periods.
             THE WALTER RATHBONE BACON SCHOLARSHIP: Awarded bienni-
                nially to a graduate or junior postdoctoral student for the purpose of
                conducting formal studies outside the U.S. $6,000. Deadline: Jan. 1.
             SHORT TIME VISITS: Financial support in small amounts is available to
                students and scholars for a short period of time, but not less than a week.

COOPERATION WITH COLLEGES AND UNIVERSITIES: The institution is interested in cooperative educational arrangements with colleges and universities. Such arrangements may follow a wide range of formats, and inquiries or proposals are invited.

THE SMITHSONIAN MEDAL: For the outstanding work in those areas of art, science, history, and technology which are the basic concern of the Smithsonian Institution. To either an individual or a team. A gold medal and monetary prize awarded annually.
Art and its history research and study in the following departments can be supported: National Museum of History and Technology, American Studies Program; Joseph Henry Papers; National Portrait Gallery; National Collection for Fine Arts,; Archives of American Art; Freer Gallery of Art; National Museum of Design: Cooper-Hewitt Collection; Hirshhorn Museum and Sculpture Garden. Institutional support services is financial in following programs: 1. Office of International and Environmental Programs, 2. Museum Programs: Office of Museum Programs, Psychological Studies Program, Office of Exhibits Central, Conservation Analytical Laboratory, Smithsonian Institution Archives, Smithsonian Institution Libraries. 3. Division of Performing Arts, 4. Information Systems Divisions, 5. Smithsonian Science Information Exchange, Inc.

vp   NAT C. SMOLIN MEMORIAL SCHOLARSHIP: For "Gifted and needy" students of painting and sculpture. SEE: Art Students League of N.Y.

ALL   SOCIAL SCIENCE RESEARCH COUNCIL, 605 Third Ave., NCY 10016. Rowland L. Mitchell, Staff Associates. Fellowships in music, for musicologists only; various restrictions. Any nationality. Write for details. MR

M   SOCIEDADE BRASILEIRA DE REALIZACOES ARTISTICAS E CULTURAIS, Ave. Franklin Roosevelt 23s/310 Centro-20,000 Rio de Janeiro, Brazil. Total prizes of $6,000 plus concerts and scholarships for singing contest.

M,D   SOCIETA DEL QUARTETTO, Casella postale 127, Vercelli, Italy. Vercelli International Music and Dance Contest. Piano, piano duets, voice and composition. Under 32 yrs except for composers. Anyone.

F-H,VP   SOCIETY FOR CINEMA STUDIES, Dept. of Cinema Studies, New York Univ., 400 South Bldg., NYC 10003. Contact: Robert Sklar.

M   SOCIETY FOR STRINGS, Meadowmount, West Port, RFD 2, Essex County, New York, NY 12993. Ivan Galamian.

P-WR   SOCIETY FOR THE STUDY OF SOUTHERN LITERATURE, c/o Sewanee Review, Sewanee, TN 37375.
EDD WINFIELD PARKS AWARD: For an outstanding study of Southern letters published by the University of Georgia Press. If merited, awarded annually to the author or editor. Prize of $500.

P-VP   THE SOCIETY OF AMERICAN GRAPHIC ARTISTS, Rm 1214, 32 Union Square, NYC 10003. Prizes awarded in national exhibitions of printmaking, etching, lithography, serigraphy, woodcut/engraving. Contact Stanley Kaplan.

WR   SOCIETY OF AMERICAN HISTORIANS, INC., Fayerweather Hall, Columbia Univ., NYC 10027. Prize for book in history or biography best combining sound scholarship and literary excellence.

M   SOCIETY OF AMERICAN MUSICIANS CONTEST, Tribune Tower, Rm 468, 435 No. Michigan Ave., Chicago, IL 60611.
   CHICAGOLAND MUSIC CONTEST: High school seniors or performers under 25 yrs; residents of Illinois, Michigan, Iowa, or Wisconsin. Prize $2,000. MR

P-WR   SOCIETY OF AUSTRALIAN WRITERS, Australia House, Strand, London, England, UK.
   SIR THOMAS WHITE MEMORIAL PRIZE: For outstanding literary work. $500 awarded annually.

WR   SOCIETY OF MIDLAND AUTHORS, 2020 N. Howe St., Chicago, IL 60614. Midland Poetry and Society Awards to residents of Midwest $250. MR

P-M   SOFIA INTERNATIONAL COMPETITION FOR YOUNG OPERA SINGERS, Bulgarian Committee for the Arts and Culture, Office of Bulgarian Music, Blvd. Stambolijski 17, Sofia, Bulgaria. For outstanding work of young opera singers no older than 33 years. Grand Prize of the City of Sofia: Gold Medal, gold ring, a diploma and 5,000 leva. Many other prizes and money awarded. Every three years.

P-M   LEONIE SONNING MUSIC FOUNDATION, c/o A. Richard Moeller, Esq., H.C. Andersens Boulevard 40, 1553 Copenhagen, V, Denmark. Application is not possible but the assumption is that the award still exists.

WR   THE SONS OF THE REPUBLIC OF TEXAS, 2426 Watts Rd., Houston, TX 77025.
   SUMMERFIELD G. ROBERTS AWARD: For outstanding literature pertaining to the period of the Republic of Texas, fiction or nonfiction, poems, essays, etc. $1,000 annually.

all   SOUTH CAROLINA ARTS COMMISSION, 829 Richland St., Columbia, SC 29201. Contact: Grants Coordinator.
   PERSONNEL DEVELOPMENT PROGRAM: Grants up to $6,000 for salary assistance for professional personnel of arts organizations. March 1 deadline for following fiscal year.
   CONSULTANTS PROGRAM: Grants under $750 provide assistance to any nonprofit organization in arts related problem. Open deadline.
   IN RESIDENCE PERFORMING ARTS: To assist community organizations sponsor performing art residencies, including workshops or other

educational activities. Amount open, no deadline, two per year.
COMMUNITY PROJECTS SUPPORT: For local arts programming by any
nonprofit organization, deadline twice yearly, amount open.
YOUTH FILM PRODUCTION GRANTS: Small grants to youth to produce
short Super-8mm films.
INDIVIDUAL ARTISTS GRANT: Project based grant to assist in creation
of work, development of artist's work, through undertaking of projects
of benefit to artist and South Carolina citizens. Amount open, deadline:
March or spring.
CONTEMPORARY ORCHESTRAL MUSIC RENTAL: Small grants to rent
contemporary music open to symphony orchestras in the state. Amount
limited, deadline about October 1.
PERFORMING ARTS TICKET SUBSIDY: Grants to provide ticket subsidy to enable disadvantaged institutionalized and elderly persons to
attend performing arts productions at low or no cost. Amount limited
to $200 per grant: deadline open.
DANCE TOURING PROGRAM: Grants awarded to assist South Carolina
sponsors of the NEA Dance Touring Program. Amount limited to 1/3
company fee, deadline: none.

ALL   SOUTH DAKOTA ARTS COUNCIL, 108 West 11th St., Sioux Falls, SD
57102. Charlotte Carver, Exec. Dir. Grants from $500-$1,000 for residents
of South Dakota (at least 2 years residency) and unavailable to previous
recipients of National Endowment or SD Arts Council grants within the last
2 years. Renewable for 3-year period.

ALL,all   SOUTH DAKOTA STATE FINE ARTS COUNCIL, 108 W. 11th St., Sioux
FAlls, SD 57102. Grants up to $1,000 for non-student artists who have con-
tributed to South Dakota arts during the previous 2 years. Deadline March 15.

f   SOUTH DAKOTA STATE UNIV., Brookings, SD 57006. Contact: Dr. Wayne
E. Hoogestraat, Dept. of Speech. SCHOLARSHIPS: KELO-TV $200; South
Dakota Broadcasters Association $200.

vp,c   SOUTHEAST MISSOURI STATE COLLEGE, Normal Ave., Cape Girardeau,
MO 63701.

VP   SOUTHEASTERN CENTER FOR CONTEMPORARY ART, 750 Marquer-
ite Dr., Winston-Salem, NC 27106. Restricted to certain states. Gives seven
grants of $2,000 each to artists 18 yrs of age or older every 18 months.

m   SOUTHEASTERN LOUISIANA COLLEGE, Hammond, LA 70401. Scholarships, renewable with audition, personal or tape. Grad Assistantships.

vp,c   SOUTHEASTERN MASS. TECHNOLOGICAL INSTITUTE, North Dartmouth, MA 02747.

vp,c   SOUTHEASTERN STATE COLLEGE, Durant, OK 74701. Several, small.

VP,VP-H   SOUTHERN ASSOCIATION OF SCULPTURS, Inc., Art Dept., Univ/South Carolina, Columbia, SC 29208. Awards up to $750 made annually. Sculpture in any medium including documentation. Deadline November.

m,vp   SOUTHERN COLORADO STATE COLLEGE, 900 West Orman Ave., Pueblo, CO 81005. Several, renewable, restrictions, undergrad.

vp,m,c   SOUTHERN ILLINOIS UNIVERSITY, Carbondale, IL 62901. Thirteen grad assistantships at $290/mo. for nine months.

m,vp,c,f   SOUTHERN METHODIST UNIV., Dallas, TX 75222. Tuition awards based on proficiency and need. Grad. Assistantships to $1,000. Broadcast-Film Art $1,000.

vp   SOUTHWEST BAPTIST COLLEGE, Bolivar, MO 65613.

WR   SOUTHWEST REVIEW, Southern Methodist Univ. Press, Dallas, TX 75222. Award of $500 for work previously published in the Southwest Review.

vp,c,m,t   SOUTHWEST TEXAS STATE UNIV., San Marcos, TX 78666. Contact: Dr. Arlis Hiebert (Music), Charles Suckle (Art). Scholarships to $300 for best music audition. Also, University Scholars Program with $1,000 per year (up to 4 years) for music, theatrical and visual arts students, and teaching assistantships for graduate students in music or theater with $2,300 per year.

T   SOUTHWEST THEATER CONFERENCE NEW PLAY AWARD, Southwest Texas State Univ., Dept. of Speech and Drama, San Marcos, TX 78666. Annual prize of $1,000, production and travel expense for unproduced full-length play or collection of one-acts.

m   SOUTHWESTERN BAPTIST THEOLOGICAL SEMINARY, School of Church Music, PO Box 22, Fort Worth, TX 76122. Various, small, grad fels. to students already in residence.

m   SOUTHWESTERN COLLEGE, Winfield, KS 67156. Several small to entering freshmen.

vp   SOUTHWESTERN UNIV., Box 272, SU Sta., Georgetown, TX 78626.

all   GOVERNMENT OF SPAIN, c/o Cultural Counselor, Embassy of Spain, 1629 Columbia Rd., NW, Apt. 625, Washington, DC 20009. Must have BA and knowledge of Spanish. Many small, 8 mos.

vp   THE SPANISH INSTITUTE, 684 Park Ave., NYC 10021. Fels. for study in art, archaeology; support also for literary works. Spanish and U.S. citizens.

P-WR   SPANISH MINISTRY OF INFORMATION AND TOURISM, Avenida del Generalisimo 39, Madrid 16, Spain.

NATIONAL TOURISM PRIZE: For literature (writers, journalists) that help the tourism trade in Spain. 50,000 pesetas.

vp   EMILY FERRIER SPEAR SCHOLARSHIP FUND.
SEE: Art Students League of N.Y. (Talent).

P-VP   SPECIAL TECHNICAL AWARD: Photojournalism.
SEE: American Society of Magazine Photographers.

ROSS PAINE SPERRY SCHOLARSHIP, c/o Univ/So. California, University Park, LA, CA 90007. $1,000.

vp,c   SPOKANE COMMUNITY COLLEGE, W. 3410Ft. George Wright Dr., Spokane, WA 99204.

vp,c   SPRING ARBOR COLLEGE, Spring Arbor, MI 49283.

vp,c   SPRINGFIELD COLLEGE, 263 Alden St., Springfield, MA 01109.

T,WR,   SQUAW VALLEY COMMUNITY OF WRITERS, Squaw Valley Creative Arts
t,wr   Society, 725 Second St., #202, SF, CA 94107. Eight screenwriters and playwrights picked for 2-week program of taping of scenes and workshops. Poets also for one week. Award is scholarship help for all disciplines. Deadline May 15. In August write to PO Box 2352, Olympic Valley, CA 95730.

vp,a   STAATLICHE HOCHSCHULE FUR BILDENDE KUNSTE BERLIN, Hardenburgstr., 33, 1 Berlin 12 (Charlottenburg), Germany. Eight awards, 2 semesters, not renewable, tenable in Berlin. Age 18-30, at least 2 semesters of professional study in home country. Monthly stipends.

vp   JOHN AND ANNA LEE STACEY SCHOLARSHIP COMMITTEE, 411 Locust, Laguna Beach, CA 92651. Students of conservative painting and drawing usually between 18-35 yrs, Americans for study in any country. MR

f,vp   STANFORD UNIVERSITY, Stanford, CA 94305. Contact: Prof. Lorenz Eitner, Chmn. Grants & Fellowships: Available in these disciplines: Painting, Sculpture, Photography, Design, and Printmaking. For students in Master of Fine Arts Programs. Partial and full tuition. Some Course Assistantships also available.

vp   STANISLAUS STATE COLLEGE, 800 Monte Vista Ave., Turlock, CA 95380.

T,M   STANLEY DRAMA AWARD, Wagner College, 631 Howard Ave., Staten Island, NY 10301. Award of $800 for unpublished play or musical recommended by a teacher of drama or creative writing, critic, director, agent or another playwright. Deadline June 1.

ALL   STATE ARTS AGENCIES. Located in various states and known as State
          Arts Councils or otherwise. Some give grants to individuals and more are
          beginning to do so. See front matter of this book for more notes on state
          activities in this area.

m   STATE COLLEGE OF ARKANSAS, Conway, AR 72032. Severalfor band,
          choir and orchestra.

a   STATE SCHOOL OF ARCHITECTURAL ENGINEERING, Stahn-Wall 11,
          307 Neinburg/Weser, Germany. Monthly stipends for 3 years. Competency
          in English and German.

a   STATE SCHOOL OF ARCHITECTURAL ENGINEERING, Irminenfreihof 8,
          55 Trier, FDR. Seventy 3-yr schols. To any national of 18-36 yrs with 2 yrs
          professional experience in building and knowledge of German and other mod-
          ern languages.

m   STATE UNIV. OF IOWA, Iowa City, IA 52240. Numerous graduate assists,
          to $2,400. Tuition schols., fels, research assist. Special compositoon schol
          $3,000.

vp,c   STATE UNIV. OF NEW YORK AT ALBANY, 1400 Washington Ave., Al-
          bany, NY 12203.

vp   STATE UNIV. OF NEW YORK AGRICULTURAL AND TECHNICAL COL-
          LEGE, Alfred, NY 14802.

m,m-h   STATE UNIV. OF NEW YORK COLLEGE AT BINGHAMTON, Dept. of
          Music, Binghamton, NY 13901. Grad fels to $3,250 plus remission of tuition .

vp,c   STATE UNIV. OF NEW YORK, College of Ceramics at Alfred, Alfred, NY
          14802.

f   STATE UNIVERSITY OF NEW YORK AT BUFFALO, Center for Media
          Study, Richmond-Quadrangle, Bldg. 4, Amherst, NY 14261. Contact: Ms.
          Chris Nygren. $3,000 graduate fellowship.

vp   STATE UNIV. OF NEW YORK, College at Oneonta, Oneonta, NY 13820.

m   STATE UNIV. COLLEGE AT POTSDAM, Potsdam, NY 13676. Various,
          graduate assistantships.

A   THE STEEDMAN FELLOWSHIP, The Steedman Committee, School of
          Architecture, Washington University, St. Louis, MO 63130. Open to archi-
          tects who have graduated from accredited schools, practiced architecture
          some years following graduation and enter the competition. Write for de-
          tails. Deadline Oct. 10.

vp   JAMES HARRISON STEEDMAN, c/o Washington Univ., St. Louis, MO
          63130. Fel. in Art, to $3,000, under 31. MR

WR,wr   WALLACE STEGNER FELLOWSHIPS IN CREATIVE WRITING, Stanford Univ., Dept. of English, Stanford, CA 94305. Four fellowships in writing and two in poetry offered to young writers who can benefit from a year's residence at the University. Each fellowship has a stipend of $5,000. Deadline Jan. 15.

vp,c   STEPHEN F. AUSTIN STATE COLLEGE, Nacogdoches, TX 75961. Various undergrad schols; grad fels.

vp,m,d, STEPHENS COLLEGE, Columbia, MO 65201. Contact: Herbert Mudie, Dir.
t,wr,-h of Adm. HONORS SCHOLARSHIPS: $2,000 a year, up to four years, several offered to new students only, for merit and accomplishment in one or more arts.

WR   THE PHILIP M. STERN FAMILY FUND, 2005 L St., NW, Washington, DC 20005. Research grants to indiv. and projects for proposed magazine articles in the fields of public affairs, science and medicine.

m   STETSON UNIV., School of Music, Deland, FL 32720. Need with musical ability, undergrads.

A   JOHN STEWARDSON MEMORIAL SCHOLARSHIP IN ARCHITECTURE, c/o Managing Committee, 1637 Race St., Philadelphia, PA 19103. $3,000 for 5-9 months in Europe or elsewhere abroad for study of ancient or modern architecture. Must be at least one year resident in Pennsylvania.   MR

vp   STILLMAN COLLEGE, 3601 15th St., Tuscaloosa, AL 35402

WR   IRVING AND JEAN STONE FELLOWSHIP, c/o Doubleday & Co. Inc., 277 Park Ave., NYC 10017. For best biographical novel of the year and best historical novel of the year. $1,000 annually.

P-VP   STOUT, CLARE, AWARD. Award: $250.
         SEE: AMERICAN WATERCOLOR SOCIETY.

P-M   STROUD FESTIVAL INTERNATIONAL COMPOSERS COMPETITION, Lenton, Houndscroft, Stroud, Gloucester GL 5DG, S England. 600 pounds and performance at the Stroud Music Festival for short work by composer under 40. Deadline April 30.

M   STUDIO CLUB OF THE YWCA, Craft Bldg., Communications, 600 Lexington Ave., NYC 10022. Annual cash awards and use of Studio Hall for recitals. MR

vp   SUE BENNETT JR. COLLEGE, London, KY 40471.

vp   SULLINS COLLEGE, Bristol, VA 24201. Students in upper half of academic work in high school eligibel for two-year scholarship.

P-A   LOUIS SULLIVAN AWARD FOR ARCHITECTURE. Award: $5,000 and plaque. SEE: AMERICAN INSTITUTE OF ARCHITECTS.

M   SULLIVAN (WILLIAM MATHEUS) MUSICAL FND., 36 W. 44th St., NYC 10036. Cash prizes in varying amounts for music study in U.S. Under 32 yrs, recommendations by teacher and 2 outstanding musicians. MR

m   SUL ROSS STATE COLLEGE, Alpine, TX 79830. Numerous scholarships, grad fels.

m   SUSQUEHANNA UNIV., Selinsgrove, PA 17876. To entering freshmen, to $650, performance ability, renewable.

P-F,f   SUTTER CINEMA, INC., 369 Sutter, SF, CA 94108.
INTERNATIONAL EROTIC FILM FESTIVAL AWARDS: $500 is awarded, four awards, for the best erotic films instead of the usual pornographic films. Anyone.

all   SWISS FEDERAL INSTITUTE OF TECHNOLOGY, SWISS-AMERICAN STUDENTS' EXCHANGE, Leonjardstr 33, 8006 Zurich, Switzerland. (a) Approx. $1,250 to U.S. grads over 22 yrs. (VP-H) Approx. $1,200 at Univ. of Basel to U.S. cits with command of German. (Unrestricted) Approx. $1,250 at Univ. of Neuchatel to U.S. national 21 yrs and over with degree and good knowledge of French.

P-WR   SWISS TEACHERS ASSOCIATION, Ringstrasse 54, 8057 Zurich, Switzerland.
CHILDREN'S BOOK PRIZE: For an excellent collection of writings by an author in the field of juvenile literature. 1,000 Swiss francs annually.

C,VP   SYLACAUGA AREA COUNCIL ON ARTS AND HUMANITIES, PO Box 1245, Sylacauga, AL 35150. $3,000 in prizes for arts and crafts exhibition. Deadline June 12.

M/   SYMPHONY ASSOCIATION OF ORANGE COUNTY, 777 South Main St., Orange, CA 92668. Voice, Piano and instrumental. Cash awards, solo appearance with orchestra. Anyone. MR Apply Mr. & Mrs. Milton Lee, Chairmen, above.

m   SYMPHONY SOCIETY OF SAN ANTONIO, Suite 102, 600 Hemisfair Plaza Way, San Antonio, TX 78205. Joske Scholarship based on competition.

a,f,m,   SYRACUSE UNIV., School of Art, Syracuse, NY 13210. Remitted tuition vp,c   plus living stipend up to $2,000. All grants are contingent upon acceptance to the Univ. graduate school. Several grad assist, up to $2,900.

WR   TABA (SEE: The American Book Awards of the American Academy of Book Awards, c/o AAP, 1 Park Ave., NYC 10016).

T   MARK TAPER FORUM, Center Theatre Group, 135 N. Grant Ave., LA, CA 90012. Some funding available to playwright selected for performance in order that he may attend. Anyone.

m   TARKIO COLLEGE, Tarkio, MO 64491. Many small, per trimester.

P-M   TCHAIKOVSKY INTERNATIONAL MUSIC COMPETITION, Organizing Committee, 15, Neglinnaya St., Moscow, USSR. PRIZES: Monetary awards every four years for the best pianist, violinist and singer of Tchaikovsky music.

M,D   TEATRO MASSIMO, E.A.T.M. Ente Autonomo Teatro Massimo, Piazza Giuseppe Verdi, Palermo, Italy. Contact: Centro Avviamento Teatro Lirico. A $3,000 study grant is renewable. For the School of Dance and the School of Opera Singers. Anyone.

P-VP   TECHNICAL ACHIEVEMENT AWARD (in photography).
        SEE: American Society of Magazine Photographers.

P-VP   TEMPLE PURCHASE PRIZE FUND.
        SEE: THE PENNSYLVANIA ACADEMY OF FINE ARTS.

f   TEMPLE UNIVERSITY, Radio-Television-Film Dept., Philadelphia, PA 19122. Contact: Prof. John B. Roberts, Chmn. Twenty-four Grad. assistantships $3,000, $3,250 per year, plus full tuition remission. Renewable for second year for work toward MA or PhD in Communications.

all   TENNESSEE ARTS COMMISSION, 222 Capitol Hill Bldg., Nashville, TN 37219. Purchasing program of artists works for a traveling exhibition. Also, $5,000 annual grants for artist who resides in Tennessee during the year.

a   TEXAS A&M UNIV., College Station, TX 77843.

m   TEXAS BOYS CHOIR COMPETITION, PO Box 1303, Fort Worth, TX 76101. $500 prize and public performance to any U.S. college or univ student under 30 yrs. for 10-18 min. music composition for boys voices. MR

vp,d,m, TEXAS CHRISTIAN UNIVERSITY, School of Fine Arts, Fort Worth, TX
t,f,c   76129. Contact: Ofc. of Financial Aid.
        THE NORDAN FINE ARTS SCHOLARSHIPS: For superior talent in Art, Ballet/Modern Dance Music and Theatre. $8,000 over four years for undergrads or $4,000 over two years for grad students. Renewable, awarded on a competitive basis and/or interview. Applications must be received by February 1, except for Art, March 15.
        ACTIVITY AWARDS: 1) Band—Awards available to some members of Horned Frog Band. Up to ½ of tuition. Renewable, recommendations by Director of Bands after audition. No deadline. 2) Orchestra and Choral Program—Awards available to those who qualify for participa-

tion in the Univ. Orchestra or the Choral Program. Up to ½ tuition. Recommendations by the directors of these activities.

T.C.U. FINE ARTS GUILD SCHOLARSHIPS: $50,593 to provide aid to talented and needy students who wish to seek professional training in one of the fine arts.

THE OLIVE EDRINGTON HEARNE MUSIC SCHOLARSHIP: $500.

JANE LANGDON MUSIC SCHOLARSHIP—$30,210.

T. SMITH MC CORKLE SCHOLARSHIP—$6,407.

PAULYNE RAY MEMORIAL SCHOLARSHIP FUND—$2,900.

JEANETTE TILLETT SCHOLARSHIP—$5,362 (for piano).

THE SAMUEL P. ZIEGLER ART SCHOLARSHIP FUND: $7,514.

THE T. SMITH MC CORKLE MEMORIAL AWARD OF $200 goes annually to the outstanding undergraduate student of organ chosen by a Faculty Auditioning Committee each spring. It is applied to the winner's tuition costs for the following year.

THEODORE PRESSER SCHOLARSHIP: $400 annually, given by the Presser Foundation for undergraduates in music. Awarded on recommendation of the Dean of the School of Fine Arts, subject to regulations of the Presser Foundation.

O.K. SHANNON SR., VIOLIN SCHOLARSHIP: $500 is awarded to the outstanding student and violinist on the basis of an audition in the preceding spring.

One assistantship in film; one in television.

m   TEXAS COLLEGE OF ARTS & INDUSTRIES, Kingsville, TX 78363. To entering freshmen, several on need; grad fels.

all   TEXAS COMMISSION ON THE ARTS AND HUMANITIES, PO Box 13406, Capitol Station, Austin, TX 78711. Artists-in-schools.

P-C   TEXAS CRAFTSMAN EXHIBITION AWARDS.
SEE: DALLAS MUSEUM OF FINE ARTS.

WR   TEXAS INSTITUTE OF LETTERS, Box 7219, Austin, TX 78712.

CARR P. COLLINS AWARD: For the best in nonfiction to a Texan, or to author of nonfiction on Texas subject, $1,000, annually.

JESSE H. JONES AWARD: For the outstanding in fiction. To Texas author or to an author of a book on a Texas subject, $1,000, awarded annually.

THE SHORT STORY AWARD: In honorium of the best short story by a Texas author (one who was born in Texas, who presently lives in Texas, or who spent the formative years in Texas). $250 awarded annually.

THE STECK-VAUGHN AWARD: For the best children's book written by a Texas author, or written about Texas. $200 awarded annually.

VOERTMAN POETRY AWARD: For the outstanding book of poetry. To a Texas poet or for poetry about Texas. $200 awarded annually.

STANLEY WALKER JOURNALISM AWARD: For the best work of journalism. $250 awarded to a Texas journalist only.

m   TEXAS LUTHERAN COLLEGE, Sequin, TX 78155. Up to $200 per semester, renewable.

P-VP   TEXAS PAINTING & SCULPTURE EXHIBITION. Awards: From $200 to $1,000. SEE: DALLAS MUSEUM OF FINE ARTS.

m   TEXAS-SWEDISH CULTURAL FND., 3400 Montrose Blvd., Houston, TX 77006. Up to $1,000 to U.S. citizens in Texas. Must have degree. Apply: Royal Consulate General of Sweden, PO Box 66327, Houston, TX 77006. MR

m,a,f   TEXAS TECHNOLOGICAL COLLEGE, Lubbock, TX 79409. Various, grad fels. KCRS Film Scholarship for $750.

m,vp   TEXAS WESLEYAN COLLEGE, PO Box 3277, Fort Worth, TX 76105. Varying number and amounts depending on performance ability.

m,vp   TEXAS WOMEN'S UNIV., Box 3865, TWU Station, Denton, TX 76204. Women only, several, grad fels.

T   THEATER AMERICANA, Box 245, Altadena, CA 91104. $300 for best 3-act play submitted. Four finalists' plays are produced.

T   THEATER ARTS CORPORATION, PO Box 2677, Santa Fe, NM 87501. $500 for two plays in the adult category and one award of $200 for a children's play. Deadline Dec. 1.

AM,T   THEATRE COMMUNICATIONS GROUP, 355 Lexington Ave., 4th Floor, NYC 10017. Opportunity for theatre artists and administrators to tour the country observing nonprofit professional theatres. The Group pays for transportation only.

T   THEATRE EMERGENCY FUND, c/o Theatre Development Fund, 1501 Broadway, NYC 10036. Very limited fund for theatre persons in an emergency.

WR   THE THEATRE LIBRARY ASSOCIATION, c/o Prof. Robert H. Ball, No. Washington St., Port Washington, NY 11050. Award to recognized work published in U.S. in legitimate theater.

T   THEATRE USA, Univ/South Alabama, 307 University Blvd., Mobile, AL 36688. Playwright and a critic of the playwright's choice is given transportation to view his play's production.

M   THEBOM (BLANCHE) FND., INC., 205 W. 57th St., NYC 10019. $1,000 to be applied to study in NYC only to young professional singer 25-30 with past or present prof. engagements. MR

vp,c   THOMAS MORE COLLEGE, Box 85, Covington, KY 41017.

m   THE THORNE MUSIC FUND, INC., 116 E. 66th St., NYC 10021. Fellow-
        ship to composers of widely recognized accomplishment and mature years.
        Amounts vary according to need, from $5,000 to $15,000. This fund has
        been given support from the U.S. Arts Endowment and in the first seven
        years of its existence has given grants in excess of $210,000. A panel of top
        leaders in music selects grantees.

c   THOUSAND ISLANDS MUSEUM CRAFT SCHOOL, 314 John St., Clayton,
        NY 13624. Contact: Marjorie M. Coyle. Scholarships that have been donated
        to the school are awarded to local students only. Schol. covers one course
        that the student is interested in.

C,VP   THREE RIVERS ARTS FESTIVAL, 4400 Forbes Ave., Pittsburgh, PA
        15213. Arts festival with $3,000 awards and corporate purchases. Artists
        from Western Pennsylvania, Deadline March 30.

P-WR   EUNICE TIETJENS MEMORIAL PRIZE. Award: $100.
        SEE: POETRY MAGAZINE.

VP   LOUIS COMFORT TIFFANY FOUNDATION, 1083 Fifth Ave., NYC 10028.
        Based on demonstrated talent.

P-F,f   TOKYO FILM ART FESTIVAL, c/o Hiroshi Teshigahara, Sogetsu Art Center
        2-21 Akasaka, Minato-ku, Tokyo, Japan. AWARDS: For the outstanding
        film with a diploma and 200,000 yen. Prizes for encouragement with a
        monetary value of 50,000 and diploma. Annually. Anyone.

WR   TONATIUH INTERNATIONAL, INC., 2150 Shattuck Ave., Berkeley, CA
        94704. Prize of $1,000, publication and royalties for work by a Chicano
        author. Deadline Dece. 31.

P-M   TOULOUSE INTERNATIONAL VOICE COMPETITION, Theatre du Capi-
        tole, 31000 Toulouse, France. Contact: The Secretariat. PRIZES: Total
        of $8,800 awarded annually to the best singers from 19 to 32 years. Dead-
        line Sept. 15.

P-M   TOURIST REVUES INTERNATIONAL, Notabile, Malta.
        MALTA INTERNATIONAL CHRISTMAS SONGS FESTIVAL PRIZES:
        175 pounds sterling awarded annually to the composers and authors who
        present the best three songs dealing with peace in the world.

vp   HOWARD TRAFTON MEMORIAL SCHOLARSHIP. SEE: Art Students
        League of N.Y. (Talent).

P-F   TRENTO INTERNATIONAL FESTIVAL OF MOUNTAIN AND EXPLORA-
        TION FILMS, c/o Giuseppe Grassi, Dir., Via Belenzani 3, 38100 Trento,
        Italy.
        GRAND PRIZE OF THE CITY OF TRENTO: Awarded to the film which

incorporates high artistic qualities, and best keeps with the human and cultural values which inspire the festival. Anyone.
PRIZE OF THE ITALIAN ALPINE CLUB: 1,000,000 lira and a goldplate for the outstanding mountaineering film. Awarded annually. Anyone.

P-M   TREVISO TEATRO COMUNALE, Treviso, Italy.
TREVISO LYRIC PRIZE: For the outstanding performance by an opera singer. 1,000,000 liras awarded annually.

P-M   TRIESTE INTERNATIONAL COMPETITION FOR SYMPHONIC COMPO-
SITION, Conservatorio di Musica "G. Tartini," Via Ghega 12, 1-34132 Trieste, Italy.
TRIESTE CITY PRIZE: For the outstanding work in symphonic composition. First prize: 2,000,000 liras. Second: 750,000 liras. Third: 250,-
000. Annually.

vp   TRINITY UNIV., 715 Stadium Dr., San Antonio, TX 78212.

P-VP   S.J. WALLACE TRUMAN PRIZE. Award: $700.
SEE: NATIONAL ACADEMY OF DESIGN.

VP   ALLEN TUCKER SCHOLARSHIPS FOR PAINTING: Administered
through the Art Students League of N.Y. (Talent).

vp,c   TUFTS UNIV., Medford, MA

vp,c,a TULANE UNIV., Newcomb Art Dept., New Orleans, LA 70118.

vp   TULLAHOMA FINE ARTS CENTER, INC., 401 S. Jackson St., Tullahoma,
TN 37388. Tuition to Motlow State Community College for high school
senior majoring in art.

P-VP   TURKISH MINISTRY OF CULTURE, Directorate General of Fine Arts,
Ankara, Turkey.
CHILDREN'S PAINTINGS OF ATATURK PRIZE: To strengthen social
and cultural ties with the other nations, and to help encourage the cre-
ativity of children by rewarding their best paintings and to offer the
world the ideas of Ataturk and Turkey. Monetary prizes are awarded
every two years.

vp   THE TUTOR PLAN OF HOME STUDIO INSTRUCTION, Box 297, Ruidoso,
NM 88345.

vp,c   TYLER SCHOOL OF ART OF TEMPLE UNIV., Beech and Penrose Aves.,
Philadelphia, PA 19126.

M   UFFICIO DE RAPPRESENTANZA DELLA SOCIETA ITALIANA degli
Autori ed Editori Segreteria del Premio Musicale Guida Valcarenghi, Foro

Buonaparte 18, 20121 Milan, Italy. Approx. $1,600 to any composer of unpublished composition never performed. Also performance. Triennial beginning '70.

vp   ULSTER COUNTY COMMUNITY COLLEGE, Stone Ridge, NY 12484.

all   UNESCO, Place de Fontenoy, Paris 7e, France. International Audio-Visual Institute for Music, Dance and Theater helps composers, authors, choreographers and designers with problems of new modes of expression which mass media offer, so as to encourage new art forms. Opportunities to learn special techniques demanded of artists in all disciplines. Kalinga Prize for the Popularization of Science offered by Mr. B. Patnaik of India; $3,000 for achievement in the dissemination of science. Anyone.

vp   UNION COLLEGE, Union St., Schenectady, NY 12308.

mt,   UNION COLLEGE, Barbourville, KY 40906. SCHOLARSHIPS: $1,000 a yr max renewable. Need for performance specialty and skill in music. Schol. for theater based on skills, both acting and technical.

m   UNION THEOLOGICAL SEMINARY, School of Sacred Music, 3041 Broadway, NYC 10027. Several, to $1,000; numerous smaller.

m   UNITED CHORAL SOCIETY, Box 73, Cedarhurst, NY 11616. Ernest Block Award $350 plus publication to American or foreign composers in choral composition sacred or secular, accompanied or unaccompanied.

WR   UNITED DAUGHTERS OF THE CONFEDERACY, 328 North Blvd., Richmond, VA 23230. Grants-in-aid for publication of unpublished book or monograph dealing with Southern history. Apply: Chmn of the Committee on Mrs. Simon Baruch Award, above.

ALL,all   U.S. ENDOWMENT FOR THE ARTS.
            SEE: NATIONAL ENDOWMENT FOR THE ARTS.

ALL-H,   U.S. HUMANITIES ENDOWMENT.
all-h   SEE: NATIONAL ENDOWMENT FOR THE HUMANITIES.

F   U.S. INTERNATIONAL COMMUNICATIONS AGENCY, Motion Picture and Television Div., U.S. International Communications Agency 1MV-R, 1776 Pennsylvania Ave., NW, Washington, DC 20547. Purchase, rental and distribution of filmmakers depicting different aspects of American life.

m,d,t,f   UNITED STATES INTERNATIONAL UNIVERSITY, School of Performing Arts, 350 Cedar St., San Diego, CA 92101. Scholarships and grants-in-aid covering partial or full tuition. Usually $700-$1,000. Deadline Feb. 15.

VP   UNITED STATES POSTAL SERVICE, Director, Citizens Stamp Advisory Committee, Office Stamps, Rm 5700, U.S. Postal Service, 475 L'Enfant Plaza

West, SW, Washington, DC 20260. Commissions for designing commemorative postage stamps.

M   UNIVERSIDAD CENTRAL DE VENEZUELA, Caracas, Venezuela. International Guitar Contest. Apply: Direccion de Cultura above. Anyone.

m,f,vp   UNIVERSITY OF ALABAMA, Broadcast-Film Communication, Drawer D, University, AL 35486. Contact: W. Knox Hagood, Chmn. Four graduate assistantships ($2,450 each), undergrad. scholarships ($450 and $510 avg.).

vp,c   UNIVERSITY OF ALBUQUERQUE, St. Joseph Pl., NW, Albuquerque, NM 87105.

m   UNIVERSITY OF ALBERTA, Edmonton, Alta, Canada. Various.

vp,c   UNIVERSITY OF THE AMERICAS, Centro de Arts, KM16 Carretera Mexico-Toluca, Mexico 10 D.F.

m,a   UNIVERSITY OF ARIZONA, School of Music, Tucson, AZ 85721. Numerous, various amounts.

vp   UNIVERSITY OF ARIZONA, College of Fine Arts, Tucson, AZ 85721.

vp,a   UNIVERSITY OF ARKANSAS, Fayetteville, AR 72701. Assistantships, various.

vp,m,t   UNIVERSITY OF ARKANSAS AT LITTLE ROCK, 33rd & Univ. Ave., Little Rock, AR 72204. Scholarships, National Defense Student Loans, Educational Opportunity Grant $200-$1,000. Based on ability and need. Deadline March 15.

m,t,vp-h   UNIVERSITY OF BIRMINGHAM, Registrar, The Univ., PO Box 363, Birmingham 15, England, UK. Several two-year awards to graduate students.

m   UNIVERSITY OF BRIDGEPORT, Bridgeport, CT 06602. Several undergraduate work assistantships in television, $1,280 each.

T   UNIVERSITY OF BRISTOL, The Registrar, Senate House, Bristol, 2, England, UK. Cilcennin Memorial Fellowship in Drama, $4,200 for three-year period. Also graduate and undergrad. fellowships.

m,a   UNIVERSITY OF BRITISH COLUMBIA, Dept. of Music, Vancouver 8, BC, Canada. Several up to $500 to entering freshmen. Graduate fellowships.

wr   UNIVERSITY OF BUCHAREST, Str. Pitar-Mos, Nor. 7-13, Bucharest, Romania. Several for advanced study at University of Bucharest in linguistics, philology, lit. arts and folklore of Romania. Anyone.

a,vp,c   UNIVERSITY OF CALIFORNIA, Berkeley, CA 94720.

vp,m,f   UNIVERSITY OF CALIFORNIA AT LOS ANGELES, 405 Hilgard Ave., LA,
CA 90025. Awards and schols to qualifying students in all areas of music.
Teaching assistantships in film at $3,150 each. L.B. Mayer Fellowship,
$3,000 each, also assistantships.

m   UNIVERSITY OF CALIFORNIA, Riverside, CA 92502. Various.

all   UNIVERSITY OF CALCUTTA, Senate House, Calcutta 12, India. Fellowships in any field of study regarding Hindu culture.

m   UNIVERSITY OF CALGARY, 26th Ave. and 26th St., NW, Calgary, Alta.,
Canada. Many, up to $1,500.

vp,m   UNIVERSITY OF CALIFORNIA, Santa Barbara, Office of Financial Aid,
Bldg. 343, Santa Barbara, CA 93106. Scholarships based on talent. Grad
fels through William and Florence Matthew Fund.

m   UNIVERSITY OF CAMBRIDGE, Girton College, Cambridge, England, UK.
Research fellowships to women of any nationality.

wr   UNIVERSITY OF CEYLON, University Park, Peradeniya, Ceylon. Fellowship every 3 years for research in any field. Scholarships for advanced study
to U.S. male graduates.

vp,c   UNIVERSITY OF CHATTANOOGA, 801 Oak St., Chattanooga, TN 37403.
Various to $300.

m   UNIVERSITY OF CHICAGO, 835 So. Univ. Ave., Chicago, IL 60637.
Fellowships to $4,000.

P-WR   UNIVERSITY OF CHICAGO PRESS, 5801 So. Ellis Ave., Chicago, IL 60637.
GORDON J. LAING PRIZE: In recognition of an outstanding book, published by the Univ/Chicago Press during the two previous years. Certificate and $1,000 awarded to the author, editor, or translator of the book
who was a member of the faculty of the Univ/Chicago at the time of
publication. Annually.

P-WR,T   UNIVERSITY OF CHICAGO THEATER, 5706 So. University Ave., Chicago,
IL 60637.
THE CHARLES H. SERGEL DRAMA PRIZE: Awarded to the author of
the best drama. Monetary prizes of $1,500 for first place, $1,000 for
second, $500 for third, all three being awarded biennially.

m   UNIVERSITY OF CINCINNATI, 636 Pharmacy, Cincinnati, OH 45221.
Various; Morse Fellowship $5,000 to composers, BA required. Apply:
College of Conservatory of Music. Several in Speech and Theater Arts:

165

Speech assistantships $2,400; Grad Program $2,800; Univ. Schol. $1,200; WCPO-TV schol. $1,000.

m,vp,a UNIVERSITY OF COLORADO, Boulder, CO 80302. Various.

vp UNIVERSITY OF COLORADO, Denver Center, 1100 14th St., Denver, CO 80202.

WR,vp,c UNIVERSITY OF CONNECTICUT, Robert O. Harvey, Storrs, CT 06268. $1,000 for magazine stories, newspaper articles, columns and editorial contributing to better understanding of American Economic System. (vp) Various in School of Fine Arts.

vp UNIVERSITY OF CONNECTICUT, Waterbury Branch, 32 Hillside Ave., Waterbury, CT 06710.

m,vp,c UNIVERSITY OF CORPUS CHRISTI, PO Box 6010, Corpus Christi, TX 78411. Various to $500.

vp,c UNIVERSITY OF DALLAS, Irving, TX 75060.

m UNIVERSITY OF DAYTON, Dept. of Music, Dayton, OH 45409. Various.

vp UNIVERSITY OF DELAWARE, Newark, DE 19720.

vp,c,f UNIVERSITY OF DENVER, 2490 So. Gaylord, Denver, CO 80210. Porduction and Teaching Schols. $1,800 plus remission. full-tuition schols $2,175.

a UNIVERSITY OF DETROIT, Detroit, MI 48221.

all UNIVERSITY OF DURHAM, Old Shire Hall, Durham, England, UK. Research fels in arts to all nationals. Post-doctoral fels.

all UNIVERSITY OF EAST ANGLIA, Registrar, Earlham Hall, Norwich, Norfolk, Nor 88c, England, UK. Approx. $1,450 to qualified grads of any Univ. for research.

all UNIVERSITY OF EDINBURGH, South Bridge, Edinburgh 8, Scotland. Richard Brown Scholarship to grads in arts of any Univ within last 5 yrs. Other fels and six postgrad studentships.

F UNIVERSITY FILM ASSOCIATION, Dept. Radio-Television-Film, Univ/ Texas, Austin, TX 78712. Contact: Robert E. Davis, Schol. Chmn. Several $500 awards annually for continuing film study at a university.

f UNIVERSITY FILM ASSOCIATION, Dept. of Cinema Studies, NYU, NYC 10003. Contact: Dr. Donald Staples, Pres. Two $500 schols annually open in the spring for awards in August.

p-f   UNIVERSITY FILM ASSOCIATION, Communication Arts Dept., Univ/ Windsor, Windsor, Ontario N9B 3P4, Canada. Schols to film students currently enrolled in a university film program. Approx. $4,500 each year. Deadline June 1.

a,vp,c,m   UNIVERSITY OF FLORIDA, 23 Tigert Hall, Gainesville, FL 32601. I. Douglas Turner, Dir. Various schols for undergrads to $2,000; grants to $4,000. Graduate help.

m,vp,f   UNIVERSITY OF GEORGIA, Athens, GA 30602. Various; grad. assistantships and fellowships up to $2,500. (f) One undergrad and one grad assistantships.

all   UNIVERSITY OF GLASGOW, Glasgow, G12 8QH, Scotland. Contact: Clerk of the Faculty of Arts. FELLOWSHIPS: For postgraduate degree study in the Arts. Maximum 1,100 pounds per annum plus fees. Two years plus possibility of third. Deadline March 31.

vp   UNIVERSITY OF HARTFORD, Hartford Art School, Bloomfield Ave., W. Hartford, CT 06117.

m,a   UNIVERSITY OF HAWAII, Dept. of Music, Honolulu, HI 96814. Many partial and full scholarships.

all,vp,f   UNIVERSITY OF HOUSTON, Cullen Blvd., Houston, TX 77004.
          OFFICE OF RESEARCH AND SPONSORED ACTIVITIES: Provides limited assistance to faculty who wish to apply elsewhere for research grants. Contact: Francis B. Smith, Dir.
          THE ART DEPARTMENT SCHOLARSHIPS: Ten scholarships each year to undergraduate and graduate students. $250 or less.
          ARTIST-IN-RESIDENCE: For a one-month stay, $2,000 plus prerequisites: apartment, studio and some expense money. Note: Applicants are not solicited, the faculty is polled for the winning artist.
          GEORGE KIRKSEY SCHOLARSHIPS: Nine awarded annually $800-$900 each—film.

m,t,vp-h   UNIVERSITY OF HULL, Registrar, Hull, England, UK. Research studentships for music, up to $1,200. Renewable. Others, for t,vp-h.

m,a   UNIVERSITY OF IDAHO, Moscow, ID 83843. Various; $400 Presser Fnd. award; $250 Eastern Star Schol.; grad fels.

vp,m,c,   UNIVERSITY OF ILLINOIS, Grad. College, Urbana, IL 61801. Kinley
a,f   Memorial Fels. to grads of College of Fine Arts, $2,500 for advanced study in U.S. or abroad. Creative and performance fels., teaching fels., assistantships in opera ($1,500). Other graduate help.

f,m,wr,   UNIVERSITY OF IOWA, Writers Workshop, Dept. of English, Iowa City, IA 52242. Scholarships, fellowships, assistantships to graduates. Writing and teaching fels up to $3,500. In music, fels up to $3,600. Some schols., renewable. In film, several teaching, production and research assistantships. Various schols, up to $3,450. Visual arts: ¼ time graduate assistantships with a stipend of approx. $1,900 for the academic year—awarded on a competitive basis to candidates who are in residence at the university. Various in broadcasting and film, art history. Substantial help in all areas.

vp,c UNIVERSITY OF JUDAISM, School of Fine Arts, 6525 Sunset Blvd., Los Angeles, CA 90028.

m,vp,c, UNIVERSITY OF KANSAS, 217 Flint Hall, Lawrence, KS 66044. Various a,f to $2,500. Six assistantships at $2,600 each for 9 mos. in film.

m UNIVERSITY OF KANSAS CITY, Conservatory of Music, 4420 Warwick. Blvd., Kansas City, MO 64111. $1,000 for unpublished string quartet composition. Anyone. Fellowships; graduate assistantships.

vp,vp-h UNIVERSITY OF KENTUCKY, Dept. of Art, Lexington, KY 40506. Graduate Art History teaching assistantships; MA, renewable. $2,800 a year and tuition, no restrictions. Deadline March 15. Graduate Studio teaching assistantships; MFA, renewable, $2,800 a year and tuition, no restrictions. Deadline March 15.

wr UNIVERSITY OF LEEDS, Leeds 2, England, UK. Gregory Fellowships: $1,200-$1,800 for study in creative writing. Nationals of any country. Apply: Registrar, above.

all UNIVERSITY OF LIVERPOOL, c/o The Registrar, Senate House, Abercromby Sq., PO Box 147, Liverpool L69 3BX, England, UK. Various aid to students in arts, music, archaeology.

vp,vp-h UNIVERSITY OF LOUISVILLE, Louisville, KY 40208. Various schols. renewable.

vp UNIVERSITY OF MAINE, 96 Falmouth St., Portland, ME 04103.

m THE VICTORIA UNIVERSITY OF MANCHESTER, The Registrar, Oxford Rd, Manchester, M13 9PL, England, UK. Grants, fellowships, graduate and postgraduate schols., exhibitions and prizes are awarded for attendance at Manchester or study abroad.

all UNIVERSITY OF MANITOBA, School of Art, Fort Garry Campus, Winnipeg, Manitoba, R3T 2N2, Canada. Several scholarships for school of art.

m,f,a UNIVERSITY OF MARYLAND, College Park, MD 20740. General scholarships; graduate Assistantships in film, to $3,300.

t,f UNIVERSITY OF MASSACHUSETTS, Dept. of Speech, Amherst, MA

01002. Teaching and service assistantships; up to $3,200 and remission of tuition. Renewable. Other toward MFA in Theatre.

wr   UNIVERSITY OF MECHED, Meched, Iran. Scholarships for study of Persian Language and Literature. Anyone.

m,vp,f,a   UNIVERSITY OF MIAMI, School of Music, Coral Gables, FL 33124. Undergrad schols. to $2,000; grad schols to $2,000. Several in film.

vp-h,wr,   UNIVERSITY OF MICHIGAN, Dept. of History of Art, Ann Arbor, MI
m,a   48104. Scholarships, fellowships, internships, stipends, etc. In music, many fels and schols to undergrads and grads. In film, some to $3,200 per year.

WR   THE UNIVERSITY OF MICHIGAN PRESS BOOK AWARD, 615 E. Univ., Ann Arbor, MI 48106. $1,000 for book published by Univ/Michigan Press that added greatest distinction to press list. Annually.

m,vp,c   UNIVERSITY OF MINNESOTA, 1200 Oakland Ave., Duluth, MN 55812.

m,a   UNIVERSITY OF MINNEAPOLIS, 107 Scott Hall, Minneapolis, MN 55455. Various; grad. fels.

f   UNIVERSITY OF MINNESOTA, Studio Art/Speech Communication, Minneapolis, MN 55414. SCHOLARSHIPS: Four teaching assistantships in Speech Comm.: $4,600; production assistant in radio-TV: $4,600; two ¼-time assistantships in Studio Art.

m,f   UNIVERSITY OF MISSISSIPPI,University, MS 38655. Various; grad assists & fels. SCHOLARSHIPS: Graduate Instructor (and Radio Station manager) $2,000 per year.

m,vp,t,   UNIVERSITY OF MISSOURI, Columbia, MO 65201. Several, to $2,400;
a,f   grad assists.; Gregory Fels. to $1,500. Two ½-time grad teaching assists $3,200 for 9 mos.

vp,wr,m,   UNIVERSITY OF MISSOURI-KANSAS CITY, 5100 Rockhill, Kansas City,
d,t   MO 64110. Contact: Dean's Ocd. Many grants and schols awarded through audition, up to $400.

vp,m,f   UNIVERSITY OF MONTANA, School of Fine Arts, Missoula, MT 59801. Numerous, to $2,400. $3,000 available to American Indians.

m,a,f   UNIVERSITY OF NEBRASKA, School of Music, Lincoln, NE 68504. Several TV schols; grad assists to $2,300; others.

vp,c,t   UNIVERSITY OF NEBRASKA AT OMAHA, PO Box 688, Downtown Station, Omaha, NE 68101. Graduate assistantship.

mv,p,c   UNIVERSITY OF NEW HAMPSHIRE, Durham, NH 03824. $400 piano major. Apply Paul Arts Center.

a,m,vp,   UNIVERSITY OF NEW MEXICO, College of Fine Arts, Albuquerque, NM
vp-h   87106. Grad. assistantships to $2,600; other small.

f   UNIVERSITY OF NEW ORLEANS, Drama and Communications, Lakefront,
           New Orleans, LA 70122. Contact: H. Wayne Schuth. Graduate assistantships
           to $2,300 plus tuition and fees.

f,m,vp,wr UNIVERSITY OF NORTH CAROLINA, Swain Hall, Chapel Hill, NC 27514.
           Graduate assistantships $925 each; grad fels $2,300 each; undergrad schols to
           $2,500. Others.

vp,c   UNIVERSITY OF NORTH CAROLINA AT ASHEVILLE, University Hgts.,
           Asheville, NC 28801.

all   UNIVERSITY OF NORTH CAROLINA AT GREENSBORO, NC 27412.
           Graduate assistantships to $4,000, renewable.

m,vp,c   UNIVERSITY OF NORTHERN IOWA, Cedar Falls, IA 50613. Contact: Ed
           Harris. Graduate Assistantships for students working toward a master's de-
           gree, $2,000 plus remission of fees for the academic year.

vp,a   UNIVERSITY OF NORTHERN COLORADO, Greeley, CO 80631. W.R.
           Erwin Jr., Dean, School of Arts. No cash, tuition waivers positions, part-
           time instructors.

m,vp,t,m, UNIVERSITY OF NORTH DAKOTA, College of Fine Arts, Grand Forks,
vp,t,f   ND 58202.
               COLLEGE OF FINE ARTS AWARDS: 15 awards of $500 each to first-time
               students only. Contact: John H. Rogers, Dean. Deadline March 1.
               FACULTY RESEARCH GRANTS: Amount varies, given to faculty of
               UND only. Contact: VP for Academic Affairs.
               SUMMER GRADUATE RESEARCH PROFESSORSHIPS: Cash grant of
               $2,000, not renewable, to UND graduate faculty only. Contact: Fellow-
               ships Officer, UND Grad. School. Deadline November 15.
           Film assistantships, anyone.

m,a   UNIVERSITY OF NOTRE DAME, Grad. School, Notre Dame, IN 46556.
           Grad Asssistantships to $2,000.

a,vp,m,c   UNIVERSITY OF OKLAHOMA, Norman, OK 73069. Various, funds of
           $20,000 available.

vp,m,a,f   UNIVERSITY OF OREGON, Eugene, OR 97403. Various; two TV Grad
           Teaching Fels. for $3,200 and $3,600.

t,m   UNIVERSITY OF THE PACIFIC, Conservatory of Music, Stockton, CA

95204. All grants in form of tuition rebate and salary stipend. Must be full-time grad student in one of the disciplines. Grants vary from partial tuition to full ($2,510). Stipends from $700-$2,500 for 9 mos. Renewable. Deadline March 1.

wr UNIVERSITY OF THE PANJAB, Lahore, West Pakistan, Pakistan. Studentships for study in English, Sanskrit, or Arabic, 2 yrs. Any grad. Apply Registrar above.

m,vp UNIVERSITY OF PITTSBURGH, Pittsburgh, PA 15213. Several to $2,600; pre-doctoral to $2,500; post-doctoral Andrew Mellon Fel. $7,000.

m UNIVERSITY OF PORTLAND, Div. of Music, 5000 Willamette Blvd., Portland, OR 97203. Several small; grad fels.

m,vp UNIVERSITY OF REDLANDS, School of Music, 1200 E. Colton, Redlands, CA 92373. Up to $1,200 to undergrads and grads.

m,vp UNIVERSITY OF REGINA, Regina, Saskatchewan S4S OA2, Canada. Contact: President's Office.

m UNIVERSITY OF RHODE ISLAND, Dr. Albert Giebler, Dept. of Music, Kingston, RI 02881. Composition award of $300 for choral work. Various scholarships.

m UNIVERSITY OF RICHMOND, Richmond, VA 23173. One full-tuition renewable.

m,t UNIVERSITY OF SOUTH ALABAMA, 307 University Blvd., Mobile, AL 36688. University fee waivers up to $178 per quarter for theatre, $170 for music. Renewable.

vp,c UNIVERSITY OF SOUTH CAROLINA, Columbia, SC 29208. Dept. of Art Grad Assistantship, renewable, reduced fees. Anyone.

m,vp,c,f UNIVERSITY OF SOUTH DAKOTA, Vermillion, SD 57069. Various; grad fels. (f) Assistantship $1,800.

vp,c UNIVERSITY OF SOUTH FLORIDA, Visual Arts, 4202 Fowler Ave., Tampa, FL 33620. Graduate assistant schol. $2,700.

vp,m,c, UNIVERSITY OF SOUTHERN CALIFORNIA, University Park, CA 90007. Undergraduates, various schols up to $2,000; graduates, fellowships up to $2,400. (f) Fourteen Assistantships, George Cukor Schol., William Morris Schol., CBS Fnd. Schols (from $100 to $3,000).

m UNIVERSITY OF SOUTHERN MISSISSIPPI, Box 31 Southern Station, Hattiesburg, MS. Graduate assistantships, $1,500-$3,000 in opera, composition, performance, history, research, conducting, musicology, theory.

171

m,a   UNIVERSITY OF SOUTHWESTERN LOUISIANA, Box 100, Lafayette, LA 70501. Numerous; grad fels.

vp   UNIVERSITY OF TAMPA, 401 W. Kennedy Blvd., Tampa, FL 33606.

wr   UNIVERSITY OF TEHERAN, Dept. of Publications and Cultural Relations, Ave. Chah-Reza, Teheran, Iran. Scholarships for advanced study of language and literature of Persia in Iran; national grads of any country. Apply: Embassy of Iran, 3005 Massachusetts Ave, NW, Washington, DC 20008.

m,vp,a   UNIVERSITY OF TENNESSEE, Music Bldg., Knoxville, TN 37916. Various performing ability; grad fels.

f,a   UNIVERSITY OF TEXAS AT AUSTIN, Radio/TV/Film Div., PO Box 7158, Austin, TX 78712. Many small.

m,vp,c   UNIVERSITY OF TEXAS AT EL PASO, El Paso, TX 79999. Several small.

m   UNIVERSITY OF TOLEDO, 2801 West Bancroft St., Toledo, OH 43606. Several, small.

all   UNIVERSITY OF TORONTO, Secretary of Graduate Studies, Toronto 5, Ont., Canada. Open fellowships, up to $4,000. Open to all nationals.

m,f   UNIVERSITY OF TULSA, 600 So. College Ave., Tulsa, OK 74104. Various, up to full tuition; numerous awards.

a,m,vp, c,f   UNIVERSITY OF UTAH, Salt Lake City, UT 84112. Many tuition waivers based on need. Various schols; grad fels.

m,vp,c   UNIVERSITY OF VERMONT, Burlington, VT 05401. Graduate teaching fels, grad residence advisorships $2,200 and tuition.

a   UNIVERSITY OF VIRGINIA, Charlottesville, VA 22903.

a   UNIVERSITY OF WALES, The Registrar, Institute of Science and Technology, Cathays Park, Cardiff, Wales, UK. Approximately $1,400 max. for 3 yrs at Wales. To any nationals, any age with degree in architecture or in which architecture is major subject.

vp,m,c,   UNIVERSITY OF WASHINGTON, Seattle, WA 98105. Several schols, some renewable; grad fels. George F. McKay Memorial Schol. Fund in composition, $5,000, presented by CBS Fnd. (f) Jim Murphy Schol in TV news, film lab and radio production. Others, to $1,800.

m   UNIVERSITY OF WESTERN ONTARIO, College of Music, London, Ont., Canada. Various schols to $250; one for outstanding student.

vp   UNIVERSITY OF WISCONSIN, Fox Valley Campus, Midway Rd., Mensha, WI 54952.

vp,wr,m, d,t,-h UNIVERSITY OF WISCONSIN, Green Bay, 2420 Nicolet Drive, Green Bay, WI 54302.

f UNIVERSITY OF WISCONSIN–MADISON, Communication Arts, 821 University Ave., Madison, WI 53706. Contact: Charles E. Sherman. Teaching assists., research assists., departmental fellowships.

m,vp,c,a UNIVERSITY OF WISCONSIN–MILWAUKEE, Milwaukee, WI 53201. Various to $600; grad assists. and fels.

f UNIVERSITY OF WISCONSIN–OSHKOSH, Speech, Radio-TV-Film Div., Oshkosh, WI 54901. Contact: Dr. Robert L. Snyder. Warner Cable TV Scholarship $500.

f UNIVERSITY OF WISCONSIN–SUPERIOR, Communication Arts, 18th & Weeks Ave., Superior, WI 54880. Contact: Dr. Donald R. Cain. Cinematographer assistantship for $1,250; one TV assistantship for $1,250; other grants.

m,vp UNIVERSITY OF WYOMING, Division of Music, Laramie, WY. Many small, undergrad; Grad fels to $2,628.

vp,wr,m UNIVERSITY OF YORK, Heslington, York, England, UK. No programs for awards in the arts at this time.

wr, hum UNIVERSITY WOMEN'S ASSOC. OF NAGPUR, Nagpur University, Nagpur, India. Fellowships and exchange schls to women for advanced study and research in India. Women grads 25 and over of any country. Apply: The Honorary Secretary, above.

wr UNIVERSITY WOMEN'S ASSOC., 6 Bhagwandas Rd., Delhi, India. Scholarships to women graduates of any nationality, to age 45. Apply Chairman, Scholarship Committee, above.

vp UPSALA COLLEGE, East Orange, NJ.

vp,c URSULINE COLLEGE, Lander & Fairmount Blvds, Cleveland/Pepper Pike, OH 44124.

all U.S. ARMY, c/o Education and Morale Support Directorate, The Adjutant General's Office, Department of the Army, Washington, DC. Awards through which military personnel may attend college and university courses in all the arts, including painting, sculpture, drama, music. Inquire as above.

VP U.S. HOCKEY HALL OF FAME, PO Box 657, Evelenth, MN 55734. Hall of Fame Art Competition with $250 purchase award. No sculpture accepted. Deadline June 1-10.

all U.S. OFFICE OF EDUCATION, Div. of Graduate Programs, Graduate Academic Programs Branch, DC 20202. Graduate Fellowship Program. Three

173

years to prospective college teachers pursuing doctoral degree. Fields unrestricted. Apply through participating grad school. Other Elementary and Secondary Education programs. Those currently teaching Apply: U.S. Office of Education, Bureau of Elem. & Sec. Ed., Div. of Educational Personnel Training, Experienced Teacher Fel. Branch, DC 20202.

P-D USSR MINISTRY OF CULTURE, Moscow, USSR.
INTERNATIONAL BALLET COMPETITION PRIZES: For outstanding achievements in the world of choreography which express a realistic approach to the art of ballet. Gold, silver and bronze medals, and monetary prizes are awarded every four years to the best dancers (both solo and duet) and to the best choreographers. Anyone.

m U.S. STEEL FND. INC., 71 Broadway, NYC 10006. Student assistant for graduate study, teacher development grants.

all UTAH STATE DIVISION OF FINE ARTS, 609 East South Temple St., Salt Lake City, UT 84102. Aid for artists-in-schools.

vp,c,f UTAH STATE UNIVERSITY, University Hill, Logan, UT 84321. One production assistantship in film, $2,600 per 12 mos; one teaching assistantship in film, $1,540 per 8 mos.

VACHEL LINDSAY ASSOCIATION, 1529 Noble Ave., Springfield, IL 62704. Elizabeth Graham.

m VALDOSTA STATE COLLEGE, Valdosta, GA 31601. Various small.

m,vp VALLEY CITY STATE COLLEGE' Valley City, ND 58072. Numerous undergrads.

m,vp,c VALPARAISO UNIVERSITY, Valparaiso, IN 46383. Undergrads $1,100 (full tuition), renewable.

vp,c VANCOUVER SCHOOL OF ART. SEE: The Emily Carr College of Art.

m,M VAN CLIBURN INTERNATIONAL PIANO COMPETITION, 3505 West Lancaster, Fort Worth, TX 76107.. Contact: Anthony Phillips.
THE VAN CLIBURN INTERNATIONAL PIANO COMPETITION: To be held in September. First Prize: $10,000, plus Carnegie Hall Debut and American concert tour, London debut and European tour. Second Prize: $6,000. Third through Sixth: $3,000-$750. Ages 18 to 29. Housing, meals, and practice facilities are provided to all contestants accepted by the Competition.

T ALFRED E. VAN HORN AWARDS, c/o National Contemporary Theatre Conference, 726 Jackson Pl., Washington, DC 20566. $500 annually for outstanding achievement in dramatic activities.

174

d   VARNA INTERNATIONAL BALLET COMPETITION AWARDS. SEE: Bulgarian Committee of Culture and Art.

m,vp,wr   VASSAR COLLEGE, Poughkeepsie, NY 12601. W.K. Rose, Fellowship Committee. Various, renewable, partial or full, based on need or merit.

P-VP   BARBARA VASSILIEFF AWARD. Award: $100. SEE: Allied Artists of America.

ALL,all   VERMONT COUNCIL ON THE ARTS, 136 State St., Montpelier, VT 05602. Up to $2,000 to artists who are residents of Vermont. Deadline April 1.

vp   VESPER GEORGE SCHOOL OF ART, 44 St. Botolph St., Boston, MA 02116.

P-M   VIANNA DA MOTTA INTERNATIONAL MUSIC COMPETITION, Avenida Conselheiro Fernando de Sousa, SRF-r/cF Lisbon, Portugal. PRIZES: Categories vary when awards are presented every two years. Monetary prize of $11,500 in 1975. For the best performers aged 17 to 30.

F   VIDEO ALLIANCE FOR THE PERFORMING ARTS, 130 W. 56th St., NYC 10019. Homer Poupart, Exec. Dir. MR

P-M   VIENNA INTERNATIONAL MUSIC COMPETITION, The Secretariat: Hochschule for Music, Lothringstrasse 18, A-1030 Vienna, Austria. Prizes: For the best performance of Beethoven piano works: 40,000; 25,000; 12,000 and 6,000 Austrian schillings awarded every four years. Joseph Haydn piano or string quartets: 60,000; 40,000 and 30,000 schillings awarded every two years. Hugo Wolf prizes for outstanding singers: 20,000; 10,000 & 5,000 schillings every two years.

P-T   THE VILLAGE VOICE, 80 University Place, NYC 10003. THE "OBIE" AWARD: For the recognition of the finest plays, actors, directors, and more. For off-Broadway and off-off-Broadway. A certificate and monetary award of $500 for the Best Play. Awarded annually.

vp,f   VINCENNES UNIVERSITY JUNIOR COLLEGE, 1001 N. First St., Vincennes, IN 47591. One work grant based on need, two schols at $500 each.

P-M   G.B. VIOTTI INTERNATIONAL MUSIC COMPETITION, The Secretariat, Societa del Quartetto, Casella Postale 127, Vercelli, Italy. Prizes: Categories change annually. 1976: Voice, piano, flute, composition. 6,000,000 liras total awarded in 1975.

all   VIRGIN ISLANDS COUNCIL ON THE ARTS, Caravelle Arcade, Christiansted, U.S. Virgin Islands 00820. Up to $2,500 for Virgin Islands residents.

M,VP,WR   VIRGINIA CENTER FOR THE CREATIVE ARTS, Box VCCA, Sweet Briar College, Sweet Briar, VA 24595. Distraction-free environment on a 445-acre estate next to Sweet Briar College where artists live in a manor house and work in renovated barns. Cost is $70 per week with a few abatements.

ALL,all   VIRGINIA COMMISSION ON THE ARTS AND HUMANITIES, 400 East Grace St., First Floor, Richmond, VA 23219. Monies for artists-in-schools and for some individual projects.

m,vp,c   VIRGINIA COMMONWEALTH UNIVERSITY, Chairman of the Contest Committee, 901 W. Franklin St., Richmond, VA 23220. $300 for 20 min. symphony composition to any U.S. registered college or conservatory student.

vp,t,a   VIRGINIA MUSEUM, Boulevard and Grove Ave., Richmond, VA 23221. Student and grad fels for education; professional fels for creation. Grants from $1,000-$3,000 per year.

t,m,vp,a   VIRGINIA POLYTECHNIC INSTITUTE AND STATE UNIVERSITY, Financial Aid Office, Blacksburg, VA 24061. Contact: Frank L. Butler, Assoc. Dir. of Admissions.

WR   VIRGINIA QUARTERLY REVIEW, 1 West Range, Charlottesville, VA 22903.
     THE EMILY CLARK BALCH PRIZE: To create interest in American literature. $1,000 awarded to an American writer on an American subject, for an unpublished work. Awarded annually, alternately for short stories and poetry.

m   VITERBO COLLEGE, 815 So. Ninth St., LaCrosse, WI 54601. Tuition schol to entering freshmen women; music schols to $600.

all   LUDWIG VOGELSTEIN FDN., INC., 340 Haven Ave., NYC 10033. Aid to "meritorious individuals and . . . work in the realms of scholarship and the arts."

all   ALEXANDER VON HUMBOLDT—STIFTUNG, Schillerstrasse 12, 532 Bad Godesberg, FDR. Research fellowships, to 35 yrs of age; at least 2 yrs of teaching experience. Apply: Federal Republic of Germany Embassy in Washington, DC or directly at above address.

f   JOSEF VON STERNBERG PRIZE.
     SEE: Mannheim International Film Festival.

P-WR,   MARJORIE PEABODY WAITE AWARD. Award: $1,500.
VP,M   SEE: National Institute of Arts and Letters.

m   WAKE FOREST UNIV., Box 7267, Winston-Salem, NC 27106. Various.

P-VP   WILLIAM H. WALKER PRIZE FOR LITHOGRAPHY.
     SEE: THE PRINT CLUB.

vp   ABRAHAM WALKOWITZ SCHOLARSHIP, est. 1963 anonymously. Awarded as a tribute to Walkowitz. SEE: Art Students League of N.Y. (Talent).

vp   WALLA WALLA COLLEGE, Art Dept., College Place, WA 99324.

WR   EDWARD LEWIS WALLANT MEMORIAL AWARD, c/o Mrs. Irving Waltman, 3 Brighton Rd., West Hartford, CT 06117. $250 for work of fiction significant to Jews.

P-VP   ELIZABETH N. WATROUS GOLD MEDAL. Award: $300 and gold medal. SEE: NATIONAL ACADEMY OF DESIGN.

m   WARNER BROS. SCHOLARSHIPS, University/Southern California, University Park, CA 90007. $2,000.

m   WARTBURG COLLEGE, Waverly, IA 50677. Various small.

vp   WASHINGTON AND JEFFERSON COLLEGE, S. Lincoln St., Washington, PA 15301.

P-VP   THE WASHINGTON SCHOOL OF ART AWARD. Award: $200 SEE: AMERICAN WATERCOLOR SOCIETY.

P-WR   WASHINGTON SQUARE UNIVERSITY COLLEGE OF ARTS & SCIENCE OF NEW YORK UNIVERSITY, Dept. of English, 19 University Place, NYC 10003.
DELMORE SCHWARTZ MEMORIAL POETRY AWARD: To help promote a promising unrecognized young writer, who hasn't published more than one book of poetry. $2,000 awarded every other year.

ALL   WASHINGTON STATE ARTS COUNCIL, 1151 Blake Lake Blvd., Olympia, WA 98504. Works are commissioned or purchased as completed pieces for use in state buildings. Also, there is a 3-year rotating program which awards $4,750 to Washington State resident artists.

vp,c   WASHINGTON STATE COLLEGE OF THE UNIVERSITY OF MAINE, O'Brien Ave., Machias, ME 04654.

m,vp,a   WASHINGTON STATE UNIVERSITY, Pullman, WA 99163. Various; grad fels.

vp,all   WASHINGTON UNIVERSITY, St. Louis, MO 63130. Contact: Office of Financial Aid.
CONWAY SCHOLARSHIPS: Two given to freshmen. Value of tuition: $3,650 in 1976-77 plus $500 each year for four undergraduate years. Based solely on artistic achievement and potential.
MYLONAS SCHOLARSHIP: Same as above, except that it is based on artistic and/or academic achievement and potential. Financial aid based

on need. Average award in 1976-77: $3,000. 41% of undergraduates aided.

P-M, p-m   WASSILI LEPS FOUNDATION PRIZE, Bi-Annual Choral Contest for American Composers, Dept. of Music, Brown Univ., Providence, RI 02912. $500 and 10% of royalties for work suitable for college age voices. Deadline May 1.

VP   WATERCOLOR OKLAHOMA, M.E. Fleming, 2600 NW 63rd, Oklahoma City, OK. Watermedia. Purchase awards of $3,000. Deadline Sept. 22.

VP   WATERCOLOR USA, Springfield Art Museum, 1111 East Brookside Dr., Springfield, MO 65807. $10,000 in cash awarded.

P-VP   THE WATERCOLOR USA AWARD. Award: $200.
SEE: AMERICAN WATERCOLOR SOCIETY.

m   WAYLAND BAPTIST COLLEGE, Plainview, TX 79072. Various.

vp,f   WAYNE STATE UNIVERSITY, Detroit, MI 48202. Various; Grad Assistantships in film: $2,900 to $5,100, plus in-state tuition.

vp,c   WEATHERFORD COLLEGE, Box 219, Weatherford, TX 76086.

vp   MAX WEBER SCHOLARSHIP. Small. Awarded as income accrues.
SEE: Art Students League of N.Y. (Talent).

vp,c   WEBER STATE COLLEGE, 3750 Harrison Blvd., Ogden, UT 84403.

m,vp,c   WEBSTER COLLEGE, 470 E. Lockwood, St. Louis, MO 63119. Several.

P-VP   CHARLES AND ESTER WEBSTER PRIZES.
SEE: SEATTLE ART MUSEUM.

vp   MARJORIE WEBSTER JUNIOR COLLEGE, 7775 17th St., NW, Washington, DC 20012. MR

M   HENRYK WEINIAWSKI INTERNATIONAL COMPETITION, 61-841 Poznan-Poland, ul. Swietoslawska. Violinists of any nationality, ages 17-30. Prize for violin makers, composition and violin. Apply: Secretariat for the Competition, above.

a   WELSH COLLEGE OF ADVANCED TECHNOLOGY, Academic Registrar, Cathays Park, Cardiff, Wales, UK. Studentships of approx. $1,400 for research in UK. To all nationals with degree in subject of study.

m,vp   WESLEYAN COLLEGE, Macon, GA 31201. Many up to full tuition; women only.

vp   WESLEYAN UNIVERSITY, Davidson Art Center, Middletown, CT 06457.

m,vp WEST LIBERTY STATE COLLEGE, Hall of Fine Arts, West Liberty, WV 26074. Various to full tuition.

m,vp,c WEST TEXAS STATE UNIVERSITY, Canyon, TX 79015. Various; Grad assistantships.

ALL,all WEST VIRGINIA ARTS AND HUMANITIES COUNCIL, Science and Culture Center, Capitol Complex, Charleston, WV 25305. Works by West Virginia artists are chosen to be exhibited in art centers. Works are purchased for the state's permanent collection. There is an emergency relief loan program. There is an apprentice training financial assistance program. Also, a technical assistance program.

m WEST VIRGINIA STATE COLLEGE, Institute, WV 25112. Various.

m,vp,c,f WEST VIRGINIA UNIVERSITY, Morgantown, WV 26506. Various schols.; Grad fels; schols and grad assists in film, several up to $2,000.

m WEST VIRGINIA WESLEYAN COLLEGE, Buckannon, WV 26201. Several, to $800; faculty assistantships.

WR WESTBURG ASSOCIATES PUBLISHERS, PO Drawer 69, Fennimore, WI 53809. $25 awards for poetry submitted by subscribers to North American Mentor Magazine. Deadline Sept. 1.

F,f WESTDEUTSCHE KURZFILMTAGE/International Short Film Festival, Grillostr. 34, D-4200, Oberhausen 1, West Germany. Contact: Wolfgang Ruf. Films on 16/35mm up to 35 minutes long judged last week in April. Cash awards of up to 30,000 DM (Deutsche Marks).

m,vp,c,wr WESTERN CAROLINA UNIVERSITY, Culloshee, NC 28723. Various.

C,VP WESTERN COLORADO CENTER FOR THE ARTS, 1803 N. 7th St., Grand Junction, CO 81501. Designer-Craftsman Show with purchase patron awards and cash prizes. Deadline March 30.

m,vp,c, WESTERN ILLINOIS UNIVERSITY, Macomb, IL 61455. Undergrad schols
t,f to $1,800; grad assists to $3,150. Anyone. (f) Tuition schols $420 each.

ALL,all WESTERN KENTUCKY UNIVERSITY, Bowling Green, KY 42101. Contact Dr. Glen Crumb, Dir. Off. of Grants and Contracts.
GRANTS: Awarded to the faculty, include: Faculty research grants; sabbatical leaves; summer fellowships; faculty and staff tuition schols.
SCHOLARSHIPS: Awarded to students: Regents scholarships; College Heights Fnd. schols.; Ogden schols.; Oddfellow schol.; Russell Miller Schols (Theatre).

m WESTERN MARYLAND COLLEGE, Westminster, MD 21157. Various; need.

179

m   WESTERN MICHIGAN UNIVERSITY, Kalamazoo, MI 49001. Several; grad fels.

vp,c   WESTERN NEW MEXICO UNIVERSITY, Silver City, NM 88061.

ALL   WESTERN STATES ARTS FOUNDATION, 428 East 11th Ave., Denver, CO 80203. Fellowships of $2,500 awarded through 1980 on basis of artists' past works in the Foundation's chosen media. Artist must be resident of either AZ, CO, ID, MT, NV, NM, OR, UT, WA or WY state.

M,m   WESTERN WASHINGTON UNIVERSITY, Bellingham, WA 98225. Many schols; one grant to Washington resident string player.

m   WESTERN WYOMING COLLEGE, Rock Springs, WY 82901.

vp,c,m   WESTMAR COLLEGE ART CENTER' Westmar College, LeMars, IA 51031.

m   WESTMINISTER CHOIR COLLEGE, Princeton, NJ 08540. Numerous.

vp,c   WESTMINISTER COLLEGE, New Wilmington, PA 16142.

m,vp   WESTMINSTER COLLEGE, 1840 So. 13th East St., Salt Lake City, UT 84105. Various.

C   WESTWOOD CERAMICS SUPPLY COMPANY, 14400 Lomitas Ave., City of Industry, CA 91746. Westwood Clay National with purchase and cash awards for ceramics. Deadline Nov. 19.

M   WGN—ILLINOIS OPERA GUILD, Auditions of the Air, WGN Continental Broadcasting Co., 2501 Bradley Pl., Chicago, IL 60657. To $3,000 to U.S. citizens 20-34 yrs. Tape with application; live auditions in NYC, CA, LA and Chicago.

m   WHEATON COLLEGE, Conservatory of Music, Wheaton, IL 60187. Various.

vp,c   WHITMAN COLLEGE, 345 Boyer Ave., Walla Walla, WA 99362.

P-WR   THE WALT WHITMAN AWARD. Award: $1,000.
SEE: ACADEMY OF AMERICAN POETS.

P-VP   WHITNEY, EDGAR A., AWARD. Award: $200.
SEE: AMERICAN WATERCOLOR SOCIETY.

F   WHITNEY MUSEUM OF AMERICAN ART, The New American Filmmakers Series, Film and Video Dept., 945 Madison Ave., NYC 10021. Award of film or video exhibition for filmmakers' works never screened in New York City.

m   WHITWORTH COLLEGE, Dept. of Music, Country Homes Estates, Spokane, WA 99218. Various small.

m WICHITA FALLS SYMPHONY ORCHESTRA FELLOWSHIP, Mrs. Owanah Anderson, Mgr., Wichita Falls, TX 76301. Up to $1,600 for study of MA in Arts or Music; recipient will serve as instrumentalist with the Symphony.

m,vp WICHITA STATE UNIVERSITY, 1845 N. Fairmount School of Music, Wichita, KS 67208. Various; grad. students to $2,700 per yr.

m WICHITA SYMPHONY SOCIETY, Naftzger Young Artists Auditions, 105 West Second St., Wichita, KS 62702. Up to $1,200 to residents of Kansas or enrolled in Kansas colleges, under 23 yrs.

P-M WIHURI FOUNDATION FOR INTERNATIONAL PRIZES, Arkandiankatu 21B, 00100 Helsinki 10, Finland. SIBELIUS PRIZE: To prominent composers who have become renowned internationally; to individuals or associations. 100,000 Finnish marks awarded every third year.

m WILLAMETTE UNIVERSITY, College of Music, Salem, OR 97301. Numerous to $1,200 for music majors; Federal work-study opportunities.

m,vp,c WILLIAM CAREY COLLEGE, Hattiesburg, MS 39401. Various.

vp,c WILLIAM WOODS COLLEGE, Fulton, MO 65251.

vp-h,m,wr WILLIAMS COLLEGE, Williamstown, MA 01267. Several schols. for undergrads and grads in Arts, Music, English. Most may be extended a second year. Williams students only.

T WILMETTE CHILDREN'S THEATER, 1200 Wilmette Ave., Wilmette, IL 60091. $300 and $200 and production for script acted by and for children. Deadline May 1.

vp, WILSON COLLEGE, Chambersburg, PA 17201.

m WILSON VOICE AWARD, Mrs. Erich P. Frank, 836 NW 42nd St., Oklahoma City, OK 73118. $300 and possible appearance with Oklahoma City Symphony Orchestra to residents of OK, AR, KS or TX or students in said states, under 28 yrs.

P-WR WINCHESTER PRESS, 205 E. 42nd St. "F," NYC 10017.
JOHN M. OLIN AWARD: In honorium of an outstanding previously unpublished book length nonfiction manuscript having to do with the great outdoors. $2,500 awarded to the author, $1,000 of which is outright and $1,500 as an advance in royalties plus publication of the manuscript. Annual.

P-VP THE WINDSOR AND NEWTON AWARD. Award: $150.
SEE: AMERICAN WATER COLOR SOCIETY.

P-WR   EDD WINFIELD PARKS AWARD. SEE: SOCIETY FOR THE STUDY OF SOUTHERN LITERATURE.

P-WR   LAWRENCE L. WINSHIP AWARD, The Boston Globe, Boston, MA 02107. Award of $1,000 for book published between July 1 and June 30 written by a New England author or with a New England theme. Deadline June 30.

VP   WINSTON-SALEM ART COUNCIL, INC., 226 North Marshall, Winston-Salem, NC 63108.

m   WINTHROP COLLEGE, School of Music, Rock Hill, SC 29730. Several.

ALL,all   WISCONSIN ARTS BOARD, 123 West Washington Ave., Madison, WI 53702. Five fellowships of $2,000 each for a Wisconsin artist who is not a student. Artist-in-Residence program also.

m   WISCONSIN COLLEGE—CONSERVATORY, 1584 N. Prospect Ave., Milwaukee, WI 53202. Up to $1,000 grant-in-aid in composition, performance and theory.

C,VP   WISCONSIN FESTIVAL OF ARTS, 1655 South 68th St., West Allis, WI 53214. Annual Festival of Arts including most existing crafts along with visual arts. Prizes of $2,500, $350 and $150. Over 18 years of age. Deadline Oct. 1.

m,vp,c   WISCONSIN STATE UNIVERSITY, Garfield and Park Aves., Eau Claire, WI 54701. Various; Grad fels $2,400 each.

m   WISCONSIN STATE UNIVERSITY, LaCrosse, WI 54601. Various, scholarship and need.

m,vp,c   WISCONSIN STATE UNIVERSITY, River Falls, WI 54022. Several.

m   WISCONSIN STATE UNIVERSITY, Stevens Point, WI 54481. Several.

vp,c   WISCONSIN STATE UNIVERSITY, Superior, WI 54880. To $2,500.

WOMEN LIBRARY WORKERS, Box 9052, Berkeley, CA 94709. Carole Leita, Coordinator.

M   WOMEN'S ASSOCIATION OF THE MINNEAPOLIS SYMPHONY, 7515 Wayzata Blvd., Minneapolis, MN 55426. Minneapolis Symphony Young Artists' Award to piano and orchestra instruments. Anyone. MR

m   WOMEN'S COMMITTEE OF THE OKLAHOMA SYMPHONY ORCHESTRA, 3233 Whippoorwill Road, Oklahoma City, OK 73120. Awards totaling $2,500 for piano, voice and strings for residents or students of OK, AR, MO, TX and KS; under 31 yrs of age.

P-T AUDREY WOOD AWARD IN PLAYWRITING. $500 and production of the play. SEE: AMERICAN UNIVERSITY.'

VP WORLD ARTS FOUNDATION, Rm 1935, 475 Riverside Drive, NYC 10027. Over $5 million for commissioning and purchase of arts of all kinds for Presbyteries worldwide. Mr. Graham Grove is head.

P-WR WORLD FEDERATION OF BERGEN-BELSEN ASSOCIATION, Box 333, Lenox Hill Station, NYC 10021.
REMEMBRANCE AWARD: For the outstanding literary work that captures most effectively the Nazi holocaust for the benefit of present and future generations $2,500 annually.

WR WORLD FESTIVAL OF NEGRO ARTS LITERARY PRIZES, National Book League, 7 Albermarle St., London W1, UK. Prizes to negro authors in all areas of writing given in connection with the Festival every 4 yrs. Any Negroes. Apply: Mr. Clifford Simmons.

WR WORLD LAW FUND. SEE: INSTITUTE FOR WORLD ORDER.

P-WR WORLD LITERATURE TOADY, 630 Parrington Oval, Rm 109, Norman, OK 73019. Nominations made by an international jury of writers for writer who will receive $10,000.

WR ABRAHAM WOURSELL PRIZE, Universitat Wien, Universitatsdirektion, Dr. Karl Lueger-Ring 1, A-1014 Wien. Prize of $8,000 for 5 yrs to support talented and struggling young creative writers. Anyone.

P-VP IRENE D. WRIGHT MEMORIAL AWARD.
SEE: SEATTLE ART MUSEUM.

M WQXR RADIO, c/o New York Times, NYC. $2,000 in prizes to young pianists. (Local.)

m WURLITZER FND, Wurlitzer Co., 105 West Adams St., Chicago, IL 60603. Up to $1,500 for study in any accredited college or univ to children or grandchildren of Wurlitzer Co. employees. MR

D,M,VP, HELENE WURLITZER FOUNDATION OF NEW MEXICO, PO Box 545,
WR Taos, NM 87571. Residencies for 3-mo periods in which rent, linen and utility is free only.

all WYOMING COUNCIL ON THE ARTS, 200 W. 25th St., Cheyenne, WY 82002. Annual $4,000 fellowship grant given on rotating basis (i.e. 1978 Visual Arts, 1979 Crafts, 1980 Photography & Film). Wyoming residents only.

m,vp XAVIER UNIVERSITY OF LOUISIANA, Palmetto and Pine Sts., New Orleans, LA 70125. Up to $1,000 to entering freshmen.

M,VP,WR   YADDO, Box 395, Union Ave., Saratoga Springs, NY 12866. Curtis Harnack, Ex. Dir. Living and studio space provided for periods up to two months, year round. No cash grants. Deadline Feb. 1. For creative artists who have achieved some measure of professional standing in their field. There are 3 composer's studios with pianos and 7 visual artist's studios. Studios are not equipped for heavier forms of sculpture (i.e. stone, ceramics, metal construction, welding).

m,vp,wr,   YALE UNIVERSITY, Art Gallery, 1111 Chapel St., Box 2006, Yale Sta.,
m,a   New Haven, CT 06520. Museum Training Fels, pre- and postdoctoral students. Yale Univ. Library: Prizes $5,000 annually for translation of poetry into English (published); others. School of Music: $50,000 divided among approx. 80 Grad students.

P-WR   YALE UNIVERSITY LIBRARY, Box 1603A Yale Station, New Haven, CT 06520.
     BOLLINGEN PRIZE IN POETRY: For an outstanding published work in the field of American poetry. $5,000 awarded biennially to citizens of the U.S. only.

P-WR   YALE YOUNGER POETS AWARD, Yale Series of Younger Poets, Yale University Press, 92A Yale Station, New Haven, CT 06520. Award of publication and royalties for written work or poetry submitted by American author under 40. Submit between Feb. 1 and Feb. 28.

M,m   YAMAHA MUSIC FOUNDATION, 3-24-22, Shimomeguro, Meguro-ku, Tokyo 153, Japan. Award is a public concert by any student of the Yamaha Music School and for a graduate of the School the opportunity to work with a professional orchestra.

m,vp   YANKTON COLLEGE, Conservatory of Music, Yankton, SD 57978. Various.

VP   YORK ACADEMY OF THE ARTS, Box 1441, 205 S. George St., York, PA 17405.

P-WR   YORKSHIRE POST "BOOK OF THE YEAR," Yorkshire Post Newspapers Ltd., PO Box 168, Wellington St., Leeds, LS1 1RF, England, UK. Prizes of 350 and 200 pounds for fiction and nonfiction books submitted by the publisher. Deadline Nov. 5. "Best First Work" award of 250 pounds for works submitted by the publisher. "Art and Music" award for best book on the understanding of music and art submitted by its publisher who must be British but the author need not be British or a British resident. Deadline Jan. 6.

m   YOUNG ARTISTS AUDITIONS, Women's Committee of the Oklahoma City Symphony, Mrs. Erich P. Frank, 836 NW 42nd St., Oklahoma City, OK 73118. Numerous, limited to residents of OK, AR, KS, TX and MO.

m   YOUNG ARTISTS AWARDS, Raymond Morin, 45 West Hill Dr., Worcester, MA 01609. Several to female performers to 25 yrs. Residents of Massachusetts and in financial need.

m   YOUNG MUSICIANS FOUNDATION, 914 So. Robertson Blvd., LA, CA 90035. $1,000 plus appearance, violin, piano, cello, viola players under 22; composers under 29; singers under 26. Apply Dr. R. Kendall, Exec. Dir., above.

P-VP   YOUNG-HUNTER, JOHN, MEMORIAL AWARD. Award: $150.
SEE: AMERICAN WATERCOLOR SOCIETY.

P-VP   YOUNG, VERDA MC CRACKEN, AWARD. Award: $200.
SEE: AMERICAN WATERCOLOR SOCIETY.

m   YOUNGSTOWN STATE UNIVERSITY, Dana School of Music, Youngstown, OH 44512. To $600, renewable. Dr. Ch. H. Aurand, Dean.

P-WR   MORTON DAUWEN ZABEL AWARD. Award: $2,500.
SEE: NATIONAL INSTITUTE OF ARTS AND LETTERS.

vp   WILLIAM ZORACH SCHOLARSHIP: Est. 1965.
SEE: Art Students League of N.Y. (Talent).

PRIMARY GOVERNMENTAL SOURCES
—National Endowment for the Arts—

One of the major goals of the legislation which set up the National Foundation on the Arts and the Humanities was stated to be "to encourage the creative development of the nation's finest talent." Congressional leaders clearly intended that non-matching "fellowship" or grant money be made available to creative individuals doing high quality work on a broad scale. Until now this has not been achieved. Although amounts of grants sometimes range up to $10,000, the number given each year is limited in each field. Appropriations affect the number given but also the policies set by the members of the National Council on the Arts as run by its Chairman, a Presidential appointee. Sometimes the grant money is rotated within fields so that some are not available in certain years. Most who receive monies are selected, after they apply, through panels set up for this purpose, chosen from the private sector. Sometimes grantees are selected from the outstanding without their having made application. Many more apply each year than can be accommodated by the tax money available, but it is worthwhile to keep applying if a first application or second or more lost out.

Here are the fields in which "fellowships" are given, along with the Program Office where one gets forms and guidelines. Write the Program Director for the one which concerns you, c/o National Endowment for the Arts, Washington, DC 20506.

Design Program: Fellowships in various aspects of interior, architectural and other design activities. (The program first was known by other names such as "Architecture/Environmental Arts," etc.)

Dance Program: Choreography

Education Program: Artists-In-Schools. (This is not strictly a "fellowship" program, but if artists in almost any field want to participate in local schools, get information as above. The following are now integrated into the programs in over 5,000 schools in selected areas of the country: designers, dancers, filmmakers, folk artists, poets, visual artists, craftsmen. There is, in education, a program for those wishing to become arts administrators, run with federal money by: Harvard Summer Institute; Graduate School of Business, UCLA; Arts Management Program at Sangamon State U/Springfield, IL; Graduate School of Business U/WI, Madison; Yale School of Drama, New Haven, CT. Apply directly to schools, not the Endowment.)

Literature Program: Writers in creative fields, i.e., poetry, novel, essays, criticism, playwriting. (Also gives money for placing writers in developing colleges.)

Museums Program: Museum staff professionals for leaves of absence; for museum training; for visiting specialists. See also Smithsonian Institution's program under the National Museum Act which gives money for: seminars/workshops, conservation studies, stipends for graduate/professional education and training, museum internships, advanced degrees, travel for professionals, special studies and research, technical assistance. For this program: Room 2467, Arts & Industries, SI, DC 20560. Also, the new Institute of Museum Services gives operation dollars and some for special projects to museums of all types. There is a pact between and among the entities giving out museum grant money not to duplicate aid.

Music Program: Composers/librettists, various amounts and categories. Jazz, various categories. Folk/Ethnic, the same. Opera singers/composers. Soloists (orchestra).

Public Media Program: Video and film artists, and "in-residence."

Theater Program: Playwrights, but individual fellowships in this field are limited.

Visual Arts Program: Painters, sculptors, printmakers, photographers and craftsmen.

Almost none of the Programs at the Arts Endowment give anything for tuition (exception is the arts management program, see above). The term "arts" in the NFAH legislation includes: "music (instrumental and vocal), dance, drama, folk art, creative writing, architecture and allied fields, painting, sculpture, photography, graphic and craft arts, industrial design, costume and fashion design, motion pictures, TV, radio, tape and sound recording, the arts related to the presentation, performance, execution and exhibition of such major art forms and the study and application of the arts to the human environment."

—The National Endowment for the Humanities—

The Humanities Endowment is the sister of the Arts Endowment under the National Foundation. The humanities, from the standpoint of Federal definition, includes, for arts constituents: "language, literature, archaeology; the history, criticism, theory and practice of the arts and the study and application of the humanities to the human environment." The Humanities Endowment has various degrees of "fellowships" or grants for which application may be made direct but most of their aid is given out to people who apply through institutions of higher learning. All major institutions of higher learning have access to and information about the programs. They, for the most part, should be contacted rather than the Endowment. This Endowment has been criticized lately for putting less and less emphasis also on the work of individual scholars, with larger percentages of the tax money going to institutions.

An exception to the rule of going through institutions in the Humanities Program is their "Youth Grant" project, wherein individuals under 25 may apply direct, setting forth projects which they would like to undertake. Write for all "Program Guidelines" to the National Endowment for the Humanities, DC 20506. For the young, prefix "Youth Grant Program." For practicing lawyers, doctors, and others outside academe who wish exposure to humanistic courses under subsidy, there is also a program. This goes through schools which give the courses, but information on which schools do what can be had also from the Endowment. There are some monies available through the newly subsidized "State" Humanities Programs. The Federal government now requires the Humanities Endowment to give out some of its appropriation each year to these State groups.

—Others in Washington—

Such quasi-governmental institutions as the Smithsonian itself, the National Gallery of Art, Hirshhorn Museum, National Collection of Fine Arts, etc. have some money to give out each year. Some of the specific programs you will find in the general listings of this book. To find out which programs are funded currently, write the institution in Washington for more information. The Smithsonian has the use of some funds abroad which used to be called "counterpart funds" and now are called "excess currencies." These are monies appropriated by Congress and converted at foreign banks by the U.S. Embassies into local currencies. Officially they are called "19FT510 Funds." Each year the Congress gives the Smithsonian the use of specific amounts of these funds in countries where they are located in that particular year. Usually the amount in a year is between $2 and $3 million under this facet of appropriation. Work abroad under some Smithsonian programs is funded in this manner.

All fifty States and the Territories receive money from the Federal government each year for arts/humanities programs. Many have their own appropriations too from their own legislatures, with amounts varying but generally growing each year overall. Some of the States have started grants-to-individuals programs, many giving them out directly. Others support community groups, regional groups or simply non-profits which in turn give out the money to individuals. (In New York, for instance, see Creative Artists Public Service Program or CAPS in the body of this work.) Change is so rapid in these programs it is best to contact your State agency. Those we have been able to pin down, from State, community regional or non-profit sources, are listed here. Selection in many instances is by panels as with the Federal agency; amounts are generally smaller for each grant. The exact title and address of state, city, community or other lower governmental agency is best checked out on the ground since the number of changes in a year is phenomenal. As a last resort, if you cannot locate the proper office, contact the office of the Governor or Mayor, most of which have cultural people in slots. Merit (quality) alone is supposed to be the criterion for obtaining a grant. You will note that we do not mention politicians in this paragraph. Take that for what it is worth!

—CETA—

CETA: Under monies appropriated for the Comprehensive Employment Training Act some cities and states have set up slots for arts-related jobs. These jobs are of various colorations and extend into many disciplines. The amounts paid for the jobs and the duration vary considerably and the whole program is an "indigent" one, rather than a positive accent one. Unemployed people "under poverty level" are serviced. Little freedom for pure creative work is afforded although artistic institutions can benefit from having the help of the people who take the jobs and, when there really is "training," the people themselves are sometimes placed in continuing employment after their eighteen months (maximum) under CETA. Some parts of the country have been placing more people from arts programs under CETA in regular positions than those in other types of programs under this authority. However, the whole idea is controversial and may eventually go the way of the WPA of Rooseveltian days.

CETA was started under the Public Works Act of 1976 and has had changes by amendments. The Arts Endowment has an office which keeps up with developments in arts jobs throughout the country but is not directly involved in implementing CETA directly. For more information write them, after first trying to find out in your home town and state (usually through the labor office or state arts council). One issue of the "Letter" carried a complete listing of offices which handle CETA in the nation.

—Routine Scholarship Aid—

There is considerable aid to help bright and talented students from higher income families, some 40,000 scholarships from more than 600 colleges (B average or higher, or SAT scores over 1,000 or ACT scores over 20). These are for all fields, not only arts, and loans, work situations, as well as grants are being made available to more and more higher education students throughout the U.S. these years. One source of information on them and their changing regulations can be found through Octameron Associates, PO Box 9437, Alexandria, VA 22302. Their booklets are nominally priced.

Besides the information here, for those Americans interested in work or study in arts/ humanities fields outside the U.S. a fine source of information is a booklet published by the Institute of International Education, Box NR, 809 United National Plaza, NYC 10017. Often scholarships awarded for home campus study are usable abroad. The IIE series is a continuing one (annual) and describes the opportunities which are for whole academic years and for shorter periods.

—INDEX OF CONTENTS BY DISCIPLINES—

Institutions are arranged alphabetically in the main text. After each, in this index, there is a general indication as to whether subsidy or aid is for "educational" or "professional" work. Sometimes, of course, these cross over and in many cases there is a fine line of distinction. In cases where it was difficult to determine the flexibility of the institution, we have indicated they might offer aid in both areas. But for the main, those offering aid primarily for "educational" purposes within a discipline, such as music, for instance, will have a lower case "m" after the name. If it would appear the help is purely in the "professional" area, the symbol is an upper case "M."

ROTCH TRAVELING SCHOLARSHIP (a)
SCHOOLS OF THE ART INSTITUTE OF
CHICAGO (a)
STAATLICHE HOCHSCHULE FUR BILD-
ENDE KUNSTE BERLIN (a)
STANFORD UNIV. (a)
STATE SCHOOL OF ARCHITECTURAL
ENGINEERING (Neinburg/Weser,
Germany) (a)
STATE SCHOOL OF ARCHITECTURAL
ENGINEERING (Trier, Germany)
(a)
THE STEEDMAN FELLOWSHIP (A)
JOHN STEWARDSON MEMORIAL
SCHOLARSHIP IN ARCHITEC-
TURE (a)
SYRACUSE UNIV. (a)
TEXAS A&M UNIV. (a)
TEXAS TECHNOLOGICAL COLLEGE (a)
TULANE UNIV. (a)
UNIV/ARIZONA (a)
UNIV/ARKANSAS (a)
UNIV/BRITISH COLUMBIA (a)
UNIV/CALIFORNIA (Berkeley) (a)
UNIV/COLORADO (a)
UNIV/DETROIT (a)
UNIV/FLORIDA (a)
UNIV/HAWAII (a)
UNIV/HOUSTON (a)
UNIV/IDAHO (a)
UNIV/ILLINOIS (a)
UNIV/KANSAS (a)
UNIV/MANITOBA (a)
UNIV/MARYLAND (a)
UNIV/MIAMI (a)
UNIV/MICHIGAN (A,a)
UNIV/MINNESOTA (a)
UNIV/MISSOURI (a)
UNIV/NEBRASKA (a)
UNIV/NEW MEXICO (a)
UNIV/NORTHERN COLORADO (a)
UNIV/NOTRE DAME (a)
UNIV/OKLAHOMA (a)
UNIV/OREGON (a)
UNIV/SOUTHERN CALIFORNIA (a)
UNIV/SOUTHWESTERN LOUISIANA (a)
UNIV/TENNESSEE (a)
UNIV/TEXAS AT AUSTIN (a)

UNIV/UTAH (a)
UNIV/VIRGINIA (a)
UNIV/WALES (a)
UNIV/WASHINGTON (a)
VIRGINIA MUSEUM (A,a)
VIRGINIA POLYTECHNIC INSTITUTE
(a)
WASHINGTON UNIV. (a)
WELSH COLLEGE OF ADVANCED
TECHNOLOGY (a)
WOOLEY SCHOLARSHIPS (a)
YALE UNIV. (a)

(ALL)

AFL-CIO EDUCATION DEPT. (all)
ALABAMA STATE COLLEGE (all)
ALABAMA STATE COUNCIL ON THE
ARTS AND HUMANITIES (all)
ALASKA STATE COUNCIL ON THE
ARTS (all)
FRENCH INSTITUTE/ALLIANCE
FRANCAISE (ALL,all)
ALPHA CHI OMEGA (ALL,all)
AMERICA THE BEAUTIFUL FUND
(ALL)
AMERICAN ASSOCIATION OF UNI-
VERSITY WOMEN (ALL)
AMERICAN MOTHERS COMMITTEE,
INC. (ALL)
AMERICAN PHILOSOPHICAL SOCIETY
(ALL-H,all-h)
AMERICAN RESEARCH INSTITUTE IN
TURKEY (ALL-H,all-h)
AMERICAN SAMOA ARTS COUNCIL
(all)
AMERICA SCANDINAVIAN FOUNDA-
TION (ALL,all)
AMVETS MEMORIAL SCHOLARSHIPS
(ALL)
ARKANSAS STATE ARTS AND HU-
MANITIES (ALL,all)
THE ART ANNUAL (ALL)
THE ARTISTS FOUNDATION, INC.
(ALL,all)
ARTPARK (ALL)
ARTS COUNCILS OF THE VARIOUS
STATES OF THE U.S. (ALL,all)

AUGUSTANA COLLEGE (ALL)
BAKER UNIV. (all)
BETHANY COLLEGE (Lindsborg, KS)
(all,all-h)
BOISE STATE COLLEGE (all)
BROOKLYN COLLEGE (CUNY) (all)
BRANDEIS UNIVERSITY(Creative Arts
Awards Commission) (ALL)
BRYN MAWR COLLEGE (ALL-H)
BUSH FOUNDATION (ALL)
CALIFORNIA ARTS COUNCIL (ALL,all)
CALIFORNIA INSTITUTE OF THE
ARTS (Valencia, CA) (ALL,all-h)
THE CANADA COUNCIL (ALL)
CAPS (ALL)
CARNATION COMPANY (ALL)
CERCLE CULTUREL DE ROYAUMONT
(ALL)
CINTAS FOUNDATION (ALL,all)
THE COLLEGE OF WOOSTER (all)
COLORADO COUNCIL ON THE ARTS
(ALL,all)
COLUMBIA UNIV. (all)
COMMITTEE OF INTERNATIONAL EX-
CHANGE OF PERSONS (ALL)
COMMONWEALTH OF PENNSYLVANIA
COUNCIL ON THE ARTS (ALL,
all)
COMMUNITY ARTS COUNCIL (ALL,all)
CONNECTICUT COMMISSION ON THE
ARTS (all)
COOPERATIVE RESEARCH PROGRAM
(all)
CORNELL UNIV. (all)
COUNCIL FOR ASSISTANCE TO THE
ARTS (ALL,all)
COUNCIL FOR INTERNATIONAL EX-
CHANGE OF SCHOLARS (ALL)
CREATIVE ARTISTS PROGRAM SERV-
ICE (ALL)
CULTURAL LAUREATE FOUNDATION
(ALL)
CUMMINGTON COMMUNITY OF THE
ARTS (ALL)
DANFORTH FOUNDATION (all)
DANISH GOVERNMENT SCHOLARSHIP
(ALL)
DELAWARE STATE ARTS COUNCIL

DEUTSCHEN AKADEMISCHEN AUS-
TAUSCH DIENST (all)
DEPARTMENT OF AGRICULTURE
(ALL)
DEPARTMENT OF AGRICULTURE (all)
DISNEY FOUNDATION (all)
DOBIE-PAISANO FELLOWSHIPS (ALL,
all)
DOMINICAN COLLEGE OF SAN
RAFAEL (all)
EMERSON COLLEGE (all)
FEDERAL ARTS ENDOWMENT (ALL,
all)
FEDERAL HUMANITIES ENDOWMENT
(ALL-h,all-h)
FINE ARTS COUNCIL OF FLORIDA
(all)
THE FLORIDA ARTS COUNCIL OF
FLORIDA (ALL)
FOREIGN AREA FELLOWSHIP PRO-
GRAM (ALL)
FULBRIGHT ACT (all)
GENERAL MOTORS SCHOLARSHIP
PROGRAM (all)
GENESEE COMMUNITY COLLEGE (all)
GEORGETOWN UNIV. (all)
GEORGIA COUNCIL FOR THE ARTS
AND HUMANITIES (all)
GERMAN ACADEMIC EXCHANGE SER-
VICE (all)
GERMAN BOOKSELLERS ASSOCIA-
TION (ALL)
GIRTON COLLEGE CAMBRIDGE (ALL,
all)
JOHN SIMON GUGGENHEIM MEMOR-
IAL FOUNDATION (all)
HALTON FOUNDATION (all)
HAWAII STATE FOUNDATION ON CUL-
TURE AND THE ARTS (ALL,all)
HENRY FELLOWSHIPS (Harvard) (all)
HENRY FELLOWSHIPS (Yale) (all)
GEORGE A. AND ELIZA GARDNER
HOWARD FOUNDATION (all)
HOWARD UNIVERSITY (Cambridge,
MA) (all)
ALEXANDER VON HUMBOLDT (all)
IDAHO STATE COMMISSION ON THE
ARTS AND HUMANITIES
(ALL,all)

ILLINOIS ARTS COUNCIL (ALL,all)
IMPERIAL EMBASSY OF IRAN (ALL)
INDIANA ARTS COMMISSION (ALL,all)
INSTITUTE OF EUROPEAN STUDIES
(all)
INSTITUTE OF INTERNATIONAL EDU-
CATION (ALL)
INSTITUTE OF PUERTO RICAN CUL-
TURE (all)
INSULAR ARTS COUNCIL OF GUAM
(all)
INTERNATIONAL RESEARCH AND
EXCHANGE BOARD (all)
IOWA STATE ARTS COUNCIL (ALL,all)
IVY FUND, INC. (all)
JAPAN FOUNDATION (ALL,all)
JELKE FOUNDATION, INC. (all)
KANSAS ARTS COMMISSION (all)
KENTUCKY ARTS COMMISSION (all)
KIMBER FARMS FOUNDATION (all)
LAKE ERIE COLLEGE (all)
LAKE FOREST COLLEGE (all)
D.H. LAWRENCE SUMMER FELLOW-
SHIP (ALL,all)
FAYE MC BEATH FOUNDATION (ALL,
all)
MAINE STATE COMMISSION ON THE
ARTS AND HUMANITIES (all)
MARSDEN FOUNDATION (ALL,all)
MARSHALL SCHOLARSHIPS (all)
MARYLAND ARTS COUNCIL (ALL)
MASSACHUSETTS COUNCIL ON THE
ARTS AND HUMANITIES (ALL,
all)
MASSACHUSETTS FOUNDATION FOR
HUMANITIES AND PUBLIC
POLICY (ALL)
WILLIAM & FLORENCE MATTHEW
FUND (all)
MEMPHIS ACADEMY OF THE ARTS
(all)
INGRAM MERRILL FOUNDATION
(ALL,all)
METROPOLITAN ARTS COMMISSION
(ALL)
MEXICAN EMBASSY (all)
MICHIGAN COUNCIL ON THE ARTS
(ALL,all)

MILLAY COLONY FOR THE ARTS
(ALL)
MINISTRY OF FOREIGN AFFAIRS
(France) (all)
MINNESOTA STATE ARTS BOARD
(ALL,all)
MISSISSIPPI ARTS COMMISSION (all)
MISSOURI STATE COUNCIL ON THE
ARTS (ALL,all)
MONTANA ARTS COUNCIL (all)
MOREHEAD STATE UNIV. (ALL)
E.M. MORRIS FOUNDATION INC. (ALL)
MUNDELEIN COLLEGE (all)
NATIONAL ENDOWMENT FOR THE
ARTS (ALL)
NATIONAL ENDOWMENT FOR THE
HUMANITIES (all-h)
NATIONAL MERIT SCHOLARSHIP
CORP. (all)
NATIONAL SCHOLARSHIP SERVICE
AND FUND FOR NEGRO STU-
DENTS (all)
NEBRASKA ARTS COUNCIL (all)
NETHERLAND AMERICA FOUNDA-
TION, INC. (all)
NEVADA STATE COUNCIL OF THE
ARTS (ALL)
NEW HAVEN FOUNDATION (all)
NEW JERSEY STATE COUNCIL ON THE
ARTS (ALL,all)
NEW JERSEY STATE MUSEUM (ALL)
NEW MEXICO ARTS COMMISSION (all)
NEW YORK STATE COUNCIL ON THE
ARTS (all)
NEW ZEALAND GOVERNMENT SCHOL-
ARSHIPS (all)
NOBEL PEACE PRIZE (ALL)
NORFOLK FOUNDATION (all)
NORTH CAROLINA ARTS COUNCIL
(ALL,all)
NORTH DAKOTA COUNCIL ON THE
ARTS AND HUMANITIES (all)
NORTHERN ILLINOIS UNIV. (all)
OKLAHOMA ARTS AND HUMANITIES
COUNCIL (all)
ORGANIZATION OF AMERICAN
STATES (all)
OSSABOW ISLAND PROJECT (ALL,all)

OTTUMWA HEIGHTS COLLEGE (all)
PRESSER FOUNDATION (all)
PURDUE UNIVERSITY (all)
QUEEN'S UNIVERSITY OF BELFAST
  (all)
RADCLIFFE COLLEGE INSTITUTE
  FOR INDEPENDENT STUDY
  (all)
READER'S DIGEST FOUNDATION (all)
RHODE ISLAND STATE COUNCIL ON
  THE ARTS (ALL,all)
RHODES TRUST (all)
ROCKEFELLER FOUNDATION (ALL)
ARTS COUNCIL OF ROCKVILLE (ALL)
ROTARY FOUNDATION FELLOWSHIPS
  (all)
THE MARK ROTHKO FOUNDATION,
  INC. (ALL)
SAN FRANCISCO FOUNDATION (ALL)
LEOPOLE SCHEPP FOUNDATION (all)
SEATTLE ART MUSEUM (ALL)
SEVEN LIVELY ARTS FESTIVAL (ALL)
SHELL SCHOLARSHIPS (all)
SMITHSONIAN INSTITUTION (ALL,all)
SOUTH CAROLINA ARTS COMMIS-
  SION (ALL)
SOUTH DAKOTA ART COUNCIL (ALL)
SOUTH DAKOTA STATE FINE ARTS
  COUNCIL (ALL,all)
SPAIN, GOVERNMENT OF (all)
STATE ARTS COUNCILS (ALL,all)
SWISS FEDERAL INSTITUTE OF TECH-
  NOLOGY (all)
TENNESSEE ARTS COMMISSION (all)
TEXAS COMMISSION ON THE ARTS
  AND HUMANITIES (all)
UNESCO (all)
U.S. ENDOWMENT FOR THE ARTS
  (ALL,all)
U.S. HUMANITIES ENDOWMENT
  (ALL-H,all-h)
UNIV/CALCUTTA (all)
UNIV/DURHAM (all)
UNIV/EAST ANGLIA (all)
UNIV/EDINGURGH (all)
UNIV GLASGOW (ALL)
UNIV/HOUSTON (all)
UNIV/LIVERPOOL (all)

UNIV/NORTH CAROLINA AT GREENS-
  BORO (all)
UNIV/TORONTO (all)
U.S. ARMY (all)
U.S. OFFICE OF EDUCATION (all)
UTAH STATE DIVISION OF FINE ARTS
  (all)
VERMONT COUNCIL ON THE ARTS
  (ALL,all)
VIRGIN ISLANDS COUNCIL ON THE
  ARTS (all)
VIRGINIA COMMISSION ON THE ARTS
  AND HUMANITIES (ALL,all)
LUDWIG VOGELSTEIN FOUNDATION,
  INC. (all)
WILLIAM S. WALTON CHARITABLE
  TRUST (all)
WASHINGTON STATE ARTS COMMIS-
  SION (ALL)
WASHINGTON UNIV. (all)
WESTERN KENTUCKY UNIV. (ALL,all)
WESTERN STATES ARTS FOUNDA-
  TION (ALL)
WEST VIRGINIA ARTS AND HUMANI-
  TIES COUNCIL (ALL,all)
WISCONSIN ARTS BOARD (ALL,all)
COLLEGE OF WOOSTER (all)
WURLITZER FOUNDATION (all)
WYOMING COUNCIL ON THE ARTS
  (all)

(AM)

ARTS MANAGEMENT (AM)
FORD FOUNDATION (am)
FOUNDATION FREIHERR-VON-STEIN
  OF HAMBURG (AM)
INTERNATIONAL MUSEUM OF PHO-
  TOGRAPHY (AM)
LANNAN FOUNDATION (AM)
MC KINSEY FOUNDATION BOOK
  AWARD (AM)
NATIONAL OPERA INSTITUTE (AM)
THE LARGER UNIVERSITIES.
  COURSES AND AID NOW BEING
  EXPANDED

(C)

ADAMS STATE COLLEGE (c)
ALABAMA STATE UNIV. (c)
ALBERTA COLLEGE OF ART, SOUTH-
     ERN ALBERTA INSTITUTE OF
     TECHNOLOGY (c)
ALLEGHENY COLLEGE (c)
ALLEN UNIV. (c)
ALMA COLLEGE (c)
AMERICAN RIVER COLLEGE (c)
ARIZONA COMMISSION ON THE ARTS
     AND HUMANITIES (C)
ARIZONA STATE UNIV. (c)
ARKANSAS STATE UNIV. (c)
ARNOT ART MUSEUM (C)
THE ART CENTER, INC. (C)
ART INSTITUTE OF CHICAGO (c)
ART SCHOOL OF THE SOCIETY OF
     ARTS AND CRAFTS (c)
ATLANTIC CITY NATIONAL ARTS
     AND CRAFTS SHOW (C)
ATLANTIC UNION COLLEGE (c)
BALDWIN WALLACE COLLEGE (c)
BANFF SCHOOL OF FINE ARTS (c)
BAYLOR UNIV. (c)
BENEDICT COLLEGE (c)
BENNINGTON COLLEGE (c)
BEREA COLLEGE (c)
BETHANY COLLEGE (Bethany, WV) (c)
BLACK HAWK COLLEGE (c)
BLOOMSBURG STATE COLLEGE (c)
BOSTON CENTER FOR ADULT EDUCA-
     TION (c)
BOSTON UNIVERSITY (c)
BRIGHAM YOUNG UNIVERSITY (c)
BROOKLYN MUSEUM ART SCHOOL (c)
CABRILLO COLLEGE (c)
CALDWELL COLLEGE FOR WOMEN (c)
CALIFORNIA COLLEGE OF ARTS AND
     CRAFTS (c)
CAMPBELLSVILLE COLLEGE (c)
CARNEGIE MELLON UNIV. (c)
THE EMILY CARR COLLEGE OF ART
     (c)
CARSON NEWMAN COLLEGE (c)
CARTHAGE COLLEGE (c)
CENTRAL CONNECTICUT STATE COL-
     LEGE (c)

CENTRAL STATE COLLEGE (c)
CENTRALIA COLLEGE (c)
CHADRON STATE COLLEGE (c)
CHAFFEY JUNIOR COLLEGE (c)
CHURCH COLLEGE OF HAWAII (c)
CINCINNATI CRAFT SHOW (C)
CLATSOP COMMUNITY COLLEGE (c)
CLEVELAND INSTITUTE OF ART (c)
CLEVELAND MUSEUM OF ART (C)
COLLEGE OF EASTERN UTAH (c)
COLLEGE OF THE HOLY NAMES (c)
COLLEGE OF NOTRE DAME OF MARY-
     LAND (c)
COLLEGE OF THE OZARKS (c)
COLLEGE OF ST. FRANCIS (c)
COLLEGE OF ST. MARY (c)
COLLEGE OF SOUTHERN UTAH (c)
COLORADO STATE COLLEGE (c)
COLORADO STATE UNIV. (c)
COLUMBIA BASIN COLLEGE (c)
COMMUNITY COLLEGE OF BALTI-
     MORE (c)
COMPTON COLLEGE (c)
CRANBROOK ACADEMY OF ART (c)
CREATIVE ARTS LEAGUE (C)
CULVER STOCKTON COLLEGE (c)
CUMBERLAND COLLEGE (c)
DALLAS MUSEUM OF FINE ARTS (C)
DANA COLLEGE (c)
DAYTON ART INSTITUTE (c)
DELAWARE ART MUSEUM (C)
DELTA STATE COLLEGE (c)
DEPARTMENT OF JUSTICE (c)
DICKINSON STATE COLLEGE (c)
DIXIE COLLEGE (c)
DRAKE UNIV. (c)
DUTCHESS COMMUNITY COLLEGE (c)
EASTERN ILLINOIS UNIV. (c)
EASTERN MONTANA COLLEGE (c)
EASTERN NEW MEXICO UNIV. (c)
EASTERN WASHINGTON STATE COL-
     LEGE (c)
EDINBORO STATE COLLEGE (c)
ELIZABETH CITY STATE COLLEGE (c)
ELMIRA COLLEGE (c)
ENDICOTT JUNIOR COLLEGE (c)
FAIRMONT STATE COLLEGE (c)
FASHION INSTITUTE OF TECHNOL-
     OGY (c)

195

FLINT COMMUNITY JUNIOR COLLEGE (c)
FLORIDA JUNIOR COLLEGE AT JACK-SONVILLE (c)
FLORIDA MEMORIAL COLLEGE (c)
FLORIDA SOUTHERN COLLEGE (c)
FORT HAYS KANSAS STATE COLLEGE c)
FORT WORTH ART CENTER MUSEUM AND SCHOOL (c)
FRIEND UNIV. (C)
GASPARILLA SIDEWALK ART FESTI-VAL (C)
GASTON COLLEGE (c)
GDANSK CITY COUNCIL (C)
GENERAL SERVICES ADMINISTRA-TION (GSA) (C)
GEORGIA COLLEGE AT MILLEDGE-VILLE (c)
GEORGIAN COURT COLLEGE (C)
GLENVILLE STATE COLLEGE (c)
GRAND PRIX INTERNATIONAL D'ART CONTEMPORAIN DE MONTE-CARLO (C)
GREENWICH HOUSE POTTERY (c)
THE HAMBRIDGE ART CENTER (C)
HAMPTON INSTITUTE (c)
HARTNELL COLLEGE (c)
HASTINGS COLLEGE (c)
HAYSTACK MOUNTAIN SCHOOL OF CRAFTS (c)
HOFSTRA COLLEGE (c)
HOUSTON BAPTIST COLLEGE (c)
HOWARD UNIV. (Washington, DC) (c)
IDAHO STATE UNIV. (c)
ILLINOIS STATE UNIV. (c)
INDIANA STATE UNIV. (c)
INDIANA UNIV. (c)
INSTITUTE FOR THE ARTS (C)
INSTITUTO ALLENDE (c)
JACKSON STATE COLLEGE (c)
JUDSON COLLEGE (c)
KENT STATE UNIV. (c)
KENTUCKY WESLEYAN COLLEGE (c)
KUTZTOWN STATE COLLEGE (c)
LASELL JUNIOR COLLEGE (c)
LAWRENCE UNIV. (c)
LINFIELD COLLEGE (c)

LITTLE ROCK UNIV. (c)
LOUISIANA COLLEGE (c)
LOUISIANA POLITECHNIC INSTITUTE (c)
LOUISIANA STATE UNIV. (c)
LOUISVILLE SCHOOL OF ART (c)
LOWELL STATE COLLEGE (c)
LOWER COLUMBIA COLLEGE (c)
LYNCHBURG COLLEGE (c)
MACOMB COUNTY COMMUNITY COL-LEGE (c)
MADOC-TWEED ART CENTER (c)
MARYLAND INSTITUTE (c)
MARYLAND STATE COLLEGE (c)
MARYMOUNT COLLEGE (Los Angeles) (c)
MASSACHUSETTS COLLEGE OF ART (c)
MECHANICS INSTITUTE (c)
MERCYHURST COLLEGE (c)
MIAMI DADE JUNIOR COLLEGE (c)
MIAMI UNIV. (c)
MILLERSVILLE STATE COLLEGE (c)
MINOT STATE COLLEGE (c)
MISSISSIPPI UNIVERSITY FOR WOMEN (c)
MODESTO JUNIOR COLLEGE (c)
MOLLOY COLLEGE (c)
MOUNT MARTY COLLEGE (c)
MOUNT MARY COLLEGE (c)
MUSEUM ART SCHOOL (c)
MUSEUM OF FINE ARTS (c)
MUSEUM OF NEW MEXICO (C)
NATIONAL COMPETITION FOR AMER-ICAN INDIAN ARTISTS (C)
NAZARETH COLLEGE (c)
NAZARETH COLLEGE OF KENTUCKY (c)
NEBRASKA WESLEYAN UNIV. (c)
NEVADA SOUTHERN UNIV. (c)
NEWARK STATE COLLEGE (c)
NEW HAMPSHIRE COMMISSION ON THE ARTS (C)
NEW MEXICO STATE UNIV. (c)
NORTH CAROLINA COLLEGE AT DURHAM (c)
NORTHEAST LOUISIANA UNIV. (c)
NORTHERN MICHIGAN UNIV. (c)

NORTHERN STATE COLLEGE (c)
NORTHWEST MISSOURI STATE COL-
LEGE (c)
NOTRE DAME COLLEGE (c)
NOTRE DAME COLLEGE OF OHIO (c)
ODESSA COLLEGE (c)
OHIO WESLEYAN UNIV. (c)
OREGON COLLEGE (c)
OREGON STATE UNIV. (c)
OTIS ART INSTITUTE (c)
OTTAWA UNIV. (c)
OUT LADY OF CINCINNATI COLLEGE
(c)
PASADENA COLLEGE (c)
GEORGE PEABODY COLLEGE FOR
TEACHERS (c)
PENNSYLVANIA FEDERATION OF
WOMEN'S CLUBS SCHOLAR-
SHIPS (c)
PEPPERDINE COLLEGE (c)
PETER'S VALLEY CRAFTSMEN (C)
PHILADELPHIA COLLEGE OF ART (c)
PHILADELPHIA COLLEGE OF TEX-
TILES AND SCIENCE (c)
PHOENIX COLLEGE (c)
PLYMOUTH STATE COLLEGE OF THE
UNIV. OF NEW HAMPSHIRE (c)
PORTLAND SCHOOL OF ART (c)
PORTSMOUTH PARKS AND RECREA-
TION DEPARTMENT (C)
PRATT-N.Y. PHOENIX SCHOOL OF
DESIGN (c)
QUEENS COLLEGE (c)
REHOBOTH ART LEAGUE (c)
RHODE ISLAND COLLEGE (c)
RHODE ISLAND SCHOOL OF DESIGN
(c)
RHODODENDRON STATE OUTDOOR
ART AND CRAFT FESTIVAL (C)
RIDGEWOOD SCHOOL OF ART &
DESIGN (c)
RIO HONDO COLLEGE (c)
ROANOKE COMMONWEALTH UNIV. (c)
ROCHESTER INSTITUTE OF TECHNOL-
OGY (c)
J.D. ROCKEFELLER III FUND (C)
ROSWELL MUSEUM AND ART CENTER
(C)

RUTGERS UNIV. (c)
SACRAMENTO STATE COLLEGE (c)
ST. MARY-OF-THE-WOODS COLLEGE
(c)
ST. NORBERT COLLEGE (c)
ST. PAUL ART CENTER SCHOOL (c)
SAN FRANCISCO COLLEGE (c)
SAN FERNANDO VALLEY STATE
COLLEGE (c)
SAN JOSE STATE COLLEGE (c)
SCHOOLS OF THE ART INSTITUTE
OF CHICAGO (c)
SCHOOL OF THE MUSEUM OF FINE
ARTS (c)
SCRIPPS COLLEGE (c)
SEATTLE PACIFIC COLLEGE (c)
SHEPARD COLLEGE (c)
SKIDMORE COLLEGE (c)
SOUTHEASTERN MASSACHUSETTS
TECHNOLOGICAL INSTITUTE
(c)
SOUTHEASTERN STATE COLLEGE (c)
SOUTHEAST MISSOURI STATE COL-
LEGE (c)
SOUTHERN ILLINOIS UNIV. (c)
SOUTHERN METHODIST UNIV. (c)
SOUTHWEST TEXAS STATE COL-
LEGE (c)
SPOKANE COMMUNITY COLLEGE (c)
SPRING ARBOR COLLEGE (c)
SPRINGFIELD COLLEGE (c)
STATE UNIVERSITY OF NEW YORK
AT ALBANY (c)
STATE UNIVERSITY OF NEW YORK
COLLEGE OF CERAMICS (C)
STEPHEN F. AUSTIN STATE COLLEGE
(c)
THOMAS MORE COLLEGE (C)
SYLACAUGA AREA COUNCIL ON
ARTS AND HUMANITIES (C)
SYRACUSE UNIV. (c)
TEXAS CHRISTIAN UNIV. (c)
THOMAS MORE COLLEGE (c)
THOUSAND ISLANDS MUSEUM CRAFT
SCHOOL (c)
THREE RIVERS ARTS FESTIVAL (C)
TUFTS UNIV. (c)
TULANE UNIV. (c)

TYLER SCHOOL OF ART OF TEMPLE
UNIV. (c)
UNIVERSITY OF ALBUQUERQUE (c)
UNIVERSITY OF THE AMERICAS (c)
UNIV/CALIFORNIA (berkeley) (c)
UNIV/CHATTANOOGA (c)
UNIV/CONNECTICUT (c)
UNIV/CORPUS CHRISTI (c)
UNIV/DALLAS (c)
UNIV/DENVER (c)
UNIV/FLORIDA (c)
UNIV/ILLINOIS (c)
UNIV/JUDAISM (c)
UNIV/KANSAS (c)
UNIV/MANITOBA (c)
UNIV/MINNESOTA (Duluth) (c)
UNIV/NEBRASKA AT OMAHA (c)
UNIV/NEW HAMPSHIRE (c)
UNIV/NORTH CAROLINA AT ASHE-
VILLE (c)
UNIV/NORTHERN IOWA (c)
UNIV/OKLAHOMA (c)
UNIV/SOUTH CAROLINA (c)
UNIV/SOUTH DAKOTA (c)
UNIV/SOUTH FLORIDA (c)
UNIV/SOUTHERN CALIFORNIA (c)
UNIV/TEXAS AT EL PASO (c)
UNIV/UTAH (c)
UNIV/VERMONT (c)
UNIV/WASHINGTON (c)
UNIV/WISCONSIN AT MILWAUKEE (c)
URSULINE COLLEGE (c)
UTAH STATE UNIV. (c)
VALPARAISO UNIV. (c)
VIRGINIA COMMONWEALTH UNIV. (c)
WASHINGTON STATE COLLEGE OF
THE UNIV/MAINE (c)
WASHINGTON UNIV. (c)
WEATHERFORD COLLEGE (c)
WEBER STATE COLLEGE (c)
WEBSTER COLLEGE (c)
WESTERN CAROLINA UNIV. (c)
WESTERN COLORADO CENTER FOR
THE ARTS (C)
WESTERN ILLINOIS UNIV. (c)
WESTERN NEW MEXICO UNIV. (c)
WESTERN WASHINGTON STATE COL-
LEGE (c)

WESTMAR COLLEGE (c)
WESTMINISTER COLLEGE (c)
WEST TEXAS STATE UNIV. (c)
WEST VIRGINIA UNIV. (c)
WESTWOOD CERAMICS SUPPLY CO.
(C)
WHITWORTH COLLEGE (c)
WHITMAN COLLEGE (c)
WILLIAM CAREY COLLEGE (c)
WILLIAM WOODS COLLEGE (c)
WISCONSIN FESTIVAL OF ARTS (C)
WISCONSIN STATE UNIV. (Eau Claire)
(c)
WISCONSIN STATE UNIV. (River Falls)
(c)
WISCONSIN STATE UNIV. (Superior) (c)

(D)

AFFILIATE ARTISTS, INC. (D)
ALDERSON BROADDUS COLLEGE
(d)
ALVIN AILEY DANCE COMPANY (D)
AMERICAN DANCE THEATER (D)
BARD COLLEGE (d)
BOSTON CONSERVATORY OF MUSIC
(d)
BROOKLYN ACADEMY OF MUSIC (D,d)
BUFFALO FOUNDATION (D,d)
BULGARIAN COMMITTEE OF CUL-
TURE AND ART (D,d)
CAMDEN COUNTY CULTURAL AND
HERITAGE COMMISSION (D)
CAPEZIO (D)
CENTRAL MICHIGAN UNIVERSITY (D)
CHAUTAUQUA INSTITUTION (d)
COLLEGE CONSERVATORY OF MUSIC
UNIV/CINCINNATI (d)
COMMUNITY ASSOCIATION OF
SCHOOLS FOR THE ARTS (d)
MERCE CUNNINGHAM DANCE CO.
(D,d)
DELL PUBLISHING CO. FOUNDATION
(D)
DEPARTMENT OF JUSTICE (d)
EASTERN NEW MEXICO UNIV. (d)
EXOTIC DANCERS LEAGUE OF
AMERICA (D)

FLORIDA ATLANTIC MUSIC GUILD,
INC (D)
FLORIDA SCHOOL OF THE ARTS (d)
FOLKWANG-HOCHSCHULE ESSEN
(D,d)
FORD FOUNDATION (d)
FOUNDATION OF CONTEMPORARY
PERFORMANCE ARTS (D)
INTERNATIONAL HUMANITIES (D,d)
IRISH AMERICAN CULTURAL INSTI-
TUTE (D)
JACKSONVILLE UNIV. (d,d-h)
JORDAN COLLEGE OF MUSIC OF
BUTLER UNIV. (d)
JUILLIARD SCHOOL (d)
ALFRED JURZYKOWSKI FND., Inc.
(D)
THE KATE NEAL KINLEY MEMORIAL
FELLOWSHIP (d)
THE MARLAND-NATIONAL CAPITAL
PARK AND PLANNING COM-
MISSION (D)
NATIONAL DANCE ASSOCIATION (D)
NATIONAL FEDERATION OF MUSIC
CLUBS (D,d)
NEW YORK UNIV. (d)
J.D. ROCKEFELLER III FUND (D)
RODGERS AND HAMMERSTEIN
FOUNDATION (D)
HERBERT AND NANNETTE ROTHS-
CHILD FOUNDATION, INC. (D)
SCRIPPS COLLEGE (d)
SIMONE SUTER SCHOOL OF DANCE
(d)
SKIDMORE COLLEGE (d)
SOCIETA DEL QUARTETTO (D)
TEXAS CHRISTIAN UNIV. (d)
UNITED STATES INTERNATIONAL
UNIV. (d)
UNIV/MISSOURI — KANSAS CITY (d)
USSR MINISTRY OF CULTURE (D)
HELENE WURLITZER FOUNDATION
OF NEW MEXICO (D)

(F)

AMERICAN FILM INSTITUTE (F,f)
AMERICAN UNIV. (f)

AMSTERDAM INTERNATIONAL FESTI-
VAL OF STUDENT-MADE
FILMS (CINESTUD) (f)
THE ANN ARBOR 8mm FILM FESTI-
VAL (F)
ARKANSAS STATE UNIV. (f)
ASHLAND COLLEGE (f)
ASOLO INTERNATIONAL FESTIVAL
OF FILMS ON ART AND BIOG-
RAPHIES OF ARTISTS (F)
AUBURN UNIV. (f)
BALL STATE UNIV. (f)
BERLIN INTERNATIONAL AGRICUL-
TURAL FILM COMPETITION (F)
BLACK HAWK COLLEGE (f)
BOSTON UNIV. (f)
BOWLING GREEN STATE UNIV. (F)
BRANDEIS UNIV. (f)
BRIGHAM YOUNG UNIV. (F)
BROOKLYN COLLEGE, CITY UNIVER-
SITY OF NEW YORK (f)
CALIFORNIA COLLEGE OF ARTS AND
CRAFTS (f)
CALIFORNIA STATE COLLEGE AT
FULLERTON (f)
CALIFORNIA STATE UNIV., San Fran-
cisco (f)
CENTRAL MICHIGAN UNIV. (f)
THE CITY COLLEGE OF NEW YORK (f)
THE CITY COLLEGE OF SAN FRAN-
CISCO (f)
CLAREMONT SCHOOL OF THEOLOGY
(f)
THE COLORADO STATE UNIV. (f)
COLUMBIA COLLEGE, (CA) (f)
COLUMBIA COLLEGE, (IL) (f)
COLUMBUS INTERNATIONAL FILM
FESTIVAL (F,f)
CRACOW INTERNATIONAL FESTIVAL
OF SHORT FILMS (F)
DEPARTMENT OF JUSTICE (f)
DINARD INTERNATIONAL FESTIVAL
FILMS FROM FRENCH SPEAK-
ING REGIONS (F)
DUTCH FILM FESTIVAL (F)
EDUCATIONAL FILM LIBRARY ASSO-
CIATION (F)
FLORIDA SCHOOL OF THE ARTS (f)

FLORIDA STATE UNIV. (F)
FLORIDA TECHNOLOGICAL UNIV. (f)
FOOTHILL COLLEGE (f)
FORDHAM UNIV. (f)
FOUNDATION OF CONTEMPORARY
PERFORMANCE ARTS (F)
GERMANY ARTISTS-IN-BERLIN
PROGRAM (F)
GODDARD COLLEGE (f)
GRAHM JUNIOR COLLEGE (f)
HUMBOLDT STATE COLLEGE (f)
ILLINOIS STATE UNIVERSITY (f)
INDIANA UNIV. (f)
INTERNATIONALE FILMWOCHE
MANNHEIM (f)
IOWA STATE UNIVERSITY PRESS (f)
ITHACA COLLEGE (f)
THE KATE NEAL KINLEY MEMORIAL
FELLOWSHIP (f)
KRANJ INTERNATIONAL FESTIVAL
OF SPORT AND TOURIST
FILMS (F)
LEIPZIG INTERNATIONAL FILM
FESTIVAL (F)
LOS ANGELES VALLEY COLLEGE (f)
LOUISVILLE SCHOOL OF ART (f)
THE MACDOWELL COLONY, INC. (F)
MADISON COLLEGE (f)
MANNHEIM INTERNATIONAL FILM
FESTIVAL (f)
MARSHALL UNIV. (f)
MASSACHUSETTS ARTS AND HUMANI-
TIES FOUNDATION (F)
MASSACHUSETTS COLLEGE OF ART
(f)
MELBOURNE FILM FESTIVAL (F)
MEMPHIS STATE UNIV. (f)
SIDNEY MEYERS MEMORIAL FUND
(F)
MICHIGAN STATE UNIV. (f)
MONTANA STATE UNIV. (f)
MONTCLAIR STATE COLLEGE (f)
MURRAY STATE UNIV (f)
MUSEUM OF MODERN ART (F)
NATIONAL TRUST FOR HISTORIC
PRESERVATION (F)
NEW MEXICO STATE UNIV. (f)
NYU SCHOOL OF ARTS, GRADUATE
INSTITUTE OF FILM & TV (f)

NY INSTITUTE OF TECHNOLOGY (f)
NY UNIVERSITY, Cinema Studies (f)
NEW YORK UNIV. (f)
NORTHERN ARIZONA UNIV. (f)
OBERHAUSEN INTERNATIONAL
FESTIVAL OF SHORT
FILMS (F)
OHIO ARTS COUNCIL (F)
OHIO STATE UNIV. (F)
OHIO UNIV. (F)
OKLAHOMA STATE UNIV. (F)
PENNSYLVANIA STATE UNIV. (f)
PHILADELPHIA COLLEGE OF ART (f)
RHODE ISLAND SCHOOL OF DESIGN
(f)
RICHMOND COLLEGE (f)
RIDGEWOOD SCHOOL OF ART AND
DESIGN (f)
RIO HONDO COLLEGE (f)
J.D. ROCKEFELLER III FUND (F)
ROGER INSTITUTE OF TECHNOLOGY
(f)
SAN ANTONIO COLLEGE (f)
SAN DIEGO CITY COLLEGE (f)
SAN DIEGO STATE COLLEGE (f)
SAN FRANCISCO STATE COLLEGE (f)
SAN REMO FILM FESTIVAL (F)
SCHOOLS OF THE ART INSTITUTE OF
CHICAGO (f)
SCHOOL OF THE MUSEUM OF FINE
ARTS (f)
SCHOOL OF VISUAL ARTS (f)
SCRIPPS COLLEGE (f)
SKIDMORE COLLEGE (f)
SOCIETY FOR CINEMA STUDIES (F)
SOUTH DAKOTA STATE UNIV. (f)
SOUTHERN METHODIST UNIV. (f)
STANFORD UNIV. (f)
STATE UNIVERSITY OF NEW YORK
AT BUFFALO (f)
STEPHENS COLLEGE (f)
SUTTER CINEMA, INC. (F,f)
SYRACUSE UNIV. (f)
TEMPLE UNIV. (f)
TEXAS CHRISTIAN UNIV. (f)
TEXAS TECHNOLOGICAL COLLEGE
(f)
TOKYO FILM ART FESTIVAL (F,f)
TRENTO INTERNATIONAL FESTIVAL

OF MOUNTAIN AND EXPLOR-
ATION FILMS (F)
UNITED STATES INTERNATIONAL
UNIV. (f)
UNIV/ALABAMA (f)
UNIV/CALIFORNIA AT LOS ANGELES
(f)
UNIV/DENVER (f)
UNIVERSITY FILM ASSOCIATION
(CANADA) (f)
UNIVERSITY FILM ASSOCIATION
(NY) (f)
UNIV/HOUSTON (f)
UNIV/GEORGIA (f)
UNIV/IOWA (f)
UNIV/KANSAS (f)
UNIV/MARYLAND (f)
UNIV/MASSACHUSETTS (f)
UNIV/MIAMI (f)
UNIV/MINNESOTA (f)
UNIV/MISSISSIPPI (f)
UNIV/MISSOURI (f)
UNIV/MONTANA (f)
UNIV/NEBRASKA (f)
UNIV/NEW ORLEANS (f)
UNIV/NORTH CAROLINA (f)
UNIV/NORTH DAKOTA (f)
UNIV/OREGON (F)
UNIV/THE PACIFIC (F)
UNIV/SOUTH DAKOTA (f)
UNIV/SOUTHERN CALIFORNIA (f)
UNIV/TEXAS AT AUSTIN (f)
UNIV/TULSA (f)
UNIV/UTAH (f)
UNIV/WASHINGTON (f)
UNIV/WISCONSIN (Madison) (f)
UNIV/WISCONSIN (Oshkosh) (F)
UNIV/WISCONSIN (Superior) (F)
UTAH STATE UNIV. (f)
VINCENNES UNIV. (f)
WAYNE STATE UNIV. (f)
WEST VIRGINIA UNIV. (f)
WESTERN ILLINOIS UNIV. (f)
WHITNEY MUSEUM OF AMERICAN
ART (F)

(M)

ABA-OSTWALD BAND COMPOSITION

CONTEST (M,m)
ACADEMIE MUSICALE CHIGIANA (m)
ACADEMY OF MUSIC (AUSTRIA) (M)
ACADEMY OF VOCAL ARTS (m)
ACCADEMIA NAZIONALE DE SANTA
CECILIA (M)
ADAMS STATE COLLEGE (m)
AEOLIAN ORGAN PLAYING COMPE-
TITION (M)
AFFILIATE ARTISTS, INC. (M)
AFRICAN ARTS MAGAZINE (M)
AGNES SCOTT COLLEGE (M)
AGRICULTURAL AND TECHNICAL
COLLEGE OF NORTH CARO-
LINA (m)
ALBANY STATE COLLEGE (m)
ALBION COLLEGE (m)
ALDERSON-BROADDUS COLLEGE (m)
ALMA COLLEGE (m)
ALVERNO COLLEGE (m)
ALVIN AILEY DANCE COMPANY (M)
AMARILLO NAT'L ARTISTS AUDI-
TIONS (M)
AMERICAN ACADEMY IN ROME (m)
AMERICAN ACCORDION MUSICO-
LOGICAL SOCIETY (M)
AMERICAN ACCORDIONIST ASSO-
CIATION (M,m)
AMERICAN BANDMASTER ASSO. (M)
AMERICAN CONSERVATORY OF
MUSIC (M,m)
AMERICAN DANCE THEATER (M)
AMERICAN FOREIGN SERVICE
ASSOC. (m)
AMERICAN GUILD OF MUSICAL
ARTISTS (m)
AMERICAN GUILD OF ORGANISTS
COMPETITION (M,m)
AMERICAN INTERNATIONAL MUSI-
CAL FUND, INC. (M)
AMERICAN MUSIC CENTER, INC. (M)
THE AMERICAN MUSIC CONFERENCE
(M,m)
AMERICAN MUSICOLOGICAL SOCIETY
(M,m)
AMERICAN OPERA AUDITIONS (M)
AMERICAN SOCIETY OF COMPOSERS,
AUTHORS & PUBLISHERS (M)
AMERICAN UNIV. (m)

AMICI DELLA MUSICA, AREZZO, ITALY (M)
MARION ANDERSON SCHOLARSHIP FUND (M)
ANTIOCH COLLEGE (m)
ANGELICUM PRIZE (M)
APPALACHIAN STATE UNIV. (M,m)
ARCHIVES DU PALAIS PRINCIER (M)
GUIDO D'AREZZO INTERNATIONAL POLYPHONIC COMPETITION (M)
ARLINGTON SYMPHONY ASSN. (M)
ARTISTS ADVISORY COUNCIL (M)
ARTISTS FOR ENVIRONMENT FDN. (M)
ARTISTS PRESENTATION SOCIETY (M)
ASBDA-VOLKWEIN BAND COMPOSITION AWARD (M)
ASHLAND COLLEGE (m)
ASPEN MUSIC SCHOOL (m)
AUSTRO—AMERICAN SOCIETY (m)
AYUNTAMIENTO DE ALICANTE (m)
AZUSA PACIFIC COLLEGE (m)
BACH INTERNATIONAL COMPETITION (M)
BACH INTERNATIONAL COMPETITION (GERMANY) (M)
BAGBY MUSIC LOVER'S FUND (M)
BALTIMORE CIVIC OPERA COMPANY (M)
BALTIMORE OPERA COMPANY, INC. (M)
BANARAS HINDU UNIV. (M,m)
BARD COLLEGE (m)
BARNARD COLLEGE (m)
BARRINGTON COLLEGE (m)
BAYLOR UNIV. (m)
JOSEPH H. BEARNS PRIZES IN MUSIC (M)
BEAVER COLLEGE (m)
BEEBE (FRANK HUNTINGTON) FUND FOR MUSICIANS (m)
THE BEETHOVEN CLUB (m)
BELOIT COLLEGE (m)
BEMIDJI STATE COLLEGE (m)
BENEDICTINE COLLEGE MUSIC DEPARTMENT (m)
BERKLEE SCHOOL OF MUSIC (M,m)

BERKSHIRE MUSIC CENTER (M,m)
BERRY COLLEGE (m)
BETHANY COLLEGE (BETHANY, WV) (m)
BETHANY NAZARENE COLLEGE (m)
BETHEL COLLEGE (MC KENZIE, TN) (m)
BETHEL COLLEGE (ST. PAUL, MN) (m)
BLACK HAWK COLLEGE (m)
MARC BLITZSTEIN AWARD (M)
BLOCH ARTIST AUDITIONS (M)
BLUFFTON COLLEGE (m)
BOK (MARY LOUISE CURTIS) FOUNDATION (m)
BOSTON CONSERVATORY OF MUSIC (m)
BOSTON SCHOOL OF MUSIC (m)
BOWLING GREEN STATE UNIV. (m)
BRADLEY UNIV. (m)
BRAEMER FOUNDATION (M)
BRANDEIS UNIV. (m)
BRENAU COLLEGE (m)
BRESCIA COLLEGE (m)
BRIAR CLIFF COLLEGE (m)
BRIGHAM YOUNG UNIV. (m)
BRISTOL CHAMBER OF COMMERCE (m)
BROADCAST MUSIC INC. (M)
BROOKLYN ACADEMY OF MUSIC (M,m)
BROWN UNIV. (m)
BUCKNELL UNIV. (m)
BUDAPEST INTERNATIONAL MUSIC COMPETITION (M)
BUENA VISTA COLLEGE (m)
BUFFALO FOUNDATION (M,m)
BULGARIAN COMMITTEE OF CULTURE AND ART (M)
BULGARIAN CONCERT BUREAU (M)
BUREAU DE CONCERTS MAURICE WERNER (M)
BUSONI INTERNATIONAL PIANO COMPETITION (M)
BUSSETO INTERNATIONAL COMPETITION FOR VERDI VOICES (M)
CALDWELL COLLEGE (m)
CALIFORNIA STATE COLLEGE AT

FULLERTON (m)
CAMDEN COUNTY CULTURAL AND
HERITAGE COMMISSION (M)
CAMPBELL COLLEGE (m)
CANADIAN COUNCIL ASSISTANCE TO
ARTISTS (M)
CANADIAN OPERA COMPANY (M)
CANADIAN WOMEN'S CLUB OF NEW
YORK (M)
MARIA CANALS INTERNATIONAL
MUSIC COMPETITION (M,m)
CANNON MUSIC CAMP (m)
CAPITAL UNIV. (m)
CARDINAL STRITCH COLLEGE (m)
CARNEGIE HALL (M)
CARNEGIE INSTITUTE OF TECH-
NOLOGY (m)
CARNEGIE MELLON UNIV. (m)
CARROLL COLLEGE (m)
CARSON NEWMAN COLLEGE (m)
CARTHAGE COLLEGE (m)
ALFREDO CASELLA INTERNATIONAL
COMPETITION (M)
CATHOLIC UNIVERSITY OF AMERICA
(m)
CBC OTTAWA ORIGINAL MUSIC COM-
PETITION (M)
CENTENARY COLLEGE OF LOUISI-
ANA (M,m)
CENTRAL CITY OPERA ASSOCIATION
(M)
CENTRAL COLLEGE (m)
CENTRAL METHODIST COLLEGE (m)
CENTRAL MICHIGAN UNIV. (m)
CENTRAL MISSOURI STATE COLLEGE
(m)
CENTRAL STATE UNIV. (m)
CENTRAL WASHINGTON STATE COL-
LEGE (m)
CHADRON STATE COLLEGE (m)
CHAUTAUQUA INSTITUTION (m)
CHICAGO CONSERVATORY COLLEGE
(M,m)
CHICAGO MUSICAL COLLEGE (m)
CHICAGO SYMPHONY ORCHESTRA
(M)
CHICO STATE COLLEGE (m)
FREDERIC CHOPIN SOCIETY (M)

CHRISTIAN EDUCATION FOR THE
BLIND, INC. (M,m)
CITY COLLEGE OF NEW YORK (m)
CITY OF MONTEVIDEO INTERNA-
TIONAL PIANO COMPETI-
TION (m)
CLARK COLLEGE (m)
CLARKE COLLEGE (m)
CLEVELAND INSTITUTE OF MUSIC
(M,m)
COE COLLEGE (m)
COKER COLLEGE (m)
COLGATE UNIV. (m)
COLLEGE CONSERVATORY OF MUSIC,
UNIV/CINCINNATI (m)
COLLEGE MISERICORDIA (m)
COLLEGE OF NOTRE DAME (m)
COLLEGES PONTIFICAUX (M)
COLORADO COLLEGE (m)
COLORADO STATE COLLEGE (m)
COLORADO STATE UNIV. (m)
COLUMBIA UNIV COLLEGE (m)
COMMUNITY ASSOCIATION OF
SCHOOLS FOR THE ARTS (m)
CONCERT ARTISTS GUILD, INC. (M)
CONCORD COLLEGE (m)
CONCORDIA CONSERVATORY OF
MUSIC (m)
CONCOURS INTERNATIONAL DE
CHANT (m)
CONCOURS INTERNATIONAL D'EXE-
CUTION MUSICAL (M)
CONCURSO VIANNA DA MOTTA (M)
CONGRESS OF STRINGS PROGRAM
(m)
CONNECTICUT OPERA GUILD (M,m)
CONSERVATOIRE DE MUSIQUE BENE-
DETTO MARCELLO (m)
CONSERVATORIO C. MONTEVERDI
(M)
CONSERVATORIO DI MUSICA DI
SANTA CECILIA (M)
CONSERVATORIO DI MUSICA G.
TARTINI (M)
CONSERVATORY OF MUSIC
LUCERNE, SWITZERLAND) (M)
CONSERVATORY OF ORENSE (M)
CONTEMPORARY MUSIC FESTIVAL (M)

CONVERSE COLLEGE (m)
CORBETT FOUNDATION (M,m)
CORNELL COLLEGE (m)
CORNISH SCHOOL OF ALLIED ARTS
(m)
TRUSTEES OF LOTTA CRABTREE (m)
CREATIVE ARTS LEAGUE (M)
GEORGE CUKOR SCHOLARSHIP,
UNIV/SOUTHERN CALI-
FORNIA (m)
CULVER-STOCKTON COLLEGE (m)
MERCE CUNNINGHAM DANCE CO'
(M,m)
CURTIS INSTITUTE OF MUSIC (m)
CUYAHOGA COMMUNITY COLLEGE
(m)
DALLAS MORNING NEWS (M)
DANA SCHOOL OF MUSIC (m)
DEFIANCE COLLEGE (m)
DELIGACION NACIONAL DE LA SEC-
CION FEMMENINA DE
FALANGE Y DE LAS JONS
(M,m)
DELL PUBLISHING CO. FOUNDATION
(M)
DELTA OMICRON INTERNATIONAL
MUSIC FRATERNITY (M)
DE PAUL UNIV. (m)
DEPAUW UNIVERSITY (m)
DELIUS COMPOSITION AWARDS (M)
DETROIT GRAND OPERA ASSOCIA-
TION (M)
ALICE M. DITSON FUND OF COLUM-
BIA UNIV. (M)
DRAKE UNIV. (m)
DRURY COLLEGE (m)
DUQUESNE UNIV. (m)
DUSEK COMPETITION OF MUSICAL
YOUTH (M)
EARLHAM COLLEGE (m)
EAST CAROLINA UNIV. (m)
EASTERN ILLINOIS UNIV. (m)
EASTERN KENTUCKY UNIV. (m)
EASTERN MICHIGAN UNIV. (m)
EASTERN MONTANA COLLEGE (m)
EASTERN NEW MEXICO UNIV. (m)
EASTERN WASHINGTON STATE
COLLEGE (m)

EASTMAN SCHOOL OF MUSIC (M,m)
EAST TENNESSEE STATE UNIV. (m)
EAST TEXAS BAPTIST COLLEGE (m)
EAST TEXAS STATE UNIV. (m)
EAST AND WEST ARTISTS ANNUAL
COMPETITION FOR COM-
POSERS (M)
ELIZABETH CITY STATE COLLEGE
(m)
ELKS FOUNDATION SCHOLARSHIP
AWARDS (m)
ELON COLLEGE (m)
ENTE AUTONOMO TEATRO ALLA
SCALA (M)
THE OSCAR ESPLA PRIZE (M)
EVANSVILLE PHILHARMONIC (M)
FARGO-MOORHEAD SYMPHONY (M)
FEDERATION OF JEWISH PHILAN-
THROPIES (M)
EMMA FELDMAN MEMORIAL COM-
PETITION (M)
FINDLAY COLLEGE (m)
FIRESTONE CONSERVATORY OF
MUSIC (m)
FISK UNIV. (m)
CARL FLESCH INTERNATIONAL
VIOLIN COMPETITION (M)
FLORENCE STATE COLLEGE (m)
FLORIDA AGRICULTURAL AND
MECHANICAL UNIVERSITY
(m)
FLORIDA ATLANTIC MUSIC GUILD,
INC. (M,m)
FLORIDA SCHOOL OF THE ARTS (m)
FLORIDA STATE UNIV. (M)
FOLKWANG-HOCHSCHULE ESSEN
(M,m)
FONDATION DES ETATS-UNIS (m)
FONDATION PRINCE PIERRE DE
MONACO (M)
FONTBONNE COLLEGE (m)
FORT COLLINS SYMPHONY SOCIETY
(M)
FORT HAYS KANSAS STATE COLLEGE
(m)
FOUNDATION OF CONTEMPORARY
PERFORMANCE ARTS (M)
FOUNDATION ROYAUMONT (M)

204

FRIDAY MORNING MUSIC CLUB
FOUNDATION (m)
FRIENDS OF HARVEY GAUL COM-
POSITION CONTEST (M)
FROMM MUSIC FOUNDATION (M)
FURMAN UNIV. (m)
GASPAR CASSADO INTERNATIONAL
CELLO COMPETITION (M)
GAUDEAMUS FOUNDATION (M)
GENEVA INTERNATIONAL COMPETI-
TION FOR MUSICAL PER-
FORMERS (M)
GENEVA INTERNATIONAL COMPETI-
TION FOR OPERA AND
BALLET COMPOSITION (M)
GEORGIA SOUTHERN COLLEGE (m)
GERMANY ARTISTS-IN-BERLIN
PROGRAM (M)
GLASSBORO STATE COLLEGE (m)
GOLDOVSKY OPERA INSTITUTE (m)
GONZAGA UNIV. (m)
GRAMBLING COLLEGE (m)
GRAN TEATRO DEL LICEO (M)
GREENSBORO COLLEGE (m)
GREENVILLE COLLEGE (m)
GREENWOOD PRESS CHORAL COM-
PETITION (M)
GUIDO CANTELLI INTERNATIONAL
COMPETITION FOR YOUNG
CONDUCTORS (M)
GUILDHALL SCHOOL OF MUSIC AND
DRAMA (M)
GUSTAVUS ADOLPHUS COLLEGE (m)
HAGUE CHOIR FESTIVAL (M)
REID HALL INC. AWARDS (m)
THE HAMBRIDGE ART CENTER (M)
HAMLINE UNIV. (m)
HARTT COLLEGE OF MUSIC (m)
HARTWICK COLLEGE (m)
HASTINGS COLLEGE (m)
JOSEPH HEARNS PRIZE IN MUSIC (M)
HEIDELBERG COLLEGE (m)
HENDERSON STATE COLLEGE (m)
HENDRIX COLLEGE (m)
HILLSDALE COLLEGE (m)
WALTER HINRICHSEN AWARD (See:
Columbia Univ.) (M)
HOCHSCHULE FUR MUSIK (M)

HOFSTRA COLLEGE (m)
HOLLINS COLLEGE (m)
HOPE COLLEGE (m)
HOUGHTON COLLEGE (m)
HOUSTON BAPTIST COLLEGE (m)
HOWARD UNIV. (Washington, DC) (m)
HUNTER COLLEGE OF CITY UNIV.
OF NEW YORK (m)
HURON STATE COLLEGE (m)
ILLINOIS OPERA GUILD (M)
ILLINOIS STATE UNIV. (m)
ILLINOIS WESLEYAN UNIV. (M,m)
INDIANA STATE UNIV. (m)
INDIANA UNIV. SCHOOL OF MUSIC
(m)
INDIANA UNIV. OF PENNSYLVANIA
(m)
INSTITUTIO DE ESTUDIOS GIENNESES
(M)
INSTITUTO MUSICALE PAGANINI (M)
INTERNATIONAL BEETHOVEN PIANO
COMPETITION (M)
INTERNATIONAL BEL CANTO COM-
PETITIONS (M)
INTERNATIONAL COMPETITION
"GEORGE ENESCO" (M)
INTERNATIONAL COMPETITION OF
INDIVIDUAL SINGING (M)
INTERNATIONAL COMPETITION OF
MUSICAL PERFORMERS (M)
INTERNATIONAL COMPETITION FOR
EXCELLENCE IN THE PER-
FORMANCE OF AMERICAN
MUSIC (M)
INTERNATIONAL CONTEST FOR
STRINGS (M)
INTERNATIONAL CONTEST FOR
YOUNG CONDUCTORS (M)
INTERNATIONAL HUMANITIES (M,m)
INTERNATIONAL INSTITUTE OF
MUSIC OF CANADA (M)
INTERNATIONAL MUSIC COMPETI-
TION (M)
INTERNATIONAL MUSIC COMPETI-
TION (GENEVA) (M)
INTERNATIONAL MUSIC COMPETI-
TION OF THE BROADCASTING
CORPS OF THE FEDERAL

REPUBLIC OF GERMANY (M)
INTERNATIONAL MUSIC INSTITUTE OF THE CITY OF DARMSTADT (M)
INTERNATIONAL ORGAN COMPETITION (M)
INTERNATIONAL PIANO CONTEST "ETTORE POZZOLO" (M)
INTERNATIONAL SINGING COMPETITION OF BELGIUM (M)
INTERNATIONAL TCHAIKOVSKY COMPETITION (M)
INTERNATIONAL VOICE COMPETITION (M)
IOWA WESLEYAN COLLEGE (m)
IRISH AMERICAN CULTURAL INSTITUTE (M)
ITALIAN NATIONAL ACADEMY OF SANTA CECILIA (M)
ITHACA COLLEGE (m)
JACKSONVILLE UNIV. (m)
JAEN INTERNATIONAL PIANO COMPETITION (M)
JAMESTOWN COLLEGE (m)
JERUSALEM INTERNATIONAL HARP COMPETITION (M)
JOHANN SEBASTIAN BACH INTERNATIONAL COMPETITIONS (M)
JOHN BROWN UNIV. (m)
JORDAN COLLEGE OF MUSIC OF BUTLER UNIV. (m)
JOY IN SINGING, INC. (M)
JUILLIARD SCHOOL OF MUSIC (m)
JUILLIARD SCHOOL (m)
ALFRED JURZYKOWSKI FND., INC. (M)
KALAMAZOO COLLEGE (m)
KAUFMAN (MINNA)-RUDD FDN. (M)
KEARNEY STATE COLLEGE (m)
JOHN F. KENNEDY CENTER FOR THE PERFORMING ARTS (M)
KENTUCKY WESLEYAN COLLEGE (m)
KING'S COLLEGE (m)
THE KATE NEAL KINLEY MEMORIAL FELLOWSHIP (m)
KNOXVILLE COLLEGE (m)
KONSERVATORIUM DER STADT WIEN

(M,m)
KOSCIUSZKO FOUNDATION (m)
KOUSSEVITSKY MUSIC FOUNDATION, INC. (M,m)
THE LAMONT SCHOOL OF MUSIC (Univ/Denver) (M)
LAWRENCE UNIV. (m)
LEBANON VALLEY COLLEGE (m)
THE LEEDS INTERNATIONAL PIANOFORTE COMPETITION (M)
LENOIR RHYNE COLLEGE (m)
LES AMIS DE L'ART LYRIQUE (M)
LES AMIS DE MOZART (M)
EDGAR LEVENTRITT FOUNDATION (M)
LEWIS AND CLARK COLLEGE (m)
LIBRARY OF CONGRESS (M,WR)
LIEDERKRANZ FOUNDATION (M)
LIEGE COMPETITION FOR STRING QUARTETS (M)
THE MACDOWELL COLONY, INC. (M)
MARGUERITE LONG AND JACQUES THIBAUD INTERNATIONAL PIANO AND VIOLIN COMPETITION (M,m)
LONG (KATHRYN) TRUST (m)
LONGWOOD COLLEGE (m)
LONGY SCHOOL OF MUSIC (m)
LOUISIANA STATE UNIV. (m)
LOYOLA UNIV. (m)
MACALESTER COLLEGE (m)
MACMURRAY COLLEGE (m)
MAISON DE LA RADIO (M)
MAISON DES ARTISTES (M)
MANHATTAN SCHOOL OF MUSIC (m)
MANKATO STATE COLLEGE (m)
MANNES COLLEGE OF MUSIC (m)
MANSFIELD STATE COLLEGE (m)
MARIAN COLLEGE (m)
MARS HILL COLLEGE (m)
THE DAVID B. MARSHALL AWARD (M)
MARSHALL UNIV. (m)
THE MARYLAND-NATIONAL CAPITAL PARK AND PLANNING COMMISSION (M)
MARYMOUNT COLLEGE (Tarrytown, NY) (m)
MARYVILLE COLLEGE (m)

MARYWOOD COLLEGE (m)
MASON (FANNY PEABODY) MUSIC
FOUNDATION, INC. (M)
MC MASTER UNIV. (m)
MC MURRAY COLLEGE (m)
MC NEESE STATE COLLEGE (m)
MEMPHIS STATE UNIV. (m)
MENDELSSOHN-BARTHOLDY
STIPENDIUM (M)
MERCY COLLEGE OF DETROIT (m)
MEREDITH COLLEGE (m)
MEROLA MEMORIAL FUND (M)
METROPOLITAN OPERA ASSOCIA-
TION (m)
METROPOLITAN OPERA NATIONAL
COUNCIL (M,m)
MICHAELS MEMORIAL MUSIC
AWARDS (M)
MIDWESTERN UNIV. (m)
MILES COMMUNITY COLLEGE (m)
MILLS COLLEGE (m)
MILTON COLLEGE (m)
MISSISSIPPI COLLEGE (m)
MISSISSIPPI STATE UNIV. (m)
MISSOURI WESTERN COLLEGE (m)
MOBILE OPERA WORKSHOP (m)
MONTCLAIR STATE COLLEGE (m)
MONTEVIDEO INTERNATIONAL
PIANO COMPETITION (M,m)
MONTREAL INTERNATIONAL MUSIC
COMPETITION (M)
MOORHEAD STATE COLLEGE (m)
MORAVIAN MUSIC FOUNDATION,
INC. (M)
MORNINGSIDE COLLEGE (m)
MOUNT ALLISON UNIVERSITY (m)
MOUNT ALOYSIUS JUNIOR COLLEGE
(m)
MOUNT HOLYOKE COLLEGE (m)
MOUNT MARTY COLLEGE (m)
MOUNT ST. MARY'S COLLEGE (m)
MOUNT ST. SCHOLASTICA COLLEGE
(m)
MOUNT UNION COLLEGE (m)
MOZART MEMORIAL PRIZE (M)
MUNICH INTERNATIONAL MUSIC
COMPETITION (M)
MURRAY STATE UNIV. (m)

MUSIC AND ARTS INSTITUTE OF SAN
FRANCISCO (m)
MUSIC AND ART FOUNDATION
AWARDS (m)
MUSIC CRITICS ASSOCIATION (m)
MUSIC PERFORMANCE TRUST FUNDS
(M)
MUSIC TEACHERS NATIONAL ASSO-
CIATION (M,m)
MUSICAL MERIT FOUNDATION OF
GREATER SAN DIEGO (m)
MUSICIANS CLUB OF NEW YORK
ANNUAL YOUNG ARTISTS
AWARD (M)
MUSICIANS FOUNDATION, INC. (M)
MUSKINGUM COLLEGE (m)
NATIONAL ARTISTS AUDITIONS (M)
NATIONAL ARTS CLUB (M,m)
NATIONAL ASSOCIATION OF TEACH-
ERS OF SINGING (M)
NATIONAL FEDERATION OF MUSIC
CLUBS (M,m)
NATIONAL GUILD OF PIANO TEACH-
ERS (M)
NATIONAL GUILD/COMMUNITY
MUSIC SCHOOLS (M)
NATIONAL INSTITUTE OF ARTS AND
LETTERS (M)
NATIONAL OPERA INSTITUTE (M)
NATIONAL SCHOOL ORCHESTRA
ASSOCIATION (M)
WALTER W. NAUMBURG FOUNDA-
TION (M)
NEBRASKA WESLEYAN UNIV. (m)
NEWCOMB COLLEGE (M)
NEW ENGLAND CONSERVATORY OF
MUSIC (m)
NEW MEXICO HIGHLANDS UNIV. (m)
NEW MEXICO STATE UNIV. (m)
NEW ORLEANS BAPTIST THEOLOGI-
CAL SEMINARY (m)
NEW ORLEANS EXPERIMENTAL
OPERA (M)
NEW MUSIC FOR YOUNG ENSEMBLES,
INC. (M,m)
NEW YORK DRAMA CRITICS' CIRCLE
(M)
NIHON GAKKI CO. (M)

NORTH CAROLINA SYMPHONY
SOCIETY (M)
NORTHEAST LOUISIANA UNIV. (m)
NORTHEAST MISSOURI STATE
COLLEGE (m)
NORTHERN ARIZONA UNIV. (m)
NORTHERN PLAINS TRI-STATE FES-
TIVAL OF MUSIC (M)
NORTH TEXAS STATE UNIV. (m)
NORTHWESTERN STATE COLLEGE OF
LOUISIANA (m)
NORTHWESTERN UNIV. (m)
NORTHWEST NAZARENE COLLEGE
(m)
NYACK MISSIONARY COLLEGE (m)
OBERLIN COLLEGE (m)
OCCIDENTAL COLLEGE (m)
OGLEBAY INSTITUTE (m)
OHIO STATE UNIV. (m)
OHIO STATE UNIV. (M)
OKLAHOMA BAPTIST UNIV. (m)
OKLAHOMA CITY UNIV. (m)
OKLAHOMA COLLEGE OF
LIBERAL ARTS (m)
OKLAHOMA MUSICIAN OF THE YEAR
AWARD (M)
OKLAHOMA STATE UNIV. (m)
OLD DOMINION SYMPHONY COUNCIL
(m)
F.E. OLDS & SON, INC. (M)
OLIVER MESSIAEN COMPETITION (M)
OUACHITA BAPTIST UNIV. (m)
OUR LADY OF THE LAKE COLLEGE
(m)
NICOLO PAGANINI INTERNATIONAL
VIOLIN COMPETITION (M)
PAN AMERICAN COLLEGE (m)
PARSONS COLLEGE (m)
PARIS INTERNATIONAL HARPSI-
CHORD COMPETITION (M)
PARIS INTERNATIONAL VOICE COM-
PETITION (M)
HOWARD PAYNE COLLEGE (m)
GEORGE PEABODY COLLEGE FOR
TEACHERS (m)
PEABODY CONSERVATORY OF MUSIC
(m)
PENNSYLVANIA STATE UNIV. (m)

PFEIFFER COLLEGE (m)
PHILADELPHIA MUSICAL ACADEMY
(M,m)
PHILLIPS UNIV. (m)
PITTSBURGH FLUTE CLUB (m)
PIUS XII INSTITUTE COMMITTEE (m)
POINT LOMA COLLEGE, DEPT. OF
MUSIC (m)
POLISH ARTISTIC AGENCY (PAGART)
(M)
POLISH MINISTRY OF CULTURE AND
ART AND FREDERIC CHOPIN
ASSOCIATION (M)
POLISH MINISTRY OF CULTURE AND
ART AND HENRYK WIENIAW-
SKI ASSOCIATION (M)
POMONA COLLEGE (m)
COLE PORTER SCHOLARSHIP (m)
PRAGUE INTERNATIONAL COMPETI-
TION FOR COMPOSERS (M)
PREIS DES SCHUBERT WETTBE-
WERBES (M)
PRESSO ACCADEMIA MUSICALE
NAPOLETAN (M)
PRINCE PIERRE DE MONACO PRIX
DE COMPOSITION MUSICALE
(M)
PRINCETON UNIV. (m)
PUCCINI FOUNDATION (M)
PULITZER PRIZE IN MUSIC (M)
QUACHITA BAPTIST UNIVERSITY
(m)
QUEEN ELISABETH OF BELGIUM
AWARDS (M)
QUEEN MARIE-JOSE PRIZE (M)
QUEENS COLLEGE (m)
QUINCY COLLEGE (m)
RAVINIA FESTIVAL ASSOCIATION (M)
RIO DE JANEIRO INTERNATIONAL
VOICE COMPETITION (M)
RIO HONDO COLLEGE (m)
RIVIER COLLEGE (m)
ROBERTS WESLEYAN COLLEGE (m)
ROCHESTER CIVIC MUSIC ASSOCIA-
TION (M)
J.D. ROCKEFELLER III FUND (M)
ROCKEFELLER (MARTHA BAIRD)
FUND FOR MUSIC, INC. (M,m)

ROCKY MOUNTAIN COLLEGE (m)
RODGERS AND HAMMERSTEIN
FOUNDATION (M)
ROLLINS COLLEGE (m)
ROSARY COLLEGE (m)
HERBERT AND NANNETTE ROTHS-
CHILD FOUNDATION, INC. (M)
ROYAL IRISH ACADEMY OF MUSIC
(m)
ROYAL OPERA HOUSE (m)
MINNA KAUFMANN RUDD FOUNDA-
TION (m)
RUTGERS UNIV. (m)
S'HERTOGENBOSCH INTERNATIONAL
COMPETITION FOR SINGERS
(M)
SACRAMENTO STATE COLLEGE (m)
SACRED HEART DOMINICAN COL-
LEGE (m)
ST. AMBROSE COLLEGE (m)
ST. ANDREWS PRESBYTERIAN COL-
LEGE (m)
ST. CLOUD STATE COLLEGE (m)
ST. JOHN'S UNIV. (m)
ST. LOUIS INSTITUTE OF MUSIC (m)
ST. MARY COLLEGE (m)
ST. MARY OF THE PLAINS COLLEGE
(m)
ST. MARY'S UNIV. (M)
ST. MARY-OF-THE-WOODS COLLEGE
(m)
ST. OLAF COLLEGE (m)
SALEM COLLEGE (m)
SAM HOUSTON STATE UNIV. (m)
SAMFORD UNIV. (m)
SAN ANGELO SYMPHONY AWARD
(M)
SAN DIEGO CHORAL CLUB (m)
SAN FERNANDO VALLEY STATE
COLLEGE (m)
SAN FRANCISCO CONSERVATORY
OF MUSIC (m)
SAN FRANCISCO OPERA ASSOCIA-
TION (m)
SAN JOSE STATE COLLEGE (m)
SCANDINAVIAN COUNCIL (M)
SCHNABEL SCHOLARSHIP FUND (m)
SCHNITGERPRIJS ZWOLLE INTER-
NATIONAL COMPOSITION

CONTEST FOR ORGAN (M)
SCHUBERT INTERNATIONAL COM-
PETITION (M)
ROBERT-SCHUMANN KONSERVA-
TORIUM (M)
SCRIPPS COLLEGE (m)
SEATTLE OPERA ASSOCIATION,
INC. (M)
SEATTLE PACIFIC COLLEGE (m)
SEATTLE UNIV. (m)
SHENANDOAH CONSERVATORY OF
MUSIC (m)
SHERWOOD MUSIC SCHOOL (m)
S'HERTOGENBOSCH MUSIEKSTAD (M)
SHORTER COLLEGE (m)
SHREVEPORT SYMPHONY SOCIETY
(M)
SIGMA ALPHA IOTA FOUNDATION (M)
SINFONIA FOUNDATION (M,m)
SINGERS CLUB (m)
SKIDMORE COLLEGE (m)
SOCIEDADE BRASILEIRA DE REALI-
ZACOES ARTISTICAS E CUL-
TURAIS (M)
SOCIETA DEL QUARTETTO (M)
SOCIETY OF AMERICAN MUSICIANS
CONTEST (M)
SOFIA INTERNATIONAL COMPETI-
TION FOR YOUNG OPERA
SINGERS (M)
LEONIE SONNING MUSIC FOUNDA-
TION (M)
SOUTHEASTERN LOUISIANA COL-
LEGE (m)
SOUTHEASTERN STATE COLLEGE (m)
SOUTHERN COLORADO STATE COL-
LEGE (m)
SOUTHERN ILLINOIS UNIV. (m)
SOUTHERN METHODIST UNIV. (m)
SOUTHWESTERN BAPTIST THEOLOGI-
CAL SEMINARY (m)
SOUTHWESTERN COLLEGE (m)
STANLEY DRAME AWARD (M)
STATE COLLEGE OF ARKANSAS (m)
STATE UNIV. COLLEGE AT BING-
HAMTON (m)
STATE UNIV. COLLEGE AT POTSDAM
(m)
STEPHEN F. AUSTIN STATE COLLEGE (m)

STEPHENS COLLEGE (m)
STETSON UNIV. (m)
STROUD FESTIVAL INTERNATIONAL
COMPOSERS COMPETITION
(M)
STUDIO CLUB OF THE YWCA (M)
SUL ROSS STATE COLLEGE (m)
SULLIVAN (WILLIAM MATHEUS)
MUSICAL FOUNDATION (M)
SUSQUEHANNA UNIV. (m)
SYMPHONY ASSOCIATION OF
ORANGE COUNTY (M)
SYMPHONY SOCIETY OF SAN
ANTONIO (m)
SYRACUSE UNIV. (m)
TARKIO COLLEGE (m)
TCHAIKOVSKY INTERNATIONAL
MUSIC COMPETITION (M)
TEATRO MASSIMO (m)
TEXAS BOYS CHOIR COMPETITION
(M)
TEXAS CHRISTIAN UNIV. (m)
TEXAS COLLEGE OF ARTS & INDUS-
TRIES (m)
TEXAS LUTHERAN COLLEGE (m)
TEXAS-SWEDISH CULTURAL FOUN-
DATION (m)
TEXAS TECHNOLOGICAL COLLEGE
(m)
TEXAS WESLEYAN COLLEGE (m)
TEXAS WOMEN'S UNIV. (m)
THEATRE COMMUNICATIONS GROUP
(M)
THEBOM (BLANCHE) FOUNDATION,
INC. (m)
THORNE MUSIC FUND, INC. (M)
THORNE MUSIC FUND, INC. (M)
TOULOUSE INTERNATIONAL VOICE
COMPETITION (M)
TOURIST REVUES INTERNATIONAL
(M)
TREVISO TEATRO COMUNALE (M)
TRIESTE INTERNATIONAL COMPETI-
TION FOR SYMPHONIC COM-
POSITION (M)
UFFICIO DE RAPPRESENTANZA
DELLA SOCIETA ITALIANA
(M)

UNION COLLEGE (Barbourville, KY) (m)
UNION THEOLOGICAL SEMINARY (m)
UNITED CHORAL SOCIETY (M)
UNITED STATES INTERNATIONAL
UNIV. (m)
UNIVERSIDAD CENTRAL DE
VENEZUELA (M)
UNIV/ALABAMA (m)
UNIV/ALBERTA (m)
UNIV/ARIZONA (m)
UNIV/ARKANSAS AT LITTLE ROCK
(m)
UNIV/BIRMINGHAM (m)
UNIV/BRIDGEPORT (m)
UNIV/BRITISH COLUMBIA (m)
UNIV/CALIFORNIA AT LOS
ANGELES (m)
UNIV/CALIFORNIA (Riverside) (m)
UNIV/CALIFORNIA (Santa Barbara)
(m)
UNIV/CALGARY (m)
UNIV/CAMBRIDGE (m)
UNIV/CHATTANOOGA (m)
UNIV/CHICAGO (m)
UNIV/CINCINNATI (m)
UNIV/COLORADO (m)
UNIV/CORPUS CHRISTI (m)
UNIV/DAYTON (m)
UNIV/FLORIDA (m)
UNIV/GEORGIA (m)
UNIV/HAWAII (m)
UNIV/HULL (m)
UNIV/IDAHO (m)
UNIV/ILLINOIS (m)
UNIV/IOWA (m)
UNIV/KANSAS (m)
UNIV/KANSAS CITY (M)
UNIV/MANCHESTER (m)
UNIV/MARYLAND (m)
UNIV/MIAMI (m)
UNIV/MICHIGAN (m)
UNIV/MINNESOTA (m)
UNIV/MINNESOTA (Duluth) (m)
UNIV/MISSISSIPPI (m)
UNIV/MISSOURI (m)
UNIV/MISSOURI AT KANSAS CITY (M)
UNIV/MONTANA (m)
UNIV/NEBRASKA (m)

UNIV/NEW HAMPSHIRE (m)
UNIV/NEW MEXICO (m)
UNIV/NORTH CAROLINA (m)
UNIV/NORTH DAKOTA (m,m)
UNIV/NORTHERN IOWA (m)
UNIV/NOTRE DAME (m)
UNIV/OKLAHOMA (m)
UNIV/OREGON (m)
UNIV/PITTSBURGH (m)
UNIV/PORTLAND (m)
UNIV/REDLANDS (m)
UNIV/REGINA (m)
UNIV/RHODE ISLAND (m)
UNIV/RICHMOND (m)
UNIV/SASKATCHEWAN (m)
UNIV/SOUTH ALABAMA (m)
UNIV/SOUTH DAKOTA (m)
UNIV/SOUTHERN CALIFORNIA (m)
UNIV/SOUTHERN MISSISSIPPI (m)
UNIV/SOUTHWESTERN LOUISIANA
    (m)
UNIV/TENNESSEE (m)
UNIV/TEXAS AT EL PASO (m)
UNIV/TOLEDO (m)
UNIV/TULSA (m)
UNIV/UTAH (m)
UNIV/VERMONT (m)
UNIV/WASHINGTON (m)
UNIV/WESTERN ONTARIO (m)
UNIV/WISCONSIN AT MILWAUKEE (m)
UNIV/WYOMING (m)
US STEEL FOUNDATION, INC. (m)
VALDOSTA STATE COLLEGE (m)
VALLEY CITY STATE COLLEGE (m)
VALPARAISO UNIV. (m)
VAN CLIBURN FOUNDATION, INC. (M)
VASSAR COLLEGE (m)
VIANNA DA MOTTA INTERNATIONAL
    COMPETITION (M)
VIENNA INTERNATIONAL MUSIC
    COMPETITION (M)
G.B. VIOTTI INTERNATIONAL MUSIC
    COMPETITION (M)
VIRGINIA CENTER FOR THE CREA-
    TIVE ARTS (M)
VIRGINIA COMMONWEALTH UNIV.
    (m)
VIRGINIA POLYTECHNIC INSTITUTE
    & STATE UNIVERSITY (m)

VITERBO COLLEGE (m)
WAKE FOREST UNIV. (m)
WARNER BROTHERS SCHOLARSHIPS
    (m)
WARTBURG COLLEGE (m)
WASHINGTON NATIONAL SYMPHONY
    (m)
WASHINGTON STATE UNIV. (m)
WASHINGTON UNIV. (m)
WASSILI LEPS FOUNDATION PRIZE
    (M,m)
WAYLAND BAPTIST COLLEGE (m)
WEBSTER COLLEGE (m)
HENRYK WEINIAWSKI INTERNA-
    TIONAL VIOLIN COMPETI-
    TION (M)
WESLEYAN COLLEGE (m)
WESTERN CAROLINA UNIV. (m)
WESTERN ILLINOIS UNIV. (m)
WESTERN MARYLAND COLLEGE (m)
WESTERN MICHIGAN UNIV. (m)
WESTERN WASHINGTON UNIV. (M,m)
WESTERN WYOMING COLLEGE (m)
WEST LIBERTY STATE COLLEGE (m)
WESTMAR COLLEGE (m)
WESTMINISTER CHOIR COLLEGE (m)
WESTMINISTER COLLEGE (m)
WEST TEXAS STATE UNIV. (m)
WEST VIRGINIA STATE COLLEGE (m)
WEST BIRGINIA UNIV. (m)
WEST VIRGINIA WESLEYAN COLLEGE
    (m)
WGN—ILLINOIS OPERA GUILD (M)
WHEATON COLLEGE (m)
WHITWORTH COLLEGE (m)
WICHITA FALLS SYMPHONY
    ORCHESTRA FELLOWSHIP (m)
WICHITA STATE UNIV. (m)
WICHITA SYMPHONY SOCIETY (m)
WIHURI FOUNDATION FOR INTER-
    NATIONAL PRIZES (M)
WILLIAM CAREY COLLEGE (m)
WILLIAMETTE UNIV. (m)
WILLIAMS COLLEGE (m)
WILSON VOICE AWARD (M)
WINTHROP COLLEGE (m)
WISCONSIN COLLEGE CONSERVA-
    TORY (m)
WISCONSIN STATE UNIV. (Eau Claire) (m)

WISCONSIN STATE UNIV. (LaCrosse)
(m)
WISCONSIN STATE UNIV. (River Falls)
(m)
WISCONSIN STATE UNIV. (Stevens
Point) (m)
WITTENBERG SCHOOL OF MUSIC (m)
WOMEN'S ASSOCIATION OF THE
MINNEAPOLIS SYMPHONY (M)
WOOLEY SCHOLARSHIPS (m)
WQXR RADIO (M)
HELENE WURLITZER FOUNDATION
OF NEW MEXICO (M)
XAVIER UNIV/LOUISIANA (m)
CORPORATION OF YADDO (M)
YAMAHA MUSIC FOUNDATION (M,m)
YALE UNIV. (m)
YANKTON COLLEGE (m)
YOUNG ARTISTS AUDITIONS (M)
YOUNG ARTISTS AWARDS (m)
YOUNG MUSICIANS FOUNDATION (M)
YOUNGSTOWN STATE UNIV. (m)

(T)

ABC THEATRE AWARD (T)
ACTORS FUND OF AMERICA (T)
ACTORS THEATER OF LOUISVILLE
(T)
ADAMS STATE COLLEGE (t)
AFFILIATE ARTISTS, INC. (T)
AGNES SCOTT COLLEGE (t)
ALBION COLLEGE (t)
ALL-MEDIA DRAMATIC WORKSHOP
(T)
THE AMERICAN ACADEMY OF ARTS
AND LETTERS (T)
THE AMERICAN PLAYWRIGHTS
THEATER (T)
ARIZONA STATE UNIVERSITY (t)
ART-ACT PLAYWRITING COMPETI-
TION (T)
BARD COLLEGE (t)
BEAVER COLLEGE (t)
BERRY COLLEGE (t)
BETTER BOYS FDN. FAMILY CENTER
(T)
BLACK HAWK COLLEGE (t)

MARC BLITZSTEIN AWARD (T)
BOSTON CONSERVATORY OF MUSIC
(t)
BRANDEIS UNIV. (t)
BUFFALO FOUNDATION (T,t)
CAMDEN COUNTY AGRICULTURAL
AND HERITAGE COMMISSION
(T)
CENTRAL MICHIGAN UNIV. (T)
CHADRON STATE COLLEGE (t)
CHELSEA THEATER (T)
COLLEGE OF NOTRE DAME OF
MARYLAND (t)
THE COMMUNITY CHILDREN'S
THEATER OF KANSAS CITY
(T)
CREATIVE ARTS LEAGUE (T)
LOLA D'ANNUNZIO AWARD INC. (T)
DEFIANCE COLLEGE (t)
DELL PUBLISHING CO. FOUNDATION
(T)
DEPARTMENT OF JUSTICE (t)
CLARENCE DERWENT AWARD (T)
EARPLAY (T)
EASTERN NEW MEXICO UNIV. (t)
FLORIDA SCHOOL OF THE ARTS (t)
FLORIDA THEATER CONFERENCE
(T,t)
FOLGER SHAKESPEARE LIBRARY (T)
FOLKWANG-HOCHSCHULE ESSEN (T,t)
FONTBONNE COLLEGE (t)
FORD FOUNDATION (t)
FOUNDATION OF CONTEMPORARY
PERFORMANCE ARTS (T)
THE MILES FRANKLIN AWARD (T)
GENEVA INTERNATIONAL COMPE-
TITION FOR OPERA AND
BALLET COMPOSITION (T)
GERMANY ARTISTS-IN-BERLIN
PROGRAM (T)
JOHN GOLDEN FUND (T)
THE HORACE GREGORY AWARD
FUND (T,t)
SIDNEY HILLMAN FDN., INC. (T)
HOUSTON BAPTIST COLLEGE (t)
INDIANA UNIVERSITY (t)
INSTITUTO ALLENDE (T)
INTERNATIONAL HUMANITIES (T,t)

212

INTERNATIONAL THEATER INSTI-
TUTE (t)
IRISH AMERICAN CULTURAL INSTI-
TUTE (T)
JACKSONVILLE UNIV. (t)
JAMESTOWN COLLEGE (t)
THE JERUSALEM PRIZE (T)
MARGO JONES AWARD, INC. (T)
JUILLIARD SCHOOL (t)
ALFRED JURZYKOWSKI FND., INC.
(T)
THE KATE NEAL KINLEY MEMORIAL
FELLOWSHIP (t)
JOSEPH MAHARAM FOUNDATION,
INC. (T)
MARK TAPER FORUM (T)
THE DAVID B. MARSHALL AWARD (T)
THE MARYLAND-NATIONAL CAPITAL
PARK AND PLANNING COM-
MISSION (T)
JENNY MC KEAN MOORE FUND FOR
WRITERS (T,t)
MILES COMMUNITY COLLEGE (t)
MISSOURI WESTERN COLLEGE (t)
MONTCLAIR STATE COLLEGE (t)
MUSIC AND ARTS INSTITUTE OF SAN
FRANCISCO (t)
NATIONAL OPERA INSTITUTE (T)
NEW ENGLAND THEATRE CONFER-
ENCE (T)
NEW PLAYWRIGHTS' THEATER OF
WASHINGTON (T)
NEW YORK DRAMA CRITICS' CIRCLE
(T)
NEW YORK UNIV. (t)
NORTHERN ARIZONA UNIV. (t)
OMAHA COMMUNITY PLAYHOUSE (T)
THE O'NEILL THEATER CENTER (T)
OPEN CIRCLE THEATRE (T)
THE PLAYWRIGHTS' LAB (T)
POLISH LABORATORY THEATER (T)
POMONA COLLEGE (t)
THE PULITZER PRIZES (T)
RELIGIOUS ART GUILD (T)
RIJKSAKADEMIE VAN BEELDENDE
KUNSTEN (t)
RIO HONDO COLLEGE (t)
J.D. ROCKEFELLER III FUND (T)

RODGERS AND HAMMERSTEIN FOUN-
DATION (T)
HERBERT AND NANNETTE ROTHS-
CHILD FOUNDATION, INC. (T)
ROYAL ACADEMY OF DRAMATIC ART
(t)
ROYAL IRISH ACADEMY OF MUSIC (t)
ST. MARY-OF-THE-WOODS COLLEGE
(t)
SCRIPPS COLLEGE (t)
SOUTHWEST THEATER CONFERENCE
NEW PLAY AWARD (T)
SAM S. SHUBERT FOUNDATION (t)
SKIDMORE COLLEGE (t)
SOUTHWEST TEXAS STATE UNIV. (t)
SQUAW VALLEY COMMUNITY OF
WRITERS (T)
STANLEY DRAMA AWARD (T)
TEXAS CHRISTIAN UNIV. (t)
THEATER AMERICANA (T)
THEATER ARTS CORPORATION (T)
THEATER COMMUNICATIONS
GROUP (T)
THEATRE EMERGENCY FUND (T)
THEATRE USA (T)
UNION COLLEGE (t)
UNITED STATES INTERNATIONAL
UNIV. (t)
UNIV/ARKANSAS AT LITTLE ROCK
(t)
UNIV/BIRMINGHAM (t)
UNIV/BRISTOL (t)
UNIV/CHICAGO THEATER (T)
UNIV/CINCINNATI (t)
UNIV/HULL (t)
UNIV/MASSACHUSETTS (t)
UNIV/MISSOURI (t)
UNIV/MISSOURI—KANSAS CITY (t)
UNIV/NEBRASKA AT OMAHA (t)
UNIV/NORTH DAKOTA (T,t)
UNIV/THE PACIFIC (T)
UNIV/SOUTH ALABAMA (t)
ALFRED E. VAN HORN AWARDS (T)
THE VILLAGE VOICE (T)
VIRGINIA MUSEUM (T,t)
VIRGINIA POLYTECHNIC INSTITUTE
& STATE UNIV. (t)
WESTERN ILLINOIS UNIV. (t)

WILMETTE CHILDREN'S THEATER (T)

(VP)

ACADEMY OF ART (vp)
ACADEMY OF FINE ARTS (VP)
ADAMS STATE COLLEGE (vp)
ADRIAN COLLEGE (vp)
AFRICAN ARTS MAGAZINE (VP)
ALABAMA STATE UNIV. (vp)
ALBERTA COLLEGE OF ART, SOUTH-
ERN ALBERTA INSTITUTE OF
TECHNOLOGY (vp)
THE EDWARD F. ALBEE FOUNDA-
TION, INC. (VP)
ALBION COLLEGE (vp)
ALLEGHENY COLLEGE (vp)
ALLEN UNIV. (vp)
ALLIED ARTISTS OF AMERICA, INC.
(VP)
ALMA COLLEGE (vp)
AMARILLO COLLEGE (vp)
AMERICAN ACADEMY OF ART (vp)
AMERICAN ACADEMY IN ROME (vp)
AMERICAN ACADEMY OF ARTS AND
LETTERS (VP)
AMERICAN ORIENTAL SOCIETY (vp)
AMERICAN RIVER COLLEGE (vp)
AMERICAN SOCIETY OF MAGAZINE
PHOTOGRAPHERS (VP)
AMERICAN UNIV. (vp)
AMERICAN WATERCOLOR SOCIETY
(VP)
ANCO WOOD FOUNDATION MERIT
SCHOLARSHIP (vp)
ANNUAL BOARDWALK ART SHOW
(VP)
ARCHEOLOGICAL INST. OF AMERICA
(VP)
ARIZONA COMMISSION ON THE ARTS
AND HUMANITIES (VP)
ARIZONA STATE UNIV. (vp)
ARKANSAS ART CENTER (VP)
ARKANSAS STATE UNIV. (vp)
ARNOT ART MUSEUM (VP)
ART ACADEMY OF CINCINNATI (vp)
ART CAREER SCHOOL (vp)
THE ART CENTER, INC. (VP)

THE ART DEALERS ASSOCIATION OF
AMERICA, INC. (VP)
THE ART DIRECTORS CLUB (VP)
ARTISTS SPACE (VP)
ART INSTITUTE OF BOSTON (vp)
ART INSTITUTE OF CHICAGO (vp)
ART INSTITUTE OF PITTSBURGH (vp)
THE ART SCHOOL (vp)
ART SCHOOL OF W.E. GEBHARDT
(vp)
ART SCHOOL OF THE SOCIETY OF
ARTS AND CRAFTS (vp)
ART STUDENTS LEAGUE OF N.Y.
(VP,vp)
ARTESIA COLLEGE (vp)
ARTISTS EQUITY ASSOCIATION OF
NEW YORK (ARTISTS
WELFARE FUND) (VP)
ARTISTS' FELLOWSHIP, INC. (VP)
ARTISTS FOR ENVIRONMENT FDN.
(VP)
ATLANTIC CITY NATIONAL ARTS
AND CRAFTS SHOW (VP)
ATLANTIC UNION COLLEGE (vp)
ATRAN FOUNDATION (VP)
AUGSBURG COLLEGE (vp)
AUGUSTA COLLEGE (vp)
AUSTIN PEAY STATE COLLEGE (vp)
AUSTRO-AMERICAN SOCIETY (vp)
SHEVA AUSUBEL MEMORIAL
SCHOLARSHIP (vp)
AVILA COLLEGE (vp)
BAKERY SCHOOL OF FINE ARTS OF
VERNON COURT JUNIOR
COLLEGE (vp)
BALDWIN WALLACE COLLEGE (vp)
BANARAS HINDU UNIV. (VP,vp)
BANFF SCHOOL OF FINE ARTS (vp)
BAYLOR UNIV. (vp)
BEAVER COLLEGE (vp)
BELOIT COLLEGE (vp)
BENEDICT COLLEGE (vp)
BENNETT COLLEGE (vp)
BENNINGTON COLLEGE (vp)
BEREA COLLEGE (vp)
BERKS ARTS ALLIANCE SHOW (VP)
BERKSHIRE MUSEUM (VP)
THELKA M. BERNAYS MEMORIAL

FUND (vp)
BERRY COLLEGE (vp)
BETHANY COLLEGE (Bethany, WV) (vp)
BIRMINGHAM-SOUTHERN COLLEGE
(vp)
BLACK HAWK COLLEGE (vp)
ARNOLD BLANCH MEMORIAL
SCHOLARSHIP (vp)
BLOOMFIELD COLLEGE (vp)
BLOOMSBURG STATE COLLEGE (vp)
BOK (MARY LOUISE CURTIS)
FOUNDATION (vp)
BOSTON CENTER FOR ADULT EDUCA-
TION (vp)
BOSTON GLOBE NEWSPAPER COM-
PANY (VP)
BOSTON UNIV. (vp)
BOWDOIN COLLEGE (vp)
BRADFORD CITY ART GALLERY AND
MUSEUMS (VP)
BRADLEY UNIV. (vp)
BRANDEIS UNIV. (vp)
MAUD BRANDON MEMORIAL
SCHOLARSHIP (vp)
BRENAU COLLEGE (vp)
BREVARD COLLEGE (vp)
THE BREVOORT-EICKEMEYER
PRIZE (VP)
GEORGE B. BRIDGMAN MEMORIAL
SCHOLARSHIP (vp)
BRIGHAM YOUNG UNIVERSITY (vp)
BRITISH GOVERNMENT, MARSHALL
SCHOLARSHIP (vp)
BRITISH SCHOOL AT ROME (vp)
BROOKLYN MUSEUM ART SCHOOL
(vp)
BROWN UNIV. (vp)
CHRISTIAN BUCHHEIT SCHOLAR-
SHIP (vp)
BUCKNELL UNIV. (vp)
BUENA VISTA COLLEGE (vp)
BUTLER INSTITUTE OF AMERICAN
ART (VP)
BYRON BROWNE MEMORIAL
SCHOLARSHIP (vp)
CBBC (VP)
CABRILLO COLLEGE (vp)
CALDWELL COLLEGE FOR WOMEN

(vp)
CALIFORNIA COLLEGE OF ARTS AND
CRAFTS (vp)
CALIFORNIA INSTITUTE OF THE
ARTS — FILM & VIDEO
SCHOOL (Burbank, CA) (vp)
CALIFORNIA STATE UNIV/Sacramento
(vp)
CALIFORNIA WESTERN UNIV. (vp)
CAMDEN COUNTY CULTURAL AND
HERITAGE COMMISSION (VP)
CAMPBELLSVILLE COLLEGE (vp)
CAPITAL UNIV. (vp)
CARNEGIE MELLON UNIV. (vp)
THE EMILY CARR COLLEGE OF ART
(vp)
JOHN CARROLL MEMORIAL SCHOL-
ARSHIP (vp)
CARSON NEWMAN COLLEGE (vp)
ELIZABETH CARSTAIRS SCHOLAR-
SHIP (vp)
CARTHAGE COLLEGE (vp)
CASE WESTERN RESERVE UNIV.
(vp)
CATHOLIC UNIV/AMERICA (vp)
THE CATSKILL CENTER FOR
PHOTOGRAPHY (VP)
CENTRAL CONNECTICUT STATE
COLLEGE (vp)
CENTRALIA COLLEGE (vp)
CENTRAL MICHIGAN UNIV. (VP)
CENTRAL MISSOURI STATE COLLEGE
(vp)
CENTRAL STATE COLLEGE (vp)
CHADRON STATE COLLEGE (vp)
CHAFFEY JUNIOR COLLEGE (vp)
CHALONER PRIZE FOUNDATION
(VP,vp)
CHARLOTTE PRINTMAKERS SOCIETY
(VP)
CHAUTAUQUA INSTITUTION (vp)
CHICAGO ACADEMY OF FINE ARTS
(vp)
CHURCH COLLEGE OF HAWAII (vp)
CITRUS COLLEGE (vp)
CITY COLLEGE OF NEW YORK (vp)
CLARK COLLEGE (vp)
CLARKE COLLEGE (vp)

CLATSOP COMMUNITY COLLEGE (vp)
CLEMSON UNIV. (vp)
CLEVELAND INSTITUTE OF ART (vp)
CLEVELAND MUSEUM OF ART (VP)
COALINGA COLLEGE (vp)
COKER COLLEGE (vp)
COLBY JUNIOR COLLEGE (vp)
BLANCHE E. COLEMAN FDN. (VP)
COLLEGE OF THE DESERT (vp)
COLLEGE OF EASTERN UTAH (vp)
COLLEGE OF THE HOLY NAMES (vp)
COLLEGE OF NEW ROCHELLE (vp)
COLLEGE OF NOTRE DAME (vp)
COLLEGE OF NOTRE DAME OF
    MARYLAND (vp)
COLLEGE OF THE OZARKS (vp)
COLLEGE OF ST. FRANCIS (vp)
COLLEGE OF ST. MARY (vp)
COLLEGE OF THE SEQUOIAS (vp)
COLLEGE OF SOUTHERN UTAH (vp)
COLORADO STATE COLLEGE (vp)
COLORADO STATE UNIV. (vp)
COLUMBIA BASIN COLLEGE (vp)
COLUMBIA TECHNICAL INSTITUTE
    (vp)
COLUMBUS COLLEGE OF ART &
    DESIGN (vp)
COMMITTEE FOR THE VISUAL ARTS
    (VP)
COMMUNITY COLLEGE OF BALTI-
    MORE (vp)
COMPTON COLLEGE (vp)
HEREWARD LESTER COOKE FDN. (VP)
COOPER SCHOOL OF ART (vp)
COOPER UNION SCHOOL OF ART AND
    ARCHITECTURE (vp)
JON CORBINO MEMORIAL SCHOLAR-
    SHIP (vp)
CORNELL COLLEGE (vp)
CORNING MUSEUM OF GLASS (vp)
CORNISH SCHOOL OF ALLIED ARTS
    (vp)
CORONADO SCHOOL OF FINE ARTS
    (vp)
CRACOW OFFICE FOR ARTISTIC
    EXHIBITIONS (VP)
CRAFT GUILD OF THE THOUSAND
    ISLAND MUSEUM (vp)

CRANBROOK ACADEMY OF ART
    (vp)
CREATIVE ARTS LEAGUE (VP)
CREEKWOOD COLONY FOR THE
    ARTS (VP)
CULVER-STOCKTON COLLEGE (vp)
CUMBERLAND COLLEGE (vp)
DALLAS ART INSTITUTE (vp)
DALLAS MUSEUM OF FINE ARTS
    (VP)
DANA COLLEGE (vp)
DARTMOUTH COLLEGE (vp)
DAVENPORT MUNICIPAL ART
    GALLERY (VP)
LILLIAN BOSTWICK DAVIS
    MEMORIAL SCHOLARSHIP (vp)
DAVIS AND ELKINS COLLEGE (vp)
DAYTON ART INSTITUTE (vp)
DEAN JUNIOR COLLEGE (vp)
DEFIANCE COLLEGE (vp)
DELTA COMMUNITY COLLEGE (vp)
DELTA PHI DELTA ALUMNI SCHOL-
    ARSHIP FOUNDATION (vp)
DELTA STATE COLLEGE (vp)
DEPARTMENT OF JUSTICE (vp)
DICKINSON ART AWARD, DICKINSON
    COLLEGE (VP)
DICKINSON STATE COLLEGE (vp)
NATHANIEL DIRK MEMORIAL
    SCHOLARSHIP (vp)
DIXIE ANNUAL (VP)
DIXIE COLLEGE (vp)
DOMINICAN COLLEGE (vp)
DOUGLAS ART CENTER (VP)
DOUGLASS COLLEGE OF RUTGERS
    UNIVERSITY (vp)
DREW UNIV. (vp)
DRUDY COLLEGE (vp)
DUMBARTON OAKS RESEARCH
    LIBRARY AND COLLEC-
    TION (VP,vp)
FRANK VINCENT DUMOND
    MEMORIAL SCHOLARSHIP (vp)
"DUCK STAMP" DESIGN CONTEST
    (VP)
THE DULIN GALLERY OF ART (VP)
DUNBARTON COLLEGE OF HOWARD
    UNIV. (vp)

DUTCHESS COMMUNITY COLLEGE (vp)
WINTHROP EARLE MEMORIAL FUND FOR ENCOURAGEMENT OF SCULPTURE (vp)
EASTERN ILLINOIS UNIV. (vp)
EASTERN MONTANA COLLEGE (vp)
EASTERN NEW MEXICO UNIV. (vp)
EASTERN WASHINGTON STATE COLLEGE (vp)
EASTMAN KODAK COMPANY (VP)
ECOLE SUPERIEURE DES BEAUX ARTS D'ATHENES (vp)
EDGECLIFF COLLEGE (vp)
EDGEWOOD COLLEGE OF THE SACRED HEART (vp)
EDINBORO STATE COLLEGE (vp)
ELIZABETH CITY STATE COLLEGE (vp)
ELMIRA COLLEGE (vp)
ENDICOTT JUNIOR COLLEGE (vp)
ENVIRONMENTAL PROTECTION AGENCY (EPA) (VP)
EVANSVILLE MUSEUM OF ARTS AND SCIENCE (VP)
WALKER G. EVERETT MEMORIAL SCHOLARSHIP (vp)
FAIRMONT STATE COLLEGE (vp)
FASHION INSTITUTE OF TECH- NOLOGY (vp)
FELTRINELLI FOUNDATION (VP)
ERNEST FIENE MEMORIAL SCHOLARSHIP (vp)
FINE ARTS WORK CENTER IN PROVINCETOWN, INC. (VP)
FLINT COMMUNITY JUNIOR COLLEGE (vp)
FLORIDA GULF COAST ART CENTER, INC. (vp)
FLORIDA JUNIOR COLLEGE AT JACKSONVILLE (vp)
FLORIDA MEMORIAL COLLEGE (vp)
FLORIDA SCHOOL OF THE ARTS (vp)
FLORIDA SOUTHERN COLLEGE (vp)
FLORISSANT VALLEY COMMUNITY COLLEGE (vp)
FONDATION DES ETATS-UNIS (vp)

FONTBONNE COLLEGE (vp)
FORT HAYS KANSAS STATE COLLEGE (vp)
FORT WAYNE SCHOOL OF FINE ARTS (vp)
FORT WORTH ART CENTER MUSEUM AND SCHOOL (vp)
FORT WRIGHT COLLEGE (vp)
FOUNDERS SOCIETY (VP)
ROBERT LAWRENCE FOWLER ART SCHOLARSHIPS (vp)
THE FRANKLIN MINT GALLERY OF AMERICAN ART (VP)
FRIEND UNIVERSITY (VP)
FRIENDS OF PHOTOGRAPHY (VP)
GABROVO INTERNATIONAL BIEN- NIAL OF CARICATURE (VP)
GANNON COLLEGE (vp)
GASPARILLA SIDEWALK ART FESTIVAL (VP)
GASTON COLLEGE (vp)
GENERAL SERVICES ADMINISTRA- TION (GSA) (VP)
GEORGETOWN COLLEGE (VP)
GEORGIA COLLEGE AT MILLEDGE- VILLE (vp)
GEORGIAN COURT COLLEGE (vp)
GERMANY ARTISTS-IN-BERLIN PROGRAM (VP)
GLENVILLE STATE COLLEGE (vp)
GOUCHER COLLEGE (vp)
GRAHAM FOUNDATION FOR ADVANCED STUDIES IN THE FINE ARTS (vp)
GRAND PRIX INTERNATIONAL D'ART CONTEMPORAIN DE MONTE- CARLO (VP)
GRAND RAPIDS JUNIOR COLLEGE (vp)
GREENFIELD COMMUNITY COLLEGE (vp)
MACCABI GREENFIELD MEMORIAL SCHOLARSHIP (vp)
GREEN RIVER COMMUNITY COLLEGE (vp)
ELIZABETH T. GREENSHIELDS MEMORIAL FOUNDATION (vp)
GREENWICH HOUSE POTTERY (vp)

SIDNEY GROSS MEMORIAL SCHOLAR-
SHIP (vp)
GEORGE GROSZ MEMORIAL SCHOL-
ARSHIP (vp)
GUILFORD TECHNICAL INSTITUTE
(vp)
HAILE SELASSIE I PRIZE TRUST
(VP)
THE HAMBRIDGE ART CENTER (VP)
HAMLINE UNIV. (vp)
HAMPTON INSTITUTE (vp)
HANOVER COLLEGE (vp)
HARNESS TRACKS OF AMERICA (VP)
HARTNELL COLLEGE (vp)
HASTINGS COLLEGE (vp)
HAYSTACK MOUNTAIN SCHOOL
OF CRAFTS (vp)
HAZELTON ART LEAGUE (VP)
HEIDELBERG COLLEGE (vp)
HERRON SCHOOL OF ART (vp)
HELEN HERZBERGER SCHOLAR-
SHIP (vp)
HIGHLAND PARK COLLEGE (vp)
HIGHLINE COMMUNITY COLLEGE
(vp)
HOFSTRA COLLEGE (vp)
HOLDEN SCHOOL OF ART AND
DESIGN (HOLDEN FOUNDA-
TION) (vp)
HOLDEN SCHOOL OF FINE AND
APPLIED ARTS (vp)
HOLLINS COLLEGE (vp)
HOLYOKE COMMUNITY COLLEGE
(vp)
HONOLULU ACADEMY OF ARTS (VP)
HOPE COLLEGE (vp)
HOUSTON BAPTIST COLLEGE (vp)
HOWARD UNIV. (WASHINGTON,
DC) (vp)
HUDSON ARTS FESTIVAL INC. (VP)
HUNTER COLLEGE OF CITY UNIV/
NEW YORK (vp)
HUNTINGDON COLLEGE (vp)
IDAHO STATE UNIV. (vp)
ILLINOIS STATE UNIV. (vp)
ILLINOIS TEACHERS COLLEGE,
CHICAGO (VP)
ILLINOIS WESLEYAN UNIV. (VP,vp)

INCARNATE WORD COLLEGE (vp)
INCORPORATED E.A. ABBEY SCHOL-
ARSHIPS FOR MURAL PAINT-
ING IN THE USA (VP)
INDIANA STATE UNIV. (vp)
INDIANA UNIV., NORTHWEST (vp)
INDIANA UNIV. (vp)
INDIANA UNIV. MUSEUM (vp)
INDIANA UNIV/PENNSYLVANIA (vp)
INSTITUTE FOR THE ARTS (VP)
INSTITUTO ALLENDE (vp)
INTERNATIONAL ART DEALERS
ASSOCIATION (VP)
INTERNATIONAL JEWISH ART
COMPETITION (VP)
IOWA LAKES COMMUNITY
COLLEGE (vp)
IOWA WESLEYAN COLLEGE (vp)
IRISH AMERICAN CULTURAL
INSTITUTE (VP)
JACKSON STATE COLLEGE (vp)
JACKSONVILLE UNIV. (vp)
JAPAN SOCIETY OF INTERNATIONAL
CULTURAL RELATIONS (VP)
JEFFERSON COLLEGE (vp)
GEORG JENSEN INC. (VP)
JUDSON COLLEGE (vp)
ALFRED JURZYKOWSKI FND., INC.
(VP)
KALAMAZOO COLLEGE (vp)
KANSAS CITY ART INSTITUTE (vp)
KANSAS STATE UNIV. (VP)
KELLOGG COMMUNITY COLLEGE
(vp)
KENT STATE UNIV. (vp)
KENTUCKY WESLEYAN COLLEGE
(vp)
KENYON COLLEGE (vp)
KILGORE COLLEGE (vp)
MARTIN LUTHER KING, JR.
GRANTS (vp)
REV. MARTIN LUTHER KING, JR.
MEMORIAL SCHOLARSHIP
(vp)
THE KATE NEAL KINLEY MEMORIAL
FELLOWSHIP (vp)
KITCHENER WATERLOO ART
GALLERY (VP)

BERNARD KLONIS MEMORIAL
SCHOLARSHIP (vp)
KNICKERBOCKER ARTISTS OF
AMERICA (VP)
YVONNE KRAMER SCHOLARSHIPS
(vp)
SAMUEL H. KRESS FOUNDATION
(VP,vp)
YASUO KUNIYOSHI MEMORIAL
SCHOLARSHIP (vp)
KUTZTOWN STATE COLLEGE (vp)
LAFAYETTE ART CENTER (VP)
LAGUNA BEACH SCHOOL OF ART
AND DESIGN (vp)
LAKE PLACID ART SCHOOL (vp)
LAMBETH COLLEGE (VP)
LANGSTON UNIV. (VP)
LASELL JUNIOR COLLEGE (VP)
ANNA LAUER SCHOLARSHIP (vp)
LAWRENCE UNIV. (vp)
LAYTON SCHOOL OF ART (vp)
LEE-STACEY (JOHN F. AND ANNA)
SCHOLARSHIP FUND (VP,vp)
JEAN LIBERTE MEMORIAL SCHOLAR-
SHIP (vp)
LIGHT WORK (VP)
LINFIELD COLLEGE (vp)
MRS. JANET O. LIPPER SCHOLARSHIP
FOR WOMEN (vp)
LITTLE ROCK UNIV. (vp)
ROBERT LONGHI FDN. FOR THE
STUDY OF THE HISTORY
OF ART (VP)
LORAIN COUNTY COMMUNITY
COLLEGE (vp)
LOUISIANA COLLEGE (vp)
LOUISIANA POLITECHNIC INSTITUTE
(vp)
LOUISIANA STATE UNIV. (vp)
LOUISVILLE SCHOOL OF ART (vp)
EMILY LOWE MEMORIAL SCHOLAR-
SHIP (vp)
JOE AND EMILY LOWE FOUNDATION
(vp)
JOE LOWE MEMORIAL SCHOLARSHIP
(vp)
LOWELL STATE COLLEGE (vp)
LOWER COLUMBIA COLLEGE (vp)

LOYOLA UNIVERSITY (vp)
LUBNER-DIMONDSTEIN STUDIO
(vp)
GLEN LUKENS AWARD (vp)
LYCOMING COLLEGE (vp)
LYNCHBURG COLLEGE (vp)
CHARLES H. MAC NIDER MUSEUM
(VP)
MACOMB COUNTY COMMUNITY
COLLEGE (vp)
THE MAC DOWELL COLONY, INC. (VP)
MADISON COLLEGE (vp)
MADOC—TWEED ART CENTER (vp)
JOSEPH MAHARAM FOUNDATION,
INC. (VP)
MANHATTANVILLE COLLEGE (vp)
MARIAN COLLEGE OF FOND DU LAC
(vp)
MARIETTA COLLEGE (vp)
MARJORIE WEBSTER JUNIOR
COLLEGE (vp)
REGINALD MARSH MEMORIAL
SCHOLARSHIP (vp)
ISABEL B. MARVIN SCHOLAR-
SHIP (vp)
MARY BALDWIN COLLEGE (vp)
MARYLAND INSTITUTE (vp)
THE MARYLAND-NATIONAL CAPITAL
PARK AND PLANNING
COMMISSION (VP)
MARYLAND STATE COLLEGE (vp)
MARYMOUNT COLLEGE (Los
Angeles) (vp)
MARYVILLE COLLEGE (vp)
MASSACHUSETTS ARTS AND HUMAN-
ITIES FOUNDATION (VP)
MASSACHUSETTS COLLEGE OF ART
(vp)
MAWY ART SCHOOL (vp)
EDWARD G. MC DOWELL TRAVEL-
ING SCHOLARSHIPS (vp)
WILLIAM G. MC NULTY MEMORIAL
SCHOLARSHIP (vp)
MECHANICS INSTITUTE (vp)
MERCYHURST COLLEGE (vp)
MEREDITH COLLEGE (vp)
MERMEC COMMUNITY COLLEGE (vp)
MIAMI DADE JUNIOR COLLEGE (vp)

MIAMI BEACH FINE ARTS BOARD (VP)
MIAMI INTERNATIONAL PRINTS
BIENNIAL (VP)
MIAMI UNIV. (vp)
MILES COMMUNITY COLLEGE (vp)
MILFORD FINE ARTS COUNCIL (VP)
KENNETH HAYES MILLER MEMORIAL
SCHOLARSHIP (vp)
MILLERSVILLE STATE COLLEGE (vp)
MILLIKIN UNIV. (vp)
MILLS COLLEGE (vp)
MINIATURE ARTS SOCIETY OF
FLORIDA (VP)
MINNEAPOLIS SCHOOL OF ART (vp)
MINOT STATE COLLEGE (vp)
MILTON COLLEGE (vp)
MISSISSIPPI ART ASSOCIATION (vp)
MISSISSIPPI UNIV. FOR WOMEN (vp)
MISSOURI WESTERN COLLEGE (vp)
MODESTO JUNIOR COLLEGE (vp)
MOLLOY COLLEGE (vp)
MONEGASQUE NATIONAL COMMIT-
TEE OF THE INTERNATIONAL
ASSOCIATION OF ART-PAINT-
ING, SCULPTURE, GRAPHIC
ART (IAA) (VP)
MONMOUTH COLLEGE (vp)
MONTCLAIR STATE COLLEGE (vp)
NANCY MOORE MEMORIAL FUND
(vp)
MOORE COLLEGE OF ART (vp)
MORNINGSIDE COLLEGE (vp)
MOSTRA INTERNAZIONALE DEL FILM
D'AUTORE (VP)
MOUNT ALLISON UNIV. (vp)
MOUNT ALOYSIUS JUNIOR COLLEGE
(vp)
MOUNT HOLYOKE COLLEGE (vp)
MOUNT MARTY COLLEGE (vp)
MOUNT MARY COLLEGE (vp)
MUNCIE ARTS ASSOCIATION (vp)
MUNICIPAL ART SOCIETY OF BALTI-
MORE (vp)
ALICE HAROLD MURPHY MEMORIAL
SCHOLARSHIP (vp)
MUSEUM ART SCHOOL (vp)
MUSEUM OF FINE ARTS (vp)
MUSEUM OF MODERN ART (VP)

MUSEUM OF NEW MEXICO (VP)
MUSIC AND ART FOUNDATION
AWARDS (vp)
MUSKEGON COUNTY COMMUNITY
COLLEGE (vp)
MUSKINGUM COLLEGE (vp)
NATIONAL ACADEMY OF DESIGN (VP)
NATIONAL ACADEMY SCHOOL OF
FINE ARTS (vp)
NATIONAL ASSOCIATION OF
SCHOOLS OF ART (vp)
NATIONAL CAPE CORAL ANNUAL
ART EXHIBITION (VP)
NATIONAL COLLECTION OF FINE
ARTS (VP,vp)
NATIONAL COMPETITION FOR AMER-
ICAN INDIAN ARTISTS (VP)
THE NATIONAL GALLERY OF ART
(VP)
NATIONAL INSTITUTE FOR ARCHI-
TECTURAL EDUCATION (VP)
NATIONAL INSTITUTE OF ARTS AND
LETTERS (VP)
NATIONAL OPERA INSTITUTE (VP)
NATIONAL PAINTING SHOW (VP,vp)
NATIONAL SCULPTURE (VP)
NATIONAL SCULPTURE SOCIETY (VP)
NATIONAL SOCIETY OF PAINTERS IN
CASEIN AND ACRYLIC, INC.
(VP)
NATIONAL WATERCOLOR SOCIETY
(VP)
NAZARETH COLLEGE (vp)
NAZARETH COLLEGE OF KENTUCKY
(vp)
NEBRASKA WESLEYAN UNIV. (vp)
NEVADA SOUTHERN UNIV. (vp)
NEWARK STATE COLLEGE (vp)
NEW COLLEGE (vp)
NEW ENGLAND SCHOOL OF ART (vp)
NEW HAMPSHIRE COMMISSION ON
THE ARTS (VP)
NEW HAVEN PAINT AND CLAY CLUB
(VP)
MARVIN NEWMAN MEMORIAL SCHOL-
ARSHIP (vp)
NEW MEXICO STATE UNIV. (vp)
NYC COMMUNITY COLLEGE OF THE

CITY UNIV/NY (vp)
NY INSTITUTE OF TECHNOLOGY (vp)
NY-PHOENIX SCHOOL OF DESIGN (vp)
NORTH CAROLINA COLLEGE AT
DURHAM (vp)
NORTHEASTERN ILLINOIS STATE
COLLEGE (vp)
NORTHEASTERN JUNIOR COLLEGE
(vp)
NORTHEAST LOUISIANA UNIV. (vp)
NORTHEAST MISSOURI STATE COL-
LEGE (vp)
NORTHERN ARIZONA UNIV. (vp)
NORTHERN MICHIGAN UNIV. (vp)
NORTHERN STATE COLLEGE (vp)
NORTHWESTERN COLLEGE (vp)
NORTHWEST MISSOURI STATE
COLLEGE (vp)
NORTHWEST NAZARENE COLLEGE
(vp)
NORTHWOOD INSTITUTE (vp)
NORWEGIAN RESEARCH COUNCIL
FOR SCIENCE AND THE
HUMANITIES (vp)
NOTRE DAME COLLEGE (vp)
NOTRE DAME COLLEGE OF OHIO (vp)
OBERLIN COLLEGE (vp)
ODESSA COLLEGE (vp)
OHIO UNIV. (vp)
OHIO UNIV.. (College of Fine Arts) (vp)
OHIO WESLEYAN UNIV. (vp)
OKLAHOMA CHRISTIAN COLLEGE
(vp)
IVAN OLINSKY MEMORIAL SCHOL-
ARSHIP (vp)
OLIVET COLLEGE (vp)
OLYMPIC COLLEGE (vp)
OREGON COLLEGE (vp)
OREGON STATE UNIV. (vp)
OTERO JUNIOR COLLEGE (vp)
OTIS ART INSTITUTE (vp)
OTTAWA UNIV. (vp)
OUR LADY OF CINCINNATI COLLEGE
(vp)
OUR LADY OF THE LAKE COLLEGE
(vp)
PACE COLLEGE (vp)
PARSONS COLLEGE (vp)

PARSONS SCHOOL OF DESIGN (vp)
PASADENA COLLEGE (vp)
GEORGE PEABODY COLLEGE FOR
TEACHERS (vp)
PENNSYLVANIA ACADEMY OF FINE
ARTS (vp)
PENNSYLVANIA FEDERATION OF
WOMEN'S CLUBS SCHOL-
ARSHIPS (vp)
PENNSYLVANIA STATE UNIV. (vp)
PEPPERDINE COLLEGE (vp)
PETER'S VALLEY CRAFTSMEN (VP)
PHILADELPHIA COLLEGE OF ART (vp)
PHILADELPHIA COLLEGE OF TEX-
TILES AND SCIENCE (vp)
PHILANDER SMITH COLLEGE (vp)
PHOENIX COLLEGE (vp)
PHOTO CLUB OF ROYAN (VP)
PIUS XII INSTITUTE COMMITTEE (vp)
PLYMOUTH STATE COLLEGE OF THE
UNIV/NEW HAMPSHIRE (vp)
POINT PARK COLLEGE (vp)
POLISH CENTRAL OFFICE OF
ARTISTIC EXHIBITIONS (VP)
POLK JUNIOR COLLEGE (vp)
PORTLAND SCHOOL OF ART (vp)
PORTSMOUTH PARKS AND RECRE-
ATION DEPARTMENT (VP)
POSITANO ART WORKSHOP (vp)
PRATT-N.Y. PHOENIX SCHOOL OF
DESIGN (vp)
PRESBYTERIAN COLLEGE (vp)
PRINCE GEORGES COMMUNITY
COLLEGE (vp)
THE PRINT CLUB (VP)
THE PRINT MAGAZINE (VP)
PROVINCETOWN WORKSHOP (vp)
QUEENS COLLEGE (vp)
RAMON MAGSAYSAY AWARD
FOUNDATION (VP)
RANDOLPH MACON WOMEN'S
COLLEGE (vp)
RED CLOUD INDIAN SCHOOL (VP)
GEORGE A. REDLING MEMORIAL
SCHOLARSHIP (vp)
REHOBOTH ART LEAGUE (vp)
FRANK J. REILLY MEMORIAL
SCHOLARSHIP (vp)

RHODE ISLAND COLLEGE (vp)
RHODE ISLAND SCHOOL OF DESIGN (vp)
RHODODENDRON STATE OUTDOOR ᐟ ART AND CRAFT FESTIVAL (VP)
RICE UNIV. (vp)
RIDGEWOOD SCHOOL OF ART AND DESIGN (vp)
RIJKSAKADEMIE VAN BEELDENDE KUNSTEN (vp)
RIJKSUNIVERSITEIT (vp)
RIO HONDO COLLEGE (vp)
RIVERSIDE CITY COLLEGE (vp)
ROANOKE COMMONWEALTH UNIV. (vp)
ROCHESTER INSTITUTE OF TECH- NOLOGY (vp)
J.D. ROCKEFELLER III FUND (VP)
ROCKLAND COMMUNITY COLLEGE (vp)
ROCKY MOUNTAIN NATIONAL WATERMEDIA EXHIBITION (VP)
ROCKY MOUNTAIN SCHOOL OF ART (vp)
ROSARY COLLEGE GRADUATE SCHOOL OF FINE ARTS (vp)
ROSARY HILL COLLEGE (vp)
BILLY ROSE FOUNDATION (VP)
ROSEMONT COLLEGE (vp)
ROSWELL MUSEUM AND ART CENTER (VP)
HERBERT AND NANNETTE ROTHS- CHILD FOUNDATION, INC. (VP)
RUTGERS UNIV. (vp)
SACRAMENTO STATE COLLEGE (vp)
ST. ANDREWS PRESBYTERIAN COLLEGE (vp)
ST. JOHN'S UNIV. (vp)
ST. LEO COLLEGE (vp)
ST. MARY-OF—THE-WOODS COLLEGE (vp)
ST. NORBERT COLLEGE (vp)
ST. PAUL ART CENTER SCHOOL (vp)
J. SANFORD SALTUS SCHOLARSHIP (vp)

SAN ANTONIO COLLEGE (vp)
DOROTHY SANDERS MEMORIAL SCHOLARSHIP (vp)
SAN DIEGO WATERCOLOR SOCIETY NATIONAL EXHIBITION (VP)
SAN FERNANDO VALLEY STATE COLLEGE (vp)
SAN FRANCISCO ACADEMY OF ART (vp)
SAN FRANCISCO ART INSTITUTE (vp)
SAN FRANCISCO FOUNDATION (VP)
SAN JOSE STATE COLLEGE (vp)
RUDOLPH SCHAEFFER SCHOOL OF DESIGN (vp)
DANIEL SCHNAKENBERG SCHOLAR- SHIP (vp)
SCHOLASTIC MAGAZINE ART AWARDS (vp)
SCHOOL OF FASHION DESIGN (vp)
SCHOOL OF FINE ARTS (Fort Wayne Art Institute) (vp)
SCHOOLS OF THE ART INSTITUTE OF CHICAGO (vp)
SCHOOL OF THE ASSOCIATED ARTS (VP)
SCHOOL OF THE MUSEUM OF FINE ARTS (vp)
SCHOOL OF THE PENNSYLVANIA ACADEMY OF THE FINE ARTS (vp)
SCHOOL OF VISUAL ARTS (vp)
SCHOOL OF THE WORCESTER ART MUSEUM (vp)
SCRIPPS COLLEGE (vp)
SEATTLE PACIFIC COLLEGE (vp)
SEVENTEEN MAGAZINE (vp)
SHELDON JACKSON COLLEGE (vp)
SHEPARD COLLEGE (vp)
ALEXANDER SHILLING FUND AWARD (VP)
THE SHIP SCHOLARSHIP (vp)
SHORTER COLLEGE (vp)
SILVERMINE GUILD OF ARTISTS, INC. (vp)
SKIDMORE COLLEGE (vp)
SKOWHEGAN SCHOOL OF PAINTING AND SCULPTURE (vp)

SLATER MEMORIAL MUSEUM (VP)
JOHN SLOAN MEMORIAL SCHOLAR-
SHIP (vp)
SMITH COLLEGE (vp)
NAT C. SMOLIN MEMORIAL SCHOL-
ARSHIP (vp)
SOCIETY FOR CINEMA STUDIES (VP)
SOCIETY OF AMERICAN GRAPHIC
ARTISTS, INC. (VP)
SOUTHERN ASSOCIATION OF SCULP-
TURE, INC. (VP)
SOUTHEASTERN CENTER FOR CON-
TEMPORARY ART (VP)
SOUTHEASTERN MASSACHUSETTS
TECHNOLOGICAL INSTITUTE
(vp)
SOUTHEASTERN STATE COLLEGE (vp)
SOUTHEAST MISSOURI STATE
COLLEGE (vp)
SOUTHERN COLOROADO STATE
COLLEGE (vp)
SOUTHERN ILLINOIS UNIV. (vp)
SOUTHERN METHODIST UNIV. (vp)
SOUTHWEST BAPTIST COLLEGE (vp)
SOUTHWESTERN UNIV. (vp)
SOUTHWEST TEXAS STATE COLLEGE
(vp)
SPANISH INSTITUTE (vp)
EMILY FERRIER SPEAR SCHOLAR-
SHIP FUND (vp)
SPOKANE COMMUNITY COLLEGE
(vp)
SPRING ARBOR COLLEGE (vp)
SPRINGFIELD COLLEGE (vp)
STAATLICHE HOCHSCHULE FUR
BILDENDE KUNSTE BERLIN
(vp)
JOHN AND ANNA LEE STACEY SCHOL-
ARSHIP COMMITTEE (vp)
STANFORD UNIV. (vp)
STANISLAUS STATE COLLEGE (vp)
STATE UNIV/NEW YORK AT
ALBANY (vp)
STATE UNIV/NY AGRICULTURAL AND
TECHNICAL COLLEGE (vp)
STATE UNIV/NY (College of Ceramics)
(vp)
STATE UNIV/NY (College at Oneonta) (vp)

JAMES HARRISON STEEDMAN FEL-
LOWSHIP IN ART (vp)
STEPHEN F. AUSTIN STATE COLLEGE
(VP)
STILLMAN COLLEGE (vp)
SUE BENNETT JUNIOR COLLEGE (vp)
SULLINS COLLEGE (vp)
SYLACAUGA AREA COUNCIL ON
ARTS AND HUMANITIES (VP)
SYRACUSE UNIV. (vp)
TEXAS CHRISTIAN UNIV. (vp)
TEXAS WESLEYAN COLLEGE (vp)
TEXAS WOMEN'S UNIV. (vp)
THOMAS MORE COLLEGE (VP)
THOUSAND ISLANDS MUSEUM
CRAFT SCHOOL (vp)
THREE RIVERS ARTS FESTIVAL (VP)
LOUIS COMFORT TIFFANY
FOUNDATION (vp)
HOWARD TRAFTON MEMORIAL
SCHOLARSHIP (vp)
TRINITY UNIV. (vp)
ALLEN TUCKER SCHOLARSHIPS
FOR PAINTING (vp)
TUFTS UNIV. (vp)
TULANE UNIV. (vp)
TURKISH MINISTRY OF CULTURE
(VP)
TUTOR PLAN OF HOME STUDIO
INSTRUCTION (vp)
TYLER SCHOOL OF ART OF
TEMPLE UNIV. (vp)
ULSTER COUNTY COMMUNITY
COLLEGE (vp)
UNION COLLEGE (Schenectady, NY)
(vp)
U.S. HOCKEY HALL OF FAME (VP)
UNITED STATES POSTAL SERVICE
(VP)
UNIV/ALABAMA (vp)
UNIV/ALBUQUERQUE (vp)
UNIV/THE AMERICAS (vp)
UNIV/ARIZONA (vp)
UNIV/ARKANSAS (vp)
UNIV/ARKANSAS AT LITTLE
ROCK (vp)
UNIV/BIRMINGHAM (vp)
UNIV/CALIFORNIA (Berkeley) (vp)

223

UNIV/CALIFORNIA AT LOS
ANGELES (vp)
UNIV/CALIFORNIA (Santa
Barbara) (vp)
UNIV/CHATTANOOGA (vp)
UNIV/COLORADO (vp)
UNIV/CONNECTICUT (vp)
UNIV/CONNECTICUT, WATERBURY
BRANCH (vp)
UNIV/CORPUS CHRISTI (vp)
UNIV/DALLAS (vp)
UNIV/DELAWARE (vp)
UNIV/DENVER (vp)
UNIV/FLORIDA (vp)
UNIV/GEORGIA (vp)
UNIV/HARTFORD (vp)
UNIV/HOUSTON (vp)
UNIV/HULL (vp)
UNIV/ILLINOIS (vp)
UNIV/IOWA (vp)
UNIV/JUDAISM (vp)
UNIV/KANSAS (vp)
UNIV/KENTUCKY (VP)
UNIV/LOUISVILLE (vp)
UNIV/MAINE (vp)
UNIV/MANITOBA (vp)
UNIV/MIAMI (vp)
UNIV/MICHIGAN (vp)
UNIV/MINNESOTA (Duluth) (vp)
UNIV/MISSOURI (vp)
UNIV/MISSOURI AT KANSAS CITY (vp)
UNIV/MONTANA (vp)
UNIV/NEBRASKA AT OMAHA (vp)
UNIV/NEW HAMPSHIRE (vp)
UNIV/NEW MEXICO (vp)
UNIV/NORTH CAROLINA (vp)
UNIV/NORTH CAROLINA AT
ASHEVILLE (vp)
UNIV/NORTH DAKOTA (VP,vp)
UNIV/NORTHERN COLORADO (vp)
UNIV/NORTHERN IOWA (vp)
UNIV/OKLAHOMA (vp)
UNIV/OREGON (vp)
UNIV/OREGON (VP)
UNIV/PITTSBURGH (vp)
UNIV/REDLANDS (vp)
UNIV/REGINA (vp)
UNIV/SASKATCHEWAN (vp)

UNIV/SOUTH ALABAMA (vp)
UNIV/SOUTH CAROLINA (vp)
UNIV/SOUTH DAKOTA (vp)
UNIV/SOUTH FLORIDA (vp)
UNIV/SOUTHERN CALIFORNIA (vp)
UNIV/TAMPA (vp)
UNIV/TENNESSEE (vp)
UNIV/TEXAS AT EL PASO (vp)
UNIV/UTAH (vp)
UNIV/VERMONT (vp)
UNIV/WASHINGTON (vp)
UNIV/WISCONSIN (Fox Valley
Campus) (vp)
UNIV/WISCONSIN AT GREEN BAY
(vp)
UNIV/WISCONSIN AT MILWAUKEE
(vp)
UNIV/WYOMING (vp)
UNIV/YORK (vp)
UPSALA COLLEGE (vp)
URSULINE COLLEGE (vp)
UTAH STATE UNIV. (vp)
VALLEY CITY STATE COLLEGE (vp)
VALPARAISO UNIV. (vp)
VASSAR COLLEGE (vp)
VESPER GEORGE SCHOOL OF ART
(vp)
VINCENNES UNIV. JUNIOR COLLEGE
(vp)
VIRGINIA CENTER FOR THE CREA-
TIVE ARTS (VP)
VIRGINIA COMMONWEALTH UNIV.
(vp)
VIRGINIA MUSEUM (VP,vp)
VIRGINIA POLYTECHNIC INSTITUTE
(vp)
ABRAHAM WALKOWITZ SCHOLAR-
SHIP (vp)
WALLA WALLA COLLEGE (vp)
WASHINGTON AND JEFFERSON
COLLEGE (vp)
WASHINGTON STATE COLLEGE OF
THE UNIV/MAINE (vp)
WASHINGTON STATE UNIV. (vp)
WASHINGTON UNIV. (vp)
WATERCOLOR OKLAHOMA (VP)
WATERCOLOR USA (VP)
WAYNE STATE UNIV. (vp)

WEATHERFORD COLLEGE (vp)
MAX WEBER SCHOLARSHIP (vp)
WEBER STATE COLLEGE (vp)
WEBSTER COLLEGE (vp)
WESLEYAN COLLEGE (vp)
WESLEYAN UNIV. (vp)
WESTERN CAROLINA UNIV. (vp)
WESTERN COLORADO CENTER FOR
  THE ARTS (VP)
WESTERN ILLINOIS UNIV. (vp)
WESTERN NEW MEXICO UNIV. (vp)
WESTERN STATES ARTS FOUNDA-
  TION (VP)
WESTERN WASHINGTON STATE
  COLLEGE (vp)
WEST LIBERTY STATE COLLEGE (vp)
WESTMAR COLLEGE (vp)
WESTMINISTER COLLEGE (New
  Wilmington, PA) (vp)
WESTMINISTER COLLEGE (Salt Lake
  City, UT) (vp)
WEST TEXAS STATE UNIV. (vp)
WEST VIRGINIA UNIV. (vp)
WHITWORTH COLLEGE (vp)
WHITMAN COLLEGE (vp)
WICHITA STATE UNIV. (vp)
WILLIAM CAREY COLLEGE (vp)
WILLIAM WOODS COLLEGE (vp)
WILSON COLLEGE (vp)
WILLIAMS COLLEGE (vp)
WISCONSIN FESTIVAL OF ARTS (VP)
WISCONSIN STATE UNIV. (Eau
  Claire) (vp)
WISCONSIN STATE UNIV. (River Falls)
  (vp)
WISCONSIN STATE UNIV. (Superior)
  (vp)
HELENE WURLITZER FOUNDATION
  OF NEW MEXICO (VP)
XAVIER UNIV/LOUISIANA (vp)
CORPORATION OF YADDO (VP)
YALE UNIV. (vp)
YANKTON COLLEGE (vp)
YORK ACADEMY OF THE ARTS (vp)
WILLIAM ZORACH SCHOLARSHIP
  (vp)

(WR)

ABINGDON PRESS (WR)

ACADEMY OF AMERICAN POETS, INC.
  (WR)
ACTORS THEATER OF LOUISVILLE
  (WR)
AFGHANISTAN, MINISTRY OF EDUCA-
  TION (wr)   (wr)
AFRICAN ARTS MAGAZINE (WR)
AFRICAN STUDIES ASSOC. (WR)
AGA KHAN FICTION PRIZE (WR)
AGNES SCOTT COLLEGE (wr)
THE EDWARD F. ALBEE FDN., INC.
  (WR)
ALDERSON BROADDUS COLLEGE (wr)
ALLIANCE FRANCAISE (WR)
ALL-MEDIA DRAMATIC WORKSHIP
  (WR)
ALL NATIONS POETRY CONTEST (WR)
AMERICAN ACADEMY IN ROME (wr)
AMERICAN ACADEMY OF ARTS &
  LETTERS (WR)
AMERICAN ACADEMY OF ARTS &
  SCIENCE (WR)
AMERICAN BOOK AWARDS (WR)
AMERICAN COLLEGE OF HOSPITAL
  ADMINISTRATORS (WR)
AMERICAN CONSERVATORY
  THEATER (WR)
AMERICAN COUNCIL OF NEARNED
  SOCIETIES (WR,wr)
AMERICAN FEDERATION OF FILM
  SOCIETIES (WR)
AMERICAN FRIENDS OF THE MIDDLE
  EAST (WR)
AMERICAN HERITAGE PUBLISHING
  CO., INC. (WR)
AMERICAN HISTORICAL ASSOC. (WR)
AMERICAN INSTITUTE OF INDIAN
  STUDIES (WR)
AMERICAN LIBRARY ASSN. (WR)
AMERICAN MUSICOLOGICAL SOCIETY
  (WR)
AMERICAN NATIONAL THEATER &
  ACADEMY (WR)
AMERICAN NEWSPAPER GUILD (WR)
THE AMERICAN PLAYWRIGHTS
  THEATER (WR)
AMERICAN POLITICAL SCIENCE ASSN.
  (WR)
AMERICAN SOCIETY OF CHURCH
  HISTORY (WR)

AMERICAN SOCIETY OF COMPOSERS, AUTHORS & PUBLISHERS (WR)
AMERICAN SOCIOLOGICAL ASSN. (WR)
ANISFELD-WOLF AWARD IN RACE RELATIONS (WR)
ART-ACT PLAYWRITING COMPETITION (WR)
THE ART DIRECTORS CLUB (WR)
ARTISTS FOR ENVIRONMENT FDN. (WR)
ASSOCIATED WRITING PROGRAMS SERIES FOR CONTEMPORARY POETRY (WR)
ASSOCIATION DES ECRIVAINS D'EXPRESSION FRANCAISE DE LA MER ET DE L'OURTE-MER (WR)
ATLANTIC MONTHLY (WR)
ATRAN FOUNDATION (WR)
AUSTRIAN FEDERAL MINISTRY FOR EDUCATION AND THE ARTS (WR)
AUSTRO-AMERICAN SOCIETY (wr)
AUTHORS LEAGUE FUND (WR)
BANARAS HINDU UNIV. (WR,wr)
BANCROFT PRIZES (WR)
BARCELONA INSTITUTE OF HISPANIC CULTURE (WR)
BELGIAN AMERICAN EDUCATIONAL FOUNDATION (WR,wr)
BEREA COLLEGE (WR)
BERGEN-BELSEN REMEMBRANCE AWARD (WR)
PRINCE BERNHARD FUND (WR)
BETA SIGMA PHI SORORITY (WR)
BETTER BOYS FDN. FAMILY CENTER (WR)
THE BLACK WARRIOR REVIEW (WR)
B'NAI B'RITH COMMISSION ON ADULT JEWISH EDUCATION (WR)
BOLOGNA UNIV. (WR)
BOOK WORLD (CHICAGO) (WR)
BOOK WORLD (NY) (WR)
BOOKS ABROAD (WR)
BORESTONE MOUNTAIN POETRY AWARD (WR)
BOSTON GLOBE NEWSPAPER COMPANY (WR)
BRANDEIS UNIV. (wr)

BREAD LOAF WRITERS' CONFERENCE (wr)
BRITISH ACADEMY (WR,wr)
BRITISH SOCIETY OF AUTHORS (WR)
BROADCAST MUSIC INC. (WR)
BROADMAN PRESS (WR)
BROOME AGENCY, INC. (WR)
BROSS FOUNDATION OF LAKE FOREST COLLEGE (WR)
BROSS FDN. OF LAKE FOREST COLLEGE (wr)
BRUNNER FACT AND FICTION, LTD. (WR)
BULGARIAN ACADEMY OF SCIENCES (WR)
BULGARIAN PEOPLE'S REPUBLIC STATE COUNCIL (WR)
MARIA MOORE CABOT PRIZE (WR)
CALEB AND JULIA W. DULA EDUCATIONAL AND CHARITABLE FOUNDATION (WR)
CANADIAN AUTHORS ASSOCIATION (WR)
CAORLE CITY COUNCIL AND THE TOURIST ASSN. OF THE CITY OF CAORLE (WR)
CARNEGIE ENDOWMENT FOR INTERNATIONAL PEACE (WR)
CARNEGIE FUND FOR AUTHORS (WR)
CAROLINA QUARTERLY CONTEST IN FICTION AND POETRY FOR NEW WRITERS (WR)
CAXTON PRINTERS (WR)
CENTRAL MICHIGAN UNIV. (WR)
CENTRO COLOMBO-AMERICANO (wr)
CENTRO MEXICANO DE ESCRITORES (WR)
CHIANCIANO CITY COUNCIL (WR)
CHICAGO REVIEW ANNUAL PRIZE AWARDS (WR)
CHUNG-ANG (CENTRAL) UNIV. (wr)
CHUNG-GU COLLEGE (wr)
CITY COLLEGE OF NEW YORK (wr)
CLASS STUDENT SERVICES, INC. (wr)
CLEVELAND PLAYHOUSE (WR)
COLLEGE OF NOTRE DAME OF MARYLAND (wr)
COLORADO QUARTERLY (WR)

COLUMBIA UNIVERSITY (WR)
COLUMBIA UNIV. TRANSLATION
 CENTER AWARDS (WR,wr)
COMMONWEALTH INSTITUTE (WR)
THE COMMUNITY CHILDREN'S
 THEATER OF KANSAS CITY
 (WR)
CONFERENCE BOARD OF ASSOCI-
 ATED RESEARCH COUNCILS
 (WR)
COORDINATING COUNCIL OF LITER-
 ARY MAGAZINES (WR)
COUNCIL ON INTERRACIAL BOOKS
 FOR CHILDREN (WR)
COUNCIL FOR WISCONSIN WRITERS
 (WR)
COWARD, MC CANN & GEOGHEGAN,
 INC. (WR)
CREEKWOOD COLONY FOR THE ARTS
 (WR)
DELL PUBLISHING CO. FOUNDATION
 (WR)
DELTA KAPPA GAMMA SOCIETY
 (WR)
DELTA PRIZE NOVEL AWARD (WR)
THE DEVINS AWARD (WR)
DOUBLEDAY & CO. INC. (WR)
E.P. DUTTON AND COMPANY (WR)
DRAMATISTS GUILD (WR)
DUTTON ANIMAL BOOK AWARD (WR)
EARPLAY (WR)
EISENHOWER EXCHANGE FELLOW-
 SHIPS, INC. (WR)
THE ELLISTON BOOK AWARD (WR,wr)
EMORY UNIVERSITY (WR)
ENGLISH ACADEMY OF SOUTHERN
 AFRICA (WR)
FABER & FABER, LTD. (WR)
FEDERATION OF FRENCH ALLI-
 ANCES (WR)
FICTION INTERNATIONAL MAGA-
 ZINE (WR)
FINE ARTS CENTER IN PROVINCE-
 TOWN, INC. (WR)
FLORENCE CITY PRIZE (WR)
FLORIDA INTERNATIONAL UNIV.
 (WR,wr)
FLORIDA THEATER CONFERENCE

(WR,wr)
FOLGER SHAKESPEARE LIBRARY
 (WR)
FOLLETT PUBLISHING CO. (WR)
FONDATION ROYAUMONT (WR)
FONTBONNE COLLEGE (wr)
THE MILES FRANKLIN AWARD (WR)
FRENCH PEN CLUB (WR)
FRIENDS OF AMERICAN WRITERS
 (WR)
FRIENDS OF LITERATURE (WR)
FUND FOR INVESTIGATIVE JOUR-
 NALISM (WR)
GERMANY ARTISTS-IN-BERLIN PRO-
 GRAM (WR)
GERMAN COMMITTEE FOR JUVENILE
 LITERATURE (WR)
JAMES HERRICK GIBSON BOOK
 AWARD (WR)
JOHN GOLDEN FUND (WR)
GREAT LAKES COLLEGES ASSOCIA-
 TION (WR,wr)
THE GREATER MONTREAL COUNCIL
 OF ARTS (WR)
THE HORACE GREGORY AWARD
 FUND (WR,wr)
GREGG DIVISION, MC GRAW-HILL
 BOOK CO. (WR)
GROVE PRESS (WR)
GUARDIAN NEWSPAPER (WR)
HAILE SELASSIE I PRIZE TRUST (WR)
THE HAMBRIDGE ART CENTER (WR)
THE HARIAN PRESS (WR)
HARPER PRIZE NOVEL AWARD (WR)
HARTFORD JEWISH COMMUNITY
 CENTER (WR)
HARPER-SAXTON FELLOWSHIPS (WR)
HARVARD UNIV. (WR)
HARVARD UNIV. PRESS (WR)
EDWARD W. HAZEN FDN. (wr)
SIDNEY HILLMAN FDN., INC. (WR)
HOLT, RINEHART AND WINSTON,
 INC. (WR)
HORN BOOK AWARDS (WR)
HUDSON ARTS FESTIVAL INC. (WR)
THE HUDSON REVIEW (WR)
THE HUMAN FAMILY EDUCATIONAL
 AND CULTURAL INSTITUTE

(WR)
HUNTINGTON LIBRARY AND ART
  GALLERY (WR-H)
IN A NUTSHELL (WR)
INSTITUT FUR EUROPAISCHE
  GESCHICTE (wr)
INSTITUTE FOR WORLD ORDER (WR)
INSTITUTE OF EARLY AMERICAN
  HISTORY AND CULTURE (WR)
INSTITUTO ALLENDE (wr)
INTER-AMERICAN PRESS ASSOCIA-
  TION SCHOLARSHIP FUND
  (wr)
INTERNATIONAL BOOK FESTIVAL
  (WR)
INTERNATIONAL FEDERATION OF
  UNIVERSITY WOMEN (WR)
INTERNATIONAL HUMANITIES
  (WR,wr)
INTERNATIONAL POETRY FORUM
  (WR)
INTERNATIONAL READING ASSO-
  CIATION (WR)
INTERNATIONAL THEATER INSTI-
  TUTE (wr)
INTERNATIONAL WHO'S WHO IN
  POETRY INTERNATIONAL
  BIOGRAPHICAL CENTRE (wr)
IONA COLLEGE WRITER'S CONFER-
  ENCE (WR)
IOWA SCHOOL OF LETTERS (WR)
IOWA STATE UNIV. PRESS (WR)
IRISH-AMERICAN CULTURAL INSTI-
  TUTE (WR)
IRISH ARTS COUNCIL (WR)
JEFFERSON POETRY AWARD (WR)
THE JERUSALEM PRIZE (WR)
JERUSALEM MUNICIPALITY (WR)
JEWISH BOOK COUNCIL OF AMERICA
  (WR)
JEWISH CHRONICLE (WR)
JEWISH PUBLICATION SOCIETY OF
  AMERICA (WR)
ALFRED JURZYKOWSKI FND., INC.
  (WR)
JANET KAFKA MEMORIAL PRIZE (WR)
ROBERT F. KENNEDY JOURNALISM
  AWARDS (WR)

KENYON COLLEGE (wr)
KEVORKIAN FOUNDATION (wr)
ROGER KLEIN FOUNDATION, INC.
  (WR)
THE KATE NEAL KINLEY MEMORIAL
  FELLOWSHIP (wr)
ALFRED A. KNOPF, INC. (WR)
KOREAN LANGUAGE RESEARCH
  SOCIETY (WR)
KOREA UNIVERSITY (wr)
KOSCIUSZKO FOUNDATION (wr)
KOSSUTH FOUNDATION (wr)
SAMUEL H. KRESS FOUNDATION (wr)
LANNAN FOUNDATION (WR)
LE CERCLE DU LIVRE DE FRANCE
  (WR)
LIBRARY OF CONGRESS (WR)
LITERARY PRIZE OF THE FEDERA-
  TION OF FRENCH ALLIANCES
  IN THE USA (WR)
LITTLE BROWN & CO., LTD. (WR)
LOUISIANA STATE UNIV. (WR)
LUCIUS N. LITTAUER FOUNDATION
  (WR,wr)
THE LYRIC (WR)
THE MAC DOWELL COLONY, INC. (WR)
LOUISIANA STATE UNIV. PRESS (wr)
MADRID INSTITUTE OF HISPANIC
  CULTURE (WR)
MAISON DE POESIE (WR)
MARIAN COLLEGE (wr)
THE DAVID B. MARSHALL AWARD
  (WR)
MARSHALL BOARD (wr)
MASSACHUSETTS ARTS AND HUMANI-
  TIES FOUNDATION (WR)
FRANKLIN K. MATHIEWS AWARD (WR)
MC GRAW-HILL BOOK CO. (WR)
THE MAC GREGOR FUND (WR)
JENNY MC KEAN MOORE FUND FOR
  WRITERS (WR,wr)
MC KINSEY FOUNDATION BOOK
  AWARD (WR)
THE FREDERICK G. MELCHER BOOK
  AWARD (WR)
MEREDITH IOWA WRITERS AWARD
  (WR)
HOUGHTON MIFFLIN CO. (WR)

MILES COMMUNITY COLLEGE (wr)
MINDANAO STATE UNIV. (WR)
MINISTERE DES AFFAIRES CULTUR-
ELLES DU QUEBEC (WR)
MINISTRY OF EDUCATION (China) (wr)
MINISTRY OF EDUCATION (Denmark)
(wr)
MINISTRY OF EDUCATION
(Iceland) (wr)
MINISTRY OF FOREIGN AFFAIRS
(Indonesia) (wr)
MINISTRY OF EDUCATION AND
CULTURE (ISRAEL) (wr)
MINISTRY OF EDUCATION (Japan)
(wr)
MINISTRY OF FOREIGN AFFAIRS
(Italy) (WR)
MISSOURI WESTERN COLLEGE (wr)
MODERN HISTORY SELECTION
AWARD (Harper & Row) (WR)
HARRIET MONROE POETRY AWARD
(WR)
MORROW HONOR AWARD (WR)
NATIONAL BANK (WR)
NATIONAL BOOK AWARDS (WR)
NATIONAL BOOK COMMITTEE (WR)
NATIONAL FEDERATION OF STATE
POETRY SOCIETIES (WR)
NATIONAL INSTITUTE OF ARTS AND
LETTERS (WR)
NATIONAL JEWISH BOOK COUNCIL
(WR)
NATIONAL OPERA INSTITUTE (WR)
NEAR EAST COLLEGE ASSOCIATION
(WR)
NETHERLANDS GOVERNMENT (WR)
NEW ENGLAND QUARTERLY (WR)
THE NEW HOPE FOUNDATION (WR)
NEW STATESMAN PUBLISHING CO.
(WR)
NOBEL FOUNDATION (WR)
NORTH AMERICAN MENTOR MAGA-
ZINE (WR)
NOVALICHES ACADEMY SCIENTIFIC
AND EDUCATIONAL FOUN-
DATION (wr)
FRANK O'HARA FOUNDATION (WR)
OHIO UNIVERSITY PRESS (WR)

F.E. OLDS & SON, INC. (wr)
EUGENE O'NEILL FOUNDATION
(WR,wr)
OPEN CIRCLE THEATRE (WR)
PADEREWSKI FOUNDATION (wr)
PANACHE (WR)
ROBERT TROUP PAINE PUBLICATION
FUND (WR)
PANACHE CONTEST (WR)
PARIS REVIEW, INC. (WR)
ALICIA PATTERSON FUND (WR)
POLISH AMERICAN POSTER CONTEST
(WR)
THE DREW PEARSON FOUNDATION
(WR)
P.E.N. AMERICAN CENTER (WR)
CARL AND LILY PFORZHEIMER
FOUNDATION, INC. (WR)
JAMES D. PHELAN AWARDS IN LITER-
ATURE (WR)
PHI ALPHA THETA (WR)
PHI BETA KAPPA (WR)
PLANETA PUBLISHING HOUSE (WR)
PLAYBOY MAGAZINE (WR)
POET LORE (WR)
POETRY MAGAZINE (WR)
POETRY SOCIETY (ENGLAND) (WR)
POETRY SOCIETY OF AMERICA (WR)
POETRY SOCIETY OF TEXAS (WR)
POLISH AUTHORS ASSOCIATION
(ZAIKS) (WR)
POLISH P.E.N. CLUB (WR)
PONTIFICIA UNIVERSIDAD JAVER-
IANA (wr)
ARTHUR KINGSLEY PORTER PRIZE
(WR)
PORTUGAL STATE SECRETARIAT
FOR INFORMATION AND
TOURISM (WR)
PRINCETON SERIES OF CONTEMPOR-
ARY POETS (WR)
POYNTER FUND (WR,wr)
PULITZER PRIZES IN JOURNALISM
AND LETTER (WR)
PUTNAM AWARDS (WR)
QUEEN'S UNIVERSITY AT KINGSTON
(wr)
QUINTO SOL PUBLICATIONS, INC. (WR)

RAMON MAGSAYSAY AWARD FOUN-
DATION (WR)
REAL ACADEMIA ESPANOLA (WR)
REDBOOK YOUNG WRITERS' CON-
TEST (WR)
REID EDUCATIONAL FOUNDATION
(wr)
REINA PRINSEN GEERLIGS PRIZE
FOR SOUTH AFRICA (WR)
RELIGIOUS ART GUILD (WR)
RELM FOUNDATION (wr)
REVISTA ULISSE (WR)
MARY ROBERTS RINEHART FOUNDA-
TION (WR)
J.D. ROCKEFELLER III FUND (WR)
RODGERS AND HAMMERSTEIN
FOUNDATION (WR)
BILLY ROSE FOUNDATION (WR,WR-H)
HERBERT AND NANNETTE ROTHS-
CHILD ROUNDATION, INC.
(WR)
ROY PUBLISHERS, INC. (WR)
ROYAL SOCIETY OF LITERATURE
(WR)
ROYAL SPANISH ACADEMY (WR)
SACRED HEART UNIV. (WR)
SAINT MARY-OF-THE-WOODS
COLLEGE (wr)
SAN FRANCISCO FOUNDATION (WR)
SCANDINAVIAN COUNCIL (WR)
SCHOLASTIC MAGAZINE, INC. (wr)
SCRIPPS COLLEGE (wr)
SEVENTEEN MAGAZINE (wr)
SHUBERT FELLOWSHIP (wr)
SAM S. SHUBERT FOUNDATION (wr)
SKIDMORE COLLEGE (wr)
W.H. SMITH AND SON, LTD. (WR)
SOCIETY OF AMERICAN HISTORIANS,
INC. (WR)
SOCIETY OF MIDLAND AUTHORS (WR)
SOCIETY OF AUSTRALIAN WRITERS
(WR)
SOCIETY FOR THE STUDY OF SOUTH-
ERN LITERATURE (WR)
SONS OF THE REPULBIC OF TEXAS
(WR)
SOUTHWEST REVIEW (WR)
SPANISH INSTITUTE (wr)

SPANISH MINISTRY OF INFORMATION
AND TOURISM (WR)
SQUAW VALLEY COMMUNITY OF
WRITERS (WR'WR)
WALLACE STEGNER FELLOWSHIPS
IN CREATIVE WRITING
(WR,wr)
PHILIP M. STERN FAMILY FUND (WR)
IRVING AND JEAN STONE FELLOW-
SHIP (WR)
THE AMERICAN BOOK AWARDS (WR)
TEXAS INSTITUTE OF LETTERS (WR)
THEATER LIBRARY ASSOCIATION
(WR)
TONATIUH INTERNATIONAL, INC.
(WR)
UNITED DAUGHTERS OF THE CON-
FEDERACY (WR)
UNIV/BUCHAREST (wr)
UNIV/CEYLON (wr)
UNIV/CHICAGO PRESS (WR)
UNIV/CHICAGO THEATER (WR)
UNIV/CONNECTICUT (WR)
UNIV/IOWA (wr)
UNIV/LEEDS (wr)
UNIV/MECHED (wr)
UNIV/MICHIGAN (wr)
UNIV/MICHIGAN PRESS BOOK AWARD
(WR)
UNIV/MISSOURI-KANSAS CITY (wr)
UNIV/NORTH CAROLINA (wr)
UNIV/PANJAB (wr)
UNIV/TEHERAN (wr)
UNIVERSITY WOMEN'S ASSOCIATION
(wr)
UNIV/WOMEN'S ASSOCIATION OF
NAGPUR (wr)
VASSAR COLLEGE (wr)
VERGILIAN SOCIETY, INC. (WR)
VIRGINIA CENTER FOR THE CRE-
ATIVE ARTS (WR)
VIRGINIA QUARTERLY REVIEW (WR)
EDWARD LEWIS WALLANT MEMOR-
IAL AWARD (WR)
WASHINGTON SQUARE UNIVERSITY
COLLEGE OF ARTS AND
SCIENCE OF NEW YORK
UNIV. (WR)

WESTBURG ASSOCIATES PUBLISHERS (WR)
WESTERN CAROLINA UNIV. (wr)
WILLIAMS COLLEGE (wr)
LAWRENCE L. WINSHIP AWARD (WR)
WORLD FESTIVAL OF NEGRO ARTS LITERARY PRIZES (WR)
WORLD LITERATURE TODAY (WR)

ABRAHAM WOURSELL PRIZE (WR)
HELENE WURLITZER FOUNDATION OF NEW MEXICO (WR)
CORPORATION OF YADDO (WR)
YALE UNIVERSITY (wr)
YALE YOUNGER POETS AWARD (WR)
YORKSHIRE POST "BOOK OF THE YEAR" (WR)